The Paradoxes
of the
American Presidency

The Paradoxes
of the
American Presidency

FOURTH EDITION

THOMAS E. CRONIN
Colorado College

MICHAEL A. GENOVESE
Loyola Marymount University

OXFORD
UNIVERSITY PRESS

Oxford University Press is a department of the University of Oxford. It furthers the
University's objective of excellence in research, scholarship, and education by
publishing worldwide.

Oxford   New York
Auckland   Cape Town   Dar es Salaam   Hong Kong   Karachi
Kuala Lumpur   Madrid   Melbourne   Mexico City   Nairobi
New Delhi   Shanghai   Taipei   Toronto

With offices in
Argentina   Austria   Brazil   Chile   Czech Republic   France   Greece
Guatemala   Hungary   Italy   Japan   Poland   Portugal   Singapore
South Korea   Switzerland   Thailand   Turkey   Ukraine   Vietnam

© Oxford University Press 2004
© Thomas E. Cronin and Michael A. Genovese 2010, 2013

For titles covered by Section 112 of the US Higher Education Opportunity
Act, please visit www.oup.com/us/he for the latest information about
pricing and alternate formats.

Published by Oxford University Press
198 Madison Avenue, New York, NY 10016
www.oup.com

Oxford is a registered trademark of Oxford University Press.

ISBN 978-0-19-986104-0

Printing Number: 9 8 7 6 5 4 3 2 1

Printed in the United States of America
on acid-free paper

BRIEF CONTENTS

CONTENTS

Chapter 4   **Presidential Power and Leadership**   99

Chapter 5   **The Presidential Job Description in a System of Shared Powers**   122

PREFACE

"Democracy can be messy, noisy and complicated," Barack Obama said soon after winning reelection.

After $6 billion and seemingly endless primaries, contentious debates, hard-hitting negative ads, and ingenious micro-targeting campaigns, Obama won a respectable victory, but Republicans retained control of the U.S. House of Representatives and most governorships.

Obama won reelection to a second term despite relatively high unemployment, slow economic growth, and unease about the country's ability to solve several economic challenges. Obama capitalized on the fact that most Americans still blamed much of the nation's economic woes on President George W. Bush. Moreover, Obama was credited with preventing a Depression and helping to revive the U.S. auto industry, reform the financial industry, and make significant progress on health care. Obama's reelection was helped a lot by strong support among Latinos, young people, and women.

"These [feisty] arguments," said Obama, "are a mark of liberty." As his second term began, Obama vowed once again to work with the leaders of both parties to create jobs, reform the tax code, improve immigration processes, reduce the national debt, and lessen our dependence on foreign oil.

Obama's reelection provided little in the way of mandate other than ensuring that the president's health care program would be more fully implemented. Moreover, the history of presidential second terms is, at best, rather murky. Talented cabinet members retire. Presidential overreach or hubris sometimes takes a toll, and, in any event, all the checks and balances and separation of power features of our constitutional system make it hard, as was intended, for presidents to marshal votes and public support for their cherished priorities.

Do we expect too much from presidents? Are we too impatient and harsh with them? Can a presidency designed in the late eighteenth century still serve us effectively in the twenty-first century? What did the framers of the Constitution get right? And what did they get wrong? Does a president have certain authority under the Constitution's executive power and commander-in-chief clauses on which Congress cannot impinge? Exactly how does the presidency work in our complicated system of separate yet shared political powers? Are the American presidency and vice presidency keys to solving our enormous challenges—or are they problems to be solved? Finally, do elections matter? Does leadership matter?

These and similar questions guided the revising and rewriting of this fourth edition.

Alexander Hamilton persuaded us that an American presidency was necessary. Others have demonstrated that the American presidency is unique and always potentially dangerous. Yet beyond this consensus—that the presidency is unique, necessary, and potentially dangerous—the American presidency remains a challenging institution to understand.

Much of the difficulty stems from the unusual character of the institution. The presidency is both unique and evolving. It defies simple explanations. It is dynamic, variable, and often a contradictory office. Lacking a precise constitutional delineation of powers, the American presidency is elastic and changing. Different occupants at different times mold the institution to the nation's needs, or to suit their own needs; at other times the office, the times, and the U.S. system of separated and shared powers constrain a president.

This book is an effort to understand the American presidency by viewing it through the lens of a series of paradoxes that shape the office. Our goal is to convey the complexity, the many-sidedness, and the contrarian aspects of the office.

A paradox is a seemingly contradictory statement that is opposed to common sense and yet may nonetheless be true. In an extreme form a paradox consists of two similar propositions, one of which contradicts the other. We use the term in a general sense—that we often hold clashing or contradictory notions of what a leader should do.

In many ways paradoxes define the presidential office, and it is the paradoxical nature of the institution that makes the search for a unified theory elusive.

This book is interpretive in that it offers a fresh look at this complicated institution and the complicated leaders who have served as U.S. presidents.

We have benefited from the presidential scholarship done by historians, political scientists, professors of constitutional law, and biographers. Footnotes and bibliography pay tribute to the research of those who have helped us understand this fascinating and paradoxical institution.

This fourth incarnation of Paradoxes of the American Presidency has been substantially updated to reflect the most recent events in American politics. While we have kept many of the features of the previous editions, we have rewritten much of this fourth edition, incorporating findings from the latest scholarship, the most recent elections and court cases, and relevant survey research.

Special thanks to Tania Cronin and Gabriela Esteva for their love and unfailing patience and support.

We thank our colleagues and the librarians at Colorado College, Whitman College, and Loyola Marymount University. Tom Cronin especially thanks Colorado College and Anabel and Jerry McHugh of Denver for support and encouragement of his research. Michael Genovese thanks Mackenzie Burr, administrative assistant at the Loyola Marymount University's Institute for Leadership Studies, and his research assistants Brianna Bruns, Matt Candau, Katherine McGrath, and Rebecca Hartley.

Both of us thank Jennifer Carpenter, our Oxford University Editor, Assistant Editor Maegan Sherlock, and Production Editor Pamela Hanley. We also thank Copyeditor Deanna Hegle and Copywriter Leigh Ann Florek. Very special thanks, too, to Ramprasad Jayakumar for his manuscript processing contributions.

In addition, we would like to thank the following reviewers for their comments: Anthony J. Eksterowicz, James Madison University; Matthew Eshbaugh-Soha, University of North Texas; Jasmine Farrier, University of Louisville; Daniel Franklin, Georgia State University; Craig Frizzell, University of Wisconsin-Parkside; Shamira Gelbman, Illinois State University; Margaret S. Hrezo, Radford University; Karen M. Kedrowski, Winthrop University; Jonathan McKenzie, Northern Kentucky University; Ann-Marie Szymanski, University of Oklahoma; Adam L. Warber, Clemson University; and Darren Wheeler, Ball State University.

Tom Cronin and Michael Genovese
tom.cronin@coloradocollege.edu
mgenovese@lmu.edu

CHAPTER 1

Presidential Paradoxes

He must have "common opinions." But it is equally imperative that he be an "uncommon man." The public must see themselves in him, but they must, at the same time, be confident that he is something bigger than themselves.

HAROLD J. LASKI, *The American Presidency: An Interpretation*
(Harper & Brothers, 1940), p. 38

Contradictions and paradoxes are a part of life—especially for leaders. "No aspect of society, no habit, custom, movement, development, is without cross-currents," writes historian Barbara Tuchman. "Starving peasants in hovels live alongside prosperous landlords in featherbeds. Children are neglected and children are loved."[1] We are everywhere confronted with paradoxes for which we seek meaning.

The same is true for the American presidency. We admire presidential power, yet fear it. We yearn for inspiration, idealism, and optimism, yet know the need for realism. We yearn for the heroic, yet are also inherently suspicious of it. We demand dynamic leadership, yet grant only limited powers to the president. We want presidents to be dispassionate learners and listeners, yet they must also be decisive. We are impressed with presidents who have calm and even fearless self-confidence, yet we dislike arrogance and respect those who express reasonable self-doubt. We want leaders to be bold and innovative, yet we allow presidents to take us only where we want to go. In a sense, we want presidents to be representative of us, yet not too representative.

How are we to make sense of the presidency? This complex, multidimensional, often contradictory institution is vital to the American system of government. Our chief challenge is that leadership is largely contextual. What works in one situation may fail miserably in another. Political laws that seem to constrain one president

1

liberate another. What proves successful in one leads to failure in another. "The traits that lead to disaster in certain circumstances are the very ones that come in handy in others," observes *New York Times* columnist David Brooks. "The people who seem so smart at some moments seem incredibly foolish in others."[2] The American presidency is thus often best understood as a series of paradoxes, clashing expectations, and contradictions and how presidents balance conflicting ideas, demands, and constituencies.

Leaders live with contradictions. Effective presidents learn to take advantage of contrary or divergent forces. Leadership situations commonly require successive displays of contrasting characteristics. "Our best presidents," writes journalist Howard Fineman, "are those who embrace and embody the contradictions and paradoxes of our country."[3] The effective leader understands the presence of opposites. The aware leader, much like a first-rate conductor, knows when to bring in various sections, when and how to turn the volume up and down, and learns how to balance opposing sections to achieve desired results. Effective presidents learn how to manage these contradictions and give meaning and purpose to confusing and often clashing expectations.

The place of leadership in American democracy has been a confused one, in part because of the evolving democratic myth that the people are sovereign. Alexis de Tocqueville, the discerning French aristocrat who toured the United States in the early 1830s, captured this puzzling aspect of American life when he said people want to be led "yet they want to remain free. As they cannot destroy either of these contradictory propositions, they strive to satisfy them both at once [with democratic constitutional government]."[4]

We generally exaggerate the capacity of presidents to shape events, granting them too much credit when things go well and too much blame when things go poorly. Historians and political scientists have learned that although a president's impact may be important, it is only occasionally decisive. We cherish the idea of a president fully deploying what Teddy Roosevelt called the "Bully Pulpit," yet most presidents learn that even soaring rhetoric yields few votes from members of Congress or Supreme Court justices. Presidential powers are not as great as many people believe, and thus presidents are often unjustly condemned as ineffective. Sometimes a president will overreach or resort to unacceptable deviousness while trying to live up to popular demands.

The constitutional founders purposely left the presidency imprecisely defined. This was due in part to fears of both monarchy and masses, and in part to hopes that future presidents would create a more powerful office than the framers were able to win ratification for at the time. They knew that at times the president would have to move swiftly and effectively, yet they went to considerable lengths to avoid enumerating specific powers and duties to calm the then widespread fear of monarchy. After all, the nation had just fought a war against executive tyranny.

Thus the paradox of the invention of the presidency: To get the presidency approved in 1787 and 1788, the framers had to leave several silences and ambiguities for fear of portraying the office as overly powerful. Yet when we need central leadership we turn to the president and read into Article II of the Constitution various prerogatives that permit a president to perform as national leader.

Today the informal and symbolic powers of the presidency often account for as much as the formal, stated ones. Presidential powers expand and contract in response to varying situational and technological changes as well as historical developments. The powers of the presidency are thus interpreted so differently that they sometimes seem to be those of different offices. In some ways the modern presidency has virtually unlimited authority for almost anything its occupant chooses to do. In other ways, a president seems hopelessly ensnarled in a web of checks and balances.

Presidents must constantly balance conflicting demands, cross-pressures, and contradictions. Perhaps some contradictions are best left unresolved, especially as ours is an imperfect world and our political system is complicated. We may not be able to resolve some of these clashing expectations. Still, we should develop a better understanding of what it is we ask of our presidents, thereby increasing our sensitivity to the limits and possibilities of what a president can achieve.

The following are some of the paradoxes of the presidency. Some are a function of confused expectations. Some are cases of our wanting one kind of presidential behavior at one time, and another kind later. Some are cases of conflict, abstract and specific. Some are cases where positive characteristics of presidential leadership become negative because they are excessive. Still others stem from the contradiction inherent in the concept of democratic leadership, which, on the surface at least, appears to set up "democratic" and "leadership" as contending concepts. Whatever the source, each has implications for presidential performance and for how Americans judge presidential success.

Paradox #1. Americans demand decisive presidential leadership that helps solve the nation's problems. Yet we are inherently suspicious of strong centralized leadership and we fear the abuse of power.

Paradox #2. We yearn for a democratic "common person" and simultaneously a leader who has uncommon genius, charisma, and star quality.

Paradox #3. We want a decent, caring, and compassionate president, yet we also admire a cunning, guileful, and, on occasions that warrant it, even a ruthless, manipulative president.

Paradox #4. We admire an "above politics," nonpartisan, bipartisan or "post-partisan" style of leadership, and yet the presidency is perhaps the most political office in the American political system: it requires an entrepreneurial master politician. Similarly we want presidents who can both unify us and take the necessary bold and unpopular decisions that are likely to upset us.

Paradox #5. We expect our presidents to provide creative, visionary, innovative, *programmatic* leadership, and at the same time to respond *pragmatically* to the will of public opinion majorities. "Be consistent, yet be flexible." Thus presidents must lead *and* follow, educate *and* listen.

Paradox #6. Americans want self-confident, resolute, presidential leadership. Yet we are inherently suspicious of leaders who view themselves as infallible or above criticism, and who don't learn from mistakes. We want presidents, in other words, with strong but not swollen egos.

Paradox #7. What and who it takes to become president may not be what and who are needed to govern.

Paradox #8. Presidents affirm the existing order and major traditions of society, yet often must also create a new order and boldly depart from the old order.

Paradox #9. Rich states in presidential elections tend to vote for the Democratic candidate while poorer states generally vote Republican, yet rich voters generally vote Republican and have done so for decades.

To govern successfully, presidents must understand these paradoxes and embrace or balance a variety of competing demands and expectations.

Paradox #1. **Americans want decisive leadership, yet we distrust authority and fear the abuse of power.**

We admire power but fear it. We love to unload responsibilities on our leaders, yet we intensely dislike being bossed around. We expect impressive leadership from presidents, yet we simultaneously impose constitutional, cultural, and political restrictions on them. These restrictions often prevent presidents from living up to our expectations.

Our ambivalence toward executive power is hardly new. The founders knew that the new republic needed more leadership, yet they feared the development of a popular leadership institution that might incite the people and yield factious or demagogic government. Indeed, if there was one thing the framers of the Constitution did not want, it was a too powerful presidency. Thus, the early conception of the American president was of an informed, virtuous statesman whose detached judgment and competence would enable him to work well with Congress and other leaders in making and implementing national public policy. This early presidency, as envisaged by the founders, did not encourage a popularly elected leader who would directly shape and respond to the public's views. On the contrary, popular leadership too grounded in the will of the people was viewed as a danger to be avoided. The founders' goal was to provide some distance between the public and national leaders, especially the president, this distance to be used to refine and improve on the popular view.[5]

But the presidency of 1787 is not the presidency of today. The twenty-first century presidency is a larger office, structurally similar to the original design yet with a much expanded set of responsibilities as well as more closely connected to popular passions. With the evolution of the nation have come evolving conceptions of the presidency.[6] For one example, the president is, many people believe, a primary national voice and representative of the American people. New arrangements for nominating and electing presidents have reinforced this conception, as have the role and magic of television.

The demand for a more immediately responsive president often conflicts with the demand for an informed, judicious statesman. The claims of politics and popular leadership have altered the early notions of presidential behavior. And as the presidency has become a lightning rod for much of society's discontent, so also have presidents sometimes sought to be all things to all people.

Still, while looking for strong, popular, presidential leadership, Americans also remain profoundly cautious about concentrating power in any one person's hands. Schooled in the tradition of negative government, Americans have historically feared the abuse of leadership power.

It often seems that our presidency is simultaneously *too strong* and *too weak*: Too powerful given our worst fears of tyranny and our ideals of a "government by the people"; too strong, as well, because it now possesses the capacity to wage nuclear war (a capacity that doesn't permit much in the way of checks and balances and deliberative, participatory government); yet too weak when we remember nuclear proliferation, the rising national debt, the collapse of Wall Street investment firms, lingering discrimination, increasing inequality, and a batch of other fundamental problems yet to be solved.

The presidency is too strong when we dislike the incumbent. Its limitations are bemoaned, however, when we believe the incumbent is striving valiantly to serve the public interest. The Lyndon Baines Johnson (LBJ) presidency typified this paradox: many who believed he was too strong in Vietnam also believed he was too weak to wage his War on Poverty. Others believed the opposite. The George W. Bush presidency suggested this as well. He exercised too much power, many people think, in some aspects of his war on terrorism, yet his powers and influence seemed puny when it came to needed social security and immigration reform, and economic stimulus initiatives. Similarly, critics on the right faulted Obama for heavy handedness on health care reform, while others saw him as ineffective on economic recovery issues.

Since President Washington took office we have multiplied the requirements for presidential leadership and made them increasingly difficult to fulfill. Students of the presidency often conclude that more power, not less, will be needed if presidents are to get the job done—especially in domestic and economic areas.

But if the presidency is to be given more power, should it not also be subject to more accountability? Perhaps so. But what controls will curb the power of a president who abuses the public trust and at the same time not undermine the capacity of a fair-minded president to serve the public interest?

Presidents are supposed to follow the laws and respect the constitutional procedures that were designed to restrict their power; still, they must be powerful and effective when action is needed. We recognize the need for secrecy in certain government actions, yet we resent being deceived and left in the dark—again, especially when things go wrong, or when presidents lie to us.[7]

Although we sometimes do not approve of the way a president acts, we approve of successful results. Thus Lincoln was criticized for acting outside the limits of the Constitution, yet he was largely forgiven due to the apparent necessity for him to violate certain constitutional principles to preserve the Union. Franklin Delano Roosevelt (FDR) was often flagrantly manipulative of his political opponents and sometimes of his staff and allies as well. In the end, history generally goes with the victor, though we want to believe that leadership effectiveness is judged by whether a person acts in terms of the highest interests of the nation.

Political scientist Andrew Rudalevige wrote a history of the reemergence of the imperial presidency, and his decidedly paradoxical conclusion is that "strong executive leadership is at once unacceptable and unavoidable."[8] Presidents will continue to be aggressive in their claims to power just as Congress, more often than not, will defer to most of these claims.

We need government, yet we resist its power when we can, and we dislike admitting our growing dependence on it. We may want strong leadership, yet if such leadership comes in the wrong form, we resent it. This results in a roller coaster ride of support for the heroic presidency model followed by condemnations of presidential power.

In sum, our constitutional order and its health depend on a paradox. "We need a president who is both sufficiently strong to take those essential actions without which we cannot be secure," writes political scientist Benjamin A. Kleinerman, and yet "sufficiently circumscribed so that such actions do not become the norm." But how can this be done? Kleinerman suggests that to resolve this paradox for a constitutional democracy, citizens "need to be willing to make tough constitutional distinctions between the necessary exercise of extraordinary powers and the dangerous aggrandizement of unnecessary powers. We need to hold our presidents to these distinctions and to elect legislators who will help us make them."[9]

Paradox #2. We yearn for the democratic "common person" who also has an uncommon genius, charisma, and star quality.

We want our presidents to be like us, yet better than us. We like to think America is the land where the common sense of the common person reigns. Nourished on a diet of "common person-as-hero" movies, for example, *Mr. Smith Goes to Washington* (1939), *The Farmer's Daughter* (1947), and *Dave* (1993), and the literary celebration of the average citizen by authors such as Whitman and Twain, we prize the common touch. The plain-speaking Harry Truman, the up-from-the-log-cabin "man or woman of the people," is enticing. In practice, however, we want presidents to succeed and we yearn for brilliant, uncommon, and semiregal performances from presidents.

While we fought a revolution to depose royalty, part of us yearns for genius and mastery. Woodrow Wilson describes Lincoln's appeal: "Lincoln never ceased to be a common man: that was his strength," writes Wilson. "But he was a common man with a genius, a genius for things American, for insights into the common thought, for mastery of the fundamental things of politics."[10]

We yearn for and demand both king *and* commoner. Our thirst for the heroic is so enduring it is as if history is meaningless without heroes. At the same time, we are told the hero is the individual the democratic nation must guard itself against. "Pity the nation that needs heroes," goes a proverb. Why is this a haunting warning? Strong leaders, it is believed, can sap, diminish, and possibly even destroy the very wellsprings of self-government. Hence the notion: Strong leaders make for a weak people.

Cicero wondered whether great oratory was a national asset or a national peril. Presidents have to be persuasive, but if they are too convincing they may con us. Sometimes we are so mesmerized by the effective communicator we fail to criticize or maintain the healthy skepticism so necessary in a political democracy.

Americans crave to be governed by a talented, self-confident, and incandescent president, yet someone who is also down to earth and humble. We want our president to be one of the folks, yet also something special. If presidents get too special, however, they get roasted. If they try to be too folksy, people get bored. We cherish the myth that nearly anyone can grow up to be president, that there are no barriers and no elite qualifications; still, we want smart, savvy, talented, uncommon leaders.

Ronald Reagan illustrated another aspect of this paradox. He was a representative all-American small town Midwesterner, yet also a Hollywood celebrity of stage, screen, and television. He boasted of having been a Democrat (which he was until the early 1960s), yet campaigned as a Republican. A veritable "Mr. Smith Goes to Washington," he had uncommon star quality. Bill Clinton liked us to view him as both a Rhodes scholar and an ordinary, saxophone-playing member of the high school band from Hope, Arkansas; as a "Jack Kennedy" and an "Elvis" figure.

Do we pay a price when we get, permit, or encourage heroic popular leadership in the White House? Does it possibly dissipate citizen and civic participation and responsibility? Many of the heroic, larger-than-life presidents have inadvertently weakened the office for their successors. The impressive and often bold performances of Jefferson, Jackson, Lincoln, and FDR made it more difficult for their successors to lead.

There is another related problem with the notion of heroic presidential leadership. Most of the time, those who wait around for heroic leaders in the White House are disappointed. This is because presidents seldom provide sustained, galvanizing, brilliant policy leadership. In practice, the people and policy movements make policy more often than presidents do; solutions percolate up rather than being imposed from the top down. Indeed, on many of the more important issues, the people generally have to wait for presidents to catch up. In the overall scheme of the untidy policymaking process the public is in fact sometimes out in front of the "leaders," as they were in the move to get out of Vietnam; as they were in women's rights, civil rights, gay rights; stem cell research, climate change and on exiting Iraq.[11]

Effective presidents, much of the time, are essentially shrewd followers; it is primarily in national emergencies such as Pearl Harbor or 9/11 that they sometimes can become consequential, pacesetting, or in-advance-of-their-times leaders.

In the end we want our presidents to be special, yet have the common touch. We don't really want them to be average, or just like us, or merely highly likable. Rather, we want someone who understands us, who can sympathize and empathize with our situation—someone we feel comfortable turning to in times of need.

***Paradox #3.* We want a decent, caring, and compassionate president, yet we admire a cunning, guileful, and, on occasions that warrant it, even a ruthless, manipulative president.**

There is a fine line between boldness and recklessness, between strong self-confidence and what the ancient Greeks called "hubris," between dogged determination and pigheaded stubbornness. Opinion polls indicate that people want a just, decent, and intellectually honest individual as our chief executive. Almost as strongly, however, the public also demands toughness.

We may admire modesty, humility, and a sense of proportion, yet most great leaders have been vain and crafty. You don't get to the White House by being a wallflower. Most have aggressively sought power.

Franklin Roosevelt's biographers, while emphasizing his compassion for the average American, also agree that he was narcissistic, devious, and had a passion for secrecy. These, they note, are often the companion flaws of great leaders. Significant social and political advances are made by those with drive, ambition, and a certain amount of brash, irrational self-confidence.

Americans insist that our country's leaders display moral judgment, yet they like decisiveness, not agonizing. George McGovern and Gerald Ford were criticized for being "too nice," "too decent." Being a "nice guy" is sometimes equated with being soft and afraid of power. The public likes strength and backbone.

Would-be presidents simultaneously have to win our trust by displays of integrity while possessing the calculation, single-mindedness, and pragmatism of a jungle fighter. Dwight Eisenhower reconciled these clashing expectations better than most presidents. Blessed with a wonderfully seductive, benign smile and a reserved, calming disposition, he was also the disciplined, strong, no-nonsense five-star general with all the medals and victories to prove it. His ultimate resource as president was this reconciliation of decency and proven toughness, likability alongside demonstrated valor. Biographers suggest that his success was at least partly due to his uncanny ability to appear guileless to the public yet act with ample cunning in private.

While Americans want a president who is somewhat religious, they are wary of one who is preachy or evangelical. Most presidents have liked to be photographed going to church or in the presence of noted religious leaders. Nixon and Reagan, who were not religious in the usual sense, held publicized Sunday services in the White House and spoke at fundamentalist religious gatherings.

Still, one of the ironies of the American presidency is that those characteristics we condemn in one president, we look for in another. A supporter of Jimmy Carter's once suggested that Sunday school teacher Carter wasn't "rotten enough," "a wheeler-dealer," "an s.o.b."—precisely the virtues (if they can be called that) that Lyndon Johnson was most criticized for a decade earlier.

We seem to demand a double-faced Janus personality. We demand the sinister as well as the sincere, the cunning and the compassionate, President Mean and President Nice, the president as Clint Eastwood or Tony Soprano, and the president as Mr. "Won't You Be My Neighbor" Rogers. We want them tough enough to stand up to Putin and North Korea, to terrorists and dictators, or perhaps to press the nuclear button, yet compassionate enough to care for the ill fed, ill clad, and ill housed, and the very poor.

Former President Nixon, in writing about leaders he knew, said a modern-day leader has to employ a variety of unattractive qualities on occasion to be effective, or at least to appear effective. Nixon carried these practices too far when he was in office, yet his retirement writings are instructive:

> In evaluating a leader, the key question about his behavioral traits is not whether they are attractive or unattractive, but whether they are useful. Guile, vanity, dissembling—in other circumstances these might be unattractive habits, but to the leader they can be essential. He needs guile in order to hold together the shifting coalitions of often bitterly opposed interest groups that governing requires. He needs a certain measure of vanity in order to create the right kind of public impression. He sometimes has to dissemble in order to prevail on crucial issues.[12]

We want decency and compassion at home, but demand toughness and guile when presidents have to deal with our adversaries. We want presidents to be fierce or compassionate, nice or mean, sensitive or ruthless, depending on what we want done, on the situation, and, to some extent, on the role models of the recent past. Yet woe to a president who is too much or too little possessed of these characteristics.

Leaders need to balance competing impulses. Because leadership is contextual, what works in one setting may fail in another. Thus, to be effective across issues and time, leaders must be agile in matching style to circumstance.

In other words, leaders have to be uncommonly active, attentive listeners: they must squint with their ears. Along with listening we expect leaders to decide, and make judgments. Leaders such as Hamlet wait too long. Others, like Shakespeare's King Lear or Sophocles' King Creon of Thebes, listen little and act in haste.

Ambition is essential if a leader is to make a major difference. And, to gain power and retain it, one must have a love of power. Effective presidents must on occasion be manipulators, recognizing the necessity of deception and arm twisting to manage a crisis or negotiate a deal.

The intentional use of coercion, force, and even killing may, under certain circumstances, be morally and legally justifiable. The moral dilemma often becomes a choice between two competing evils. Political theorist Michael Walzer writes that on some occasions leaders find that the right thing to do may also be wrong. Calling this a "moral paradox," Walzer says a particular act by a leader "may be exactly the right thing to do in utilitarian terms and yet leave the man who does it guilty of a moral wrong."[13]

Machiavelli jolts us when he says leaders must sometimes overcome their moral inhibitions and learn not to be good. How do we judge the bombing of Japan or Kosovo or the appropriateness of torture and waterboarding? Do favorable results excuse the acts in question? What are the moral standards? Who judges on these "dirty hands" political issues?[14]

The key, usually, is whether the leader is seeking only self-aggrandizement. Leadership divorced from worthy purposes is merely manipulation and deception and, in the extreme, repressive tyranny. We insist that leaders, whatever their style, act with integrity to achieve the common goals for the nation and help realize the needs of all Americans.

Still, a paradox remains: "Power, or organized energy, may be a man-killing explosive or a life-saving drug," wrote Saul Alinsky. "The power of a gun may be used to enforce slavery, or to achieve freedom."[15] So it is with leadership. Good leaders respect the preciousness of human life. Elements of calculation, abrasiveness, manipulation, and egoism are endemic in leadership. But a president must also be able to consider people in all of their relationships, in the wholeness of their lives, and not just as a means for enhancing profit or productivity.

A person who permits a cynical shell to harden around the heart will not long be able to exercise creative leadership. Presidents who are hell-bent on success sometimes fail to ponder whether the ends justify their means.

It was said of the nineteenth-century statesman Henry Clay that he was so brilliant and capable and yet also so corrupt that "like a rotten mackerel in the moonlight, he both shines and stinks." That depiction lives on because it is clever and it speaks to a moral ambiguity most Americans find hard to comprehend. "We look for heroes to represent us, although we rarely find them," writes prize-winning journalist Alan Ehrenholt. "We take certain perverse pleasure in unmasking hypocrites and dispatching blowhards who fail to deliver on their promises. The leaders we have trouble dealing with are those of obvious talent and genuine achievement who turn out to have displayed ethical insensitivity—or worse."[16] Nixon, Clinton, and George W. Bush are only the beginning of such a list.

Few things, Abraham Lincoln reminded us, are wholly good or wholly evil. Most public policies or ideological choices are an indivisible compound of the two. The best presidents are balanced individuals; they are sure of themselves, yet not dogmatic; they are self-confident, yet willing to acknowledge and learn from their mistakes.

Effective presidents understand that compassion and toughness are not inherently contradictory. There are times for compassion, yet equally there are times when one must be resolute. To be cunning does not necessarily mean one is unjust so much as one has a keen sense of timing. The specific context of the situation requires that presidents balance these two sides of their personality and character.

Paradox #4. **We admire an "above politics," nonpartisan, bipartisan, or "postpartisan" style of leadership, and yet the presidency is perhaps the most political office in the American political system: it requires an entrepreneurial master politician. Similarly we want presidents who can both unify us and take the necessary bold and unpopular decisions that are likely to upset us.**

The public yearns for a George Washington or a second "era of good feelings"— anything that might prevent partisanship or politics as usual in the White House. Former French President Charles de Gaulle once said, "I'm neither of the left nor of the right nor of the center, but above." Similarly, Jefferson once said "we are all Federalists, we are all Republicans." Yet the job of president demands that the officeholder be a gifted political broker, ever attentive to changing political moods and coalitions, and assiduously working to strengthen his or her political coalitions.

Several early presidents condemned parties while blatantly reaching out for party support when they needed to get their programs through Congress. "It is one of the paradoxes of the office," writes historian Robert J. Morgan, that a president "must seek to balance his position as chief of his party with an equal need for support of his policies from all quarters of the nation regardless of partisan lines. He owes his office to the efforts of the party which put him there and, yet, once in power, his success as a leader rests in no little measure upon his securing a broad base of popular approval."[17]

Franklin Roosevelt illustrates this. Appearing so remarkably nonpartisan while addressing the nation, he was in practice one of the craftiest manipulators and political-coalition builders to occupy the White House. He could punish friends and reward enemies or vice versa. He did not always succeed—for example, when he tried to "pack the Court" in 1937 and to purge some Democratic members of Congress in 1938.

A president is expected at times to be the least political and most bipartisan of national figures yet at other times the same president must act as the craftiest of politicians on the national stage. Presidents are not supposed to act with their eyes on the next election, yet their power position demands it. They are neither supposed to favor any particular group or party nor wheel and deal or twist too many arms. Instead, a president is supposed to be "president of all the people," above politics, "a uniter, not a divider," as George W. Bush once pledged.[18]

A president is also asked to lead a party; to help fellow party members get elected or reelected; to deal firmly with party barons, interest-group chieftains, and congressional political brokers. A president's ability to gain legislative victories depends on his or her skills at party leadership and on the size of his or her party's congressional membership. Jimmy Carter lamented that "It's very difficult for someone to serve in this office and meet the difficult issues in a proper and courageous way and still maintain a combination of interest-group approval that will provide a clear majority at election time."[19]

To take the president out of politics is to assume, incorrectly, that a president will be generally right and the public generally wrong, that a president must be protected from the push and shove of political pressures. But what president has always been right? Over the years, public opinion has often been as sober a guide as anything else on the political waterfront. Having a president constrained and informed by public opinion is, lest we forget, a defining characteristic of a democracy.

Politics, properly conceived, is the art of accommodating the diversity and variety of public opinion to meet public goals. Politics is the task of building durable coalitions and majorities. It isn't always pretty. A president must reward loyalty. No president can escape party politics. Presidents must first be nominated by their party. Presidents who are effective must closely work with party leaders in Congress and the states. A president, to be sure, must be much more than a party leader, yet if he or she is not at least this, he or she will fail.

In their attempts to be unifying leaders, presidents often avoid polarizing conflicts. One of the lessons of history, however, is that early confrontation of controversial issues may avoid later violence. Further, sharpening conflict is often an important leadership responsibility. After he had left the White House, Harry Truman said a president "who is any damn good at all makes enemies. I even made a few myself when I was in the White House, and I wouldn't have been without them."

Presidents go to considerable lengths to portray themselves as unconcerned with their own political futures. Yet the presidency is a highly political office; it cannot be otherwise. Moreover, its political character is for the most part desirable. A president separated from, or somehow above, politics might easily become a president who doesn't listen to the people, doesn't respond to majority sentiment or pay attention to views that may be diverse, intense, and at odds with his or her own. Presidents may not always wish to obey the will of the majority—in fact, leadership sometimes requires them to publicly argue against majority sentiment—but they cannot be unmindful of the will of the people.

A standard diagnosis of what's gone wrong in an administration will be that a presidency has become too politicized. Yet it is futile to try to take the president out of politics. A more useful approach is to realize that certain presidents try too hard to hold themselves above politics, or at least to give that appearance, rather than engage in it deeply, openly, and creatively. A democratic president has to act politically regarding controversial issues if any semblance of government by consent is to be achieved, yet presidents at the same time need objective, professional, and multiple sources of expertise. Presidents need their political and permanent campaign advisers, yet they need much more.

A president should be a national unifier and a *harmonizer* while at the same time the job requires priority setting and advocacy leadership. Such tasks are near opposites.

Presidents have to build coalitions and seek consensus. Presidents cannot be too far ahead of their times if they are to be successful. The United States is one of the few nations in the world that calls on its chief executive to serve as its symbolic, ceremonial head of state *and* as its political head of government. Elsewhere, these tasks are spread around. In some nations there is a monarch and a prime minister; in others there are three visible national leaders—a head of state, a premier, and a powerful party chief.

In the absence of an alternative office or institution, we ask our president to act as a unifying force in our culture. It began with George Washington, who artfully performed this function. He was a unique symbol of our new nation. He was a healer and an extraordinary man for several seasons. Today we ask no less of our presidents than that they should do as Washington did.

We have designed a presidential job description, however, that sometimes forces presidents to act as national dividers. Presidents must necessarily divide when they act as the leaders of their political parties, when they set priorities to the advantage of certain goals and groups at the expense of others, when they forge and lead political coalitions, when they move out ahead of public opinion and assume the role of national educators, when they choose one set of advisers over another, when they decide we should enter into a military campaign. A president, as a creative executive leader, cannot help but offend certain interests. Those presidents who have proposed bold measures on civil rights, immigration, and health care, for example, eventually lost public support for themselves and their parties.

George W. Bush and Barack Obama both paid a price for political boldness. Bush's decision to wage war in Iraq divided the country and ultimately hurt his party. But he was convinced he did the right thing. Similarly with Obama, Obama fought for comprehensive health insurance reform; he swung big and he paid for it with major losses in his party in the 2010 election and diminished public approval ratings, before bouncing back in 2012. These presidents divided, yet both believed they were providing leadership the nation needed.

The nation is torn between the view that a president should primarily preside over the nation and merely serve as a convener or referee among the various powerful interests that actually control who gets what, when, and how, and a second position, which contends a president should gain control of government processes and powers so as to use them for the purpose of furthering public, as opposed to private, interests.

The president is sometimes seen as the great defender of the people, the ombudsman or advocate general of "public interest." But this should be viewed as merely a claim, for many presidents have acted otherwise, even antagonistically, to mass or popular preferences.

Leaders are forever having to decide how much harmony or stirring up is needed to achieve objectives. All organizations need action and decisiveness, yet they also need shared values, community, and integration.

***Paradox #5.* We want our presidents to provide visionary, innovative, *programmatic* leadership and at the same time to respond *pragmatically* to the will of public opinion majorities; that is, presidents must lead *and* follow, educate *and* listen.**

We want both pragmatic and programmatic leadership. We want principled "conviction" leadership *and* flexible, adaptable leaders. *Lead us*, yet also *listen to us*. We want presidents with creative plans who will also respond to facts and be able to improvise according to varying contexts.

Most people can be led only where they want to go. "Authentic leadership," writes James MacGregor Burns, "is a collective process." It emerges from an appreciation of the mutually shared goals of both followers and leaders. The test of leadership, says Burns, "is the realization of intended, real change that meets people's enduring needs." Thus a leader's key function is "to engage followers, not merely to activate them, to commingle needs and aspirations and goals in a common enterprise, and in the process to make better citizens of both leaders and followers."[20]

Leadership at its best unlocks the talent and energy of the nation. Strong presidential leadership can provide a vision that empowers us to rise above the routine and make real contributions to our common purpose. Yet Americans rebel against too much of any hierarchical leadership, and we emphatically resist being led too far in any one direction.

We expect vigorous innovative leadership when crises occur. Once a crisis is past, however, we sometimes act as if we neither need nor want those leaders around. We expect presidents to provide bold initiatives "to move us ahead," yet we resist radical new changes and usually embrace "new" initiatives only after they have achieved some consensus.

Most of our presidents have been conservatives or "pragmatic liberals." They only cautiously venture much beyond the conventional consensus of the times. They follow public opinion rather than shape it. John F. Kennedy (JFK), the author of the much-acclaimed *Profiles in Courage*, was criticized for presenting more pro-file than courage. Kennedy responded to his critics by pointing out he had barely won election in 1960 and that great innovations should not be forced on the public by a leader with a slender mandate.[21]

Leadership requires radiating hope, grounded in reality. Be visionary, yet be able to fight for the achievement of your visions. Be dedicated to "visions" and be passionately committed to carrying them out. Be flexible enough to change direction quickly. The art of the possible is wanted. The challenge is how to bring about the doable and the desirable, while at the same time encouraging innovation. A constant balance, reconciling dreams and reality, intuition and logic, is needed.

Americans may admire consistency in the abstract, but in politics consistency has its costs. Everett Dirksen, a popular Republican U.S. senator from Illinois, liked to say, "I'm a man of fixed and unbending principle—but my first fixed and unbending principle is to be flexible at all times."

Franklin D. Roosevelt proclaimed that the presidency is preeminently a place for moral leadership. Yet he was also an opportunist and pragmatist just as Lincoln and Theodore Roosevelt were before him and as Kennedy, Reagan, Clinton, and Obama would later be.

These men knew that political leadership responsibilities in America meant sometimes being detached, vague, and uncommitted, while at other times taking a stand and being passionately committed. They knew, too, that changing their minds—or what we often derisively call "flip-floppery"—was also in order. Lincoln changed his mind on how to deal with slavery. FDR changed his mind on a balanced budget and on neutrality in World War II. Nixon, thankfully, changed his mind on dealing with China. Reagan was a "tax cutter" who actually raised taxes about ten times, and he also evolved a lot on how best to relate to the Soviets. He also, fortunately, changed his mind about negotiating with the evil Soviet leaders. Leaders sometimes change their minds because circumstances have changed. Sometimes, too, they change because they have learned new facts or understand new realities. Of course, they also change their minds because of political expediency. It is only the stubborn, overly self-confident and politically deaf leader who is unwilling to compromise and change course. We insist on consistency, yet creative compromising is sometimes appropriate.

Changing one's mind in politics has a noble history. Both the public and the press need to give a little more room to leaders who admit they were wrong on some matter. Indeed, it may be dangerous to elect a president who never changes his or her mind. "The evidence on this point is obvious…" writes *Newsweek*'s Jonathan Darman. "President George W. Bush watched his dad reverse himself on the 'Read my lips: no new taxes' pledge and pay the price, losing his re-election. His son overcompensated by refusing to reverse course on anything—even when the weight of facts and history and reason commanded it. A flip-flop or two from George W. Bush might have gone a long way."[22]

Our paradoxical desire for programmatic yet pragmatic leadership is compounded by the reality that what we find desirable in one president we may condemn in another. This factor often renders the lessons of history immaterial, and makes such a thing as standard pragmatic or programmatic leadership difficult, if not impossible. A president who becomes too committed risks being called rigid; a president who becomes too pragmatic risks being called wishy-washy.

We want idealism *and* realism, optimism *and* levelheadedness, principled commitment *and* opportunistic agility. Be inspirational, we tell a president, but also be realistic—don't promise more that you can deliver. Don't equivocate, yet keep on learning and be willing to make sensible adjustments. We ask our presidents to stir our blood and rekindle a sense of glory about our nation, yet also appeal to our reason. Too much inspiration sometimes can lead to dashed hopes, disillusionment, and cynicism.

The preeminently successful presidents radiated courage and hope and stirred the hearts and minds of Americans with an almost demagogic ability to simplify and convince. "We need leaders of inspired idealism," said Theodore Roosevelt, "leaders to whom are granted great visions, who dream greatly and strive to make their dreams come true, who can kindle the people with the fire from their own burning souls."[23]

Presidents who do not raise hopes are criticized for letting events shape their presidency rather than making things happen. A president incapable of radiating hope, optimism, and confidence is rejected as un-American. For people everywhere America has been the land of promise, of possibilities, of dreams. No president can stand in the way of this truth, regardless of the current dissatisfaction about the size of big government in Washington and its incapacity to deliver the services it promises.

Do presidents overpromise because presidential aspirants are congenital optimists, or because they are pushed by a demanding public? Or are competing candidates engaged in an escalating spiral of promise heaped on promise as they try to outbid each other for votes? Surely the public demands it, yet only self-confident optimists need apply in the first place. Whatever the source, few presidents have been able to keep all their promises.

Charlie Brown of Peanuts cartoon fame once said, "I have very strong opinions, but they don't last long." So also American public opinion shifts—sometimes quickly, sometimes slowly. There are times when we want presidents to be engaged actively as innovators, and on other occasions we would like to see them sit back and let things run their course.

"Politicians are, at different times, driven by grand notions and mere necessity," is how political commentator Chris Matthews speaks to this paradox of the programmatic versus pragmatic leaders. "Speak of the next election when they're dreaming loftily, and you risk being dismissed as a hack. Speak of high purpose when they're hearing the footsteps of a rival, and you invite instant dismissal."[24]

Contexts are always changing. Presidents sometimes find themselves in a period when the yearning for affirmative government or defense buildup are quickly followed by calls for tax cuts and a general downsizing of government.

Effective presidents need to be able to read these changing contexts and develop a "contextual intelligence" to tack one way or the other. Management scholar Roger Martin says leaders must learn how to integrate the obvious advantages of one possible approach without completely cancelling out the advantages of alternative approaches. Martin recommends an "integrative thinking" leadership style, which involves "generative reasoning, a form of reassessing that inquires into what might be than what is."[25]

One of the hardest things for presidents is whether to swing for the fences, speak from the heart and to take bold stands even when the country and their party might not be ready. Obama faced precisely this dilemma in 2010 and 2011. His own Simpson-Bowles Deficit Commission outlined bold ideas for cutting government spending , raising taxes, and helping to get the deficits under control. Obama's political instinct told him that if he fully embraced their recommendations he would have been torn to political shreds, perhaps even more than he had been with "Obamacare." So Obama ducked and weaved and essentially went small, not big and bold. Thus, in the event, Obama looked timid. He failed to use what leverage the bully pulpit might have availed. The press and many in the business world assailed him saying there was no leadership from the nation's "leader." "He's chief executive officer of the United States," said former U.S. Comptroller General David Walker; "He has a disportionate obligation to lead."[26] Even Obama's famous supporter, Warren Buffet, called the shelving of the deficit commission's report "an absolute tragedy."

Should Obama instead have told people what they didn't want to hear and led them where they didn't want to go? Every president faces these dilemmas and hard choices. Obama eventually, but gradually, began to embrace his debt commissions general ideas—but he was cautious in doing so.

One final note here. People yearn for courage and the heroic. But what we call Act III elected leaders rarely provide policy purity or coherence or the ideological consistency many of us may want. Another president from Illinois similarly had a limited political goal in a major moral issue of his day. Lincoln didn't like slavery, yet he knew that any embrace by him of full political equality for black Americans was incompatible to his being elected president and maintaining the fragile collection of Northern and border states he needed to win the war. So he was pragmatic and incremental at the time, even if we retrospectively view him nowadays as visionary.[27]

Paradox #6. Americans want resolute, self-confident presidential leadership. Yet we are inherently suspicious of leaders who are arrogant, above criticism, and unwilling to learn from mistakes. We want presidents, in other words, with strong but not swollen egos.

We cherish our three branches of government with checks and balances, countervalence, and dispersed and separated powers. We want presidents to be successful and to share their power with Congress and other responsible national leaders. We oppose the concentration of power, dislike secrecy, and resent depending on any one person to provide all of our leadership.

Yet Americans, at least on occasion, also yearn for dynamic, heroic presidents—even if they do cut some corners. We celebrate gutsy presidents who made a practice of manipulating and pushing Congress. We perceive the great presidents to be those who stretched their legal authority and challenged if not dominated the other branches of government. It is still Jefferson, Jackson, Lincoln, and the Roosevelts who get top billing. Whatever may have been the framers' intentions for the three branches, most experts believe that most of the time, especially in crises, our system works best when the presidency is strong and when we have a self-confident, assertive president.

We want presidents who are fearless and undaunted about exerting their will, but at what point does this become mulishly antidemocratic, even authoritarian? There is, of course, a fine line between confidence and arrogance, firmness and inflexibility.

We want presidents to consult widely and consider the advice of cabinet members and top advisers. We like the idea of collegial leadership and shared responsibility. But do we want presidents to sacrifice their own ideas and priorities to those of their cabinet officers? Generally not. We elect the president, not advisers.

While we want presidents to be open-minded, we also admire the occasional "profile in courage" type of decision. One of the most fondly remembered Lincoln stories underscores this point. President Lincoln supposedly took a vote at a cabinet meeting and it went entirely against him. He announced it this way: "Seven nays and one aye, the ayes have it." Much of the time, however, Abraham Lincoln followed the leadership of Congress, his advisers, and the general public. Still, as Harold Laski once observed, "A president who is believed not to make up his own mind rapidly loses the power to maintain the hold. The need to dramatize his position by insistence upon his undoubted supremacy is inherent in the office as history has shaped it. A masterful man in the White House will, under all circumstances, be more to the liking of the multitude than one who is thought to be swayed by his colleagues."[28]

Critics faulted Barack Obama for overreaching on his controversial Affordable Care Act of 2010. The American public was obviously divided and Republicans vigorously opposed Obama's proposals.[29] Even Obama and his advisers wondered, in retrospect, whether they had done the right thing. But the Supreme Court gave it support and Obama stalwartly campaigned in 2012 saying "We did the right thing. We have to move forward not backward," adding that no American should go broke because of bad health. His attitude was somewhat similar to what LBJ had said when some of his political advisers advised him to wait until later to aggressively push for the Civil Rights Act of 1964. A president, aides advised, shouldn't spend time and power on lost causes, no matter how worthy these causes. "Well, what the hell's the presidency for?" replied LBJ.[30]

Humility is admirable, yet excessive humility paralyzes. Significant advances in the world have generally been made by confident innovators. "Any self-doubts the leader may have, especially in the battlefield, must be concealed at all costs," wrote military historian John Keegan. "The leader of men in warfare can show himself to his followers only through a mask...made in such form as will mark him to men of his time and place as the leader they want and need."[31]

Rare is the great commander, the truly successful executive, or the politician who is not self-centered and conceited. A leader must be self-confident enough to believe he or she is indispensable. Untempered confidence, however, is dangerous. Hitler oozed it. So did Melville's mad Captain Ahab. Both had vision, purpose, and enormous drive.

The question is whether big leadership egos are subject to reasonable self-control. Self-discipline is key. An unrestrained ego that constantly needs to be fed and isn't placed in disciplined service to worthy public purposes invariably corrupts.

Bush White House Press Secretary Scott McClellan (2003–2006) was about as loyal a Bush operative as they come. In retrospect McClellan says that Bush and his chief advisers shaded and exaggerated the truth on several issues—most notably the decision to go to war in Iraq. Bush, McClellan writes, was never one to look back once a decision was made. "Rather than suffer any sense of guilt and anguish, Bush chose not to go down the road of self-doubt or take on the difficult task of honest evaluation and reassessment."[32]

McClellan and other writers believe Bush's "dead certain" attitude on Iraq stemmed from his fear of looking weak, his fear of repeating his father's mistake of flip-flopping on a major issue, and his "determination to win the political game at virtually any cost."[33]

Former Secretary of Defense Robert S. McNamara (who served JFK and LBJ) similarly, in retrospect, believed that major mistakes were made in starting and conducting the Vietnam War due to hubris and a failure to fully understand our alleged enemy and their motivation.

We misjudged the nationalistic intensions of the Vietnamese and we had a profound ignorance of their history and culture, McNamara said. He also said the decision-making process was flawed in a number of ways. Finally, "Where our own security is not directly at stake," McNamara writes, "our judgment of what is in another people's or country's best interests should be put to the test of open discussion in international forums. We do not have the God-given right to shape every nation in our image and as we choose."[34]

Leaders must believe in themselves, yet they cannot afford to discredit the ideas, plans, counsel, or criticism of others. Leaders who encourage thoughtful dissent in their organizations are, according to most studies, likely to produce better organizational decision making. Effective presidents encourage and reward criticism without retaliating against the critics. Hitler eliminated his critics. Ahab ignored his. In *Antigone*, Sophocles' King Creon listened almost entirely to himself, which proved fatal. His son, Haemon, chided him in vain, saying, "Let not your first thought be your only thought. Think if there cannot be some other way. Surely, to think your own the only wisdom and yours the only word, the only will, betrays a shallow spirit, an empty heart."

But Creon dismisses his son's advice, saying, "Indeed, am I to take lessons at my time of life from a fellow of his age?" He ignores everyone else as well until it is too late.

Unsuccessful presidents are like Creon. A fine line separates self-confidence from conceit, boldness from recklessness, positive and entrepreneurial ambition from narcissistic personality disorder, mindless adherence to the course from reevaluation and redirection. The challenge is how to blend the competing impulses and combine them effectively.

Life and history are complicated and paradoxical. That's why we have constitutionalism and regular elections. "The reason we have democracy is that no one side is right all the time," writes David Brooks. "The only people who are dangerous are those who can't admit, even to themselves, that obvious fact."[35]

Paradox #7. What and who it takes to become president may not be what and who are needed to govern the nation.

To win a presidential election takes ambition, money, years of hard work, masterful public relations strategies, as well as luck. It requires making promises and the formation of an electoral coalition. To govern a democracy requires much more. It requires the formation of a *governing* coalition, and the ability to compromise and bargain on a much more expansive field.

Obama spent much of his transition period emphasizing that there was a time for campaigning, yet the time had now come for governing. Ken Duberstein, a former Reagan White House chief of staff sums up part of this paradox by noting that presidential campaigns are all about "destroying your adversary" while governing requires the art of "making love with your adversary."[36]

"People who win primaries may become good presidents—but 'it ain't necessarily so,'" wrote columnist David Broder. "Organizing well is important in governing just as it is in winning primaries. But the Nixon years should teach us that good advance men do not necessarily make trustworthy White House aides. Establishing a government is a little more complicated than having the motorcade run on time."[37] Or, he might have added, being adept at smearing negative campaign ads.

Ambition and determination are essential for a presidential candidate, yet too much of either can be dangerous. A candidate must be bold and energetic, but in excess these characteristics can produce a cold, frenetic candidate. To win the presidency obviously requires a laser-like single-mindedness, yet our presidents must also have a sense of proportion, be well rounded, have a sense of humor, be able to take a joke, and have hobbies and interests outside the realm of politics.

To win the presidency many of our candidates (Kennedy, Clinton, and Obama, to cite a few) have to pose as being more progressive or even populist than they actually are; yet to be effective in the job they are compelled to appear more cautious and conservative than they often want to be. One of Carter's political strategists said, "Jimmy campaigned liberal, but governed conservative." Bill Clinton admitted near the end of his first year, "We've all become Eisenhower Republicans."[38]

Another aspect of campaigning for the White House is the ambiguous position candidates take on issues to increase their appeal to the large bulk of centrist and independent voters. The following is a typical view replete with paradox: "I want my presidential candidate to have clear-cut policies, to be as clear and precise as possible on positions, not hazy and ambiguous—to run a campaign that educates people and persuades them to adopt the candidate's position. But I also want my candidate to win."[39]

Policy positions are seldom comprehensively outlined; bumper-sticker slogans and entertaining TV ads are designed to please most people and offend few. Such presidential pledges as LBJ's "We will not send American boys to fight the war that Asian boys should be fighting," Richard Nixon's "open presidency" (1968) and "peace is at hand" (1972), George W. Bush's "I'm a uniter, not a divider," and Obama's upbeat but vacuous "change we can believe in" are illustrative.[40]

One of the most difficult aspects of campaigning is to win without proving you are unworthy of the job you are seeking. A common temptation is for candidates, including some incumbents, to run a "bureaucrats-are-bums," "anti-Washington" outsider kind of campaign. There is something more than a little deceitful, and certainly a lot that is ironic, in a presidential candidate who is trying to get to Washington by saying that he or she is running "against Washington," and one hoping to be elected the most powerful office in the world by proclaiming that he is against big government. An irony is that Ronald Reagan and George W. Bush both campaigned against big government yet left bloated deficits, a proliferation of defense programs, and a vastly bigger government than anyone ever would have imagined back in 1980 and 2000.

We expect a president to be able to work effectively with Congress and civil servants. Candidates who bad-mouth Washington officials will breed resentment; if they get to the White House, they will have a difficult time winning sustained cooperation from these same officials. Candidates who get too pious about how ethical standards have to be raised in Washington will be called hypocrites if their top aides are caught in compromised conflict-of-interest positions.

We often want both a "fresh faced" outsider as a presidential candidate *and* a seasoned, mature, experienced veteran who knows the corridors of power and the back alleyways of Washington. Frustration with past presidential performances leads us to turn to a "fresh new face" that is uncorrupted or at least less corrupted by Washington politics and its "buddy system." But inexperience, especially in foreign affairs, has sometimes led to blunders by outsiders.

New nominating rules combine with the requirements of the media and this "high tech" campaign age to sharpen the clash between what is required of a successful candidate and the successful president.

To be a winning candidate, a would-be president must put together an electoral coalition involving a majority of voters advantageously distributed across the country, especially in a dozen or so "battleground states." The candidate must thus appeal to all regions and interest groups and cultivate the appearance of honesty, relaxed sincerity, and experience. This is not all bad. It's good to travel around the country, meeting people, learning about their problems and testing ideas on diverse audiences. Who can doubt that Barack Obama wasn't a more informed and probably more representative leader for all his travels in 2007 and 2008 as he learned about people and issues from Iowa and New Hampshire through South Carolina, Colorado, Indiana, Oregon, and Pennsylvania? He had to stand up to pressure, prove his stamina, and let diverse publics learn about him even as he learned from them.

Once elected, however, the electoral coalition has served much of its purpose, and a governing coalition is the order of the day.

Recent presidents have found it difficult to abandon or transcend what is now called the permanent campaign. This is the case in part because our presidential campaigns are both so long and so highly professionalized. There are other factors at play, yet the campaigning mode of operation readily carries over to the White House.

Campaigning to win the White House is "antideliberative"; that is, it is a fight, a contest, a marketing, and an adversarial debate to win needed electoral votes. Governing "involves deliberation, cooperation, negotiation, and compromise over an extended period" as opposed to waging an either/or short-term competition.[41]

In short

> Campaigns prosecute a cause among adversaries rather than deliberate courses of action among collaborators. Campaign communications are designed to win rather than to educate or learn. Thus, the incentives for leaders are to stay on message rather than to engage with opponents and to frame issues rather than inform their audience about anything in detail. Similarly, campaigning requires projecting self-assurance rather than admitting ignorance or uncertainty about complex issues and counter attacking and switching the subject rather than struggling with tough questions...the more campaigning infiltrates into governing, the more we should expect the values of a campaign perspective to dominate over values of deliberation.[42]

Producing legislation acceptable to a broad public is often much harder than destroying political rivals. The former is the work of governance; the latter is the work of polarizing, partisan political campaigning—and we have seen a lot of that over the past generation.

Consequently, what it takes to become president may differ from what it takes to *be* president. To become president takes a determined, and even a driven person, a master fundraiser, a person who is glib, dynamic, charming on television, and

Election Night, 2012. President Obama addresses supporters at a victory rally in Chicago. AP Photo/Jerome Delay.

somewhat hazy on the issues. But, once president, the person must be well rounded, careful in reasoning, more transparent, and more specific in communications.

Paradox #8. Presidents are order *affirming*, order *shattering*, and order *creating*.

Presidents celebrate traditional American values and the American way of doing things, yet an effective president often has to help us create bold new traditions and a new order where, as Lincoln reminded us, the dogmas of the past become irrelevant to new challenges.

Presidents serve as a primary agent of modernization in the United States. No nation can stagnate and long endure. But political change is resisted. Since we fear change, and a variety of political roadblocks stand in the way, how are needed reforms enacted? To promote change, presidents must simultaneously affirm and create order. They begin by affirming the past, and they use that past to improve on the present and recreate it on the basis of past values.[43]

Abraham Lincoln understood this. In his Gettysburg Address and Second Inaugural Address, Lincoln affirmed the nation's commitment to past values, yet reinvented the future by reinterpreting those values to reflect modern necessity. He paid tribute to the framers of the Constitution while elevating the principles of the Declaration of Independence above the Constitution. In effect, he promoted a conservative revolution: conservative in that it grounded itself in the security of known values from the past, yet revolutionary in that it reordered those values to place political democracy and equality above all else. Lincoln affirmed the reordered traditional values of the collective past as a way to affirm a new vision for the future.[44]

Franklin Roosevelt came to the White House in 1933 as a result of a major repudiating 1932 election. That election, in addition to vanquishing Herbert

Hoover, led to a Democratic U.S. Senate with a 60 to 37 margin and a Democrat House with 310 Democrats to 117 Republicans.

Roosevelt had to devise economic security and development programs. He, his cabinet, and Congress redefined the government agenda—both reaffirming traditional American values such as liberty and freedom yet also emphasizing economic opportunity and economic security.

The times encouraged the politics of change yet political skill and agility—which FDR provided—helped pass the landmark Social Security Act of 1935. It was both radical and yet community enhancing, bold yet reassuring.

Ronald Reagan in his two election victories helped redefine his era. He sought to slow the march to a welfare state and celebrate individual freedoms as conceived by the constitutional framers. "No one understood better than Reagan the transformative political effect of bringing the order-shattering and order-affirming elements of presidential action into alignment" writes political scientist Stephen Skowronek.[45] Reagan himself understood this when he acknowledged, "They called it the Reagan Revolution. Well, I'll accept that, but for me it always seemed more like the great rediscovery, a rediscovery of our values and our common sense."[46]

In a way, all presidents are compelled to couch reform and modernization in the comforting, familiar clothing of past values. To be forward-looking we must affirm the past. Change, to be acceptable, must be grounded in deeply rooted American values. Political scientist Skowronek concludes that great presidents and their great performances "have been the most wrenching in their assault on the system." They have, in effect, shaken things up and been disrupters or disturbers of peace. "All told, the relationship between the presidency and the American political system is not at all a comforting one. It is always paradoxical and often perverse."[47]

Paradox #9. **Rich states in presidential elections tend to vote for the Democratic candidate while poor states tend to vote Republican, yet rich voters generally vote Republican and have done so for decades.**

While rich states (states such as Connecticut, California, and New York) have grown more strongly Democratic in recent decades, rich voters are consistently more Republican than lower income voters.

Political scientist Andrew Gelman examines this as the red-state, blue-state, rich-state, poor-state paradox. It is important, he says, to understand the marked differences within states. Rich people in poor states are more prone to vote Republican than rich people in rich states. States differ in a number of ways, socially, economically, and religiously. Born-again fundamentalists are concentrated, for example, in lower income states such as the South.[48]

Rich people in richer states tend to be somewhat more culturally liberal and apparently more likely to be swing voters than in poorer states. Indeed, "Rich Republicans are, if anything, socially more liberal than poor Americans, but the rich are more likely to vote Republican and more likely to define themselves as conservative."[49]

The income gap between rich and poor states has declined in recent years, but the individual inequality gap has increased within affluent states such as Connecticut, Colorado, Maryland, and California.

Yet another contributing factor to the red-state, blue-state, rich-state, poor-state paradox is the role of religion and regular church going. Rich people, it turns out, are somewhat less likely to be religious believers though this is apparently more the case in the West and East Coast than in the South and Midwest. Regular church goers are more likely to vote Republican.[50] The Deep South, Utah, and the Mississippi Valley are the most religious regions of the country, and they happen also to be consistently supportive of Republican presidential candidates. "Religiosity [defined as frequent church going and praying] has partisan overtones that it did not have in the past. While there are notable exceptions [Latinos and African American Baptist communities], the most highly religious Americans" write Putnam and Campbell, "are likely to be Republican."[51] So voters who identify themselves as having no religion are much more likely than others to consistently vote for Democratic presidential candidates.

The red-state, blue-state, rich-state, poor-state paradox defies simple explanations. Income matters. Religion matters. Race plainly matters. But so also geography and a variety of social and cultural differences help define each state. It is important not to exaggerate the ideological and cultural views in red states as opposed to blue states. Yes people in red states go to church more often and were more opposed to gays serving in the military, for example. But political scientist Morris Fiorina and others conclude that on most policy questions the red-state, blue-state divide has been overstated by the media who always seem to be looking for conflict. On the contrary most Americans share a pragmatic middle position and are against government waste *and* corporate welfare, *and* favor conservation principles *and* decreased immigration. Indeed, there is more of a divide between men and women than between red and blue states on policy issues. Yet on election day, red and blue states, again excepting several purple states, predictively tilt Republican or Democrat, respectively.

In addition, of course, the state of the economy and the particular appeal of the candidates in any given election, as we will discuss in the next two chapters, matters a lot. Incumbent parties generally benefit if the economy is robust or at least seen to be improving. And candidates who are perceived as more likeable, more informed, more real and honest generally win over the all-important independent or "swing voters." Still, at least a third of Americans nowadays live in predictably "red states" and at least another third live in "blue states," leaving approximately a dozen states as so-called "purple" or battleground states (states such as Ohio, Virginia, Iowa, and Colorado). The challenge for presidents, of course, is how to get voters to think less as red states or blue states, or Republican or Democrats, than to think of themselves as Americans. That's no small challenge.

CONCLUSION

Leadership, like life, is replete with paradoxes. Healthy individuals learn to manage the paradoxical elements in their personal lives. Effective leaders understand their jobs as embracing and resolving paradoxes and managing the contradictions of public life.

All leaders face countervailing pressures that pull them in different directions. "I have discovered the secret that after climbing a great hill," Nelson Mandela said, "one only finds that there are many more hills to climb."[52]

Presidents need to be optimists yet realists. Sunny Ronald Reagan made optimism a seemingly indispensable ingredient for presidential leadership. Presidents all say they are optimistic and accuse their opponents of being pessimistic. "A typical American politician," cracks pundit Michael Kinsley, "would sooner admit to being a bigamist than a pessimist." But, adds Kinsley, "we don't want a president who sees the silver lining in every cloud. We want a president who sees the cloud and dispels it. We want someone who will make the objective situation justify optimism, not someone who is optimistic in any objective situation."[53]

Political leaders with high emotional intelligence and robust empathy recognize the moods and needs of the moment, and fashion their leadership style to respond accordingly. This requires leaders capable of discerning the requirements of the moment as they shape policies and deal with both the context of the times and the mutually shared aspirations of their countrymen. This requires "style-flexing"—something few leaders can do. You first need to recognize the contradictions, and then devise strategies to deal with problems.

A key element of leadership is to identify the needs of the times and to solve the problem at hand. Leaders cannot be passive observers; they must improvise, synthesize, facilitate, and recontextualize. Psychologist Howard Gardner suggests that effective leaders learn to knit together information and ideas from competing sources into a creative and coherent strategy. "As synthesizers, they will need to be able to gather together information in ways that work for themselves and can be communicated to other persons."[54] Thus effective presidential leadership invariably involved infusing vision, purpose, and energy into an administration, but it also involved the ability to renew and reinvent new strategies to deal with a myriad of exacting challenges.

This requires a multidimensional leader. Lincoln was such a leader. He was arguably the most "complete" person ever to serve in the White House. He had good judgment, empathy, political skill, cunning, wit, intellect, resilience, and determination. He managed the vast contradictions of the Civil War with skill, imagination, ruthlessness, compassion, and disciplined focus. Lincoln was usually the master of contradictions, not their victim.[55]

The formal and informal powers of the presidency are impressive if both are used skillfully. Yet they are of little consequence unless exercised in accord with constitutional principles and in service to the nation's mutually shared aspirations.

Leading amid paradoxes requires leaders to (1) read the signs; (2) adapt strategy to the demands and needs of the context; (3) work to persuade followers; (4) understand the importance of balance and mediation; (5) understand the importance of timing; (6) devise a governing strategy; (7) manage the machinery of government; and (8) reevaluate, reexamine, and improvise. Effective leaders are smart diagnosticians, artful prescribers, effective agreement builders, and masterful jugglers of life's and history's paradoxes.

FOR DISCUSSION

1. Come up with one additional paradox that the authors may have overlooked.
2. Discuss an example or two of how these paradoxes shape or influence how presidents do their job?

DEBATE QUESTIONS

1. That the paradoxical nature of the American Presidency makes it harder to develop a unified theory of presidential leadership.
2. That an appreciation for the paradoxes of the presidency and for leadership in general should make us more tolerant of presidential mistakes.

FURTHER READINGS

Cronin, Thomas E., and Michael A. Genovese. *Leadership Matters: Unleashing the Power of Paradox*. Boulder: Paradigm, 2012.

Gelman, Andrew, David Park, Boris Shor, Joseph Bafumi, and Jeronimo Cortina. *Red State, Blue State, Rich State, Poor State: Why Americans Vote the Way They Do*. Princeton, NJ: Princeton University Press, 2010.

Handy, Charles. *The Age of Paradox*. Boston: Harvard Business School Press, 1994.

Martin, Roger. *The Opposable Mind*. Boston: Harvard Business School Press, 2007.

Nye, Joseph S., Jr. *The Future of Power*. New York: Public Affairs, 2011.

Skowronek, Stephen. *Political Leadership and Political Time*, 2nd edition. Lawrence: University Press of Kansas, 2011.

Critical Thinking

John F. Kennedy once said that, "We all enjoy the comfort of opinions without the difficulty of thought." Airing our opinions, announcing assertions, that is the easy part. But our task is to move beyond mere assertion and get to the hard work of thinking deeply.

The United States was "invented" in 1787 by men of the Enlightenment. The "Age of Reason" rejected myth and superstition, hoping to replace them with reason. And yet, we are both rational *and* emotional beings. The critical thinking boxes in each chapter are designed to sharpen decision making by getting the reader to think more deeply; apply sharper tools to our analysis; move beyond bias, prejudice, or distorted thinking; and rely on evidence in making decisions.

A critical thinker is a skeptic, not a cynic. A skeptic seeks more evidence, asks more questions, gathers and assesses information, is open-minded and curious, questions his or her assumptions, and tests their conclusions against neutral criteria and standards. A critical thinker bases his or her decisions on evidence.

CHAPTER 2

How We Evaluate Presidents

> Greatness is a compliment generally conferred in retrospect. We have
> lucked out several times in our history when implausible characters
> showed unexpected greatness…a country lawyer from Illinois, a
> spoiled patrician in a wheelchair; to name two.…Even more miracu-
> lous…both Lincoln and FDR were elected by promising more or less
> the opposite of what they did.
>
> MICHAEL KINSLEY, *Time*, October 27, 2008, p. 68

Americans were tough on King George III, and we continue to be exacting in
how we treat our own governing elites. We love our country, yet we often talk
as if we hate our government. Presidents as symbols of government are regularly
scrutinized and blamed for the ills of society. That presidential approval is often a
function of national *and* global economic cycles or foreign policy events that are
largely beyond a president's influence doesn't matter. Presidents have to appear
prepared, informed, and "in charge" as much as is possible or pay an exacting
penalty.

The average American doesn't have a strong grasp of American history.
Americans like certain presidents whom they know or at least about whom they
have heard positive firsthand stories. Thus recent Gallup poll popular favorites are
John F. Kennedy, Ronald Reagan, Bill Clinton, Franklin D. Roosevelt, as well as
Abraham Lincoln. Democrats, as we will see later in this chapter, admire Kennedy,
Lincoln, and FDR. Republicans, if they could do it, would put Reagan, Lincoln, or
Eisenhower back in the White House today.

American historians and biographers generally agree that Lincoln, Washing-
ton, and Franklin D. Roosevelt were our best presidents. Runners-up include
Jefferson, Jackson, Teddy Roosevelt, and Woodrow Wilson. Presidents Truman,
Reagan, and Eisenhower get at least favorable mention as well.

A paradox in how we evaluate presidents is the confused standards by which we judge leaders. While we are "results oriented," we are also rightly concerned about means. We demand that presidents succeed, and we criticize them if they do not. But they must not demand too much of us, push the system too far, call for too many sacrifices, or trample on our rights and liberties. We want heroic leaders with soaring visions yet we also want presidents who pay close attention to our views. We want presidents to lead, yet also to be responsive to us, and what we think matters. We demand that presidents think and act constitutionally, yet we expect them to do "whatever it takes," especially in national security matters. We yearn for effective leaders to become president, yet only sometimes do we want them to have the powers and resources necessary to do the job.

We have come to understand that presidential power can be used to achieve both noble and ignoble ends. Limited tenure, as required by the Twenty-Second Amendment, and additional statutory checks and accountability procedures such as inspector generals and ethics codes, are some of the devices we use to try to keep strong power from becoming irresponsible power.

The growth of presidential power came in fits and starts over our first 140 years. But since Franklin D. Roosevelt, the office and its power have steadily grown. We may have modified or even abandoned some earlier constitutional principles. In addition, times have changed, popular expectations have changed, and Congress has passed laws and delegated increased responsibilities to presidents, especially during crisis periods.[56]

What follows is a discussion of how what we want from presidents has changed over time.

WHAT THE FRAMERS EXPECTED

The framers of the Constitution were torn between their fears of executive tyranny and the urgent need for executive power. They feared the possibility of an arbitrary and ruthless leader. However, even the most vigorous champions of a strong executive insisted that the president would not become a monarch. Alexander Hamilton in *Federalist # 69* compared the powers of a president with those of a king, and he argued persuasively that presidents would possess much less power than the English monarch.

The framers were deliberately vague about the precise character of presidential powers, yet they provided the office with a potential for growth. Over the short run, they wished a president to be mainly a partner in a triumvirate, to be restrained by the judicial and especially by the legislative branch. They took care in drafting the Constitution to construct a governmental system that did not depend on a strong, popular leader. Even to admit the need for strong leadership was to leave open the possibility for the exercise of discretion and thus power. Unchecked power was considered dangerous.

Alexander Hamilton optimistically argued in 1788 that the office of president would seldom fall to anyone not in an eminent degree endowed with the requisite qualifications. Indeed, he predicted that the office would be regularly filled by individuals noted for ability and virtue. In fact, however, presidents have varied dramatically in skill and character. A more realistic James Madison wrote that "enlightened statesmen will not always be at the helm" (thus the need for all the Madisonian checks and balances).

The framers of the Constitution were not of one mind, and the final constitutional provisions were compromises, sometimes guesses. They necessarily had to leave much to be worked out.

One expectation, however, has remained constant. We want prudent and intellectually wise leaders who exercise their powers to the fullest when emergencies arise. We want presidents who will place the country and the Constitution ahead of their own personal or partisan interests. At the same time, both framers and citizens worried that a president capable of exercising robust executive power in a crisis situation could also become a demagogue and the worst kind of tyrant. The tension between energetic executive power and popular control is an enduring one. Hence, checks, both formal and informal, would always be needed to safeguard liberty. An appreciation of this paradox has given rise to an ambivalence toward presidents and presidential power.

The framers, in a burst of intellectual cleverness, devised a constitutional system that made dynamic presidential leadership exceedingly difficult, except in times of crisis. Alexander Hamilton, however, believed prosperity would be realized not from the absence of power, but from the presence of decisive executive power and leadership.

The framers obviously hoped for wise and virtuous statesmen to be presidents, individuals who would work closely with Congress and respond to the "sense of the community." Implicit, if not explicit, in their early expectations was the notion that each president, as well as members of Congress, would be preoccupied with what ought to be done rather than with what shortsighted temporary majorities might desire. They thus sought to insulate the president from the pressures of popular whim, and likewise to protect the other branches from the dangers inherent in a president armed with the support of masses and a large military.

The reason for providing distance between the people and the presidency is clear. It was to allow ample scope for leadership and statesmanship. In a constitutional democracy, or republic, public opinion would not always be identical with the public interest. There is at least the hint in Hamilton's conception of national leadership that sometimes a president would have to have the power "to do what the laws would do if the laws could foresee what should be done, as well as the power to make exceptions in the execution of the laws, exceptions governed by a judgment as to whether it would be good to apply them or not."[57]

Hamilton's prediction came true more quickly than he may have imagined. President George Washington set some precedents for unilateral executive action not exactly envisioned by the framers. He saw to it that he alone would lead the executive branch of government. In foreign affairs he issued the Neutrality

Proclamation of 1793 without the consent of Congress. He withheld information from Congress he thought should not be disclosed for reasons of national security. Congress willingly conceded to Washington most of the executive powers he exercised, especially those in foreign policy matters. By making the president commander-in-chief and allowing him to appoint ambassadors and to negotiate treaties, the framers provided important foreign policy and symbolic roles for the newly invented presidency.

Once Washington established these early practices, however, executive assertiveness was limited. Monarchial fears of the anti-federalist opponents of the Constitution were not realized. With few exceptions, Adams, Jefferson, Madison, and Monroe regularly deferred to Congress. The framers, and the American voters of the day, did not expect extensive domestic and economic policymaking leadership as much as administrative efficiency. Washington, in taking executive action yet always acknowledging the power, partnership, and centrality of Congress, set the prudent example.

What was expected of our early presidents was an executive role with neither tyrannical nor hereditary powers, restrained by representatives of the people and the Constitution, yet able to protect the people, at least on occasion, from their own representatives. Under George Washington, Americans in the 1790s got what they wanted.

WHAT WAS EXPECTED IN THE NINETEENTH CENTURY?

Early presidents did not have to conduct presidential campaigns as we know them today. Due to the natural restrictions of travel and the absence of modern media tools, they remained distant from the average citizen. To be sure, presidents traveled about the country for occasional ceremonial visits. The early presidents also held weekly social gatherings and were accessible even to casual visitors in the nation's capitol. Many presidents deemed it a requirement of the job to take an occasional "bath in public opinion," to paraphrase Lincoln.

Still, presidents in this period were not expected to provide popular leadership. Elected representatives, it was believed, would be better able to make important decisions than the average citizen. Being physically removed from the workings of government, the public had fewer or at least more general expectations of their representatives, and of the president. Moreover, the impact of the national government on the average citizen was decidedly less than it is today.

The typical nineteenth-century president was expected to be a "constitutional executive," a dignified presider over the administrative branch who would not tread on the responsibilities of the other branches. The nineteenth century eventually witnessed remarkable industrial growth based primarily on individual initiative, and that growth generally flourished free of governmental regulation. Freedom *from* government seemed to permeate most aspects of economic and social life (even though the national government provided for various public works like canals, postal service and army protection).

The doctrine of laissez-faire was widely accepted. Government might and did help, yet only in a limited way. Public expectations of the president were not geared toward greatness but toward efficiency in those limited responsibilities assigned to the office.

General Andrew Jackson, the seventh president and the first real "outsider" to win the presidency (in 1828), unquestionably altered prevailing conceptions of the office. In common with George Washington, Jackson was charismatic, imposing, and a national celebrity because of several military ventures, most notably because of his much celebrated military triumph over the British in the 1815 Battle of New Orleans.

"Old Hickory" (one of his nicknames because it was said he was as tough as a hickory branch) or "The Hero of New Orleans," as he was also called, was an irascible duelist, gunslinger, Indian-slaying Westerner from Tennessee. He owned 150 or more slaves, lived well on a vast estate of thousands of acres, and was not especially known for populist political views prior to his presidency. But he and his followers believed he was "robbed of the presidency" in 1824 when, or so his supporters believed, Henry Clay and John Quincy Adams rigged the election in the House of Representatives for Adams, denying the presidency to the popular plurality winner Jackson.

Jackson became the "people's candidate"—the champion and representative of the farmers and mechanics—and railed against the establishment made up of the wellborn, the bankers and the privileged classes so exemplified by its Harvard-educated son of a president, John Quincy Adams.

As president, Jackson called for the popular election of presidents and portrayed the presidency as an office that could represent the general public's views better than, or at least as well as, the other branches of government. Biographer Jon Meacham writes that his larger argument was that a president should not simply defer to the will and wishes of the Congress or the judiciary. Instead, Jackson was saying, the president ought to take his own stand on important issues, giving voice as best he could to the interests of the people at large.[58]

More activist than his predecessors, Jackson fought South Carolina's nullification efforts, vetoed the rechartering of what he considered the elitist privilege-serving Second Bank of the United States, waged a preemptive military strike in Sumatra, and much more.

Jackson was a polarizing politician, yet he handily won reelection in 1832 and was one of the few American presidents to enjoy a successful second term and leave the White House as popular, perhaps more popular, than when he arrived. Jackson's efforts in opposing states' rights when it came to nullification helped postpone a likely civil war—at least for a generation—yet on slavery, Indian rights, and other progressive issues, he was hardly a populist reformer. He was a political giant yet a flawed one. "Jackson, who believed in the virtues of democracy and individual liberties so clearly and forcefully for whites," writes Jon Meacham, "was blinded by the prejudices of his age, and could not see—or chose not to see... —that the promise of the Founding, that all men are created equal, extended to all."[59]

To say that nineteenth-century presidents had less to do does not mean emergencies did not arise. The Civil War was the greatest challenge the nation and our constitutional system ever faced. Rather, it means that the public seldom viewed presidents the way we do today.

With the exception of the Jackson's experience just discussed and Lincoln's crisis leadership, the presidency was rarely a dominant and often not an especially visible leadership institution in America. For much of the first half of the century, government was shaped by congressional leaders such as Daniel Webster, Henry Clay, and John Calhoun. Andrew Jackson, forceful executive though he was, did not approve of a forceful national government prior to taking office. Abraham Lincoln, before he was elected president, counseled against a strong presidency. And save in matters of war or security, President Lincoln regularly deferred to Congress and his cabinet.[60]

The Whig party (1834–1856) blossomed during the Jackson presidency, and it won the presidency on a couple of occasions following Jackson and Van Buren. The Whigs favored the national bank, financing extensive public works, and similar measures designed to promote an industrially driven market economy.

But the Whigs were vigorously opposed to Jackson's contention that the president should be the "sole representative of the American people." They blasted Jackson as a near tyrant, calling him "King Andrew the First," and passed in the U.S. Senate a measure censuring him for assuming "upon himself authority and power not conferred by the Constitution and laws."

In a nutshell, Whigs held that Congress should be the policymaking branch since they were the true representatives of the people. Presidents should primarily see to it that laws are properly administered. The Whigs were a party of the rich, respectable church goers and the upper middle class and at least for a while enjoyed widespread success in state legislatures and in Congress. Staunch advocates for liberty and republican government, their heyday was in the 1840s, but the slavery issue would ultimately divide the party.[61]

Other factors also made the public expect less of presidents in the nineteenth century than today. Presidents before McKinley (1897–1901) were not expected to make the United States a world power. Thus, when we look back and judge presidents, we rate them largely according to domestic affairs, often forgetting they had considerably fewer responsibilities than today.

Not until Theodore Roosevelt did the general public consciously expect a president to provide sustained assertive leadership. Populist manifestoes of the late nineteenth century began to change attitudes, as people turned to mass movements, popular political figures, and the central government as possible remedies for their economic problems. The populist crusade to elect Democrat William Jennings Bryan in 1896, 1900, and again in 1908 was illustrative of this new development. Attitudes toward presidential leadership had begun to change.

Teddy Roosevelt used the "bully pulpit" of the presidency to set the nation's programmatic agenda, and in doing so over time he also expanded expectations for the office. Woodrow Wilson echoed and extended Roosevelt's conception. Wilson wrote that the presidency should respond to and help enact the progressive sentiments of the people. Since the country had expanded in so many ways, so too the government and the presidency must expand. The people, Wilson suggested, should look to the president to serve as a spokesman and conscience of the nation.[62]

Were Roosevelt and Wilson responsible for changing the expectations of the presidency, or were they merely in office when the public began to expect and demand more? Probably more the latter than the former, yet both factors were at work.

PUBLIC EXPECTATIONS TOWARD PRESIDENTS IN RECENT TIMES

Public attitudes toward the presidency are subject to certain cycles. After strong presidents, who are often crisis or war presidents or who helped enact especially bold, controversial politics, the public yearns for a lessened presidential role, a general return to normalcy. After a weak leader, and especially after a series of weak leaders, we yearn for strength. Presidents live in the shadows of their predecessors, and presidents often pay for the "sins" of a predecessor. After the presidencies of Theodore Roosevelt and Woodrow Wilson, the Harding-Coolidge-Hoover administrations assumed a more passive posture.[63]

Coolidge once said that nine out of ten problems brought to his office could be safely ignored and did not require his attention. Franklin Roosevelt, who came to office in the depths of the Great Depression, had different conceptions and acted accordingly. After Franklin Roosevelt served, however, there was a backlash; the public supported the Twenty-Second Amendment in an apparent effort to punish the institution (as well as reaffirm the two-term tradition). After the Johnson-Nixon administrations there was another backlash to presidential power, as Ford and Carter appeared to provide a return to normalcy and rectitude in the White House. However, Ford and Carter paid for the political excesses of Nixon by being more constrained by an energized Congress.

Seldom does a president actually relinquish any formal powers associated with the office. The more passive ones may not use the powers in a vigorous way, but even the three Republican presidents of the 1920s (Harding, Coolidge, Hoover) attempted to protect the powers of the office they inherited by "consciously trying to steer a middle course between the extreme activism of Wilson and the passivity that had defeated Taft."[64]

President Franklin D. Roosevelt set a precedent for executive leadership that became a benchmark as the national government became more and more involved in everyday life. Roosevelt established a pattern that most chief executives would inevitably follow: proposing legislation, lobbying to get proposals enacted, rallying public opinion in support of his measures, creatively using radio, and inserting himself into ongoing international diplomatic negotiations.

In the beginning of the Republic there was at best grudging acceptance that a president would intervene in the affairs of the Congress.[65] Now it is assumed and expected that presidents will initiate and seek to win support for their measures. The FDR performance irretrievably altered people's views of presidents and the presidency. General Dwight Eisenhower added the reputation of a national hero to the luster of the office. Then, partly due to the glamour of the Kennedy administration, people and scholars were further captivated by the magic of the office.

Lyndon Johnson won a landslide reelection in 1964 and enjoyed an almost two-year honeymoon with Congress. He sponsored vital civil rights legislation, and he got the Great Society programs off to a rousing start. The power of the modern presidency appeared robust. Public and scholarly celebration of the presidency reached a peak.

Then came Vietnam, increased secrecy and duplicity, the Nixon Watergate scandals, obstruction of justice, and an increasingly frustrated American public. For a period, this dissatisfaction was reflected by a profound anti-Washington sentiment. Public approval of presidents declined, and expectations of presidents were temporarily lowered.

Presidents Johnson, Nixon, Ford, and Carter were criticized and found wanting. Yet, after a brief infatuation with the idea of turning to Congress for national leadership (notably in the 1973–1979 period), Americans revived their demand for more assertive presidential leadership. Ronald Reagan won election in part because he played on this yearning. Reagan's self-assurance, charm, optimism, wit, and seeming decisiveness struck a responsive chord among a demoralized public. Reagan's likeability, his talent for speaking plainly, his ability to convey his love of the country, and his ability to give the people he was talking to, whether an individual or the public at large, the impression of liking them made him a rare political phenomenon. Reagan called for and promised a more powerful presidency, and he charmed and often entertained the nation.[66]

Political scientists have suggested it is also important to evaluate presidents in the context of the nation's historic political cycles. Some presidents, like FDR and Reagan, come to power as the result of the rise of new political coalitions. These new coalitions may have developed in response to major problems that governments are asked to solve. But once in power for a presidential term or so this dominant coalition often faces divisions and degenerates in ways that make it difficult for their successors to lead.

Both Andrew Jackson and Franklin Roosevelt came to power as a result of new coalitions and new challenges for government, whereas Franklin Pierce and Jimmy Carter came to power at times when the dominant political coalition had degenerated into myopic sects that seemed impervious to the challenges facing the nation.[67]

Economists similarly suggest that the economic condition a president inherits and how the economy fares during and soon after a presidency also matter. Bill Clinton's presidency, among recent presidents, generally wins high scores in this regard. The Reagan presidency rates well too as consumer confidence rose during his two terms. Yet the value of the American dollar fell in the Reagan years. We also became a debtor nation in those years. Republican presidents like the Nixon, Ford and Bush presidencies fared less well than Democratic administrations in terms of the value of the dollar, economic growth, and job creation. But economists often differ depending on exactly what measures they weigh as most critical.[68]

These cyclical or "political time" theories can be complicated, yet they are helpful in warning that it is difficult to compare and contrast presidents as if they all faced similar circumstances and enjoyed similar political environments and resources.

Here are a few factors that affect how we evaluate and understand presidents and public opinion:

- The American public has rewarded presidents who "provided," or at least presided over, periods of peace and prosperity, and who displayed courage and leadership.
- Presidents go to great lengths to win public support for themselves and their initiatives because they believe that public support is a strategic resource in winning support in Congress, in the bureaucracy, in diplomatic endeavors, as well as, occasionally, in the courts.
- Public approval of presidents is less shaped by charisma or election results than by the times, the economy, the context of the challenges presidents have to face, and their success in dealing strategically with such challenges.
- A president can be popular and a splendid communicator yet also ineffective. What the public thinks about presidents is not always what historians and political biographers will conclude. Thus Kennedy, Reagan, and Clinton were often popular with the public yet are viewed as average or even "overrated" presidents by many students of the presidency.
- Finally, presidential leadership involves more than slavishly following public opinion; Americans expect presidents on occasion to rise above doing what might be conventionally popular in favor of doing the right thing—that is, to lead us, to educate us, and to bring out our better, more idealistic selves. Thus, we may ask a president to serve or even pander to our short-term or selfish interests, yet we define leadership as more than this.

QUALITIES AMERICANS LOOK FOR IN PRESIDENTS

We have a tough, unwritten code of conduct for our nation's chief executive. We demand much. Part of this is because many Americans nowadays cherish the idea of American Exceptionalism—the idea that America is somehow a superior, exemplary nation, perhaps even blessed by God to the point the way for other nations. Part of this also comes from our inflated image of what "the great" presidents did. Our selective memories about the past glories and victories under our favorite presidents result in our holding incumbents to unusually high standards.

Many Americans and some scholars, with an inadequate understanding of constitutionalism, favor an increased concentration of power in the American presidency and argue that in an age of terrorism the country is in better hands when executive branch power is left unfettered by intrusionist legislative, judicial, or international constraints. Such views both exaggerate the integrity and competence of most presidential administrations and do a serious injustice to our separation of powers shared governance system.[69]

When looking for a new president, Americans search for a leader who is honest and bright and who can bring us together and bring out the best in us. This is an especially tough assignment in a country shaped by stalwart individualism, embedded partisanship, polarized media outlets, and an abiding irreverence for politics and centralized government.

Most of us yearn for so many talents and qualities in our prospective presidents that it comes close to wanting "God—on a good day"—or at least a pleasant amalgam of Lincoln, the Roosevelts, Churchill, Mandela, Mother Teresa, Rambo, and the Terminator. However much we may expect of presidents, we are highly unlikely to ease up on them.

Experts usually rate experience, judgment, agility, vision, and intellectual capacity over honesty. But this is not the case with the average person. *Honesty, credibility, consistency, and good moral character* are the qualities people generally want in presidential candidates. Voters say they want a leader whose words they can both understand and believe, and someone they can trust. It also helps (see Table 2.1) if they are likable, "real," and understand the challenges facing average people.

When George H. W. Bush enjoined the public to "Read my lips, no new taxes," and later felt compelled to break that vow, the public was unforgiving. When candidate Bill Clinton promised a middle-class tax cut but broke that vow, and when he acknowledged lying under oath, he lost political capital as well as credibility. The general public was highly critical of George W. Bush's misleading justification for going to war in Iraq when no weapons of mass destruction were found. Similarly, many Americans faulted Barack Obama for not delivering on more of his campaign promises.

If the public rates honesty as the top quality a president should have, they also want their president to have compassion, intelligence, empathy, relaxed sincerity, decisiveness, and decision-making ability. Knowledge of economic issues and international affairs are also cited frequently.

LEADERSHIP THE PUBLIC WANTS

The public as well as pollsters ask the following tough questions of presidents: Is the president willing to make tough gutsy decisions? Can the president get things done? Is the president an effective manager of the government? Can the president deal effectively with Congress? Does the president share our values and relate to average Americans? Is the president an effective leader?

Most Americans, but not all, believe the nation would be better off if presidents and other national leaders followed public opinion more closely. The Gallup Poll organization finds that about 75 percent of Americans, in surveys, think the

TABLE 2.1 What the Public Wants in Their President

PERSONAL QUALITIES THE PUBLIC WANTS

Honest/straightforward	33%
Integrity	10
Moral character/family values	5
Intelligence	5
Honorable	4
Trustworthy	4
Christian	3

PRESIDENTIAL QUALITIES THE PUBLIC WANTS

Leadership strength	16%
Competent, governing ability	10
Can listen, be representative	9
Vision for country	5
Consensus-builder, bring country together	2

QUALITIES THE PUBLIC THINKS ARE "ABSOLUTELY ESSENTIAL"

Strong, decisive leader	77%
Good moral character	68
Effective manager	63
A uniter	59
Consistent policies	47
Foreign policy experience	46
Will pay attention to public opinion	43
Faithful to spouse	37
Lot of government experience	34
An inspiring speaker	24

SOURCE: www.gallup.com/poll 27088. April 4, 2007. Gallup survey of 1,006 nationally represented adults, conducted in late March 2007.
NOTE: The first two lists were compiled from open-ended questions. The third list is from a question that asked respondents to rate each of 16 qualities as either "absolutely essential," "important but not essential," or "not that important." (Margin of sampling error, plus or minus 3 percent.)

country would be better off if their leaders followed the public's view more closely. This finding holds true for at least the past three decades regardless of party affiliation. Those with more college and graduate education are somewhat less supportive of this idea that national leaders should closely follow public opinion.

This data raises the old question the founding fathers debated about how representative they wanted our elected officials to be. The constitutional framers, as we discussed, held that elected representatives should act as "trustees" of public sentiment and do what they believed was best in the public's behalf. But, nowadays, as this Gallup data suggests, three-quarters of the public espouse the view that elected representatives, including presidents, should be "delegates" of their constituents, and should strive to ascertain the public will and presumably translate this into public policies.

These and related public opinion findings, reflecting the heightened distrust in the national government, imply Americans have more confidence in themselves when it comes to making important public policy judgments than they do in their national legislative or executive branch elected officials.[70]

The problem with this contemporary sentiment is that Americans are deeply divided on many important issues, from health care to immigration. Moreover, the general public seldom has well-developed, not to mention well-informed, views on a whole host of national security and international relations issues. Thus, what exactly should our foreign policy be toward Pakistan, China, Somalia, or Iran? On such issues the people understandably look for guidance and education to leaders in both our elected branches as well as in the State and Defense departments, more than to their neighbors for informed leadership.

HOW AMERICANS JUDGE INCUMBENT PRESIDENTS

President Lincoln said that public sentiment and support are indispensable for a president to succeed. Lincoln, who lived through the most trying of times without Gallup, Wall Street Journal/NBC, and CNN polls reporting his considerable public disfavor, would warn us today that in evaluating presidents we should be careful not to take polls too seriously, for the sources of positive or negative evaluations are often superficial. He would doubtless also say the influence between a people and their president is reciprocal: presidents must be both leaders and followers of public opinion.

The Gallup organization, since the late 1930s, has been asking random samples of adult Americans, "Do you approve or disapprove of the way [the incumbent president] is handling his job as president?" Nowadays, Gallup is joined by a dozen or more polling or media organizations probing how liked or disapproved a president is. See Figure 2.1, and notice the gyrations and the gravity pull of diminished approval over the course of most presidential terms.

This question allows us to learn, at least in part, whether presidents meet public expectations or not and whether or not a president seems responsive and accountable to citizens.

Over the past seventy years we can discern at least a few patterns:

➡ Presidents tend to be more popular in their first year than they are later.
➡ Presidential approval ratings often rise during the "honeymoon" early months in office.
➡ Over time, however, approval ratings usually drop, with a number of zigs and zags caused by specific events, conditions, or crises.
➡ Presidents typically lose popularity during midterm elections, when the "guns" of the opposition party are aimed directly at the White House.
➡ Domestic crises, especially recessions, typically cause approval evaluations to drop.

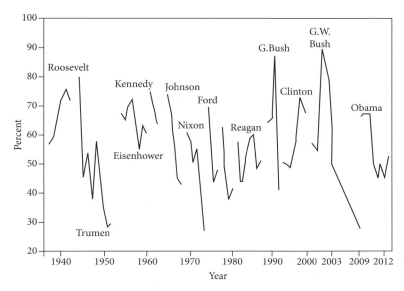

Figure 2.1. Presidential Gallup poll approval ratings, 1938–2012. (Created by the authors using data from Gallup).

→ International or terrorist crises, regardless of what a president does, typically cause us to rally around our president in the short run.

→ Presidents often enjoy a rebound late in the first term—especially when they begin to be evaluated in comparison with likely opponents.

→ If a president is reelected, the pattern often repeats itself, although approval ratings drop more quickly and tend to be lower in second terms.

→ Polls do not necessarily accurately reflect how a president is doing the job. And at least a good part of poll fluctuations are beyond the influence or control of a president.

"The course of presidential popularity proceeds up and down in varying sequences of intensity and duration, yet always more inevitably downward," writes political scientist Lyn Ragsdale. "The one obvious difference between the presidential ride and the amusement park ride is that presidents do not finish where they began. Instead they start higher, finish lower, and presumably have less fun."[71]

While these patterns are persistent, they are not inevitable. Moreover, it is premature to be definitive when we are examining just a dozen or so presidencies. The American people find it convenient to blame presidents for a whole range of problems, regardless of whether the problems are subject to presidential influence and solution or not. Presidents receive blame, and sometimes praise, for events, like the price of gas, over which they have little or no control.

Most people are politically inattentive and mostly notice the gaffes and mistakes, while failing to appreciate successes. Decline in approval of a president is partly a function of the inability and unlikelihood of presidents to live up to the buildup they receive during the presidential honeymoon (and the hopes and promises they raised during the campaign). Heightened expectations are invariably followed by disappointment. Sometimes the disappointment warrants despair and retribution; people often unfairly turn on presidents almost as if they were the sole cause of everything that is wrong in their lives.

Another paradox for a president stems from the public's desire to want contradictory things from government. The public wants budget cuts yet not service cuts (for themselves, at least); we want tax cuts yet also want entitlement programs such as Social Security and Medicare to be fully funded.

Presidents want to unite and lead the nation as well as to maintain high public opinion and approval; but each of them confronts the dilemmas and paradoxes of a plural democratic presidency in the era of 24-hour instant news cycles. They have to listen to myriad groups on myriad issues—"many of which are contradictory, while appearing to devise solutions to the problems in such a way as to maintain the nation's unity and to retain their presidential images as natural leaders of all the people."[72]

Presidential resources tend to wane as the years roll by. Every presidential honeymoon comes to an end. Prominent politicians who are rivals for the office begin, after a short grace period, to criticize a president's positions, partisan followings crystallize, and the ranks of those who disapprove of the president begin to grow. Presidential promises, at least some of them, go unachieved. Presidential achievements often fail to get acknowledged. Factions in a president's own party inevitably develop. Press criticism increases.

A predictable cycle develops. Presidents usually lose political capital when their approval ratings sink. A president in this predicament is tempted to avoid divisive issues in favor of not making waves. But problems often become greater.

Because modern media coverage gives so much emphasis to the presidency, it serves to quicken and intensify these reactions. Because presidents can usually gain immediate publicity, they are expected to communicate their views and solve problems without delay. Precisely because they are supposed to be shapers of public opinion, they are expected to inspire the country to great causes and sensible, low-cost solutions.

Whatever they do, the more presidents strive to achieve favorable support in public opinion polls, the more they are tempted to engage in short-term transitory policies—policies that may not necessarily be good for the country in the long run.

A few observers worry that presidents preoccupied with falling approval ratings may be tempted to resort to "darker" or Machiavellian projects. Consider the following:

> Faced with impossible expectations, presidents may be left little choice but to create the image that they are fulfilling expectations, using the powers of office to stage symbolic events, public relations derbies to effect favorable perceptions,

resulting in nothing more than an "image-is-everything presidency."... In the extreme, some fear the possibility that the president may use his power in the international sphere in hopes of uniting a rally event to direct attention from other less favorable considerations, trying to induce the so-called "wag the dog" effect.[73]

In the aftermath of the September 11, 2001, terrorist attacks on the United States, President George W. Bush's popularity soared to over 90 percent. This led Democrats and much of the media to be cautious in their criticism of the president. But Bush lost nearly 40 percentage points from this all-time public approval high by the time he ran for reelection in 2004. And he tumbled even lower, to around 23 percent approval, in his last year in office.

Why did Bush's approval rating fall nearly 65 points in just over four years? He had pledged to unite the country and bridge the partisan divide, especially in Washington. He failed to do this—indeed, the partisan divide became larger than ever.[74] Bush misled the public on Iraq and mismanaged the federal government's response to Hurricane Katrina and the mortgage and credit crisis meltdowns of 2007 and 2008.[75] In the end Bush was often perceived as a poor listener, and an ineffective manager. Even the Republican ticket in 2008 criticized several Bush programs as failures.

Obama, like George W. Bush, ran on the promise of bridging the partisan divide and unifying the country. But divided party lines quickly took their toll on how people judged his presidency. He courted Republicans in his first year, but to no avail. Republicans in Congress unanimously opposed his Affordable Care Act and similarly opposed his economic stimulus and debt reduction initiatives.

President Obama also lost support among those who call themselves independents. They had been crucial to his election in 2008. He had started out with 63 percent of independents approving his performance. This declined to about 40 percent before he won nearly a majority of them in 2012 reelection.

An anemic economic recovery, continued high unemployment, and the housing crisis hurt Obama's standing. Obama became viewed as too big a spender and unable to deliver on his campaign promise that he would change how Washington operates.

Ironically, even Obama's "successes" earned him little political credit. He fought valiantly for a major health care insurance overhaul, but for this he was punished as favoring big government and opposing personal liberty. He successfully, most economists agreed, helped stabilize and rescue both the auto industry and the country's big banks but again received a lot criticism for these efforts. He kept his pledge to wind down the war in Iraq, which Americans supported, yet his efforts in this area seemingly went unrewarded. Even his capture and elimination (with the courageous help of Navy Seals) of Osama bin Laden won him only a fleeting public approval boost.

Americans became as divided, in partisan terms, about Obama as they had been about George W. Bush. But, writes political scientist Gary C. Jacobson, the sources of polarization were different. "For Bush, the strongest force was his foreign policy, particularly the Iraq War. For Obama, it has been his domestic initiatives, particularly regarding the health care system; his foreign and military policies have proven notably less divisive."[76]

WHY DISAPPROVAL RATINGS RISE

Presidents usually have the support of a majority of Americans just after their inauguration. A rallying around the newly elected president customarily takes place. Most people, including many who did not vote or who did not vote for the victor, give new presidents the benefit of the doubt. Most Americans want to have positive feelings about the presidency. Plus, inauguration ceremonies generally promote patriotism, national pride, and optimism in the new governing team. Presidents serve a variety of functions for the American public. A president serves (or at least can serve) as a symbol of national unity, stability, and the American way of life, as an outlet for feeling good about America, and as a means of simplifying complexity.

Because the president serves as both head of government (the nation's chief politician) and head of state (the symbolic representation of the nation), the president is simultaneously the chief divider of the nation and its chief unifier. Ronald Reagan was a masterful head of state. In the aftermath of the Challenger disaster, Reagan took on the role of the high priest and national healer for a nation devastated by tragedy. This role allowed Reagan, the nation's top politician, to rise above politics (at least for a while) and serve as a symbol for the nation.

Invested in the office of the presidency is high respect, but also high expectations (typically exaggerated by presidential campaign promises). Yet the president's powers are seldom commensurate with the responsibilities or the public's expectations. This invariably leads to frustration, and also to a decline in popularity. Likewise, if the public continues to demand that the government deliver on contradictory expectations (e.g., lower taxes yet provide more government services), presidents are put in no-win situations. Given this paradox, what's a president to do?

Presidents and their message managers are tempted to spin, distort, and manipulate the news. Political scientists Paul Brace and Barbara Hinckley say that excessive reliance on appearances has led to the development of a "public-relations presidency...concerned primarily with maintaining and increasing public support."[77]

The heroic view of what might be accomplished is promoted by journalists who write or talk about the possibilities of the first one hundred days and in doing so sometimes attribute to the president the entire responsibility for the nations' economy. The problem is compounded by Americans who want—and sometimes need—to believe their presidents can regularly make a transformational difference. Polls suggest that people believe a president can make a difference; that Franklin D. Roosevelt did make things happen; that America would have been much different if John F. Kennedy had not been assassinated; and that presidents can reduce unemployment or inflation, increase governmental efficiency, pursue an effective foreign policy, and strengthen the national defense and homeland security.

To win the presidency, presidents make promises. Once in office, they find themselves battling with the Congress and colliding with the Supreme Court on occasion, unable to exert as much influence over the federal bureaucracy as they had presumed, and are constrained by public opinion, the press, interest groups, rogue nations, and other forces. A president's power today to make and implement policies is limited by the partisan and decentralized character of politics and government in America, which often results in gridlock. America's growing interdependence with the rest of the world, with all the negative fallout from globalization as well as the rise of worldwide terrorism, also can limit the flexibility of the office.

Thoughtful people realize that presidents are indeed constrained by a number of factors and should be constrained. That said, they still hold presidents responsible. Presidents are a convenient, highly visible scapegoat for the nation's problems. We oversimplify issues, we personalize them, and television is constantly featuring the president on the news. When things go wrong, people notice. When things go right, people are usually complacent. Reality may be far more complex, but it is easier for busy people to ascribe blame to a specific person—the president.

Americans evaluate presidents on the basis of social, economic, and international policy *outcomes*. Yet the public's perceptions of presidential performances are usually inexact. Their evaluation is based on a combination of their own situation and on their general judgment of how the nation is doing, and how they think the nation will do. "When the economy falters, support for the president erodes, not so much because citizens blame the president for their private hardships, however vivid, immediate, and otherwise important they might be, but because citizens hold the president accountable for the deterioration of national economic conditions."[78]

Lyndon Johnson lost public approval more because of the civil rights disturbances and divisiveness of his Vietnam policies than because of economic developments; the economy was actually good at the time of his major popularity losses. Nixon lost his popularity and his claim to office not because of economic factors, but because of all the things associated with the Watergate scandal. Another reason presidents lose popularity is because we have faulty memories. We forget past presidents also had difficulty controlling events and solving problems quickly. We also forget that all leaders, even our heroes, have made mistakes. We often judge our presidents according to a model of the perfect, ideal, or heroic president.

People often acknowledge they hold unfair or unrealistic expectations. Thus when people are asked, "Why do you think presidents almost always lose popularity the longer they stay in office?," they give these reasons:

➡ Presidents can't please everybody.
➡ People only see their good points at first.
➡ Presidents are scapegoats for our problems.

→ Presidents can't spend money we and they don't have.
→ They make too many promises they can't keep.
→ Presidents often have to make unpopular decisions.
→ Presidents are not as powerful as people think.
→ People don't always look at the overall record of a president.

In sum, people judge them on their record, and especially on whether or not they follow through on their pledges. Our support for presidents is influenced also by how long they have been in office, and questions of peace, prosperity, and integrity. Also, especially in recent years, partisanship looms large in how we judge incumbent presidents. Thus, while most Republicans favored Bill Clinton's impeachment, Democrats supported him in high numbers. Democrats far more than Republicans, on the other hand, lost confidence in George W. Bush and especially his handling of the war in Iraq. Democrats favored most of Obama's policy initiatives but Republicans quickly became critical of almost anything Obama proposed. Note in Figure 2.2 how one's party identification is highly correlated with how people judged Barack Obama.

WHAT CAN A PRESIDENT DO?

Can presidents appeal for public support and improve their standing with the public and use this to help enact their legislative initiatives?

Leading the public is supposed to be a key responsibility as well as a key source of power for presidents. Yet the ability to *inspire* the nation and generate sustained public support takes enormous time and effort. Those who think this ability is somehow automatically conferred upon assuming office are mistaken.

Presidents with popular support can sometimes exert pressure on Congress to adopt their programs. Lyndon B. Johnson did this on landmark civil and voting rights legislation in the mid-1960s. Reagan did it on tax cuts and defense

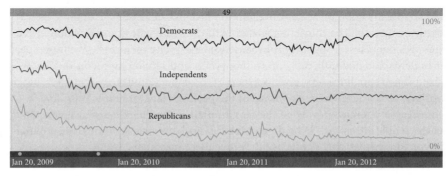

Figure 2.2. Obama's Approval by Party Affiliation. President Barack Obama's Approval, by Party Affiliation. (Created by the authors using data from Gallup Presidential Job Approval Center).

spending measures in his first term. Obama did it with his first economic stimulus initiative. Yet there are many more cases where presidents failed to win public support and consequently failed to secure congressional approval for their priorities. Thus, LBJ lost the public's support on Vietnam, Clinton lost it on health care, and George W. Bush failed to win public support for his social security and immigration policies.[79]

Is presidential popularity a predictable source of presidential power? Some scholars believe it can be a convertible source of political power—namely, that a president can convert popularity into congressional votes, better treatment by the media, greater party loyalty, and less criticism from political opponents. Many legislative achievements have occurred during presidential honeymoons and when presidents were riding high in the polls. Also, if a president can convince Congress that he or she is popular and that to defy the White House is politically dangerous, that president has more political capital. *Perception* often counts as much as (and sometimes more than) *reality*.

In any event, presidents are keenly aware of fluctuations in their popularity, and they routinely engage in efforts at dramatizing themselves and their initiatives in hope of currying increased public approval.[80]

But the relationships between presidents and the public they serve is complex. While presidents try to respond to the public's policy preferences, they are wary of doing so if the policy outcomes will not be to their liking. Political scientist Jeffrey Cohen persuasively points out, "If presidents try to curry public favor by implementing policies that follow public wishes, and if these policies fail, it will be the president, not the public, that bears the brunt of the blame."[81]

Presidents protect their reputations as well as their priorities. They seldom pander to the public when it is not in their interest to do so. Political scientist Brandice Canes-Wrone concludes presidents can and occasionally do appeal to the public as a way to influence congressional receptiveness to a presidential priority, yet presidents do not typically pander to mass public opinion if they believe it is misinformed or misguided and would hurt the national interest.[82]

Trying to understand the complications of when to lead, when to follow, and when to hold back or merely respond symbolically is the subject of a growing body of research. Complicating all this are the major changes taking place in the media. The golden age of radio and traditional network television has been replaced by 24-hour cable television, YouTube, Twitter, Facebook, Internet bloggers, and a whole range of alternative news sources. It is harder now for a president to get media coverage and frame issues as they would like. And the public has become more skeptical if not cynical toward all of the media. Presidents keep "going public," yet the public either isn't listening or is increasingly skeptical. "Rather than being the voice of the nation, presidents in the new media age appear more spokespeople for special interests than they did in the golden age," writes Jeff Cohen. "When presidents are less able to lead the public, they seek other ways to get Congress to act favorably on their policies. With less opportunity or ability to lead the public in the era of the new media, presidents instead seek the support of interest groups, special publics, and their partisan base."[83]

Presidents nowadays reach fewer people via television than was the case a generation or more ago because viewers uninterested in politics "have many alternative entertainment outlets. In addition, critics of the president have many more venues through which to voice their criticism ..." as George Bush and Barack Obama found out.[84]

Political scientist George Edwards concludes that while presidential popularity is obviously an asset for a president, presidential speechmaking to rally the general public to put pressure on Congress usually has little effect.[85] Edwards recommends that a president may well want, in many circumstances, to engage in quiet negotiations, or deliberative discussions, with leaders in Congress. "Staying private," as opposed to using a bully pulpit to "go public" and thereby bypassing Congress might "contribute to reducing gridlock, incivility, and thus public cynicism," says Edwards.[86]

Still, rightly or wrongly, many Americans want to believe presidents should provide vision and frame the policy agenda in Congress. Franklin Roosevelt said, "All our great presidents were *leaders* of thought at a time when certain historic ideas in the life of the nation had to be clarified." His cousin Theodore Roosevelt boasted, "People used to say of me that I...divined what the people were going to think. I did not 'divine'...I simply made up my mind what they ought to think, and then did my best to get them to think it."[87]

Effective leaders take risks as George Washington did driving the American Revolution, as Lincoln did in the Civil War as FDR and LBJ did on social and humanitarian issues. Those who merely want to be loved sometimes sacrifice conviction for wanting to be loved. Harding was popular yet also a failure. JFK was popular yet often cautious until his third and last year. FDR once said, "Judge me by the enemies I've made." Historian Arthur M. Schlesinger, Jr., suggests that effective presidential leadership is provided by those who follow their convictions and, at least on important issues, ignore middle-of-the-road pragmatism. "We hear much these days about the virtues of the middle of the road. But none of the top nine [highly rated presidents] can be described as a middle-roader," writes Schlesinger. "Middle-roading may be fine for campaigning, but it is a sure road to mediocrity in governing. The middle of the road is not the vital center: it is the dead center.... The Greats and Near Greats all took risks in pursuit of their ideals. They all provoked intense controversy. They all, except Washington, divided the nation before reuniting it on a new level of national understanding."[88]

HOW THE PUBLIC JUDGES PRESIDENTS

The unwritten presidential job description, the one we carry around in our heads, calls for a president to be a visionary problem solver, a unifying force for the nation, a healer and sage. Thus, every four years we search anew for a fresh superstar who is blessed with the judgment of Washington, the brilliance of Jefferson, the genius of Lincoln, the political savvy of FDR, the youthful grace of JFK, and the sunny optimism of Ronald Reagan. Expectations always rise as elections near. Yet an exaggerated sense of what can be called "the textbook president" or "national Spider-man" inevitably blinds us to the limits of what a president can accomplish.

As noted, the public has favorable memories of certain presidents and these memories often differ from how expert political historians rank presidents.

One difference in the evaluation between the public and experts is the perspective of time. Historians like to wait for twenty or thirty years and see how a president's policies played out. They also want to read the memoirs of the president and other top advisers and examine archival materials. The public, on the other hand, is plainly influenced by what historians call *presentism*. The people are more likely to remember presidents who were good ones in their own or their parents' lifetimes rather than past presidents who were notable in the judgment of history. People who remember the youth and excitement of John Kennedy or the charm and patriotism of Ronald Reagan, especially in comparison to their successors who seem ineffective, dishonest, or boring, rank Kennedy and Reagan as greater than Thomas Jefferson (see Table 2.2).

Popularity while in office is not necessarily a useful gauge for judging historical reputation. Thus, Harry Truman received some of the lowest popularity ratings in history, yet his reputation today is more positive. Political scientist James Ceaser reminds us

> It is worth emphasizing how little approval ratings have to do with any lasting judgment of presidential performance. A president's legacy derives from his accomplishments or failures. As an instrument of presidential power, a high approval rating has some value as a reminder to others of the potential "cost" they might have to pay in opposing a popular president. Yet it is important to remember that an approval rating is a lag, rather than a lead, indicator. What determines the score will be the public's assessment of conditions, performance, and persona. An astute President should accordingly be prepared in most cases

TABLE 2.2 The Public's Favorite Presidents

Question: "Suppose you could bring back any of the U.S. presidents, living or dead, to be the next president of the United States. Who would you want to be the next president?" (February 2008)

John F. Kennedy	23%
Ronald Reagan	22
Bill Clinton	13
Abraham Lincoln	10
Franklin D. Roosevelt	8

Source: The Gallup Poll Briefing, Princeton, NJ. February 18, 2008, p. 68.
Note: $N = 1,007$; For Democrats the favorites were JFK, Bill Clinton, and FDR. For Republicans the favorites were Ronald Reagan, JFK, and Lincoln.

to sacrifice his standing today, if by doing so he can affect positively the future assessment of these factors.[89]

All rankings of presidents, whether by the public or by experts, reinforce our inclination to attribute more power to presidents than they really had.

What Americans expect of a president depends on varying factors. Not the least of these is who is president, who has been recently in office, and what the times demand. If recent presidents appear to have been weak, the public will likely call for more decisiveness. If the recent presidents seem to have overreached, the public demands more humility, honesty, or a collaborative president.

The public does not always base its evaluation of presidents on policies, issues, or achievements. The public likes past and present presidents who elicit positive emotion—optimism, hope, strength, warmth, excitement—and made them proud to be Americans. Political psychologist Drew Westen argues that, whether we are looking at candidates or judging presidents, we should never underestimate the role that positive emotions play: "Positive emotions rally voters to the polls and convince the uncommitted that they have someone and something to be excited about. The most successful politicians know how to elicit a range of positive feelings—enthusiasm, excitement, hope, inspiration, compassion, satisfaction, pride..."[90]

Historians, on the other hand, are more concerned with how a president handled the economic demands and national security of the day, the content of a president's program, and the president's success in carrying it out. Experts also admire political skill, agility, and style.

Both expert and average citizens alike are influenced by the cycles of American politics. People cannot emancipate themselves from their own age. Historians and biographers are expected to transcend the present, yet they, too, seldom succeed entirely.

HOW EXPERTS JUDGE PRESIDENTS

What constitutes presidential greatness? Experts judge presidents on the basis of the scope of the problems they faced, their efforts (actions) and intentions (vision) in dealing with these problems, what they were able to accomplish, and long-term results. Experts admire presidents who are smart, skilled politically, and willing to tell people what they may not want to hear and who can lead these same people to where they may not, at least in the short term, want to go. Experts downgrade presidents whose administrations were rife with corruption, or who were lacking in character.

The process of rating presidents is fraught with potential biases. The actions of presidents look different from different historical vantage points. There are dangers in trying to assess the effectiveness and achievements of a presidency too early, say within twenty years. Sometimes a spate of new biographies about a former president will cast a favorable light on a presidency or, conversely, may downgrade a previously respected administration. Harding, for example, was popular at his death in office yet was rated as ineffective by historians. Truman was unpopular in 1952 yet gained stature two generations later.

The charge is made, too, that most of the experts polled in these surveys are university professors or writers who are liberal or Democratic in their political orientation. While this is true, studies find the ranking by conservatives and liberals generally similar. Serious disagreement in the ranks of the top ten most favored presidents mainly involved the relative placement of Franklin D. Roosevelt. Conservatives sometimes place FDR in third rather than second place. Still, the charge cannot be entirely ignored. Experts on the presidency are generally biased in favor of activist Democratic presidents.[91]

Surveys conducted in 2000 and again in 2005 by the conservative Federalist Society and cosponsored by *The Wall Street Journal* deliberately included both law school professors and more scholars of a Republican persuasion. These detailed surveys of over seventy experts found Washington, Lincoln, and FDR as the great presidents, with Jefferson, Theodore Roosevelt, and Jackson as leading near-great presidents. Republicans Ronald Reagan and Dwight Eisenhower rose in these rankings at the same time as Democrats Woodrow Wilson and JFK earned lower ratings than in earlier surveys. Overall, however, the Federalist Society's rankings were relatively similar to those in the Arthur Schlesinger, Jr., *New York Times Magazine* survey of historians[92] (see those results in Table 2.3).

C-SPAN, both in 2000 and again in 2009, conducted a survey of historians and presidential scholars "intended to reflect a broad experience in the study of the U.S. Presidency across ideological and demographic spectra." Their survey results in 2000 ranked the top presidents in the following order: Lincoln, FDR, Washington, Teddy Roosevelt, Truman, Wilson, and Jefferson. The only surprise in that survey was that JFK and Reagan were ranked a bit higher in the "near great" category than Jackson and Polk.

In 2009 C-SPAN's survey of nearly 65 presidential scholars ranked the best presidents in this order: Lincoln, Washington, FDR, Teddy Roosevelt, Truman, Kennedy, and Jefferson. Kennedy moved up, Wilson moved down.

Do great crises encourage great presidential performance? Madison, Pierce, Buchanan, Andrew Johnson, Hoover, and George W. Bush all faced crises, yet their

---

TABLE 2.3 *Historian* Ratings of Presidential Performance

Great:	Lincoln, FDR, Washington
Near Great:	Jefferson, Jackson, Wilson, Theodore Roosevelt, Truman, Polk
Average (High):	John Adams, Eisenhower, Cleveland, McKinley, Kennedy, LBJ, Monroe
Average (Low):	Madison, J. Q. Adams, Van Buren, Hayes, Arthur, Harrison, Taft, Ford, Carter, Reagan, Bush
Below Average:	Tyler, Taylor, Fillmore, Coolidge
Failure:	Pierce, Buchanan, A. Johnson, Grant, Harding, Hoover, Nixon

SOURCE: Arthur M. Schlesinger, Jr., "The Ultimate Approval Rating," *The New York Times Magazine* (December 15, 1996): 48–49. Copyright © 1996 by the New York Times Co. Reprinted by permission.

responses seemed lame or ineffective. On the other hand, Lincoln, Wilson, FDR, and Truman all rank as great or above average because they responded to crises effectively. Although severe crises do not necessarily bring forth great leadership, the so-called "greats" served in periods of military, social, and economic upheaval, and the way they met these tests justifiably enhanced their reputations. The old question of whether great times make for great leadership or great leaders make great times is never satisfactorily settled, in part because even admired presidents experienced failures too.

An energetic presidency is, however, different from an imperial presidency. LBJ, Nixon, and George W. Bush overreached and will be judged harshly by historians.

Another factor that renders rankings problematic is the difficulty in judging some presidents solely on their performance in office. Achievements over a lifetime are often a complicating factor. Thus Washington, Jefferson, Madison, and Eisenhower were distinguished Americans apart from their presidencies. Grant was a great general but a weak president. Madison was a superb constitutional architect yet an average president. Hoover had been an outstanding success in business and a splendid war relief administrator and cabinet member, but was far less successful as a president. While it is difficult to separate the presidential years from an overall career, experts seem able to do so.

An additional problem is this: Can we objectively compare presidents from different eras? Just as presidents cannot be experts on all areas of policy, historians cannot be experts on all presidents. And, as noted earlier, biographers and historians have to be mindful of the varying cultural and political climates in which presidents served. Yet, isn't this what is necessary to make fair, objective judgments? Seldom are different presidents faced with the same situations. Thus, for example, we honor Jefferson and Polk for adding vast areas to the territory of the United States, yet recent presidents cannot duplicate those feats.

CAN WE PREDICT PRESIDENTIAL EFFECTIVENESS?

It would be nice to have a simple formula for predicting presidential leadership success, but no one has come up with one, and it is unlikely.

One political scientist examined past political experience to see whether more experienced political leaders might provide us better presidents. He was motivated, in part, by Hillary Clinton's campaign strategists in 2008 who boasted that because of her years in the White House (as First Lady) and in the U.S. Senate (as a senator from New York) she was "Ready to lead on day one." The implication, none too subtle, was that Senator Obama was less experienced and less ready to lead.

But John Balz found there was no evidence that political experience improves the likelihood of White House effectiveness. He found, on the contrary, that certain types of political experience, such as service in Congress and as mayor, were actually correlated with poorer White House performance. In the end, he concludes, "other personal and historical factors are likely to be more important,"[93] than just simply that they had spent long careers in politics.

Other writers have speculated about whether successful business executives make for better presidential or top governmental executives. In other words, can business success equal national political success? Our best business success who became president was Herbert Hoover. Top Ford CEO Robert McNamara had a controversial tenure as Secretary of Defense. Successful real estate mogul Donald Trump nominated himself occasionally as a possibly great president but many people questioned his political judgment and leadership temperament. Governing may have much in common with running a business, yet it is not exactly the same thing.

Jamin Soderstrom compiled exhaustive resumes for our previous presidents. He especially weighed legislative, executive, military, and foreign policy experience, but also gave credit for business experience, intellectual achievements, and writing and speaking ability. According to his findings, several great presidents, at least according to expert polls, were among those with the best resumes. George Washington, Franklin Roosevelt, Theodore Roosevelt, Thomas Jefferson, and Dwight Eisenhower were in this category. However, Soderstrom's resume analysis also placed Richard Nixon, Herbert Hoover, and the two Adamses as among the dozen with top resumes. Further, two of the widely agreed on "failed presidents," Pierce and Buchanan, met his "qualified threshold" and indeed were ranked, at least in terms of having impressive resumes, ahead of Reagan, Jackson, and Truman.[94]

Soderstrom concludes that even highly qualified candidates may sometimes be the wrong choice for the White House.

Political scientist Fred Greenstein says we should assess past and future presidents on their policy vision, political skill, communication ability, and organizational strengths. These are conventional tests. But he adds: cognitive style and emotional intelligence. By "cognitive style" he suggests we should examine a person's ability to process information and avoid becoming overwhelmed in details. By "emotional intelligence" he refers to a leader's ability to control one's emotions and turn them to constructive uses. "Examples of presidents whose defective emotional intelligence impaired their leadership include Woodrow Wilson, whose rigid refusal to compromise led to the defeat of the Versailles Treaty [and] Richard Nixon, whose suspiciousness and impulse to strike out at perceived enemies destroyed his presidency."[95]

Another student of presidential evaluation shares this list of "What to Avoid in Presidential Candidates": Stay Away from Cynics and Whiners, Keep Away from Know-It-Alls, Steer Clear of Candidates With a Narrow Focus, Be Leery of Unrelenting Ideologues, Stand Guard Against Bearers of Grudges, and Beware Those Who Don't Fully Understand Our System of Separate Branches Sharing Power.[96]

An exclusive club: George H. W. Bush, Barack Obama, George W. Bush, Bill Clinton, and Jimmy Carter. AP Photo/J. Scott Applewhite.

WHAT IS PRESIDENTIAL GREATNESS?

An attempt to define "presidential greatness" is necessarily subjective. It is a value judgment. We all have biases. We all live in a fixed historical era. We almost always approach the task with an eye on contemporary problems and with a partisan or ideological bias of some kind. Still, it is tempting, if not irresistible, to attempt such a definition.

Experts judge presidents as effective or outstanding when they have acted greatly in challenging times. Great presidents, they believe, had an appreciation of the dynamics of history as well as a deep sense of the needs, anxieties, and dreams of the American people. Did the president have the courage to fight for what was right? Did they bring out the best in the American people? Did they recruit a first-rate cabinet and advisory team? Did they display common sense, agility, decisiveness, and good judgment in picking priorities, associates, and fights? Did they secure both the blessings of liberty and peace? Lesser presidents often shy away from, rather than join, a conflict. They fear that decisiveness or polarization will lead to blood in the streets, even though history often teaches that courageous and early confrontation of divisive issues often avoids even worse violence later.

Also, moral courage stands out. Were they willing and able to stand up and be counted, as Lincoln and FDR were, when the nation and the nation's allies were challenged by the forces of hate and oppression? Conservatives revere Reagan for his boldness in standing up to the Soviet Union, the bureaucracy, and unions.

An almost universally accepted aspect of leadership is the willingness and ability to take risks, to act boldly when situations necessitate vision. Presidents are asked to educate and shape public opinion—even as they consult it. The question, to be sure, is more difficult than it first seems, because determinations of what is popular and what is right are hard to make. Still, we can look back and find examples of presidential courage, of bucking the popular trends, and conclude satisfactorily that these actions were correct.

George Washington faced intense hostility over the Jay Treaty, yet he saw it through. John Adams was prepared to break up his party to avoid war with France, and he did both. Lincoln defied public opinion by removing General McClellan of the Army of the Potomac, and Truman displayed similar courage nearly a century later in removing General Douglas MacArthur from his top military command in Korea. Though these actions were unpopular, history vindicated them.

Experts look for accomplishments and whether or not the president provided leadership to advance the nation's interests. Most experts understandably evaluate past presidents on whether or not that president provided leadership to advance the nation's interests. But experts are seldom unified on what the nation's main interests are. Liberals admire those presidents who championed what they call the positive role of government to help all the people, not just the powerful stakeholders in society. Conservatives admire presidents who championed liberty, "free-market" economics, and a less-regulated society. Everyone admires leaders who were willing, on occasion, to say no to their friends.

Everyone agrees that the best presidents put in place policies that encouraged long-term economic growth, expanded equality of opportunity, preserved and expanded civil liberties and human rights, and provided for long-term national security.

Deciding whose presidential leadership is "good" or "bad" or constitutionally "appropriate" or inappropriate is not easy. Imagine—as a thought experiment— that you have been sent an evaluation form to analyze this president: He failed to win a majority popular vote, yet still governed as if he had a strong mandate from the people. He led the United States military into enemy territory where thousands of soldiers fell to local guerilla fighters. During the war he restricted access to the U.S. Constitution's guarantee of habeas corpus and in other ways violated the rights and freedoms of U.S. citizens. And after a while this president became very unpopular. "You're probably thinking this president's leadership doesn't sound very impressive. There's only one problem with that conclusion: both George W. Bush and Abraham Lincoln fit this description."[97]

An iconoclastic evaluation, with libertarian orientation, reminds us that most of us are suckers for someone with great charisma. But, Ivan Eland argues, that dull, drab, or quiet presidents have actually served us better—especially if you look closely at what the charismatic and dull presidents did. Ivan Elaud concludes that the ever-popular John F. Kennedy is one of the most overrated individuals in U.S. history. "He took rash actions that led to the Cuban Missile Crisis, which almost incinerated the world, and he was reluctant to push civil rights for African Americans." And on the much liked Ronald Reagan[98]

> Ronald Reagan, adored by conservatives, was not all that conservative and did not "win" the Cold War. His harsh anti-Soviet policies and massive defense build-up wasted money, reversed Richard Nixon's policy of détente with the U.S.S.R., and

unnecessarily raised the existential threat of nuclear war. His tax cuts were fake because they weren't accompanied by cuts in spending. To win conservative support for his military expansion, he allowed domestic expenditures to be increased much more than defense spending. Thus the federal government doubled in size under Reagan's watch.... Even worse, in The Iran-Contra Affair, he authorized illegal arms shipments to state sponsors of terrorism in order to secretly generate funds for the Contra army in Nicaragua; this secretly undermined Congress' most important remaining role under the Constitution—holding the power of the purse.[99]

Libertarian Elaud concludes that Presidents John Tyler, Grover Cleveland, Martin Van Buren, Rutherford Hayes, and Chester Arthur are at least as worthy as those currently on Mount Rushmore. Yes, he admits, most of his excellent presidents are remembered as bland, gray personalities, but they largely respected the Constitution's intention of limiting government and restraining presidential war-making power. His evaluations, not surprisingly, won high praise from Congressman and 2012 presidential candidate Ron Paul who rather consistently warned people to beware macho-imperial presidents and to maximize individual liberties by reducing and curbing unnecessary government.

What did the great presidents do? George Washington, more than any other individual, converted the paper Constitution into an enduring document. With commanding prestige and character he set the precedents that balanced self-government and leadership, constitutionalism and statesmanship. Washington's success made possible the success of the Republic. That Washington owned as many as three hundred slaves and became wealthy as a result of their labor is hard for many modern Americans to accept. He held contradictory and varied ideas about the institution of slavery, and only at the end of his life did he begin to set his slaves free.

Jefferson was a skilled organizer and a resourceful chief executive and party leader. He made his share of mistakes, yet he adapted the office to countless new realities. His expansion of territory with the Louisiana Purchase, an achievement breathtaking in its consequences, assures him special status. Lincoln saved the Union and will be remembered as the foremost symbol of liberation, freedom, and tenacious leadership in our hour of ultimate crisis. FDR saw the nation through its worst economic crisis and rallied the nation and the world to defeat Nazism and Hitler. In a time of dictatorships, he managed a democratic response to the depression.

These accomplishments are admirable. Still, they raise many questions. If presidents alone were responsible for all those notable and enduring accomplishments, it is little wonder that our expectations of presidents are so high. Plainly, a variety of people and institutions (cabinet members, advisers, the military, diplomats, etc....) contributed to these achievements.

History seldom adequately honors the economic and social movement leaders, reform activists, and "disrupters" as opposed to "incrementalists" who often provide as much or more of an era's leadership than does the president of the time.[100] Great leadership depends on its surroundings, on teams of leaders, and on people who demand leadership. Luck—sometimes "dumb luck"—also plays a part in greatness. Timing and knowing how to embrace and exploit paradoxes and context is also crucial.[101]

Our fascination with the presidential effectiveness and failure reveals much about ourselves, about qualities we admire and those we dislike. It tells us, too, about our dreams and national character. We yearn for heroism and courage in literature, film, sports, and in our own lives. And so too we look for certain heroic "Mount Rushmore" qualities in our presidents. We delight in presidents who have triumphed when they faced ultimate tests. We admire presidents who are smart and compassionate and who think and act constitutionally. We are diminished by those who reveal the darker side of human nature and public life.

Leadership at the presidential level is full of risks. Sometimes risk taking does not pay off, as with Johnson's Vietnam policies. FDR risked his political life and reputation by arranging secret naval deals with the British, and his policies were handsomely rewarded. Nothing may be more dangerous than to be constantly guided by instant and temporary national poll results; for although the public often affords a president popularity on the basis of means, it is ends that ultimately determine the common good. One instance of a president appearing to pander to the polls and public sentiment came from President Ford. At a press conference he was asked if he favored a stiff tax on a gallon of gasoline as a form of price rationing to dampen demand. Columnist George Will recalls Ford's answer and condemns his reasoning: "'No, today I saw a poll that showed that 81% of the American people do not want to pay more for a gallon of gasoline.... Therefore,' said Ford, 'I am on solid ground in opposing it.' The problem is that all ground seems solid when your ear is to it, and as Winston Churchill said, 'It is hard to look up to some-one in that position.'"[102]

A democratic republic puts its faith in the people—faith that they will not merely elect presidents who will be responsive to their desires, but who will both educate them and do what is right. Americans want to be heard, yet they also want leaders who will exercise their judgment. We honor leaders who refuse to be intimidated by contrary public opinion data. Although presidents, to be sure, must take care not to be so self-assured they become insensitive to advice, they also need a certain inner sense of what has to be done. In the end, the best presidents are likely to be those who can accurately interpret the sentiments of the nation and rally the people and other political leaders to do what must be done, and what the public will later respect. These presidents will commonly be strong political leaders with a vision, as well as policy proposals, of where they think the nation should go. We will ask of them, Did they preserve, protect, and enrich the liberty, the rights, and the economic opportunities of all the people? Did they so engage with the public to educate and build support for what was right and to encourage the many alternative sources of leadership in a nation with such ample talent?

CONCLUSION

The United States has had some excellent presidents, yet Americans have reserved the label "great" to just one per century: Washington in the eighteenth century, Lincoln in the nineteenth century, and FDR in the twentieth century. Along the way, we have liked Teddy Roosevelt, JFK, and Ronald Reagan, yet affection toward these presidents is a different matter than their place in history.

The presidency may have been designed to be more of an administrative than a political or leadership position. This has of necessity changed, and public views of what presidents should do are different now than they were in the 1790s or even a few generations ago. We expect a lot from our contemporary presidents. We know they cannot all be "Mount Rushmore" presidents, yet we still want the best for our nation's sake and our own. We say we want leadership, yet we are often reluctant followers—and we can become impatient critics.

The public does not evaluate presidents in the same way that historians, biographers, or political scientists do. Presidents have always faced probing if not cynical treatment from journalists, especially the longer a president is in office. Today's media are critical of incumbent presidents as they strive to be watchdogs and expose the inevitable spin every White House dishes out. Public support for presidents follows certain patterns, yet these patterns are somewhat unpredictable and the exceptions are sometimes as interesting as the patterns themselves. When ranking and judging presidents we often learn more about the raters than the rated. As this chapter has also shown, even the most serious efforts at judging presidencies invariably involve some subjective or partisan biases.

The enduring challenge for presidents remains: Summon us to live up to our highest shared ideals of a generous, benevolent country that is a shining beacon for liberty and freedom; take prudent risks and anticipate and head off fiascoes; and pay close attention to our immediate shared aspirations such as national security, energy security, job creation, fair taxes, trade, prosperity, and equality of opportunity.

FOR DISCUSSION

1. In general, how do historians differ from the average person in judging and rating presidents?
2. What are the chief factors that typically influence why presidents lose public approval the longer they are in office?

DEBATE QUESTIONS

1. That George W. Bush and Barack Obama will be judged as below average presidents.
2. That presidents should sometimes ignore public opinion, and do what they believe is right.

FURTHER READINGS

Abramawitz, Alan I. *The Disappearing Center*. New Haven, CT: Yale University Press, 2010.

Bardes, Barbara A., and Robert W. Oldendick. *Public Opinion*, 4th ed. Lanham, MD: Rowman & Littlefield, 2012.

Bose, Meena, and Mark Landis, eds. *The Uses and Abuses of Presidential Rankings*. Hauppauge, NY: Nova, 2003.

Edwards, George C. *Overreach: Leadership in the Obama Presidency*. Princeton, NJ: Princeton University Press, 2012.

Fiorina, Morris P., et. al. *Culture War? The Myth of a Polarized America*, 3rd ed. Boston: Longman, 2011.

Hetherington, Marc J. *Why Trust Matters*. Princeton, NJ: Princeton University Press, 2005.

Jacobson, Gary J. *A Divider, Not a Uniter*, 2nd ed. New York: Longman, 2011.

Merry, Robert W. *Where They Stand: The American Presidents in the Eyes of Voters and Historians*. New York: Simon and Schuster, 2012.

Stimson, James A. *Public Opinion in America*. Boulder, CO: Westview Press, 1999.

Taranto, James, and Leonard Leo, eds. *Presidential Leadership: Rating the Best and the Worst in the White House*. New York: A Wall Street Journal Book, 2005.

Critical Thinking

STATEMENT: Barack Obama is the best president in the post-World War II era

PROBLEM: To prove—or disprove—this statement, what theories, evidence, assumptions, and information might I need? What data and reasoning are sufficient to make a compelling or at least plausible case?

CHAPTER 3

How We Elect Presidents

If Jefferson is elected, the Bible will be burned, the French "Marseil-laise" will be sung in Christian churches, and we may see our wives and daughters the victims of legal prostitution; soberly dishonored; speciously polluted.

REVEREND TIMOTHY DWIGHT, President, Yale University

Americans love their country, celebrate democratic ideals, and generally prize the American presidency, yet we are disgruntled about the way we elect presidents, and the candidates who run. Many Americans have been bewildered by the contentious presidential election of 2000, disappointed at the negative attacks in 2012, baffled by the Electoral College, and embarrassed by the huge role money and the media play in presidential elections. People see the selection process as an often self-defeating system, more like a demolition derby, as much a process of eliminating good people rather than encouraging strong candidates to run for the White House. Many worry as well at a paradox noted in chapter 1, that the qualities needed to win the White House are not necessarily the same as those needed to govern the country.

The process by which we select presidents is complex and controversial. Complex because there is not one law that covers presidential selection, but many. In some cases the federal government or national parties establish rules; in other cases, each state has laws governing presidential selection. For the most part it is the states that establish rules for elections. This means that there can be fifty different sets of laws governing the election. And given the Electoral College, a presidential election is really fifty different, separate races.

The process is controversial because the campaign is very long, very costly, and rarely seems to produce nominees about whom we get excited. Cynics contend that we usually end up voting for the lesser of two evils, or the evil of two lessers.

Many of our presidential paradoxes apply to the way we elect presidents. The qualities we look for in a president (Paradox 2) are often at odds with one another. Yes, we want a "common man"—one of us—yet we insist that they also be extraordinary, above the rest. We want caring, compassionate, empathetic leaders who are also tough, even ruthless, when necessary (Paradox 3). Americans want a leader to bring us together, yet to govern—even to get elected—is to be partisan, to be a divider at times (Paradoxes 4 and 5). Finally (Paradox 8), the skills and attributes that make one an effective candidate, are at times at odds with what it takes to govern effectively.

This chapter describes how we elect our presidents. We explore the following questions: Who becomes president? What do we look for in prospective presidents? What must a person do to be taken seriously as a presidential candidate? How important are the primaries and caucuses? Are national conventions still needed? What about the so-called advantages of incumbency? Why do people vote or not vote for a president? What about the controversial Electoral College and its role in presidential elections? And finally, does the selection process do what we need in democratic and quality-of-outcome terms? After all, a presidential election is about more than merely determining who will assume office. It is also, or should be, the great conversation a democracy has concerning its future.

The 2008 race was truly precedent shattering. The two final candidates vying for the Democratic party nomination for president were both from previously

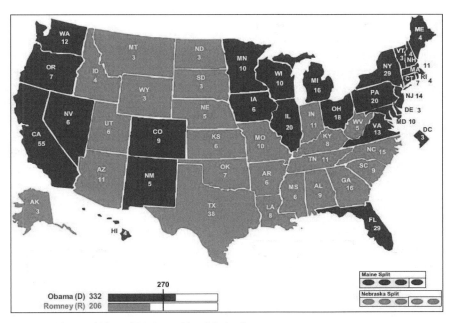

Map 3.1 Electoral Map of 2012 presidential election.

excluded groups: a woman and a black male. Senators Hillary Clinton and Barack Obama broke barriers, opened up our democracy, and struck a significant blow for equality. Likewise, the choice of Sarah Palin as the Republican nominee for vice president added to the precedent shattering nature of the election. It is hard not to look back at that race—regardless of your party affiliation—and not be impressed with how significant an event the '08 race was for America. A black male with the middle name of Hussein won the presidency with 53 percent of the popular vote and nearly 70 percent of the electoral college vote (365 electoral votes). A corner was turned in America.[103]

Four years later, President Obama faced a very difficult set of electoral circumstances. An incumbent with a record to defend, 2012 was more about his accomplishments than about the promise of hope and change. The Bush and Obama stimulus may have prevented the U.S. from slipping into an economic depression, but unemployment remained high, growth was sluggish, and budget deficits soared. Did the president deserve four more years?

After a campaign that lasted three years and cost around three billion dollars, the 2012 race gave President Obama another term, and compelled Republicans to reassess their strategy as well as their core beliefs. As the nation was changing demographically, the Republicans refused to keep up with the changes. Could President Obama govern a divided nation? Would the Republicans hunker down and remain obstructionist or would they seek accommodations as they reinvented themselves?

WHO BECOMES PRESIDENT?

Presidents are usually middle-aged, white, male Protestant lawyers of European lineage from the larger states. Thirty-seven of our presidents trace ancestry to the British Isles, three were Dutch, and two were German. All but one, John Kennedy, were Protestants. About half have been lawyers and served in Congress. Most others held state or community elective office. Several were military heroes. Twelve were generals.

Long gone are the days when party leaders could alone select a candidate. Today, with the proliferation of state primary and caucus elections, the candidate who is well financed and can devote themselves to one or two years of full-time campaigning often has an advantage over public figures who occupy office.

In a sense, there is an "on-deck" circle of at most thirty to forty individuals in any given presidential election year: governors, prominent U.S. Senators, a few members of the House of Representatives, and a handful of recent governors or vice presidents who have successfully kept themselves in the news media. These men, and an occasional woman, form the core of electables whom "The Great Mentioner," that mythic conglomeration of prominent media figures and pundits, is willing to anoint as serious candidates.[104]

No doubt there are talented business entrepreneurs, educators, or other outstanding individuals who might make as capable a president as any of the activist politicians who inevitably become the serious candidates. Seldom, however, are these nonprofessional politicians willing to enter the political thicket in their fifties or sixties. Dwight Eisenhower in the 1950s, and billionaire H. Ross Perot, who won 19 percent of the popular vote in the 1992 and 8 percent in 1996, are the exceptions to the rule. Most potential presidential candidates do not want to spend two or three years on the campaign trail or raise the more than 100 million dollars needed to run. Others may be reluctant to disclose their finances and subject their families to the brutal public scrutiny involved in a presidential race. Both General Colin Powell and Indiana Governor Mitch Daniels acknowledged their wives' objection to their running for president was a factor in their decision not to seek the presidency. The demanding presidential campaign, especially with the more than thirty primary elections, is unappealing even to seasoned politicians.

The general public harbors a disdain for politicians. "If God had wanted us to vote" goes the saying, "He would have given us candidates." When asked about their career aspirations for their children, parents rate "politician" low on their list.

By about January of each presidential election year two or three front-runners emerge from the pack of ten or so to go on to the semifinal—the nominating convention. Both the parties and the public are usually presented with a virtual *fait accompli*. In practice, name familiarity, access to large financial resources, and the substantial spare time necessary to prepare for the primaries give certain candidates advantages over others.

According to the Constitution, a presidential candidate must be at least thirty-five years old, must have lived within the United States for fourteen years, and must be a natural born citizen. Whether a person born abroad of American parents is qualified to serve as president has never been fully decided. Such a person would probably be considered "natural born" even if not native born.

Beyond the constitutional requirements, American voters have a tough, unwritten set of demands for anyone presumptuous and driven enough to want to become president. We are often disappointed in the quality of our candidates because we invariably measure them against an idealized composite of what our greatest presidents and world leaders did, rather than against what our past presidents looked like prior to their becoming presidents. We remember past presidents primarily for their victories and on their best days.

Most of us yearn for so many talents and qualities in our presidents that it comes close to wanting "God—on a good day." We want vision, character, experience, organizational competence, intelligence, stamina, agility, inspiration, judgment, wisdom, emotional stability, and strength, and we want someone who shares our political beliefs.

When looking for a new president, we also want a leader who can bring us together and bring out the best in us. Yet this is a tough assignment in a nation shaped by stalwart individualism and irreverence for government and centralized institutions, and today hyperpartisanism.

We justifiably look at candidates with an unforgiving eye, but perhaps we are unfair with pop quizzes, trick questions, and denunciation of candidates for doing things we ourselves might have done. Yet another paradox is that we simultaneously want a candidate to be like us and better than us.

Our ideal candidate, in addition to sharing our dreams and policy values, would have the following attributes:

Courage. The willingness to take risks and try to serve all the people and not just those who bankrolled his or her candidacy; the intellectual courage to do what is right even when it is not popular or easy; and the guts not to give up after legislative or political defeats.

Experience and competence in bringing people together in teams to solve major political problems; great skill as negotiator and builder of policy agreements.

Political savvy. An understanding of the necessity of politics and the ability to be an effective politician; one who works regularly with people of all political views and who recognizes that coalition building is a central as well as constant part of the job.

An **understanding** of history and constitutionalism, a solid grasp of how governments and markets work and how trade and diplomacy operate, and a respect for the U.S. Constitution and the constraints it puts on leadership and government. Helpful, too, would be a sophisticated understanding and respect for the diverse political culture in the United States.

The **ability** and judgment to recruit wise advisers and effective administrators and the wisdom to delegate to teams of colleagues. This requires, too, an understanding of the strategic tools for governing and an ability to empower public servants and volunteers at all levels of government.

Listening, learning, and teaching skills. Paradoxically, a leader has to both listen to us and lead us. We want leaders who give us a sense not only of who they are, but more important, of who we are, and what we as a nation might become.

Programmatic ideas and wisdom; and the ability to define plans, clarify options, and help set the nation's policy agenda. A president has to be preoccupied with the large, compelling issues of our day (economic opportunities for everyone, freedom, trade, nuclear proliferation, racism, equality, etc.)—a forest person, not overwhelmed by the trees or leaves.

Communication and motivational skills. Ideas and wisdom are of little use if a president cannot rally the public and empower teams and constituencies to enact new plans. Having speaking and media conference skills and the ability to inspire and build new political coalitions is crucial.

Tenacity and discipline balanced with emotional strength and humility. Self-confidence and self-esteem are also essential. A thick skin helps in this generally thankless job, as do the ability to laugh at oneself and to admit flaws and mistakes. Not wanted are persons who are defensive, rigid, torn by self-doubt or self-pity, or who blame their problems on "enemies."

Intellectual honesty. We want presidents we can trust, who have a basic respect for others and a commitment to serve the public interest: a sense of decency, integrity, and fair play.

Morale-building and community-building skills. The presidency is far more than just a political or constitutional job; it is also an institution and office that has to help us through crises and transitions and help unify us when we experience national setbacks and tragedies. Presidents at their best help remind us of our mutual obligations, shared beliefs, and the trust and caring that can hold us together in traditions and duty.

Do we ask too much of our presidential candidates? Sure. History conditions different cultures to expect different things of their leaders. In the United States we exaggerate the capacity of what even heroic presidents can do to change the course of events.

But we won't lower our expectations.

WHY VOTERS VOTE THE WAY THEY DO

Most scholars believe the chief factors influencing how people vote in presidential elections are their *party orientation*; their *public-policy preferences*; the way they perceive the *integrity, character, and judgment* of the candidates; and *retrospective judgments* on the performance of the incumbent or their political party.[105]

The American system was invented by men from the Enlightenment, during the Age of Reason. And democracy is grounded in the belief that humans are rational, thinking beings. The study of political science is largely based on the premise of the rational actor. But are voters rational? Neuroscientist Drew Westen argues that "*The political brain is an emotional brain*," [italics in original] and it is "not a dispassionate calculating machine objectively searching for the right facts, figures, and policies to make a reasoned decision." He further argues that "In politics, when reason and emotion collide, emotion invariably wins"; and that "people's positive and negative associations to a candidate were better predictors of their voting preferences than even their judgments about his personality and competence." In short, he says, people "vote with their guts."[106]

Rather than casting a rational vote for president, we sometimes base our vote on emotions and feelings. "The data from political science are crystal clear," Westen writes; "people vote for the candidate who elicits the right feelings, not the candidate who presents the best arguments." Therefore, "managing positive and negative feelings should be the primary goals of a political campaign." In the end, "successful campaigns compete in the marketplace of emotions and not primarily in the marketplace of ideas."[107] Candidates who can "frame" issues, present a compelling narrative, touch the emotions of the electorate, and draw voters in

The President suspended electioneering just prior to election day to monitor disaster relief efforts after Hurricane Sandy. AP Photo/Pablo Martinez Monsivais.

emotionally often have the best chance of winning. The heart, not the head, is the way to win votes.[108] The Obama 2008 campaign combined issue initiatives such as his Iraq position and health care coverage with emotional appeals about hope and change.[109]

Parties are still important factors when votes are counted. Americans are not as partisan as they were in the twentieth century; they are now are better educated, have multiple sources of political information, and are no longer as dependent as they once were on party leaders for welfare, patronage, or certain other intermediary services. Still, nearly two-thirds of Americans identify themselves as Democrats or Republicans. Most of the time, Republicans vote Republican and Democrats vote Democrat. Republicans, however, are a more cohesive party in the general election. Thus 90 percent of Republicans voted for McCain–Palin in 2008, while 89 percent of Democrats voted for the Obama–Biden ticket.

Issues or public policy preferences play an even more complicated role in how people cast their presidential vote. In certain years, like 1800, 1860, 1896, 1936, 1964, and 1992, issues played a larger, more clear-cut role. In other years, 1956 and 1960, 1984, and 2000, issues weren't as important. Sometimes both major candidates take the same position on a major issue, as in 1968 when both Richard Nixon and Hubert Humphrey said they favored ending the war, honorably, in Vietnam. In 2008 and

2012, with the economic meltdown looming over the heads of voters, the issue of who might better handle the economy proved significant in voters' decisions.

Issues seem to be less important in many elections because of the tendency for both parties to offer candidates who take moderate policy stands to appease widespread public opinion. Thus, both candidates often echo the public mood rather closely. Moreover, candidates' policy preferences are often deliberately ambiguous. Clear-cut policy stands are infrequent and inconspicuous, as candidates devote much more attention to their concerns about general goals, problems, and past performance.

While candidates often try to avoid specific controversial issues, such issues do serve a broader and in many ways more important function: They allow candidates to simplify complexity for voters. Effective candidates provide meaning and purpose in a confusing world. They help make sense of the times. A candidate, or president, who can give comfort, assurance, and hope amid this confusion can generate loyal and wide support.

Honesty and integrity top the list of desired characteristics. We are keenly aware, more so because of Watergate, the Iran-Contra scandal, and Bill Clinton's and George W. Bush's various failings, of the need for a president to set a tone and to serve as an example of credibility. Dishonesty and duplicity are qualities we dislike.

Most voters prefer a moderate candidate. They generally vote against extremists of any kind. This has led to an aphorism that "the only extreme in American politics that wins is the extreme middle." Ronald Reagan is somewhat of an exception to this rule, yet the public seldom saw Reagan as an extremist; his rhetoric was often comforting and nurturing to the point that he appeared to be mainstream. In 2008 and 2012, Republicans tried to paint Barack Obama as too radical and dangerous, but because of Obama's reassuring style, those charges did not stick.

Personality and character also count. In local elections people often just rely on party labels. But with governors, U.S. Senators, and especially presidents, and with the availability of extensive television coverage, people plainly exercise their own personal judgment about who is most fit to serve in office.

Both candidates in 2012 were introverts. The public had grown accustomed, if not completely pleased, with the President's "cool", analytical style. Governor Romney, on the other hand, had a harder time passing the "likeability" test. His reserved style and elitist tendencies were off putting to many, and he was never able to warm up to the average voter.

Some people deplore the fact that a candidate's personality and style are evaluated as equal to or more important than issues and substance. But a candidate's personality is a perfectly legitimate and, indeed, a proper subject for voters to weigh. There is little doubt that a candidate's sense of self-confidence and personal style of conduct can and usually do affect how he or she would behave in office. Presidents have significant discretionary power, and their personalities can and do affect the way they decide public policy and handle crises.

The basic insecurities of certain presidents have also led to failure in the White House. We have reason to be alert to whether a candidate can accept criticism and whether he or she demands absolute loyalty from subordinates. We have suffered from presidents who have encouraged "group think" and developed "enemy lists."

In 2012, the proliferation of big money into the race raised questions of whether one or both candidates had become captured by an elite plutocracy. The 2012 race cost roughly three billion dollars, leaving average voters to wonder if anyone was representing their interests, or if both candidates had sold out to big money.

Elections are also judgments about the past and hopes for the future. We base our vote in part on a retrospective assessment of how well or poorly we think the incumbent president or their party did in governing the nation. We base our vote in part on how confident we are in where the country is going. If we believe the state of the economy is going in the right direction, especially in the election year, we are likely to reward the incumbent party.

What then do we look for in our presidents? We want persons who are self-confident and self-aware, not given to defensive and compulsive behavior.

Political scientist James David Barber's provocative analysis of presidential personality urged voters to look carefully at a candidate's character. The issues of an election year will change, but the character of the president will last. Politics, he says, is politicians. There is no way to understand the former without understanding the latter. We need to look closely at the rhetoric, skill, and world view of presidential candidates. Barber said Wilson, Hoover, Johnson, and Nixon displayed tendencies toward compulsiveness and rigidity and were not as desirable as FDR, Truman, and JFK. These latter candidates combined a high volume and fast tempo of activity with marked enjoyment of politics and people. These "activist-positives," as Barber calls them, manifested strong self-esteem and distinct success in relating to their environment.[110]

Barber's analysis, while helpful, has its limitations. It would not have encouraged us to consider favorably Abraham Lincoln. And Barber's theory is less than helpful when applied to Gerald Ford, Jimmy Carter, and George H. W. Bush, all of whom Barber initially viewed as healthy active-positive types, yet all of whom proved to be merely average, at best, in presidential effectiveness. In short, psychological style and personality do not necessarily predict a president's performance and effectiveness.

Since all elections are judgments about past performance, an incumbent president is judged in good part on the quality of the job done. Character matters, yet performance generally matters more.

In 2012, both candidates were highly scrutinized by the media, and every blemish was revealed and put under a microscope. Candidate Romney's "47%" remark, and President Obama's "you didn't build that" comment were both taken out of context and exploited, and yet both statements revealed something about the inner beliefs of each candidate.

To what extent are questions of private moral character relevant to presidential politics? While the president is, in many ways, a moral or symbolic spokesperson for the nation, must the person who fills the office be personally "pure" to be a good president? It doesn't seem so. The public may want its presidents to be of the highest character, yet a look at the private lives of our great presidents reveals plenty of personal foibles.[111]

One of the few modern presidents who might have passed today's "character test" is Richard Nixon. In his private life, Nixon was seemingly upright. In his public life, however, Nixon left much to be desired. In a test of character, "which Nixon passes and FDR fails, something is evidently amiss with our current prejudices about the kind of character we desire in political leaders."[112]

Precisely what do we mean by character? Some people with roguish private lives exhibit great public integrity. Others of spotless private life exhibit public qualities of duplicity. Today, journalists and rival candidates search the backgrounds of candidates, looking for any indiscretion. If found, that candidate is likely drummed out of the race. Is it fair to base our judgments of character on isolated events that may have occurred years ago, and from which the candidate may have drawn useful lessons?

Questions about presidential character are as old as the office itself. In 1800, ministers denounced Thomas Jefferson from their pulpits as "godless," and in the 1820s, Andrew Jackson was pilloried as a barbarian and adulterer.

The election of 1884 provides a fascinating case study of character and politics. In that election, Democratic candidate Grover Cleveland was charged with fathering a child out of wedlock. Cleveland took responsibility and agreed to pay for the child's upbringing. This became a prime campaign issue for his opponent James G. Blaine. The dilemma was that while Cleveland had character questions about his private life, his public or political reputation was spotless. Blaine on the other hand had a decent private life, but was generally thought of as a public crook. The voters selected Cleveland.

Presidents, like the rest of us, are human, they make mistakes. Some learn from their mistakes, others don't. The perfect person does not exist. Our presidents come with a wide array of strengths and weaknesses. To disqualify one candidate because it was revealed they made mistakes years ago seems shortsighted.

Can a president be too nice, too honorable? Both Ford and Carter were decent people. Would they have been more effective if they had been more Machiavellian?

Judging character is especially difficult given the varied motives of those who pursue political careers. Some enter politics for the wrong reasons—to fill a void or in search of recognition. Others go into politics for more noble reasons—to accomplish good things for the nation. It is often difficult to tell.

One clue into character may be how a person deals with adversity or defeat. FDR's polio would have overwhelmed most people, but Roosevelt overcame adversity, and in doing so, was even more convincing when he told us we had nothing to fear but fear itself. In Roosevelt's case, adversity made him stronger. His character was forged in the fire of personal crisis.

While no single definition of character adequately covers all our needs, the following qualities are certainly admirable in the person who becomes president: courage of conviction, internal moral compass, respect for others, commitment to the public good, respect for democratic standards, trustworthiness, generosity of spirit, compassion and empathy, optimism, hope, and emotional strength, sense of decency and fair play, and inner strength and confidence.

In the end, questions of presidential character serve as yet another example of the paradoxical nature of presidential politics. What we applaud in one president we condemn in another. In the end, the real test of presidential character may well be, "Did this president bring the best out in all of us?"

However much we seek the well-rounded leader, we usually get ambitious, vain, and calculating candidates who often do not know what is to be done (though they are willing to try). The people who run and win view presidential campaigns less as dialogues or programs for adult education than as a fight to win office, a fight to get there. Once they get there, they will experiment and see what works. The voters may like a person who knows all the answers—but few candidates will make commitments that are not reversible once in office.

THE INVISIBLE PRIMARY

Not too many years ago political analysts held that nothing that happened before the New Hampshire presidential primary (held in February of presidential election years) had much meaning. In times past, it was a confession of weakness for a presidential candidate to get too organized before the New Hampshire primary. Now, however, candidates work for three, and even four, years before that primary to prepare for their race. Thus Jimmy Carter announced his candidacy for the White House on December 12, 1974, almost two full years before the 1976 election, and he admits he made his decision in 1972, four years before the election. Many of the Republicans who ran for their party's 2012 nomination got started in 2009. Mitt Romney began running for the presidency at least as early as 2007. By 2011, a long list of Republicans formed exploratory committees, testing the presidential waters. Hence, "the invisible primary"—the determining preliminary events of an election that actually occur a year or more before the Iowa caucus and the New Hampshire primary.[113] Since 1936 active candidates ranked as most popular within their own party in the Gallup poll taken one month before New Hampshire's primary have won their party's nomination almost every time. This happened again in 2012. Pre-primary activity is indeed significant. A candidate needs to be convincing on at least several "tracks" before he or she gets contender status. All of the following are needed:

→ To become as well known as possible
→ To raise substantial sums of money
→ To attract and organize a staff

➡ To pay numerous visits to key caucus and primary states, especially Iowa and New Hampshire

➡ To identify core issues and build a supportive constituency

➡ To become identified as a spokesperson for a few key issues

➡ To devise a "winning" strategy

➡ To speak at scores of party functions (the rubber-chicken circuit)

➡ To devise an effective relationship with the media

➡ To develop a psychological preparedness and a self-confidence that radiates hope and likability

These do not necessarily occur in this order, and this short list does not exhaust the self and organizational testing of this period. However, without these a candidate has little chance of being taken seriously.

The first need of a would-be president is to become known.[114] No other effort commands as much time as the battle to gain name recognition. Candidates like Roosevelt, Eisenhower, Kennedy, Reagan, Gore, George W. Bush, and Mitt Romney to a lesser extent (Romney had a father who ran for the presidency in 1967 and 1968, and he himself had run a decent race in 2008) had a leg up on most others because they had become celebrities or had inherited a well-known political name even before they ran for the presidency. Candidates like Carter, Dukakis, Clinton, Obama, and Santorum, on the other hand, had to go out and become known the hard way—by crisscrossing the nation, visiting city after city, and giving unremitting, bone-numbing speeches and interviews.

The second major need for a presidential candidate is money. Large sums are needed to pay for staff, travel, and later in the campaign for crucial television and radio advertising. In 2008, Barack Obama raised more money than had ever been raised to run for president. In 2012, all candidates combined yet again set a record for fundraising. Money is convertible into many other resources. It is exceedingly difficult to raise money for a presidential race unless you look like a "winner" or unless you take especially strong positions on controversial issues. A conservative such as Barry Goldwater, George Wallace, or Ronald Reagan can more easily raise early money than a moderate candidate. Making matters worse, the national media generally follow the "star system" of giving primary coverage to those who are already well known or to the controversial candidates who command intense followings.

The "entry cost" for merely getting into the race today is well over $100,000,000. This discourages many considering a run. With money serving as a gatekeeper, only wealthy individuals (Steve Forbes in 1996, Mitt Romney in 2008 and 2012) or those willing to invest time—and perhaps their principles—in extensive fundraising need apply for the job of president. In 2008, Barack Obama was able to raise an astonishing $770 million. How many potential candidates, eyeing the race in 2012, decided not to even try given the staggering cost of presidential elections?

The process of raising money in large sums is a compromising and often corrupting one. The burden of having to raise millions for a presidential race is at the heart of why many able persons do not consider running for the office.

It is also at the heart of why some people are turned off by our political process. All this raises serious questions about the selection process. When does a political contribution become a bribe? When does systematic campaign soliciting become equivalent to a conspiracy to extort funds? At what point does our democracy become an auction? The late Hubert Humphrey, who twice ran for president, put it bluntly:

> Campaign financing is a curse. It's the most disgusting, demeaning, disenchanting, debilitating experience of a politician's life. It's stinky. It's lousy. I just can't tell you how much I hate it. I've had to break off in the middle of trying to make a decent, honorable campaign and go up to somebody's parlor or to a room and say, "Gentlemen, and ladies, I'm desperate. You've got to help me....
>
> And you see people—a lot of them you don't want to see. And they look at you, and you sit there and you talk to them and tell them what you're for and you need help and, out of the twenty-five who have gathered, four will contribute. And most likely one of them is in trouble and is somebody you shouldn't have had a contribution from.[115]

Reliance on big money has made the presidential selection process vulnerable to charges of corruption. In the aftermath of the Watergate scandal, the Congress passed legislation for public financing of presidential elections. Enacted in 1974, the campaign finance reform effort called for public disclosure of all contributions exceeding one hundred dollars, established ceilings on contributions, created a system of federal subsidies, and established spending limits. This law was challenged in court, and in *Buckley v. Valeo* (424 U.S. 1, 1976) the Supreme Court determined that while the Congress could regulate contributions and expenditures of campaign organizations, it could not prevent or limit independent individuals or groups from exercising free speech (and spending) rights.

The Congress then passed the Federal Election Campaign Act (FECA) to revise existing laws to keep them in line with constitutional standards. These new guidelines have been in effect since the 1976 presidential election. Since that election, campaign organizations have discovered loopholes in the law that allow campaigns to get around the law.[116]

First the "independent" money exemption allows individuals and organizations to spend money for or against candidates as long as the effort is not conducted with the advice or assistance of a candidate's campaign organization. This has opened the door for independent spending on behalf of a candidate, or, as is more likely, negative campaign ads against a candidate. Second, the spending of what is called "soft money" allowed party organizations to raise and spend money for a variety of purposes in support of the campaign.

Buried inconspicuously beneath the public, visible primary campaign is the less visible yet all important "money primary." In 2012, in the lead up to the January Iowa caucuses, the Republican field of candidates demonstrated that because of the "weekly" debates, a low-polling candidate, even if unable to raise adequate funds, could stay in the race and use the frequent debates to reach voters. But once the primaries began, money became essential for success.[117]

In 2010, the Supreme Court in a 5–4 decision in the case *Citizens United v. Federal Election Commission*[118] overruled important campaign spending precedents by allowing corporations (and labor unions) to contribute money to political campaigns. Asserting that corporations have the same rights as persons, the Court determined that the First Amendment rights of free speech—which included money—apply to corporations and that the government may not ban political spending (speech) by corporations in elections.

The Court's majority asserted that their decision was a vindication of the First Amendment's basic free speech right. The Court's dissenters warned that unleashing corporate money in campaigns would corrupt democracy.

The 2010 decision marked a sharp shift in the Court's approach, overruling two precedents. Up to that point the Court decided in *Austin v. Michigan Chamber of Commerce* (1990)[119], and *McConnell v. Federal Election Commission* (2003),[120] that corporate and labor campaign contributions could be restricted. The decision was a major victory for Republicans and big businesses. The 2012 presidential election was the first where *Citizens United*'s new rules applied.[121]

This led to the development of what are called the "Super PAC's" (Political Action Committees). These Super PACs are supposed to be "independent" of individual candidates, yet the line is often blurred. Restore Our Future promoted Governor Mitt Romney. This Super PAC spent millions of dollars—mostly in negative television ads—attacking Romney's opponents. In this way an attack ad cannot be linked directly to the candidate who benefits because Super PACs are independent of the campaign and the candidates. Obama had his Super PACs as well.

Super PACs allow candidates to circumvent campaign finance laws. A current law limits what individuals can contribute to a candidate to $2,500. Normal PACs (corporations, unions, etc.) are limited to giving $5,000 to any single candidate. *Citizens United* made a mockery of this. Now, individuals and organizations can spend unlimited amounts of money to support—or attack—a candidate. The only requirement—a cosmetic one at that—is that the organization not directly work with a candidate.

While both liberal (Dream Works CEO Jeffery Katzenberg gave $3 million to Priorities USA Action) and conservative (the Koch brothers gave $200 million to their Super PAC, Americans for Prosperity) Super PACs have sprung up, spending in 2012 heavily favored Republicans.

To put U.S. campaign spending into perspective, the 2010 general election in Great Britain cost roughly $130,000,000 for all its races. The U.S. 2012 presidential race alone cost roughly $3 billion.

While it would be unfair to say that money literally buys elections, it is nonetheless clear that money plays a significant role in influencing who the eventual winner will be and framing several of the key issues. Almost always, the primary candidate who spends the most money wins.

Campaign contributions are often given to reward and influence candidate positions. Steel magnate Henry C. Frick complained of Teddy Roosevelt, "We bought the son of a bitch and then he did not stay bought."[122] Yet campaign contributions are seen as investments in the future, and contributors do expect, and often get, a return on their investments.

Incumbent presidents have always used the lure and trappings of the office to elicit campaign contributions, but no president in the past twenty years elevated it to the art form practiced by the Clinton White House.[123]

In 2008, Democratic nominee Barack Obama raised eyebrows when he bypassed public funding for the general election, believing, correctly, that he could raise and spend substantially more money outside the public financing parameters. Obama's rejection of the public funding regime will doubtless spell its doom for the public option.

In 2012, the right wing of the Republican Party failed to unite behind any single candidate. This gave Mitt Romney an advantage, though the others pulled Romney more to the right on a number of issues and forced him at one point to claim he was "severely conservative." As one conservative after another rose and fell—first Michele Bachmann, then Rick Perry, then Herman Cain, then Newt Gingrich, then Rick Santorum—it became clear that splitting the vote, and the money, was dooming the right wing of the party.

Increasingly, campaigns are utilizing the Internet in the race for the White House. YouTube did not exist in 2004. In 2008, it had a significant impact in the presidential contest. In addition to being a "first-stop-shopping" source for "gotcha" video clips (one of the early 2008 Republican frontrunners, Sen. George Allen of Virginia, had his campaign collapse after a video clip of Allen calling someone in the audience "a macaca" aired on YouTube, and John McCain's "Bomb Iran" likewise damaged his campaign), campaigns consciously utilized access to YouTube to get their message out, especially to young voters.[124]

New campaign technologies dramatically impact both the way campaigns are conducted and how citizens connect to the campaign and candidate.[125] New technologies give us more quantity, but do they give us more quality? As new forms of social media rise, interest in "serious" news has declined.[126] New media—the Internet, YouTube, blogging, social networking, Twitter—has a generational bias as well.

The rise of online news sources has contributed to the decline of newspapers, network news, even local television (see Table 3.1). It has also led to the ability to cocoon oneself from even hearing news or opinion different from your own. A liberal can read like-minded blogs. A conservative can watch Fox News, or listen to Rush Limbaugh, and never be bothered by a different perspective. In this way, we have no common reference points. We speak past each other, isolated on our own comfortable islands, safe from the challenges a healthy public discourse requires.

A novel attempt to use the new media to impact the selection process occurred in 2012 with the emergence of a group called Americans Elect (AE). The stated goal was to hold a national online convention, open to all registered voters, to select what they referred to as a nonpartisan presidential ticket. Hoping to tap into the many frustrated voters who see the hyperpartisanship of contemporary

TABLE 3.1 Changing News and Information-Gathering Habits in the United States, 1993–2008

Percent of People Who Regularly Watch, Read, or Listen to:	1993	1996	2000	2004	2008
Newspapers	58	50	47	42	34
Radio News	47	44	43	40	35
Cable News	—	—	33	38	39
Local TV News	77	65	56	59	52
Nightly Network News	60	42	30	34	29
Network Morning News	—	23	20	22	22
Online News	—	2	23	29	37

SOURCE: Richard L. Fox and Jennifer M. Ramos, *iPolitics: Citizens, Elections, and Governing in the New Media Era* (New York: Cambridge University Press, 2012), p. 9.

politics as appalling, AE hoped to create an electronic highway for voters to bypass the two major parties, but at the end, failed to generate sufficient support.

The new media has shaped campaigns. Barack Obama's post-Reverend Wright speech on race attracted more than five million viewers. The musician will.i.am produced a "Yes We Can" music video that attracted over 15 million hits. CNN even partnered with YouTube to produce a presidential debate with questions coming from YouTube users.

The Internet was also skillfully used by the Obama campaign to both reach other voters and form a virtual community of connected supporters, but also to raise significant sums of money from a wide range of donors.

From campaigning to governing, the Obama team experimented with new ways of governing and new ways of connecting the President to citizens, as well as citizen to like-minded citizens, creating a virtual community of political cohorts. The village green has morphed into the village screen, and Barack Obama's innovative use of e-mails, text messages, YouTube, Facebook, and other social-networking sites continues past the campaign to a bold experiment in governing. Obama's Internet strategy has "rewritten the rules on how to reach voters, raise money, organize supporters, manage the news media, track and mold public opinion, and wage-and-withstand political attacks."[127] It was, as Mark McKinnon, senior advisor to President Bush remarked, "the year we went into warp speed [on the use of the Internet]. The year the paradigm got turned upside down and truly became bottom up instead of top down."[128]

In the 1930s, Franklin D. Roosevelt utilized the "new" medium of radio to reach out directly to voters. In the 1980s, Ronald Reagan effectively used television to bypass the press and go directly to the public. Barack Obama used the "new" medium of the Web to make a "direct" connection to voters, closing the gap between candidate and citizen and creating a virtual community of supporters.

Attracting loyal staff, identifying key issues, becoming identified with vital issues, and devising a sensible strategy are also all vital to the successful launching of a candidacy. Often underestimated is the capacity to establish a good working relationship with reporters and television interviewers. In an age of candidate-centered campaigns, where political parties are of decreasing importance, the electoral role of the media has greatly increased. Some candidates, great speakers who are superb at raising funds, perform poorly when interviewed by the press. Sometimes, too, the great stump speaker looks foolish and too "hot" on television. Others are gaffe prone or come across as too programmed and/or wooden.

What might be called the psychological test—how a candidate reacts to the strain, the temptations, and the intense public scrutiny of the campaign—is one of the most important measures of a candidate. Arthur Hadley asked, "How much does the candidate want the presidency? How much of his private self and belief will be compromised to the public man? To what extent will he abandon family, friends and other normal joys of life, and how does he handle this isolation?[129]

The exacting invisible primary period is always an exhausting ordeal and a formidable test, as well, of whether an individual can hold up physically and can control himself emotionally. Barack Obama gained energy, voice, and self-confidence as he endured and grew during the grueling primary season of 2008; the Republican field in 2012 seemed to push each other further to the right, perhaps weakening electability in November.

PRESIDENTIAL PRIMARIES

Presidential primaries began as an outgrowth of the Progressive movement's efforts in the early twentieth century to eliminate "boss rule" and to encourage popular participation in government. Presidential primaries began to take shape after 1905 when the La Follette Republicans in Wisconsin provided a system for the direct election of members of the state's delegation to the national nominating convention. Now most of the big, electoral-rich states are using some type of presidential primary.

The concept of popular participation in the nomination of the presidential party nominees evolved slowly. First we relied on the congressional caucus system, which did not allow for direct popular participation at all. Until 1828 members of Congress from each party met and selected the person they wanted as their nominee. With the growth of democratic sentiment and the coming of the Age of Jackson, the national nominating convention system began to emerge as the replacement. In 1828 state legislatures and state party conventions were relied on to nominate party nominees. After that national conventions took hold, although it was not until 1840 that national party conventions were accorded full recognition.

Not until 1912 did primaries began to be used regularly (about twelve states used them that year) in enough places to begin to have a serious impact on the presidential nominations. Many party leaders, however, have never been enthusiastic about primaries, in large part because they believe they undermine the two-party structure by strengthening the hand of candidate loyalists and issue-oriented zealots at the expense of the party regulars. Primaries allow people to vote who may have little or no loyalty to the party and no interest or stake in the party's future.

The importance of primaries has waxed and waned during the past century, but they have become increasingly important. The primaries are now essential in winning the nomination. Most delegates are won in these primary contests.

The rules for primaries vary from state to state and from party to party. Usually, however, like in Ohio or Florida, voters elect delegates directly or by showing a preference for a presidential candidate. Some of the early primaries, such as those in New Hampshire and South Carolina, can be important in giving a psychological lift to a front-runner or a new challenger. Later primaries can be important in giving the final edge to one candidate over others as the front-runner heads into the national convention. The later primaries, as in the case of California, usually have less impact, since the front-runner often has a sufficient number of committed delegates.

In recent years the system of presidential primaries has become one of the most debated aspects of the presidential selection process. Critics say it is a case of "democracy gone mad," and a "questionable method of selecting presidential candidates." It is especially good, critics say, at eliminating candidates.

Nearly always, the criticism of the primaries ends up focusing on these alleged flaws: the system takes too long, costs too much, highlights entrepreneurial personalities at the expense of issues, makes pseudo-enemies out of true political allies, invites factionalism, undermines parties, often favors colorful ideological candidates over moderates, and frequently does not even affect the outcome of the nomination process. Critics point to the Goldwater and McGovern nominations as prime examples of flaws in the primary system.

Primary voters are older, have higher incomes, are more educated, and are more politically active than those who do not vote in primaries. Turnout is relatively low (yet much higher than in caucuses), though we witnessed a greater turnout, especially in some of the Democratic primaries, in 2008 and some of the Republican primaries in 2012. This leads some analysts to conclude that as a democratic institution designed to stimulate popular participation, the presidential primary has limited effectiveness, and has turned off rather than turned on potential voters.

The frequent and sustained criticism of primaries leads some observers to suggest that we should abolish or at least reform them. Many people support a national primary, a one-shot winner-take-all event in August or September of election year. Others favor regional (multistate) primaries or a return to state conventions as a better means by which to select competent presidential nominees. Still others favor letting smaller states go first, then midsize states, followed by the big states.[130]

The primary system has its blemishes, yet it has also served us reasonably well. Although "the people" do not fully control the nominating process, it is clear that primaries have increased the public's potential to influence who will be convention delegates and has opened the process to some candidates and ideas that might otherwise have been excluded.

Primaries have decreased the party leaders' control over the nomination process. Students of our party system are worried about this. They would prefer a system that sends responsible party regulars of the state and local parties to the national convention, not bound by rigid instructions from a primary verdict, but as representatives, free to seek out the national interest according to their best judgment. They believe these party regulars would be delegates concerned with the majority of the party's rank and file and also with the acceptability and electability of a candidate as well as that candidate's ability to serve effectively as president. This view celebrates party regulars as those who are most informed and best qualified to select the nominee.

Another criticism of the primary system stems from the undue weight placed on the first primary in New Hampshire and the first caucus in Iowa. Do these small states reflect the nation or does the conservative nature of the states give undue advantage to more conservative candidates? In an effort to offset the power of the New Hampshire primary, many states have "front-loaded" their primaries, that is, moved them up in the calendar so as to have a greater impact.

It is true that primaries do allow, on occasion, for a Goldwater or a McGovern to be nominated. But primaries also allow for fresh faces and young new blood to emerge, as happened in 1960, 2008, and 2012. The 1976 and 2008 campaigns showed that the Democrats, for example, could emerge from the primaries as a fairly unified party. By giving candidates several opportunities to present themselves to the public, our present procedures make it possible for a candidate to win substantial support during a relatively short period of time. This is how Rick Santorum was able to rise from single-digit status to become one of the two leading Republican candidates in 2012. Abolishing this aspect of the presidential selection process could limit the infusion of new blood into the presidential race.

While 2008 was a bit of an exception, the generally modest participation in the primaries prompts reform suggestions. Universal voter registration or the Motor-Voter bill (allowing people to register to vote at the time they register for a driving license) slightly increases participation. A Sunday voting day or a national holiday on voting day may also encourage voting. Newspapers and television could do a better job of getting to the heart of candidates' views, exploring inconsistencies, and piecing together the candidates' positions on various policies.

To win their party's nomination, candidates in primary races—unless there is a clear and undisputed front-runner—must compete for the votes of party activists who vote in primaries at a higher rate than do mainstream party members. As activists tend to be more ideologically extreme, Democrats—to attract partisan activists—must usually move farther to the left, and Republicans farther to the right. Once the nomination has been secured, they usually scurry to the center, as Romney did in the fall of 2012, to appeal to the more numerous moderate and independent voters of the general election.

In the 2012 Republican primary race, several candidates deftly danced away from previous positions so as to better appeal to conservative activists for whom certain policy issues were a litmus test. Mitt Romney, as Governor of Massachusetts, passed a health care plan similar to "Obamacare," yet when facing Republican primary and caucus voters, did a Texas two-step, arguing that the Massachusetts plan bears little resemblance to President Obama's program and that as president he would repeal Obama's program. His pirouette continued when he described "Obamacare" as "a government takeover of health care," but "Mass-care" (which is similar to the Obama plan) as a way to "help people get and keep their health insurance."[131] This sparked humor magazine *The Onion* to print its mock headline: "MITT ROMNEY HAUNTED BY PAST OF TRYING TO HELP UNINSURED SICK PEOPLE".

Likewise, in 2012, Tim Pawlenty who dropped out of the race almost before it began, felt compelled to do a one-eighty on global warming. As Governor of Minnesota, Pawlenty was a vocal supporter of cap-and-trade. He went so far as to record a radio commercial in 2008 pleading with Congress to "cap greenhouse gas pollution now." As a 2012 primary candidate, Pawlenty did an about-face, saying he was wrong to support cap-and-trade, calling it "a disaster." Cap-and-trade was a particularly upsetting issue to Republican Tea Party activists, and Pawlenty bowed to them in hopes of gaining votes. Likewise, Texas Governor Rick Perry hardened his stance on abortion after being constantly criticized by the anti-abortionist wing of the Republican Party.

Driving candidates to the extremes may be necessary in the primaries but they can spell disaster in the general election. So concerned with this dilemma was former Republican national chairman Haley Barbour, Governor of Louisiana, that he warned his party that often "purity is the enemy of victory."

When an incumbent president faces a tough challenge from his own party, as Jimmy Carter faced in 1980 with Senator Ted Kennedy, or Gerald Ford in 1976 with Ronald Reagan, they emerge severely weakened and usually will end up losing in the general election. An inside challenger forces the incumbent to take stands that will appeal to the base yet not always play well in the general election. They also face challenges and criticism that may weaken them in the eyes of the public and—as the primary may serve as a test-run for the general election—give the opposing party a good sense of which criticisms work and which do not. Also, the unchallenged incumbent does not have to spend much money, keeping his campaign treasury full for the general election. And the incumbent will not have to actively campaign, saving precious time and energy for the battle ahead.

On the Republican side, Mitt Romney rose as the early favorite but was vigorously challenged by a series of candidates on his right. Many of the most conservative members of the party either did not trust or did not like Romney and were not persuaded that he was conservative enough to be the party standard bearer.

In 2012, Mitt Romney followed his Iowa caucus "win" (later announced as a Santorum victory) with a comfortable, though not commanding, victory in the

January 10 New Hampshire primary, the first time a nonincumbent has ever won both Iowa and New Hampshire in the same year. Romney, looked on with suspicion by many Republican evangelical Christians and Tea Party advocates, benefitted from the fact that no single rival on the far right was able to unify the conservative base of the Party. With several more conservative candidates carving up the vote on the right wing of the Party, Romney was able to cobble together 39.3 percent of the vote and emerge the winner.

The next primary, held on January 21 in South Carolina, appeared to be the last chance to derail Romney. Super PACs for Rick Perry and Newt Gingrich blasted Romney in a barrage of television ads. It worked. Gingrich won with 40 percent of the vote to Romney's 28 percent.

But with superior organization and more money, Mitt Romney was able to outlast all his opponents. One by one they fell, until the last candidate standing was Romney. By mid-April, the contest for the Republican nomination was all but over. Another Washington D.C. "outsider" had been nominated to "clean up that mess in Washington".

Our paradoxical approach to electing presidents can further be seen in our hunger to elect an "outsider" to the White House. Where at one time experience, demonstrated ability, and policy knowledge all mattered, today these candidates who run as outsiders, against the "Washington establishment," as a Sheriff who will ride into town and clean up that mess in Washington, have the advantage.

It began after Vietnam and Watergate. Four of the five presidents elected before these tragic events had served as U.S. Senators. The fifth, Dwight D. Eisenhower, had a great deal of Washington experience and as Allied Commander in Europe. After Vietnam and Watergate four of the six presidents had no Washington experience, and all ran "against the system." Governors replaced Senators in the White House. Outsiders replaced insiders. The inexperienced in the workings of Washington replaced DC veterans.

In 2012, outsiders Rick Perry (Governor of Texas), businessman Herman Cain (chief executive of a pizza company), Jon Huntsman (former Utah Governor), and Mitt Romney (former Governor of Massachusetts) figured prominently in the Republican field. The insiders (most former members of Congress) did less well.

One of the virtues of the primary system is that candidates are required to present themselves to the people. Candidates have got to organize their thoughts, to clarify and define key issues. They are required to communicate with all kinds of people and to react under pressure. Most of the time, it is an excellent learning experience for both candidates and the public. It also allows room for the people to sharpen and alter their initial views of candidates.

The long, expensive, sometimes testy 2008 Democratic primary race between Clinton and Obama may have seemed excessive to some, yet it did force both candidates to face off against one another, and gave voters the opportunity to do comparison shopping. With all its flaws, we *did* know both candidates much better at the end of the process, and were able to make a more informed choice. A similar, if somewhat more bruising experience, happened in the Republican primaries of 2012.

Primaries were designed to give the people the right to be involved in the choice of their party's nominee and should not be abandoned because qualified persons choose not to run. While more must be done to encourage the best people to seek the office, we need not sacrifice the democratic integrity of the process to attain our goals. The convention can still draft a "dark horse" if there is no popular favorite. Primaries may be imperfect, yet so are democratic societies. They are an inexact, expensive, and overlong way of coming up with nominees, but the system is not as flawed as critics contend.[132]

Return to state conventions or the ancient congressional caucus procedure (where the party leaders in Congress selected candidates) would serve only to increase the influence of political bosses and special interests, who find it easier to bring pressure to bear on a few individuals in those old "smoke-filled rooms" than on entire electorates. Moving to a national or even a regional primary would lessen contact between candidate and voter, virtually prevent the less well-known candidate from running, and increase reliance on television advertising.[133]

CAUCUSES

While most of the delegates to presidential nominating conventions are selected in primaries, caucuses also have a significant impact on the electoral process. A caucus is a meeting of citizens who select delegates to represent them—and their chosen candidate—in state conventions where the actual delegates are selected.

The Iowa caucus, which occurs before the first primary (in New Hampshire), is especially important in that, as the first test of the candidates' organization, appeal, and electability, they tend to elevate some and eliminate other candidates from the race. While a relatively small and electorally less significant state, Iowa nonetheless has clout as the first electoral contest of the campaign season.[134]

In January of an election year, Iowans meet in over 2,000 precincts to elect delegates to the county convention. Then, another meeting is held in each of the 99 counties of the state. These county conventions select delegates to the state's congressional district convention and the state convention. These conventions select state delegates to the national party convention.

In contrast to primaries, where an individual casts a vote in secret in a voting booth, caucuses are group or community exercises in political participation. They allow for interaction, party building, and community building. They are, however, time-consuming, and critics argue that some—the sick and elderly, military stationed out of state, people working two jobs, and parents of small children—are effectively prevented from participating. Unlike primary elections, there is no absentee or mail ballot voting in a caucus.

A candidate who has a strong state organization, a bit of money, and who is willing to spend several weeks in the dead of winter sloshing around in the snows of Iowa can emerge out of "nowhere" to become a legitimate contender. Several lesser known candidates have been able to emerge from the pack in Iowa. Jimmy Carter in 1976 surprised pundits by winning the Iowa caucuses and emerging as the party front-runner.[135] Similarly, former Republican Senator Rick Santorum emerged from his relentless personal campaigning across the whole of Iowa in 2012.

Several other states such as Nevada, Colorado, Washington, Maine, and Idaho have used caucuses to select their delegates.

NATIONAL CONVENTIONS

Over time, national conventions have performed (or tried to perform) the following functions. They have nominated presidential candidates acceptable to most factions within the party. By winning plurality victories in the primaries a candidate can secure the nomination without being acceptable to virtually all elements within a party. It is only the acquiescence of these other interests at the convention that signals to the party's rank and file that the nominee is the legitimate party standard-bearer. Carter and Ford won that legitimization at the 1976 conventions; Al Gore and George W. Bush did so in 2000. Goldwater and McGovern failed at their conventions in 1964 and 1972, respectively.

It has always been the purpose of a convention to select or ratify nominees who possess a strong likelihood of winning voter support in November. The goal is to produce a winning ticket. A more general function of conventions is the task of trying to unify a party that is not inherently unified. Conventions are not a time to examine differences but to promote unity in the face of disagreements and diversity. It is naturally in the party's interest to build enthusiasm and rally the party faithful to work for the national ticket.

Conventions also hammer out party platforms. Platforms are generally less meaningful than the campaign statements of the presidential candidates, but they are a useful guide to the major concerns of a party. They are often inclusive "something-for-everyone" reports. A platform is invariably a compromise of sectional views, diverse caucuses (women, blacks, etc.) and the policy preferences of dominant party elites. The winning candidate is often willing to concede a plank in the platform to the wishes of one of the runner-ups in the primaries. This can be a quid pro quo offer to a faction or a candidate-based organization within the convention that must be won over to unite the party.

If the party has an incumbent president, the platform is often drafted in the White House or approved by the president and his top policy advisers. Seldom does the party adopt a platform critical of its incumbent president.

Criticism of the national party nominating conventions has been loud and frequent. President Eisenhower called them a national disgrace, and social critic H. L. Mencken once wrote that "there is something about a national convention that makes it as fascinating as a revival or a hanging."[136] Critics contend conventions are too big, noisy, unwieldy, unrepresentative, irresponsible, boring, and a waste of time. Others say they function with too much concern for selecting a winner rather than the best qualified person. Similarly, critics say vice presidential choices are often made too hastily, with too much regard for balancing the ticket and not enough regard for selecting a person who may eventually become president. The selections of Agnew (1968), Eagleton (1972), Quayle (1988), and Palin (2008) are often cited as examples.

Television and the proliferation of presidential primaries have altered the role of modern conventions. Today, conventions are less about selecting candidates and more about political theater and marketing; less about where the party wishes to lead the nation and more about entertainment.

Yet another complaint about national conventions came about in the wake of the Democratic party's reforms of the early 1970s. A commission was established to try to improve the delegate selection processes and to "open up" the Democratic party. The basic goal of these reforms was to end the traditional dominance of regular party leaders and to make the Democratic convention more representative of the party rank and file.

A key criticism, however, is that according to the new rules many, and perhaps even a majority, of the delegates to the convention are not acting as responsible members of a party, with all the memories, past participation in, and commitment to its future. Instead, they are acting as members of a candidate-centered organization whose loyalties are almost exclusively to specific candidates and their issues. This may lead, critics charge, to allowing the "zealots" to rule.[137]

This is a serious charge, yet it does not stand up to critical analysis. Greater openness does not mean the end of influence by party leaders, only that they would have more competition for influence. Nor are issue activists inclined to be party wreckers.

While party activists and convention delegates are more ideological to the left or right than the general public, it is not true that this leads them to nominate extremists for the presidency. Of the ten individuals nominated over the last six election cycles, only Ronald Reagan somewhat leaned to the political extreme, yet he rarely seemed extreme to the voters who elected him twice.

One wag commented that "Democrats have to control their left-wing extremists and Republicans have to worry about their right-wing extremists." And we should not be surprised when committed true believers get active in politics in pursuit of their cherished agenda items.

On balance, the national conventions have served us rather well, if imperfectly. New rule changes, the far greater role of television, and the reality that nominees are more and more "selected" and "nominated" in the state primaries require us to reexamine the traditional functions of the convention. Although substantial change has taken place, the conventions still serve many intended goals. Despite their deficiencies, they have nominated some capable leaders: Lincoln, the Roosevelts, Wilson, Eisenhower, and JFK among them. Conventions have had many triumphs and few outright failures.

Conventions remain a uniquely American pageant. Where most Western democracies select their leader (prime minister) from a closed party caucus, away from the hustle and bustle of mass politics, in the United States selecting a president is the people's job, as messy and chaotic as this process may be.

Many of the criticisms of the convention process are really criticisms of elections in general. Elections may not be our finest hour, they may not always address our better selves, they may not be the ideal way to select leaders, yet they remain the most reliable of the known available devices.

INCUMBENCY: ADVANTAGE OR DISADVANTAGE?

It is often thought that we have a two-term presidential tradition and therefore incumbent presidents enjoy an advantage. But, in fact, only 12 of our 43 presidents, prior to Obama, served out fully eight consecutive years in office. Most U.S. presidents have served one term or less or one term plus a year or two.

Still, for a sitting president, the benefits of incumbency are easily distinguishable: instant recognition, full access to government research resources, the ability to dominate events and make news and attract constant media exposure, party organizational structure at one's disposal, the ability to dispense government contracts, and some ability to manipulate the economy.

Regardless of a president's record of accomplishment, an incumbent president is supposed to benefit from a public relations machine that shows the president as a person of action, a commander in chief, a traveling statesman, and a strategic crisis manager. Not the least of a president's assets is a loyal White House staff that, in the unavoidable blurring of presidential and political functions, performs a myriad of services. Presidents and then national party can usually also raise money far more easily than the opposition, and the resources of the office provide millions of dollars' worth of publicity.

A rival for the presidency is generally a political candidate and little more. He or she is a seeker whose motives are unclear, a pursuer with a feverish gleam in his or her eye. Such candidates covet what their rival already possesses. The most they can give are criticisms and promises.

Perhaps the most important asset for the incumbent is the selective or manipulative use of government contracts, patronage, and other political controls over the economy. President Nixon's manipulation of milk prices is alleged to have aided his campaign treasury in the 1972 election. In what was called "the incumbency-responsiveness program," Nixon aides sought to maximize their control over the federal government's enormous resources to their best advantage. Federal grants were evaluated according to political benefits. Political appointments and ambassadorships were sometimes promised in exchange for large campaign contributions. And corporations were "encouraged" to contribute to the upcoming Nixon campaign in a near-extortionist manner.

But is incumbency really that much of an advantage? Political scientist Edward Tufte finds positive support going back to 1918 for the not surprising hypothesis "that an incumbent administration, while operating within political and economic constraints and limited by the usual uncertainties in successfully implementing economic policy, may manipulate the short-run course of the national economy in order to improve its party's standing in upcoming elections and to repay past political debts."[138] Today, however, presidents have less opportunity to manipulate the economy in this manner. With an enormous national debt and budget challenges, presidents have less discretionary money and fewer resources to throw at the voters in the months before to an election. Incumbents can and often have lost. Indeed, incumbency is sometimes as much a burden as a benefit. Since the Jacksonian era, which inspired the rise of mass political parties and the party convention system, five presidents have been denied party renomination: Tyler, Fillmore, Pierce, Andrew Johnson, and Arthur. Another nine, John Adams, Van Buren, Cleveland, Benjamin Harrison, Taft, Hoover, Ford, Carter, and George H. W. Bush, were defeated for a second term after winning their party's nomination. Against these fourteen failures, incumbent presidents have been successful in winning both the nomination and the election only sixteen times, including three reelection triumphs by Franklin Roosevelt.

One of the paradoxes of recent years can be seen in the incumbency advantage being transformed into the incumbency disadvantage. In 1968, incumbent Lyndon Johnson was compelled not to seek renomination when faced with mass protests over his Vietnam policy. His successor, Richard Nixon, was forced to resign from office one step ahead of impeachment. Nixon's successor, Gerald Ford, nearly lost his nomination bid and ended up losing the election in 1976, and the man who defeated him, Jimmy Carter, also faced a serious nomination challenge and lost in his 1980 bid for reelection. Reagan's successor George H. W. Bush lost in his 1992 reelection bid to Bill Clinton. Plainly being the incumbent can sometimes be dangerous to the president's political health.

Incumbency, then, is a double-edged sword. It can help a president who presides over a period of prosperity and peace and projects an image of being in charge of events. But it can just as readily act against a president associated with troubled, perplexing times, who does not seem to be in full possession of his office. If prosperity favors the incumbents, depression favors the challengers. Distrust of politicians and low morale in the nation favors the challengers; strong confidence in the national government favors the incumbent.

An incumbent is necessarily on the defensive: His record is under detailed scrutiny, his administration's every flaw and unfulfilled promise exposed to microscopic examination. The American people can conveniently, if often unfairly, blame a whole range of problems on a president, whereas the astute challenger presents a smaller target.

The incumbent is often judged against the idealized model of the perfect president, and not unnaturally, is found wanting. Paradoxically, the incumbent may at times be the symbol of the nation's pride, but just as readily be the nation's most convenient scapegoat.

INCUMBENCY AND THE OBAMA PRESIDENCY:
LAME DUCK, SITTING DUCK, OR DEAD DUCK?

In 2008 Senator Barack Obama, the little-known outsider, campaigned on the themes of hope and change. Many voters, especially young voters, were drawn to his style and message. But the 2008 election was more a rejection of the Bush and Republican performance in office than an endorsement of Obama and his agenda. Most elections, most of the time, are retrospective judgments about the performance of the incumbent president and their party.

In 2012, President Obama was the incumbent, and voters went to the polls to reward or punish the president based on their evaluation of his performance in office. As with all presidents, the record was mixed: some successes, some failures. His successes were impressive: an economic stimulus package, health care reform, ending the Iraq war, Wall Street regulation, the killing of Osama bin Laden, driving Muammar Gaddafi from power in Libya. But the failures were significant as well: a weak economic recovery, an ongoing war in Afghanistan, massive Democratic losses in the 2010 midterm elections. Additionally, the rise and intensity of opposition—a unified Republican opposition, the rise of Tea Party activists—meant that there would be a great deal of political push back against the president.

President Obama and his campaign team, of course, stressed the positive, and Vice President Biden's campaign stump line "Osama bin Laden is dead, General Motors is alive"—captured in bumper sticker simplicity—the message the administration wished to convey to voters. Early on, voters appeared willing to "fire" the president. But Governor Romney was unable to make a sufficiently strong case for his candidacy.

The president's early lead evaporated after a dismal performance in the first presidential debate and the race evolved into a virtual toss-up. But as election day approached, Hurricane Sandy struck the East Coast with devastating impact. Obama went into "presidential mode" and tackled hurricane aftermath and recovery. By being and appearing "presidential" Obama stemmed the Romney momentum and went into election day with small leads in the key swing states.

GENERAL ELECTIONS: WHAT MATTERS?

In 2000, while 105 million voters (or 51.3 percent) turned out to vote, at least another 100 million who were eligible to participate in the selection of the president did not vote. In 2004, 59 percent of eligible voters actually voted. In 2008, that number rose to roughly 61 percent.

In 2012, voter turnout was approximately 57.5%, and while enthusiasm was markedly down from 2008, the Obama ground game was so strong that it made up for the lack of passion in most voting groups. For example, in the key battleground state of Ohio, the Obama campaign had 139 field offices, while the Romney campaign had 40.

TABLE 3.2 Why People Say They Don't Vote

Too busy, conflicting schedule	17.5%
Illness or disability (own or family's)	14.9%
Not interested, felt vote would not make a difference	13.4%
Out of town or away from home	8.8%
Other reason, not specified	11.3%
Did not like candidates or campaign issues	12.9%
Refused or don't know	7.0%
Registration problems	6.0%
Forgot to vote (or send in absentee ballot)	2.6%
Inconvenient polling place or hour or lines too long	2.7%
Transportation problems	2.6%
Bad weather conditions	0.2%

Source: U.S. Bureau of the Census, "Current Population Service" at www.census.gov.

As is well known, people with higher family incomes are more likely to vote than those with lower incomes. Older people, with the exception of the infirm, vote more often than younger people. Women vote in higher percentages than men. White turnout nowadays is only slightly higher than African-American turnout, but Hispanic voting is decidedly lower. The more formal education one has, the more likely one is to vote.

Why do so many people not vote in presidential elections? The easiest explanation is that people are lazy and apathetic about national issues. Paradoxically, however, American citizens are more aware of and interested in political issues than are citizens in most other democracies, yet American participation is far lower.

There are a variety of reasons for not voting. Most states require advance voter registration. As can be seen in Table 3.2, some people say they are too busy, too ill, or don't feel the outcome of the election will make that much difference.

One analysis of voter turnout suggests it is also partly due to the fact that political parties have declined in importance, that the media dwells so much on the negative aspects of candidates and campaigning, and that presidential campaigns go on for so long that elections become a mind-numbing experience. One proposed remedy might be to shorten the nominating process, yet this is unlikely to make a significant difference. Others suggest a system of early voting, as practiced in 34 states, to encourage higher turnout. Still others favor same-day voter registration and online voting.

In general, voters who vote participate out a sense of duty, believing that it is a part of their civic responsibility. Most also believe that their vote sometimes matters, that their political and economic interests are at stake (see Table 3.3). They want their party nominee to win because they either strongly or mildly adhere to the policies championed by their party. (See Figure 3.1 for information on voter turnout patterns.)

TABLE 3.3	Voter Turnout in U.S. Presidential Elections
Year	% Turnout
2012	57.5%
2008	61.0
2004	59.0
2000	51.3
1996	49.0
1992	55.1
1988	50.3
1984	53.3
1980	52.8
1976	53.5
1972	55.2
1968	60.9
1964	61.9
1960	62.8
1956	59.3
1952	61.6

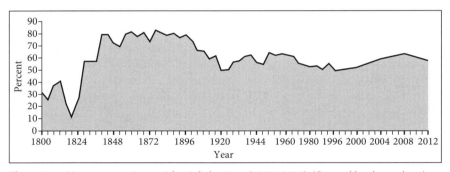

Figure 3.1. Voter turnout in presidential elections (1800–2012). (Created by the authors)

So *political parties* do matter. In addition, *candidate appeal* and *special issues* being debated in a particular election can matter a lot. But for issues to really matter requires the issues in question matter to a large number of voters and that the main candidates take clearly opposing stances on the issues. But rarely do candidates focus on only one issue, and candidates often blur their issue positions to broaden their appeal.

Candidates such as Dwight Eisenhower in 1952, John F. Kennedy in 1960, Ronald Reagan in 1980, and Barack Obama plainly benefited from candidate appeal.

Presidential candidates are not free agents who can choose among strategies at will. Strategy is seldom based on mere choice, it is usually forced by circumstance. For example, about every eight or twelve years there is a strong underlying desire to throw out the party in office. (In 1920, 1932, 1952, 1960, 1968, 1980, and 1992 voters seemed in part to be punishing those in office who were unable to improve things.) Slogans such as "It's time for a change" or "Throw the rascals out" are a familiar refrain as voters turn incumbents out of office with an almost predictable alternation. Since the 1950s, only George H. W. Bush was able to defy the "eight years is enough" rotational phenomenon.

Most voters have made up their minds as to how they will vote by the end of the national conventions (late August or early September of election year, a good eight or ten weeks before election day.) The basic organizational effort of a candidate must be aimed at stirring up the support of voters at the grass roots. The strategy that makes the most sense is to get out all possible supporters and potential supporters and independents and to target only secondary resources at converting the opposition. Supporters need general reassurance on both substantive and stylistic matters, but opponents want to know specific policy plans and program ideas.

A lot depends on how candidates conduct themselves. We carefully watch how they answer tricky questions and whether they keep their cool with hecklers as well as in heated presidential debates. Looking "presidential" is an important part of the voter's equation when deciding on a preferred candidate.

More than anything else, presidential electoral politics is coalitional politics. Interest groups help to get others involved in a campaign. They can help mobilize voters on Election Day. Groups are seldom neutral. They lean to one party or one kind of candidate over others. Groups want access to the political system and they want someone favorable to their interests in the White House.

Candidates find the general election fraught with dynamic tensions. Issue-oriented enthusiasts urge them to "speak out on the vital issues." Party regulars urge them to work closely with the party bosses. Television consultants urge them to devote most of their time to brief television spots and talk-show appearances. Public relations aides urge them to invoke patriotic symbols and quote from prestigious heroic sources. Campaign managers generally urge that debating all the issues and trying to educate the public is not the best way to win a campaign. Issues that attract some groups drive others away. (See Figure 3.2.)

TABLE 3.4 Democratic Vote in Presidential Elections by Race and Ethnicity, 1976–2012

	1976	1980	1984	1988	1992	1996	2000	2004	2008	2012
White	48	36	34	40	39	43	42	41	43	40
Black	83	83	91	89	83	84	90	88	95	93
Latino	82	56	66	70	61	72	62	53	67	69
Asian	N/A	N/A	N/A	N/A	41	46	55	56	62	74

Sources: 2000 data are from the Voter News Service Exit Poll as reported on cnn.com/election/2000/epolls/us/poco.html; 2004 data are from the Edison Media Research and Mitofsky Exit Poll as reported on cnn.com/election/2004/pages/results/states/USp/oo/epolls.o.html

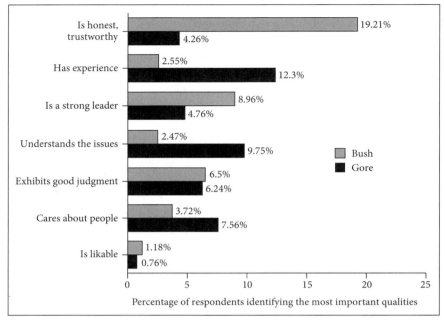

Figure 3.2. Qualities that mattered most in the 2000 presidential election. (Created by the authors)

The study of voting patterns in presidential elections reveals several notable findings. Sometimes referred to as "gapology," voting studies reveal several gaps between Democratic and Republican votes.[139] (See Table 3.4.)

There is a "race gap" that is especially apparent in white versus African-American voters. In 2004, George W. Bush won 58.7 percent of white votes (which comprised 77.1 percent of all votes) yet only 27.6 percent of non-white votes. Nine out of ten African-American voters supported John Kerry in 2004, and roughly 95 percent of black votes went with Barack Obama in 2008 and 2012.

There is also a "marriage gap." In 2004 Bush received 58 percent of the married vote, and John Kerry received 59 percent of votes from the unmarried. In 2008, John McCain received only 52 percent of the married vote.

One can also see a "church attendance" gap, with three-fifths of those who regularly attend church services voting Republican in 2004. In 2008 there was roughly a 10 percent gap favoring John McCain. In the '08 race, 54 percent of Protestants voted for McCain, 54 percent of Catholics for Obama, 78 percent of Jewish voters supported Obama, and 74 percent of white evangelical voters supported McCain.

One often hears of the "gender" gap, and while not as determinative as the previously cited gaps, women do tend to vote more Democratic and men more

Republican. In 2008, men voted at a 49 percent rate for Obama and women voted for him at a 56 percent rate.

A "generation" gap is sometimes evident. Voters 50 and older tend to vote Republican; under 40 tend to vote Democratic. The generation gap in voting was especially evident in 2008 with the 18–29-year-old vote going almost 2-1 for Obama. Older voters, 65 and older, voted 53 percent for John McCain. Yet it is instructive to remember that in 1984, Ronald Reagan won every voter age group, including a majority of younger voters.

There is also a "rural-urban" gap, with rural voters more likely to vote Republican and urban voters Democratic. Again, in 2008, this gap closed a bit as the vote for Barack Obama in rural areas rose by 5 percent but dropped by 3 percent in small towns.

In 2012 there was an 11% gender gap with women favoring Obama. And there was also a male gender gap, as men voted for Romney at a 52–45% rate. Fifty-eight percent of whites voted for Romney, 93% of black for Obama, and 69% of Hispanic went with Obama. These gaps are well within the range of gaps from the previous few presidential elections.

Do elections matter? They do, although elections seldom give a president or a country a specific mandate. A national election in the United States is rarely a plebiscite or referendum on a number of specific issues. Because of candidate's policy ambiguity, we often vote without a clear idea of what the candidates will do if elected.

Candidates who win by a large margin usually claim a mandate from the people. Such a claim is often unjustified, however, especially in elections such as those in 1972 and 1984 where the "landslide" was more a factor of the personal popularity of a president or the negative perceptions about the defeated than positive support for major new policy directions.

Presidents invariably try to convince the Washington community they have some sort of mandate, believing that if the public and Congress believe that there is such a mandate they will have an easier time governing. A mandate is based on three features: the *size* of a president's electoral victory; the *type* of election (issue oriented or personal); and the *number* of candidates from the president's party elected to Congress (the president's coattails and the aggregate numbers.)

The debate over whom to vote for usually centers around which candidate is best equipped to handle the job and the problems at hand rather than around the detailed specifics of how to solve the big issues of the day. Thus, our elections represent mandates to get the job done, yet we leave the means up to the judgment of the president. Elections sometimes set limits on what can be done, but they usually only moderately determine the precise future course of public policies.[140]

Unlike their parliamentary counterparts, elections in the United States do not confer *power*. They merely grant office, which grants the opportunity to seize power. Presidents must work at translating an electoral victory into political power.

THE ELECTORAL COLLEGE DEBATE

The controversial and virtually tied presidential election of 2000 was troubling. Some of our worst fears about the anachronistic Electoral College came true. Popular vote winner Al Gore lost to electoral winner George W. Bush. Bush carried 30 states and won 271 electoral votes. Gore won 20 states and the District of Columbia and won 267 electoral votes.

The Florida vote ended up in nearly a statistical tie, yet all 25 electoral votes went to Bush, rather than a proportional allocation of 12.5 electoral votes to each of the leading contenders.

There were at least two puzzling aspects of the election in 2000. Bush and Gore all but ignored California, New York, and Texas, the three largest states in terms of population and electoral votes. These states were conceded well in advance—California and New York to Gore and Texas to Bush.

Both before and after the 2000 election, the American public has told pollsters they favored abolishing the Electoral College and moving to the more simple and presumably much more democratic "one-person-one-vote" direct election procedure for selecting a president. Between 60 and 70 percent of Americans regularly support this. Yet weeks after the Bush–Gore election was settled, there was little public clamor and even less political maneuvering for amending the U.S. Constitution to bring about this change.

As we were reminded in 2000, presidents are elected by the Electoral College, not directly by the voters. Many people and many political observers grumble about the Electoral College system, yet little seems to get done about it. Even people like Nobel Prize winning former president Jimmy Carter think it is a waste of time to talk about changing it. "I would predict," said Carter, "that 200 years from now, we will still have the Electoral College."[141] Yet, leading scholars who have examined the Electoral College and its consequences generally conclude we need a better way to pick our presidents.

The Electoral College system was adopted for a variety of complicated reasons at the Constitutional Convention on 1787 and was more an afterthought than a carefully constructed method of selection. Ever since it has been one of the most regularly debated provisions in the Constitution.[142]

HOW THE ELECTORAL COLLEGE WORKS TODAY

In making their presidential choice in November, voters technically do not vote for a candidate but choose between slates of "presidential electors" selected by state political parties. In almost all of the states, the slate that wins a plurality of popular votes in the state casts all the electoral votes for that state. In Maine and Nebraska, the plurality of the votes in congressional districts determines two and three of their four and five electoral votes, respectively. This is called the district plan.

Candidates cannot afford to lose the popular vote in many of the most populous states. The Electoral College system plainly gives a disproportionate power to the largest states.

Each state has one electoral vote for each senator and each representative. The District of Columbia has three votes, which it was granted by the Twenty-Third Amendment to the U.S. Constitution. There are 538 votes in today's Electoral College, and one must earn 270 or more to win. George W. Bush's much debated 271-vote electoral victory was plainly a close call.

Thus, according to this system, a president is not officially elected on election day. Victorious slates of electors travel to their respective state capitols on the first Monday after the second Wednesday in December—no wonder most people don't remember how this system works!—where they cast ballots for their party's presidential ticket. Ballots are then sent from the state capitals to Congress, where early in January they are formally counted by House and Senate leaders and the next president is finally announced.

There is yet another unusual and rather undemocratic aspect to the Electoral College. In the event that no candidate secures a majority of electoral votes, the decision would then go to the House of Representatives. This has happened twice, once in 1800 and again in 1824. It was a possibility in 1968, 1992, and again in 2000. In the House, the delegation from each state casts a single vote. If a delegation is evenly divided, this state forfeits its vote. Thus, the influence of a third-party "spoiler" candidate can on occasion pose a significant threat to the two main parties because the House of Representatives chooses a president from among the top three candidates. Consecutive ballots are taken until a candidate wins a majority (26) of the state delegations.

THE CASE FOR RETAINING
THE ELECTORAL COLLEGE

Defenders of the Electoral College contend we should not lightly dismiss a system that has served us reasonably well for so long.

The Electoral College continues to attract devoted supporters. Political scientist Norman Ornstein argues that as imperfect as the Electoral College may from time to time seem, overall it has served the republic quite well for over two hundred years.[143] And conservative columnist George Will argues that the Electoral College supports "America's federalist republic," with an emphasis on federalism.[144]

Attorney Tara Ross, of the American Enterprise Institute argues that the framers saw democracy as dangerous, and instead invented a "federalist republic," of which the Electoral College is a key component. For Ross and other proponents of the Electoral College, the framers "deliberately created a federalist republic, rather than a pure democracy," and the historical results "support as a successful election device," that "created a stable, well-planned and carefully designed system—and it works."[145] Why risk the intended or unintended consequences of change?

Defenders are fond of the old saying that "the evil best known is the most tolerable" and "when it is not necessary to change, it is necessary not to change." They also cite John F. Kennedy, who once defended the Electoral College by arguing that the question does not merely involve certain technical details of the election process, but a whole solar system of subtle, interrelated institutions, principles, and customs.

Defenders emphasize that ours is a federal system, not a unified, centralized, hierarchical, or nationalized system. They remind us that our nation was founded as a republic with a number of checks and balances, and that the Electoral College is one of those balancing checks.

Supporters of the Electoral College process claim eliminating this system might

- ➡ weaken the existing two-party system and encourage splinter parties, possibly triggering numerous contingency elections
- ➡ weaken the federal character of America's constitutional system
- ➡ encourage presidential candidates to pay less attention to smaller states as they concentrate on major metropolitan areas
- ➡ encourage even more simplistic media-oriented campaigns

Perhaps the greatest fear of moving from the Electoral College system to a direct vote system is that relatively small third parties or single-cause candidates might be able to magnify their strength. "In direct elections," writes historian Arthur Schlesinger, Jr., "they could drain enough votes, cumulative from state to state, to prevent the formation of a national majority—and to give themselves strong bargaining positions in case of a run off."[146]

Defenders of the Electoral College argue, often passionately, that the current system is an essential part of the subtle structure of federalism. This, they contend, has helped thwart factionalism and helped encourage liberty. The Electoral College also imposes a state-oriented strategy on presidential candidates. Each candidate must forge a coalition of supporters within each state, especially the big states. This method gives us a disproportionately large amount of influence to smaller, less populated states.

THE CASE AGAINST THE ELECTORAL COLLEGE

Critics of the Electoral College cite several problems, among them, that the vote of the people (popular) might be undermined, that faultless electors could violate the will of voters, that there is a small-state advantage, and that contingency elections in the House could lead to chaos and questions of legitimacy on the party of the winner. The *New York Times* editorialize that the Electoral College "is an antidemocratic relic."[147] And a 1967 report by the American Bar Association called the Electoral College "archaic, undemocratic, complex, ambiguous, indirect, and dangerous."[148]

Further, given that many states are solidly red (Republican) or solidly blue (Democratic), presidential elections are conducted primarily in "purple" states (those eight or ten that are "in play"), ignoring most of the nation. The purple states are battleground states, the rest mere spectator states.[149]

One of the most compelling critiques of the Electoral College system is offered by political scientist George C. Edwards III. Edwards persuasively argues against the Electoral College, favoring direct popular election of the president.[150] After systematically debunking the main claims of Electoral College advocates—that the current system protects the interests of smaller states and some minority voters, supports federalism, strengthens the two-party system, protects against voter fraud, and gives the newly elected president a clearer mandate—Edwards explores several other options for selecting presidents: the *Automatic Plan* (bypass an Electoral College and directly award delegates to each state's winning candidate), the *District Plan* (awarding votes to the winner in each Congressional district, plus giving two additional electoral votes to the overall winner of the state), the *Proportional Plan* (awarding votes in each state based on the proportion of votes received with each state), and the *National Bonus Plan* (giving 102 additional electoral votes to the popular vote winner). In the end, Edwards argues that "political equality" is the key feature of a viable electoral democracy, and as such, since "every voter's ballot does not carry equal weight,"[151] in the current system, only the direct election of a president meets standards of democratic fairness.

THE CASE FOR THE DIRECT ELECTION OF PRESIDENTS

The direct election method means that the person who gets the most votes wins. There is no Electoral College. Advocates of the direct popular system contend everyone's vote should count equally, people should vote directly for the candidate, and the candidate who gets the majority of votes should be elected.

With the Electoral College method, a president can be elected who has fewer popular votes than his opponent, as was the case in 1824 when John Quincy Adams, with 30.92 percent of the vote, defeated Andrew Jackson with 41.34 percent of the vote. This happened again in 1876 when Rutherford B. Hayes, with 47.95 percent of the popular vote, won over Samuel J. Tilden, with 50.97 percent of the vote; and in 1888, when Benjamin Harrison, with 47.82 percent, won over Grover Cleveland, with 48.62 percent. And, of course, it happened most recently in 2000 when George W. Bush won 47.9 percent of the popular vote, while Al Gore won 48.4 percent. This can happen because all of a state's electoral votes are awarded to the winner of the state's popular vote regardless of whether the winning candidate's margin is one vote or three million votes.

Ironically, the major "defect" here, the unit-rule provision, is not a part of the Constitution. This winner-take-all formula (unit rule) is merely a state practice, first adopted in the early nineteenth century for partisan purposes, and gradually accepted by the rest of the states to ensure maximum electoral weight for their state in the national election. Maine and Nebraska, however, have modified this winner-take-all allocation rule.

But because the rest of the states use the winner-take-all rule, the Electoral College benefits the large "swing" states at the expense of the middle-size states. The unit-rule arrangement magnifies the relative power of residents in large states. As political scientist Larry Longley suggested, each of the voters in the ten largest states might, by their vote, "decide not just one popular vote, but how a bloc of 33 to 54 votes are cast—if electors are faithful." Hence, the Electoral College has a major impact on candidate strategy.

As the presidential election of 2000 reminded us, the logic of the Electoral College forces the serious candidates to concentrate only on the competitive "battleground" states. In fall 2000, only about 15 states were still "in play," effectively eliminating the vast majority of the states, including, as noted, California, New York, and Texas, from the election process.

The smaller states are advantaged by the "constant two" electoral votes. Thus, Alaska may get 1 electoral vote for every 40,000 popular votes, whereas Minnesota may get 1 for every 200,000 popular votes. In the 1990s, "the seven states with 3 electoral votes each had a ratio of 268,000 or fewer citizens per electoral vote, while every state with 13 or more electoral votes had a ratio of 475,000 or more citizens per electoral vote."[152]

In contrast to the complexities and dangers of the Electoral College system, the direct-vote method is appealing in its simplicity. Since it is based on a one-person-one-vote principle, it more clearly makes a president the agent of the people and not of the states. Governors and senators are elected by statewide direct popular voting, and they are supposed to be agents of the state. The president, however, should be president of the people, not president of the states—or at least this is what reformers say.

Most of those who favor a direct popular election of the president base their views on the undemocratic character of the Electoral College. They say it doesn't treat voters equally, it discourages turnout, and it discriminates against third parties and independent presidential candidates. They point out that those living in large states and small states get more influence. They point out that Democrats in Kansas or Idaho and Republicans in the District of Columbia or Massachusetts are discouraged from even turning out to vote since votes are cast in a bloc and the chances of their party winning are small.

Thus there are major questions of fairness and democracy that constantly get raised in the debate over the Electoral College and its alternatives. A direct popular vote would eliminate undesirable and undemocratic biases. Stephen J. Wayne wrote, "It would better equalize voting power both among and within states.... The large, competitive sates would lose some of their electoral clout by the elimination of winner-take-all voting. Party competition within the states and perhaps nationwide would be increased. Candidates would be forced to wage campaigns in all fifty states. No longer could an area of the country be taken for granted. Every vote would count in a direct election."[153]

Critics of the Electoral College invariably also attack the contingency election procedure and would change the contingency procedure to a popular runoff. The current system provides that if no presidential candidate wins an absolutely majority of the electoral votes (270 under present arrangements), the members of the House of Representatives choose a president from the top three vote getters. The members vote as part of their state delegation with each state having just one vote. Thus, Alaska and California, Delaware and New York, Wyoming and Texas get one vote.

If this contingency procedure had to be used in future elections, it would obviously be a big boon for small states. But more important, critics lament, it would be an incredibly undemocratic way to select a president. Further, the intrigues in the House might prove unseemly, especially in a three-person, three-party race.

Thus, proponents of the direct vote say it is the most forthright alternative and far preferable to the present system. They contend that voters, when they are choosing a president, think of themselves as national citizens, not as residents of a particular state. The direct popular vote system, proponents claim, is simple, democratic, and clear-cut.

Although we may not especially like or even understand fully the Electoral College system, we are likely to be stuck with it, for better or worse, for at least the next generation or two. Still, plenty of reform suggestions will continue to be debated, and deserve to be debated. They are summarized as follows:

1. The direct vote system just discussed.[154]
2. The district system, as used in Maine and Nebraska.
3. A proportional allocation of the vote within the states, similar to that used in many European countries. Thus, in Florida in 2000, Gore and Bush would have received 12.5 state electoral votes each, rather than all 25 going to Bush.[155]
4. A national bonus plan, which would award 102 bonus electoral votes to the winner of the popular vote—a system that strives to preserve the best aspects of the Electoral College yet virtually guarantees that the popular vote winner wins.[156]

In the aftermath of the confusing 2000 presidential election, a wide array of ideas surfaced, many dusted off from earlier efforts at reform. Most efforts were, as noted, some type of direct vote or proportional allocation. One intriguing, if unlikely, proposal called for a new format for voting that asks voters to choose not only their first choice, but also their second and third choices. If no candidate receives 50 percent, the candidate with the fewest votes among the top three would be eliminated. Those who voted for the eliminated candidate would then have their second choice receive their vote. This is repeated with lesser candidates until only two candidates remain and there is a clear winner. It is, in essence, a built-in "instant runoff" procedure, a runoff without having to hold a new election.[157] While this and similar ideas attracted interest, it was instructive how quickly demands for reform faded and the United States went on as usual, as if the bizarre events of the presidential election of 2000 had never happened.[158]

FROM ELECTION TO GOVERNING

Campaigns, while interesting in and of themselves, are designed to determine who shall govern. Ironically, elections tell us *who* shall govern, yet they do not automatically confer the power to govern to the newly elected. In a separation-of-powers system, elected officials are given the *opportunity* to govern, but not necessarily the *power* to govern.

Some scholars believe that getting elected requires one set of skills and governing another. This distinction has led some recent presidents to engage in what is called "the permanent campaign" where a president is constantly in campaign mode as a means to drum up support to govern. This "going public" strategy is sometimes done at the expense of "going Washington" (bargaining, cajoling, and deliberating at length with congressional insiders) and may actually make governing more difficult. Understandably, however, presidents engage in both strategies.

Power in the American system is akin to a greased pig contest at the county fair. There, you grease up a pig, put it in a pen, and have a dozen or so children run after the pig, trying to catch it and bring it to the judge's table to get their hard earned prize. The problem is, the pig doesn't want to be grabbed, and even if you can grab the pig, it squirms and is slippery, and difficult to hold on to. And there are a bunch of other kids who are grabbing at your arms, and pulling the pig out of your hands, trying themselves to gain control of the pig. In the greased pig contest, the game is funny and entertaining. If you are the president, grabbing for power rarely seems funny.

To answer that question, we must examine the incoming president-elect's "level of political opportunity" or political capital, the fuel that drives the American system. Not all presidents are created equal. Some enter office with a full tank of high octane gas, while others assume office depleted and running on fumes. Franklin D. Roosevelt came into office with a wealth of political capital, Gerald Ford did not. Thus, the stage was set for FDR to succeed, while the cards were stacked against Ford.

How does one convert electoral victory into political clout? One's level of political opportunity is largely derived from factors extrinsic to the president himself. In trying to calibrate political capital, first look at conditions or circumstances. Are these routine or crisis times? If routine, expect the president to be constrained by the separation of power's checks and balances. If a crisis, the president's powers expand: Witness George W. Bush prior to, then after, 9/11.

Next, what is the size of the election victory? If a double-digit victory, power expands. Were there clear issues discussed and promoted in the election or was it largely an election about personality? If several key issues were promoted by the victor, he may claim that he was elected to accomplish his policy agenda and thereby gain some clout.

How long were the president's coattails? Did they bring other members of their party into the House and Senate as a function of their attractiveness at the top of the ticket? We measure coattails by how much of a difference there was between the vote in a district or state for the president and for the candidate running for Congress. If the presidential outpolled the local candidate, he had coattails and can claim that one of the reasons the local candidate won was because of the pull the presidential candidate had in that district. All this may give the president an opportunity to claim a *mandate* for governing. If others in the political universe think the president has a mandate, they may be less likely to oppose a president's policies.

Does the public demand change? If so, the president has another power leg on which to stand. Is the political opposition in Congress united and determined or divided and uncertain?

Finally, is the incoming administration ready to "hit the ground running" with a few clear policies they will focus on, or do they hit the ground stumbling, and have a vast and undisciplined list of "must haves" on the legislative agenda? The general rule is a short, disciplined, focused agenda is best. During the honeymoon period, early victories on key agenda items will pave the way for future success, as the impression is cemented that this is a president to be reckoned with.

Not everything is extrinsic to the president. An array of personal and skill factors also help shape power. Experience counts, as do management skills and the ability to persuade. Judgment is essential. Charisma helps. One's power or strategic sense is valuable. Empathy is a key. So too is the team one puts together.

CONCLUSION

Our presidential selection process is neither tidy nor easy to understand. It is and will continue to be under criticism because of its expense and length, because of the biases of the Electoral College, and because many people believe it tests candidates more for their fund-raising and media skills than for the ability to govern and make tough economic and foreign policy choices.

The election process has evolved in varying and often unpredictable ways since the framers met in Philadelphia. It seeks to achieve a variety of often contending and conflicting purposes. Yet it is one of the grand compromises so often found in the structure of the American political system that seek to paper over regional, political, and even ideological differences. Old tensions of how strong a central government we really want and of how strong and powerful a central leader we are willing to tolerate are never far behind the scenes. Questions of just how much democracy we really want and how much we actually trust the judgment of the average citizen are often involved in our attitudes about the presidential election system. The politics produced by this complicated process is not always pretty, is not always democratic, and, as we have tried to suggest, has its share of paradoxes. Yet the whole selection process is part of the continuing American quest to preserve a politics of compromise, coalitions, moderation, and pragmatism.

The 2012 presidential election may not have been our finest hour; but there were glimmers of hope: negative attack ads proliferated the airwaves; efforts at voter suppression were troubling; big money gave the appearance of a corrupt bargain by both campaigns; the ground game (especially for Obama) was a major factor in the race; and in the end, the people spoke. Perhaps Winston Churchill speaking from the floor of the British House of Commons on November 11, 1947, said it best: "Democracy is the worst form of government, except for all the other forms that have been tried from time to time."

FOR DISCUSSION

1. Given that the presidency is an impossible job, what sorts of experiences or training best prepares someone for the office?
2. What are the arguments for and against abolishing the Electoral College and directly electing presidents? Should we move in that direction?

DEBATE QUESTIONS

1. That money is a corrupting force in American electoral politics.
2. That voting in the United States should be required, by law, of every adult citizen.

FURTHER READINGS

Brown, Lara M. *Jockeying for the American Presidency: The Political Opportunism of Presidents*. Amherst, NY: Cambridge Press, 2010.
Conley, Patricia H. *Presidential Mandates: How Elections Shape the National Agenda*. Chicago: University of Chicago Press, 2001.
Edwards, George C. *Why the Electoral College Is Bad for America*. New Haven, CT: Yale, 2004.
Heilemann, John, and Mark Halpern. *Game Change*. New York: Harper Collins, 2010.
Plouffe, David. *The Audacity to Win*. New York: Penguin, 2009.
Wayne, Stephen J. *Is This Any Way to Run a Democratic Election?*, 3rd ed. Washington, DC: CQ Press, 2007.

Critical Thinking

STATEMENT: Our presidential selection system punishes many potential candidates who have qualities we admire, and often rewards those with the qualities we do not necessarily admire.

PROBLEM: What qualities do Americans say they want in a president? What factors in the presidential selection process reward or punish a candidate's positive or negative characteristics?

CHAPTER 4

Presidential Power and Leadership

It is said that the presidency of the United States is the most powerful office in the world. What is not said or even generally understood is that the power of the chief executive is hard to achieve, balky to manage, and incredibly difficult to exercise.

JOHN STEINBECK, *America and Americans*

"**P**ower" is a much used yet little understood concept. The problem is particularly vexing when we wrestle with the concept of presidential power. What do we mean by power? How much does a president have? How much power should the president wield in a constitutional democracy?

Several of our presidential paradoxes apply directly to the dilemmas of power and leadership. Begin with number one: Americans want powerful leadership, yet we distrust authority and fear the abuse of power. We want our presidents to solve problems, yet refuse them the power equal to our demands and expectations. As stated in the opening chapter, "we admire power yet fear it."

One of the most striking paradoxes is that we expect presidents to govern successfully, yet refuse to trust or support them. Since the 1950s, trust in government has generally declined (see Figure 4.1). While there was a rally effect after 9/11, trust quickly dropped to its lowest point since we began taking measurements. How can a president govern in such an atmosphere?

Also the very term *democratic leadership* is paradoxical. How can a democracy—government of, by, and for the people—look to one person, or even a small team of people, for leadership? It sounds so antidemocratic.[159] The words *leader* and *leadership* imply that someone provides direction. The word *democracy* implies widespread participation and rule by the people. Aren't these irreconcilable?

While there is certainly a tension between democracy and leadership, it can be a creative tension that enhances both democracy and leadership. Yet, all too

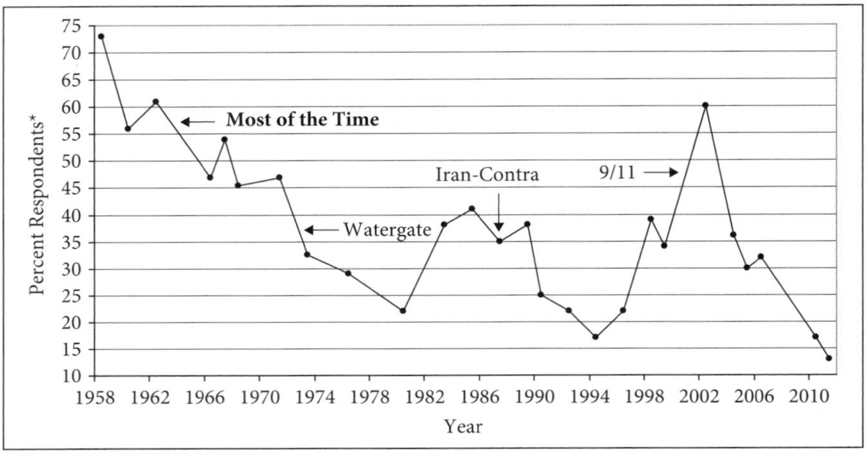

Figure 4.1. Trust in Federal Government 1958–2011. * QUESTION: How Much of the time do you think you can trust government in Washington to do what is right? Just about always, most of the time, or only some of the time? (Created by the authors using data from Gallup)

often this potentially creative tension degenerates into forms of behavior that can undermine both democracy and leadership.

Before we examine what democratic leadership looks like, we will discuss presidential power and leadership, for while democratic leadership may be our goal, the road to achieving it can be difficult.

Several hurdles stand in the way of strong presidential leadership. A system organized around a separation of powers as opposed to a fusion of power (e.g. Great Britain and Canada fuse legislative and executive power) structurally inhibits strong leadership. America's political culture also undermines strong leadership.

Ours is in many ways an anti-authority and therefore an anti-leadership culture. Political scientist Samuel Huntington refers to "the American Creed," which consists of a commitment to individualism, egalitarianism, democracy, and freedom.[160] All are admirable goals, yet not especially supportive of strong leadership or strong deferential followership. Political scientist Clinton Rossiter captures this paradox when he writes, "We have always been a nation obsessed with liberty. Liberty over authority, freedom over responsibility, rights over duties—these are our historic preferences.... Not the good man, but the free man had been the measure of all things in this "sweet land of liberty"; not national glory, but individual liberty has been the object of political authority and the test of its worth."[161]

How does this American creed shape our views on leadership? While it creates a fundamentally anti-leadership disposition, the American propensity for individualism generates a type of hero worship that encourages a heroic model of the presidency. Thus we honor Washington the patriot, Jefferson and Jackson the great democrats, Lincoln and FDR the saviors. But such hero worship masks, in some ways, our notable fear of power and resistance to authority.

Still, in general, we distrust leaders. Historian Max Lerner writes that "American thinkers have been at their best in their anti-authoritarianism."[162] From Jefferson to Henry David Thoreau, and more recently exemplified by Libertarian Ron Paul and maverick Ralph Nader, America's influential thinkers reflected deep strains of individualism and irreverence toward political leaders. The implications of this for leadership were not lost on the thoughtful French observer of the American scene, Alexis de Tocqueville, who wrote

> When it comes to the influence of one man's mind over another's, that is necessarily very restricted in a country where the citizens have all become more or less similar…and since they do not recognize any signs of incontestable greatness or superiority in any of their fellows, and continually brought back to their own judgment as the most apparent and accessible test of truth. So it is not only confidence in a particular man which is destroyed. There is a general distaste for accepting any man's word as proof of anything.[163]

It is difficult, except in a crisis, for presidents to ask the people to make major sacrifices for the common good, to move beyond self-interest. When Jimmy Carter back in the 1970s asked citizens to turn their thermostats down to 68 degrees Fahrenheit in an oil crisis, he was rebuked. When President Bill Clinton called on the American people to provide military peace forces in Haiti and Bosnia, Americans were hesitant if not hostile to his requests.

President George W. Bush, perhaps realizing that the American public responded harshly to calls for sacrifice, told voters in the immediate aftermath of the 9/11 attacks on the United States not to tighten our belts, pay higher taxes to fund a new war against terrorists, or otherwise settle for less, but to "Get on board. Do your business around the country. Fly and enjoy America's great destination spots. Go down to Disney World in Florida. Take your families and enjoy life, the way we want it to be enjoyed."[164]

In his memoirs, Bush noted, "I was surprised by critics who suggested I should have asked for more sacrifice after 9/11. I suppose it's easy for some to forget, but people were making sacrifices. Record numbers of volunteers had stepped forward to help their neighbors."[165]

The United States lacks a defined "public philosophy" of the role of government in a post-Cold War age of Terrorism. The lack of public philosophy often reflects a lack of consensus as to what we as a people should do, where we as a nation need to move. In the absence of a national consensus, presidents have a difficult time moving our separated system.

Our sense of a shared community, or a social contract, has generally remained murky. We are not "one nation indivisible" as much as a collection of individuals. Most of the time, we rarely pull together for the common good. In part, we are a "nation," a loose knit collection of individuals, and in part we are a confederation of tribes.[166]

While Americans occasionally demonstrate patriotic fervor, they seldom demonstrate a deep-seated sense of community. When the public lacks a strong sense of community, leaders have a difficult time pulling the nation together (except in a crisis) to respond collectively, politically, as one nation.

THE MOODS AND CYCLES OF AMERICAN POLITICS

Leadership seldom occurs in a vacuum. There are different "seasons" of leadership, times when presidents are afforded more or less room to exercise power.[167]

These cycles take many forms: a business cycle of economic growth followed by recession; a political pendulum of liberalism followed by a conservative period; strong presidents followed by weak ones; a mood swing of public confidence in government followed by a retreat into private more self-centered interests; a foreign policy shift from isolationism to international involvement. Such cycles are, for the most part, beyond the control of presidents, yet they do have an impact on presidential power.

Presidents are occasionally afforded considerable leverage. Then there are times when presidents are kept on a short leash. In the aftermath of the war in Vietnam and of Watergate, the public turned against the government and presidential power and we questioned everything a president did. Thus Presidents Ford and Carter were restricted in their opportunities to exercise power. The public was more suspicious, the press was more skeptical, the Congress was willing to reassert its authority, and if that weren't enough, the economy was sluggish. Even if Ford and Carter had been skilled, gifted politicians, their level of political opportunity was so low, there was little way they could have been successful at governing.

FDR, by contrast, a skilled politician, benefited from a level of opportunity that was unusually high. He came to office when the public yearned for strong leadership and when Congress was willing to accede power to the president. Hence the mixture of high skill and high opportunity encouraged FDR to pursue power.

"Political time" is also important.[168] During periods of social upheaval, certain types of leadership will be more necessary, while during periods of normalcy, a different type of leadership may be required. Moreover, a different sort of leadership is required during periods of crisis. There is not one leadership style for all seasons. Effective leaders improvise accordingly.

Several cycles are especially relevant to presidential leadership. One is the succession cycle. Major policy shifts are most likely when new leaders come to power.[169] Thus, leadership change is connected to policy change. Another cycle is the cycle of decreasing popularity. Over time, presidents tend to lose popular support (as noted earlier), which makes it more difficult for them to put together political coalitions as time progresses. Another presidential cycle is the cycle of growing effectiveness.[170] A president's learning curve is at its lowest at the beginning of the term and rises as time goes by. Yet a president's power is usually at its zenith early in the term, when knowledge is lowest.

The cycle that seems most relevant to presidential leadership deals with the long-term ebb and flow of American politics. Historians suggest this cycle is like a pendulum swinging back and forth. The United States alternates between periods of "conservatism versus innovation" and "diffusion versus centralization"; such mood swings reflect "a continuing shift in national involvement, between public purpose and private interest."[171]

The roots of this repeating cycle doubtless lie deep in human nature and the U.S. structure of government, and the pattern follows roughly a thirty-year alternation between the pursuit of public purpose and of private interest. In the twentieth century there were a few periods of high governmental activism in support of public purpose: Theodore Roosevelt and Woodrow Wilson from 1901–7 and 1913–15, respectively; Franklin D. Roosevelt from 1933–35; and John F. Kennedy and Lyndon Johnson from 1963–66. Alternatingly, we have experienced periods of conservative restoration such as the 1920s, the 1950s, the 1980s.[172]

Political change is in essence a connection between leader (office holder) and follower (citizen) at different points in time. This allows us to broaden our horizons to the interconnected nature of political change in a democracy. Leaders do not always lead; followers do not always follow. Different political climates require different types of political leadership, and a different set of political skills.

Much of a president's power is contextual, that is, different contexts or situations present presidents with different power opportunities. Some presidents have a high level of political opportunity; others a low level. Some presidents' goals and agendas match the age in which they govern; others are at odds with the times.[173]

One's level of political opportunity is based on factors such as crisis versus normal conditions (as the post 9/11 political environment demonstrated, a crisis president expanded powers), the results of the previous election (landslide vs. a close election), the number of a president's political party in Congress (a large majority vs. divided government), issue ripeness, and a public demand for action. *Opportunity*, combined with *resources*, and *skill*, determine how much power a president is likely to have.

THE VAGARIES OF PRESIDENTIAL POWER

All presidents on assuming office receive similar formal constitutional powers. The founding fathers arranged for an office broadly defined as well as vaguely outlined. Power was available, yet it would be subject to various checks. A president is open to challenges or possible vetoes from a number of political institutions.

As political scientist Edward S. Corwin and others pointed out, there is a plasticity in our fundamental conception of presidential powers.[174] The exact dimensions of executive power at any given moment are largely the consequence of the incumbent's character and energy combined with the overarching demands of the day, the challenges to the system. Some presidents have been maximizer: Jackson, Lincoln, and the Roosevelts, for example. Certain of them became shrewd party leaders. Some saw themselves as direct agents of the American people, as the people's choice with mandates to carry out in exchange for the conferring of power. Still others employed the "take care that the laws be faithfully executed" clause of the Constitution to broaden the notion of executive power well beyond the boundaries envisioned by most of the framers of the constitution. Plainly, an office underdefined on paper has become enlarged with the accumulation of traditions and with the cumulative legacy of some often brilliant achievements.

Tocqueville observed that if executive power was weaker in the United States than in European countries (in the early 1800s), the reason was more in circumstance than in laws. He added that "it is generally in its relations with foreign powers that the executive power of a nation has the chance to display skill and strength."[175] If the United States had remained a small nation, isolated from the other nations of the world, the role of the executive would doubtless have remained weak, certainly much weaker than the presidency we have come to know. Had the presidential office not been capable of expanding, the nation may well not have survived. Presidential powers and leadership have been essential for progress.

One of the more persisting of presidential paradoxes from the standpoint of presidents is the realization that the office carries much less power, however power is defined, than the candidates had thought when they ran for office. Lyndon Johnson did his best to pyramid available power resources to the office soon after he found himself there. But he never stopped complaining that its responsibilities always exceeded his powers. LBJ did not have much advice for his successor, yet he did have these words of caution:

> Before you get to the presidency you think you can do anything. You think you're the most powerful leaders since God. But when you get in that tall chair, as you're gonna find out, Mr. President, you can't count on people. You'll find your hands tied and people cussin' you. The office is kinda like the little country boy found the hoochie-koochie show at the carnival, once he'd paid his dime and got inside the tent: "It ain't exactly as it was advertised."[176]

Presidential power is not fixed, it is not static. It fluctuates depending on the demands of the times, skills of the president, types of issue areas, and needs of the public.

In normal or routine times when dealing with domestic matters, presidential power is limited. In such circumstances the separation of powers system distributes and shares powers between the three branches. At such times, presidents resemble Sisyphus from Greek mythology, condemned for eternity to roll a boulder up a hill only to have it roll down just before reaching the summit, when he must return to the base of the hill and repeat, over and over, this frustrating and inevitable unsuccessful venture.

However, in crisis or war, presidents often seize or are delegated significant, even imperial powers. In a crisis, the checks and balances of the separation of powers recede and the president has at least the chance to wield greater power.

And therein lies the irony. In domestic policy during normal times the president may have too little power. In foreign policy during a crisis he may wield too much power. Thus we have the "Goldilocks problem" of presidential power. In normal times presidential power is "too cold"; in a crisis "too hot." It is hard to get it "just right."

Political scientist Richard Neustadt appreciated how hard it was for presidents to be effective. *Presidential Power*,[177] first published in 1960, is a veritable manual of personal power: how to get it, how to keep it, and how to use it. Presidents Kennedy and Johnson, among others, were influenced by Neustadt's thinking.

Presidential Power was a call for presidents to exercise their power wisely and fully. How do his views hold up in the twenty-first century? After Vietnam, Watergate, Iran-Contra, the Clinton impeachment, and a new foreign policy of "preemptive war," and Obamacare, does Neustadt's analysis still inform? Have the intervening decades validated or undermined his basic premises? Neustadt's *Presidential Power* was rightfully hailed as a pioneering contribution to our understanding of the operational realities of presidential leadership.

Presidential Power broke away from the traditional emphasis on leadership traits, the compartmentalized listings of functional tasks, and the then-dominant tendency to study the presidency in legal or constitutional terms. Instead, Neustadt used organizational and administrative behavior as frames of reference for the study of what presidents must do if they want to influence events and why and how presidents often lose the ability to influence. His stress was on the shared powers of the office rather than the separation of powers. He emphasized the reciprocal character of influence, the constant personal calculations that motivate people to cooperate or not to cooperate with presidential initiatives.

His message was that the presidency is neither as powerful as many people think nor should its strengthening be feared as many others believe. Neustadt called on future presidents to acquire as much power as they could, for formal institutional powers were fragile, even puny, compared with the president's responsibilities.

Neustadt said presidential power is the power to *persuade*, and the power to persuade comes through *bargaining*. Bargaining, in turn, comes primarily through getting others to believe it is in their own self-interest to cooperate. Presidents are depicted as being constantly challenged by threats to their power and constantly needing to enhance their reputation as shrewd bargainers. Tenacity and proper timing are also essential.

Neustadt put great emphasis on "professional reputation" as a source of presidential influence. A president who was, in Machiavelli's classic formulation, both loved and feared, could be a powerful leader. [178]

Neustadt viewed Franklin D. Roosevelt as a many-splendored prototype. Roosevelt had that rare combination of self-confidence, ambition, political experience, sense of purpose, and Neustadt's elusive term, "sensitivity to power," that was necessary to harness formal authority with effective personal performance and thus make the presidency work. "Roosevelt has a love affair with power in that place. It was an early romance and it lasted all his life."[179] "[He] saw the job

The President's Daily Briefing

The President's Daily Briefing, or President's Daily Brief, is a document given every morning to the President with a summary of important events that require the President's attention. Since 1964, the PDB was complied in the Central Intelligence Agency with other agencies adding material from time to time. The PDB was often delivered to the President by the CIA Director himself, and the Director might discuss with the President the impact of certain events and the need for presidential attention or action. On occasion, the director of the CIA would bring colleagues along to the briefing who might be able to shed additional light on significant controversies or problems that are outlined in the PDB. In 2005, responsibility for putting the PDB together and delivering it to the President was transferred to a newly established post, the Director of National Intelligence. Often, the PDB is the opening of a conversation among high-ranking executive branch officials regarding what action to take or what issues to pursue.

Primarily intended to alert the President as an early warning mechanism for emerging international threats and developments, the PDB is also delivered to other high-ranking officials. While there is no statutory requirement as to who shall receive these PDBs, and while it is up to the President himself to decide who shall be included in the list of those who receive the PDB, often the Secretary of State, the President's National Security Advisor, and the Secretary of Defense will be among those to receive the PDB. The PDB is "top secret" and on very rare occasions will be designated for the sole use of the President with "For the President's eyes only" stamped on the cover.

Source: *National Security Archive*, Washington DC, *nsarchiv@gwu.edu*.

PRESIDENT'S DAILY BRIEFING: August 6, 2001

Declassified and Approved

for Release, 10 April 2004

Bin Ladin Determined to Strike the US

Clandestine foreign government and media reports indicate Bin Ladin since 1997 has wanted to conduct terrorist attacks in the US. Bin Ladin implied in US television interviews in 1997 and 1998 that his followers would follow the example of the World Trade Center bomber Ramzi Yousef and "bring the fighting to America."

After US missile strikes on his base in Afghanistan in 1998, Bin Ladin told followers he wanted to retaliate in Washington, according to a xxxxxxxxxxxx service.

An Egyptian Islamic Jihad (EIJ) operative told an xxxxxx service at the same time that Bin Ladin was planning to exploit the operative's access to the US to mount a terrorist strike.

The millennium plotting in Canada in 1999 may have been part of Bin Ladin's first serious attempt to implement a terrorist strike in the US.

Convicted plotter Ahmed Ressam has told the FBI that he conceived the idea to attack Los Angeles International Airport himself, but that Bin Ladin lieutenant Abu Zubaydah encouraged him and helped facilitate the operation. Ressam also said that in 1998 Abu Zubaydah was planning his own US attack.

Ressam says Bin Ladin was aware of the Los Angeles operation.

Although Bin Ladin has not succeeded, his attacks against the US Embassies in Kenya and Tanzania in 1998 demonstrate that he prepares operations years in advance and is not deterred by setbacks. Bin Ladin associates surveilled our Embassies in Nairobi and Dar es Salaam as early as 1993, and some members of the Nairobi cell planning the bombings were arrested and deported in 1997.

Al-Qa'ida members—including some who are US citizens—have resided in or traveled to the US for years, and the group apparently maintains a support structure that could aid attacks. Two al-Qa'ida members found guilty in the conspiracy to bomb our Embassies in East Africa were US citizens, and a senior EIJ member lived in California in the mid-1990s.

A Clandestine source said in 1998 that a Bin Ladin cell in New York was recruiting Muslim-American youth for attacks.

We have not been able to corroborate some of the more sensational threat reporting, such as that from a xxxxxxxxxx service in 1998 saying that Bin Ladin wanted to hijack a US aircraft to gain the release of "Blind Shaykh" 'Umar 'Abd al-Rahman and other US-held extremists.

Figure 4.2. The President's Daily Briefing

of being President as being FDR."[180] In short, Roosevelt had the will to power, the driving ambition, and the uncommon sense of knowing how to deal with people.

Neustadt was impressed with the way Roosevelt juggled assignments, kept people guessing, and put men of clashing temperaments and ideas in charge of his major projects. FDR loved dividing authority and keeping his organizations temporary and overlapping. To some people this might have been the art of manipulation, but to Neustadt it was the essence of leadership. Roosevelt remained the Neustadt model.

Neustadt's analytic treatment of presidential power was a description of how to strengthen the hand of a president one liked. Neustadt's propositions, slightly rephrased, are as follows:

1. To be a leader, a president must have a will for power. If he lacks a desire for power and a penchant for shrewdly handling people, he is not suited for the office.

2. The skill of a president at winning others over to his support is a necessary energizing factor to get the institutions of government into action.
3. A president cannot be withdrawn, above the battle, above politics, or simply work from within the confines of his own ideas; a sensitivity to the thoughts and feelings of others, and an ability to create solutions that compromise contesting points of view, are what distinguishes effective from ineffective leadership.
4. The members of Congress act the way they think they have to in order to win or claim credit, get reelected, and "look good." A president's job is to get members of Congress and other influential members of the government community to think his requests are in their own best interests.
5. A president has to exploit events and crises to gain attention. Most Americans grow attentive only as they grow directly concerned with what may happen in their lives.
6. A president should never rely on others to determine his power stakes. He should be his own intelligence officer, his own expert on crucial power relationships. A president who delegates the job of being chief politician to others is a president who will be less influential.
7. Popularity and public prestige produce favorable credit for a president among the professional Washington community. Public disapproval, on the other hand, encourages resistance from the Washington community (defined as members of Congress, bureaucrats, the press, governors, diplomats, etc.).
8. Presidential power is not easy to come by and even the most skillful of presidents will have to be flexible, always sensitive to the need for multiple channels of information, always frugal in using power resources to get their way, and always employing the art of persuasion in a bargaining situation, thereby avoiding at almost all costs the direct issuing of a confrontational command.

Presidential Power held out hope that a shrewd and artful leader could and would be a powerful Hamiltonian engine of change. An aggressive, ambitious, strategic politician, determined to get his way and ever distrustful of the motives of others, seemed to be the remedy for the post-Eisenhower years. A key problem of the presidency at the time was how the presidency could regain control over the drifting Washington policy apparatus. Forceful leadership was needed, Neustadt said, and only the president could fill the leadership vacuum.

Neustadt's contribution to the understanding of the presidency is his notion that the power of a president rests on his ability to persuade others. Because a president shares authority with other institutions, he cannot merely command. Thus, he must constantly bargain and negotiate in an effort to achieve results.

UNRESOLVED QUESTIONS

The most frequent criticism of Neustadt's analysis is that it seemed too preoccupied with the acquisition of power and stockpiling the power, divorced from any discussion of purposes to which power should be put. Such an emphasis on means without a clear discussion of ends left the impression that the art of leadership is mainly the art of manipulation. Neustadt was faulted too for his failure to emphasize the role that a "sense of direction" plays in presidential leadership, and how a president would call on or consider ideological values in his power exchanges.

One critic went so far as to suggest the Neustadt "baptizes" political ambition just as Dale Carnegie or Wall Street manuals baptize greed. Many readers would have liked a more thoughtful discussion of the ends of presidential power, of the ethical boundaries. What are the higher claims on a president and how does the creative president join together the ethic of responsibility and the ethic of ultimate ends?

A second criticism of Neustadt's book was that it is too approving of the personalization of presidential power. It seems to say, find the right president and teach him or her what power is all about and progress will be realized. It portrays presidents as potential saviors. If only we had the "second coming" of Franklin Roosevelt, all would be well. It comes close to suggesting we need a heroic, charismatic, larger-than-life figure on whom to lean to make the system work.

Two problems arise from this emphasis on FDR and on presidents as the answer to our needs. First, Neustadt failed to take into account the degree to which presidents are almost invariably stabilizers or protectors of the status quo rather than agents of retribution or progressive change. Neustadt gave little attention to the way the prevailing American elite values, and market capitalism, often limit a president's freedom. One gets the impression from reading Neustadt that he thought a president can and should roam at will, providing he is shrewd enough to be able to persuade others that their interests are the same as his. In fact, however, all of our presidents have had to prove their political orthodoxy and their acceptability to a wide array of established powers, especially corporate leaders, entrenched interest-group leaders, and so on. Thus, Neustadt raised hopes that the presidency would be an instrument for the progressive transformation of American politics.

Just how much and how often we can turn to the White House and hope that a benevolent, bright, and energetic president will provide truly inspired leadership? Surely this is what Obama supporters in 2008 were hoping from their candidate. Sometimes we must recruit such a leader, yet a reading of history suggests that breakthroughs and leadership often come from the bottom (or at least the middle) up. Civil rights workers, consumer organizers, women's rights activists, environmentalists, tax-revolt champions, and antiwar protestors are illustrative of the catalysts that more often than not bring about policy change in the United States.

In Neustadt's defense it can be said that although his treatise reads like a hymn of praise for FDR, the author really did not go so far as to say "Defer completely to your president and trust him." He appears, at least most of the time, merely to say that without a good engineer the train just won't go.

Did Neustadt's call for strong presidential leadership betray a liberal bias? For most of the post–World War II era, the heroic/strong presidency that Neustadt promoted was considered the model for political progressives of his day. Neustadt and others advocated a powerful activist presidency in the pursuit of more government intervention in problem solving. From the 1950s through the 1970s, conservatives advocated more limited government, less presidential power, and a smaller role for the federal government.

But as testimony to the seductive lure of the heroic presidency model, by the 1980s even conservatives had been converted to presidential power. The heroic presidency could, conservatives found, be used to pursue the conservative agenda. Emboldened by Ronald Reagan's rhetorical skills and the promise of the "Reagan Revolution," conservatives saw the presidency as a vehicle for political power. From that point on, through most of the George W. Bush presidency, conservative presidentialists emerged as a powerful force in the Republican party, and Neustadt's strong presidency view became a philosophy for multiple political leanings.[181]

PERSUASION AND POWER

Who can doubt that prestige and persuasion comprise key elements of presidential leadership? And yet, persuasion *does not* exhaust the opportunities of presidents to lead. Presidents also have *power*, the ability to act, to command, to assert, to initiate. Presidential leadership is about persuasion *and* power, leadership and command.[182]

The American political system positions the president in an advantageous spot. While he shares power with Congress, and many of the key elements of power are blended, split, and shared by the president and Congress, the president is thereafter well positioned to initiate action, to assert authority, and thus to lead or even preempt Congress.

By using executive orders, national security directives, initiating action, acting unilaterally, or by invoking administrative methods, presidents can increase their governing powers and if Congress does not fight back, often win. While the Madisonian system requires the president to govern with Congress, certainly there are formal powers as well as political opportunities that sometimes allow presidents to govern alone.

James Madison anticipated that individuals would seek to aggrandize power. This led to the establishment of a separation of powers designed to give competing institutions power and leverage to counterbalance aggrandizing efforts. In the modern era, however, Congress has sometimes been remiss in standing up for its institutional powers, and presidents have been able to acquire power, sometimes unchallenged.

If, constitutionally, presidents are dealt a relatively weak or limited power hand, there are still ways for them to engage in direct, unilateral actions and exercise power.[183] A president with skill, persuasive ability, prestige, popularity, and strong personal attributes can add to his arsenal of power by taking direct or unilateral action.[184]

It is not *either* the personal presidency *or* the direct action presidency. Smart, effective presidents employ the lessons of Neustadt and unilateralism. They survey the political landscape and utilize the strategy most likely to prove effective.

The direct actions a president can employ that might lead to successfully leveraging of unilateral power include

1. Taking the initiative
2. Executive Orders
3. Signing Statements
4. Prerogative Authority

Presidents may be constitutionally as well as politically vulnerable, but they are not helpless. They may employ an array of unilateral actions that might—under the right conditions (e.g., crisis, war, or when they have unified government)—give them independent power to act above and beyond the constitutional limits of the office.

POWER-MAXIMIZING STRATEGIES

Any discussion dealing with presidential power must deal with presidential weakness as well as strength. The founders left the president vulnerable to several potential veto points, most notably from the Congress. The framers did not want executive impotence—had that been their goal they could have stuck with the Articles of Confederation. But they also feared tyranny. They chose instead an executive office of limited powers that operated in a separation-of-powers model that fragmented power. Of course, such a system had consequences for the president's ability to lead.

Left to its own devices, the presidency has limited powers and is thereafter vulnerable to the will of Congress and others. At times, a president can act alone. Yet a president is usually dependent on the compliance or cooperation of others to achieve his or her goals. The presidency gives the occupant of the White House little more than the opportunity to govern.

Presidents cannot merely command, they must persuade. But they must do much more. For presidents to be effective, and govern within the bounds of democratic leadership, they must also develop a "strategic sense." They must know what to accomplish and how to accomplish it. And, their means and goals must aim to further the will of the people, empower citizens, and strengthen democratic accountability. Success is not measure merely by getting one's way but also by the ends to which policies are directed.

By strategic sense,[185] we mean the ability to devise an overall plan that is designed to integrate means and ends, that shows what to do and how to do it, and that links smaller tactical steps to a broad guiding vision.

To overcome the roadblocks built into the system, a president must develop a strategic sense of governing. Some elements of presidential leadership remain fairly constant over time—the Constitution, the separation of powers. Others are variable—the skill level of the president, the context or situation at hand, the nature of the president's mandate, the president's party strength in Congress. The president must develop a strategy designed to maximize political capital.[186]

Presidential leadership refers to a complex phenomenon involving influence—the ability to move others in desired directions. Successful leaders are those who can take full advantage of their opportunities, resources, and skills. Institutional structures, the immediate situation, the season of power, the political culture, the regime type, and the dynamics of followership define the opportunities for the exercise of leadership. The resources at a leader's disposal include constitutional and statutory powers, intermediaries, media, level of popularity, nature of the congressional majority, and policy arena. We often mistake resources for power. A successful leader converts resources to power. This does not happen automatically. To convert resources to power requires skill.

The leader's style, political acumen, experience, political strategy, management skills, vision, ability to mobilize political support, character traits, and personal attributes provide a behavioral repertoire, a set of skills. Opportunities, resources, and skills interact to determine the potential for success or failure in attempts to lead and influence. Presidents who can play to the optimum their cards of opportunity, resources, and skill have a chance of succeeding.

But few presidents are FDR, and few face the opportunities for leadership FDR had. Power is dispersed, it "exists only as a potential. Leadership is the means by which the president can exploit that potential. This is no easy task."[187]

A president has vast responsibilities, with high public expectations and limited power resources. But as an institution, the presidency has proven to be elastic; it stretches to accommodate skilled leaders in situations of high opportunity, but contracts to hem in less skilled leaders.

The variable nature of presidential power has left presidency scholars a bit schizophrenic regarding the proper scope and limits of presidential power. When presidents performed credibly (1930s to early 1960s), they called for an enlarged institution. As presidents faltered (1960s to 1980s), they called for restrictions on presidential power; and when the United States faced terrorist attacks in 2001, demands were heard for an enlarged presidency. This variability is reactive, it is based on the subjective judgments derived from the short-term political performance of presidents. Such evaluations miss the key point: the normal state of the presidency is one of constrained power. To be successful, a president must overcome nature, or at least the nature of power built into the system. Thus, it is better to look at the requirements for leadership generically, at the preconditions necessary for the exercise of political leadership, than merely to react to the current temporary occupant of the Oval Office. In doing this we can see which threads run through the presidency as well as see how well a president performed.

The founders wanted a government of energy, yet a specific type of energy, energy that resulted from deliberation and collaboration. What model or type of leadership is required to move such a system?: a model based on consensus, not *fait accompli*; influence, not command; agreement, not independence;

cooperation, not unilateralism. Such a model of power requires presidents to think strategically.[188]

PRESIDENTIAL LEADERSHIP

The words *leadership* and *power* are often used interchangeably. This is misguided. Leadership suggests influence; power is command. Leaders inspire and persuade; power wielders order compliance. Leaders induce followership; power holders force compliance. Officeholders have some power by virtue of occupying an office. Leaders, on the other hand, must earn followership. The officeholder uses the powers granted by the virtue of position. The leader tries to reshape the political environment, "he seeks to change the constellation of political forces about him in a direction closer to his own conception of the political good."[189]

Occasionally, a president can act on his own authority, "independent" of others. But such unilateral acts (except in a crisis) are the exception, not the rule. In most cases, presidents share power. Therefore, the informal "powers" usefully discussed by Neustadt become important to presidents who wish to promote political change.

All presidents have some power, some ability to command. Yet such power is short term and limited. It ceases to exist the moment the president leaves office. Its effects can often be undone by a new president.

A president's formal power, for so long the focal point of presidential studies,[190] includes constitutional authority, statutes, delegated powers, and those areas where others follow a president's command. But with the publication of Neustadt's *Presidential Power*, the ability to persuade took center stage in presidential studies. Rather than take an "either/or" approach to the debate over formal versus informal powers, one should see these two potential sources of strength as complementary, as presidential options in the pursuit of their goals. While presidents derive some of their power from constitutional sources, they derive other parts from political and personal sources. Effective presidents use all the resources available to them. True leadership occurs when presidents are able to exploit the multifaceted nature of opportunities to both command and influence.

For better or worse, only presidential leadership can regularly overcome the natural lethargy built into the American system and give focus and direction to government. Congress can, on occasion, take the lead on select policy, as was the case when the Congress overcame presidential opposition from Ronald Reagan and imposed economic sanctions on the white minority government of South Africa. The Newt Gingrich-led Congress in 1995 provides a few examples. But such cases are infrequent. Congress simply is not institutionally well designed to provide consistent national leadership over extended periods of time. In the late twentieth and early twenty-first centuries, the citizens have most often looked to the White House for leadership and direction. If the president does not lead, gridlock usually results. Like it or not, presidential leadership usually remains the key for moving the machinery of government.

THE BUILDING BLOCKS OF PRESIDENTIAL LEADERSHIP

Vision

The most important "power" a president can have is to rally the public around a clear and compelling *vision*. A meaningful, positive vision that is rooted in building blocks of the past addresses needs and hopes of the president, and portrays an image of a possible future that opens more doors to presidential leadership than all the skills and resources combined. A powerful vision can transform a political system, recreate the regime of power, and chart a course for change. Vision energizes and empowers, inspires and moves people and organizations.[191]

Few presidents use to the fullest what Theodore Roosevelt referred to as "the bully pulpit" to develop a public philosophy for governing. Rather than attempting to educate and lead the public, most presidents serve as managers or clerks of public business. But if presidents wish to craft significant change, they must use the bully pulpit to promote a moral and political vision in support of change.[192]

Visions are empowering. They are derived from the core values of a community, flow from the past, and are about the future. Visions inspire, give meaning and direction to a community, and are roadmaps. Visions are about achieving excellence. A visionary leader gives direction to an organization and gives purpose to action. Visionary leadership charts a course for action.

Visionary leaders are remembered and have an impact after they have left office. Thus, long after FDR, Martin Luther King, Jr., and Ronald Reagan were gone, the power of their ideas and the impact of their words remain symbolic and emotional forces in the political arena. Ronald Reagan was able to inspire followers because he was skilled at presenting his vision. In contrast, the Bushes often had trouble providing a compelling vision that rallied the nation.

Few people are better positioned to present a vision to the public than a president. Already the focus of much media and public attention, presidents can become "highlighters" of important issues to be addressed as a part of the president's agenda.

Skill

For successful political leadership, skill is important, yet skill is never enough. Even the most skilled of presidents face formidable roadblocks. Skill can help determine the extent to which a president takes advantage of or is buried by circumstances, but circumstances set the parameters of what is possible regarding leadership. President Reagan referred to the "window of opportunity," his way of talking about open or closed circumstances for exercising presidential leadership. Skilled presidents face a closed window (e.g., the opposition party controlling Congress during a period of economic troubles where the president's popularity is low) will be limited in what they can accomplish. Presidents of limited skill, when the window of opportunity is open, will have much greater political leverage, even though their skill base is smaller. It is thus entirely possible for a president with limited skill to be more successful than a president with great skill. If one is dealt a weak hand, there is only so much skill can do.[193]

Ronald Reagan, an inspirational leader who challenged the voters with a new vision and new direction for the nation, had a significant impact on the politics of his era. © Shepard Sherbell/CORBIS SABA.

This is not to say that skill is unimportant. But in the constellation of factors that contribute to success or failure, skill is but one, and probably not the most important, element.

Before an election one often hears political cynics whine, "It really doesn't matter who gets elected, they all end up doing the same thing anyway." Social science lends some support to this view. After all, social scientists widely believe the institution, role, expectations, time, and other factors play a significant role in determining behavior. The cynic has a point, yet it should not be taken too far. Individuals are constrained, but individuals do matter, and leaders matter.[194]

One way of looking at the skill/opportunity dilemma is to focus on what is referred to as a president's "political capital." Is a president's political capital like a bank account where a one-time deposit is made at the beginning of his term and he invests carefully and draws on that account prudently, lest he run out of resources? Or can a president add to his bank account from time to time, renewing his political resources?

President George H. W. Bush believed that his capital was a fixed sum, and in spending it, he dissipated it. Bill Clinton, on the other hand, viewed political capital more flexibly. He sometimes spent it, then tried to replenish his assets as best he could. As President Clinton noted

> ...even a President without a majority mandate coming in, if the President has a disciplined, aggressive agenda that is clearly in the interest of the majority of American people—I think you can create new political capital all the time, because you have access to the people through the communications network. If you have energy and sort of an inner determination that keeps you at the task, I think you can re-create political capital continuously throughout the Presidency. I have always believed that.[195]

Do individual leaders make a difference? Sometimes. As political scientist Erwin C. Hargrove writes, "Surely the issue is not, Do individuals make a difference? but under what conditions do they make a difference? The relative importance of leaders varies across institutions and across time and place.... The task of scholarship is to integrate the study of individuals with the social and institutional forces that move them and that they, in turn, may influence."[196]

At what point do individuals matter?: often when skill is an important variable in presidential success. It is nonetheless important to note that "effectiveness in achieving goals was enhanced if skill and task were congruent."[197] To that we would add a third element: the level of political opportunity. Skill, matched to task when the window of political opportunity is open, may lead to goal attainment.

The impact of individual presidents who made a difference in specific policy areas is unmistakable: Lyndon Johnson and civil rights, Richard Nixon and China, Jimmy Carter and human rights, Ronald Reagan and tax cuts, George H. W. Bush and the Gulf War, Bill Clinton and the Brady bill (gun control) and NAFTA (North American Free Trade Agreement), George W. Bush and the war on terrorism, and Barack Obama and health care. These presidents made choices, moved in new directions, and made a difference. Yes they were limited, yet they were able to overcome the natural lethargy of the system and succeed in selected policy arenas. That in most areas and on most issues presidential behavior appears more similar than dissimilar should not obscure the essential fact that on some issues at some times, some presidents do make a difference.

Determining what role skill played in these events is a slippery task. Could another president have opened the doors to China? Perhaps, yet maybe not. Could any president emphasize human rights in his foreign policy? Certainly. So where are we left? When does skill matter and how can we recognize or measure political skill? Regrettably, it is too elusive a concept to measure precisely. High levels of skill, task congruence, and high opportunity sometimes lead to presidential success, and low levels of these often lead to failure.

If skill is of some importance, it is useful to ask, what skills are most useful to a president? Political experience is often cited as a requirement for effective leadership, and while this sounds like common sense, the correlation between experience and achievement is not clear. Some of our most experienced national leaders were, in many respects, failures (Hoover, LBJ, Nixon, and George H. W. Bush come to mind). Overall, more experience is better than less experience, although by no means a guarantee of successful performance. Thus, other factors determine to a great degree the success or failure of a president.

Ronald Reagan, Bill Clinton, and George W. Bush serve as excellent examples of amateurs, in Washington, DC, terms, who sometimes behaved amateurishly in the White House. Reagan in Beirut, Clinton in Somalia, and Bush in Iraq all made fundamental errors. In all cases, leaders with little or no foreign policy experience made blunders that probably could have been avoided. More experienced hands might have known better.[198]

Presidents also need people skills. They must know how to persuade, bargain, cajole, and co-opt. They must be masters of self-preservation. They must be able to motivate and inspire, to gain trust and influence. And occupants of the White House must master the art of "presidential schmoozing."

Personality skills are also a significant part of the arsenal of presidential requirements. All presidents have a strong drive for power. Some hold it within healthy bounds; others, like Nixon, destroy themselves. To be effective, presidents should be self-confident, secure, and flexible. Presidents consumed by self-doubt, insecurity, and rigidity are often dangerous and more apt to abuse power.

Presidents also need self-knowledge. We all have weaknesses, but we need not let our weaknesses consume us. Good presidents recognize their strengths and weaknesses, and attempt to deal constructively with weakness. Thus, presidents who are inexperienced in foreign policy may need to compensate by surrounding themselves with experienced foreign policy insiders.

Managerial skills are also important if a president is to succeed. Upon taking office, presidents tend to see only the personal as important; the historical and institutional are often downplayed.

A president must also have enormous personal discipline. By this we mean they must be intelligent, have stamina, show sound judgment, and carefully focus their efforts. Good presidents are also creative, empathetic, and expressive. They need to be optimistic. They must also have sense of humor, and learn to control their temper. President Reagan's self-effacing sense of humor served him especially well; it disarmed opponents and won over much of the public.

Political Timing

The "when" of politics also matters greatly: when the legislation is introduced, when the public is ready to accept change, when Congress can be pressured to act, when to lead and when to follow, when to push and when to pause. A sense of political timing, part of the "power sense" all great leaders have, helps a president know when to move, when to retreat, when to hold firm, and when to compromise. The transition and honeymoon are especially important periods.

Getting a good start ("hitting the ground running") is a key element of political success, and during the transition, the eleven-week period between the November election and the January inauguration, some of the most important work of an administration is done. Here the groundwork is laid for much that will follow and a tone is set that shapes the way others see the new administration. During the transition, the president makes key decisions on who the top advisors will be, who will fill important cabinet positions, how the staff will be instructed, what decision style will be employed, whether to pursue a partisan strategy or try and woo the opposition, how to mobilize the public, and what issues the administration will push during the first year.

"Power is not automatically transferred, but must be seized. Only the authority of the presidency is transferred on January 20; the power of the presidency—in terms of effective control of the policy agenda—must be consciously developed."[199] To seize power, presidents must adopt a strategic approach to the transition, one that leave little to chance and that deals self-consciously with the use of power.

A president's first one hundred days and first six to ten months are crucial periods for setting the agenda. It is important to win at least a few key legislative victories as soon as possible.

Strong presidents such as Woodrow Wilson, Franklin Roosevelt, Lyndon Johnson, and Ronald Reagan began with explicit goals and pushed Congress to enact bold new programs. Indeed, each new president is in effect invited in the first year to share a vision and a national agenda with attentive Washington, national, and international audiences.

When Reagan took office, for example, his administration self-consciously chose to focus on a select few big-ticket items: tax cuts and increased defense spending. Nearly all else, including important foreign policy matters, were put on the back burner. This allowed the Reagan administration to concentrate its energies and also conveyed an image that this president could succeed. He appeared to be, and for a time was, influential.

In contrast, George H. W. Bush virtually relinquished the advantages offered by the honeymoon period. He got off to a slow start and appeared more concerned with managing a response to events as they happened than with shaping events by his actions. His early weeks were marked by caution.

A president's strategic sense must also take into account other key elements of presidential power maximization: popularity and public opinion, relations with and the number of the president's party members in Congress, media relations, management skills, control of the agenda, and coalition and consensus building.

THE "CONDITIONS" OF POWER

Presidents have formal and unilateral or direct powers; they also have political and personal resources that can be employed to gain leverage. Just how much "power" they have at any given moment depends on the interaction of several key factors:

1. Policy Area: Presidents have more power in foreign affairs than in domestic or economic policy.
2. Routines vs. Crises: In war or during a crisis, presidents have more power than under normal conditions.
3. Skill Can Matter: Highly skilled presidents who develop and implement an effective "strategic map" can get added leverage.
4. Boldness Counts: Presidents who are assertive (but not bullies) can initiate actions and employ unilateral acts to gain power.
5. A Congressional Majority: Unified government, especially if one has a significant numerical majority in Congress, can be a great benefit to a president.

In the end, presidential power is largely conditional. Many key factors are out of the control of a president. Conceptualized together these factors yield a relative scale of presidential power that captures the key variables that lead to strength or weakness.

ARE WE TOO PRESIDENCY-CENTRIC?

When things are going well, we praise presidents and celebrate presidential power. Yet we have little patience when things go badly and usually point the finger of blame—whether merited or not—directly at the president.[200]

Apart from the blame game perspective, are there principled critiques of presidential power that merit our attention? Three recent critiques, one from the political right, and the other from the left, deserve to be confronted if we are to grasp both the potential and the problems inherent in presidential power.

On the right from a libertarian-oriented position, Gene Healy argues that the presidency has become more powerful than the Framers anticipated or wished, and that the swelling of presidential power has led to "romanticization of the presidency," with the president as "our guardian angel."[201] "Is that vision of the presidency," he asks, "appropriate for a self-governing republic? Is it compatible with limited constitutional government?" Healy concludes, not surprisingly, "that it is not."[202]

In the end, Healy calls for a "constitutional presidency," one more in line with the model invented by the framers. Healy is aware of the many forces that have contributed to the growth of presidential power, and may also be aware that he is tilting at windmills, yet this much needed voice offers a correction to those conservatives who promote the "unitary executive" or presidentialist model of presidential power.

On the left, Dana D. Nelson contends that the more we rely on and look to the president as our savoir and problem solver, the less will we rely on authentic democratic responses to our problems. In this sense, presidential power is dangerous to democracy. She says that

> We citizens have a powerful, civically and presidentially trained misunderstanding of the relation of the president to democracy. The president, cast from the early 1800s as the "leader of democracy," has often been either a bad surrogate for or downright antagonistic to the self-governing interests, abilities, and efforts of the people. The president's antidemocratic function in U.S. democracy has become normalized both symbolically and structurally.[203]

By elevating the presidency we demolish democracy. By deferring to and investing our hopes in a president, we rely less on ourselves and less on our collective capacity to exercise democratic power.

In a third critique, Lou Fisher[204] warns us of the dangers in idealizing the presidency. He reminds us that the presidency is a constitutional office, defined and redefined over time, yet still embedded within a constitutional framework.

These writers pose useful questions and make us stop and think; yet as long as the president is seen as a world leader, and the United States as a military and economic superpower, calls for a reduced role for the president seem implausible.

CONCLUSION

Bold, effective, sustained presidential leadership is uncommon. In those rare periods of leadership, presidents are able to animate citizens and mobilize government, develop a vision and establish an agenda, move Congress and lead the bureaucracy. Such presidents recast the arena of the politically possible. It has not happened often. The forces arrayed against a president usually have the upper hand. The power of lethargy is considerable.

The preconditions for effective presidential leadership are rarely in syncopation: skill, the right timing, a consensus, a governing coalition, popularity, vision, and a mandate. Presidents, to be effective leaders in a democratic system, must bring Hamiltonian energy to a Madisonian system for Jeffersonian and Rooseveltian ends. Few presidents can achieve this.

To succeed, presidents must be masters of the light (education, vision, mobilization) and the heat (power, bargaining). Given the incredible array of skills and circumstances necessary for presidents to succeed, no wonder many of them fail to live up to our expectations.

Some of the difficulty rests with individual presidents who lack valid programmatic ideas as well as sufficient political skill. Part of the challenge rests with the structural design of the American constitutional system, which separates and fragments power.

A tension will always exist between the need for leadership and the demands of democracy. Proponents of robust democracy realize that leadership has rarely fit comfortably with democracy in America.

Thomas Jefferson believed that the primary duties of a leader in a democracy were "to inform the minds of the people, and to follow their will."[205]

Informing the minds of the people speaks to the role of leader as educator. In a democracy, the leader has a responsibility to educate, enlighten, and inform the people. He or she must identify the problems and mobilize the people to act. By informing or educating the citizenry, the leader also engages in a dialogue, the ultimate goal of which is to involve the leader and citizen in the process of developing a vision, grounded in the values of the nation, that will animate needed action.

FOR DISCUSSION

1. In creating the American system of government and in inventing the presidency, were the framers correct about

   a. Human nature;
   b. The need to control power;
   c. The utility of a separation of powers system;
   d. The rule of law and limited government; and
   e. The amount of power given to the president in the Constitution?

2. Which is more important, the informal power of the president or the formal powers of the office?

DEBATE QUESTIONS

1. That the presidency is not too big a job for one person to handle.
2. That the public expects and demands too much of its presidents.

FURTHER READINGS

Burns, James MacGregor. *Leadership*. New York: HarperCollins, 1978.

Cronin, Thomas E., and Michael A. Genovese. *Leadership Matters: Unleashing the Power of Paradox*. Boulder, CO: Paradigm, 2012.

Genovese, Michael A. *Memo to a New President*. New York: Oxford, 2008.

Howell, William G. *Power Without Persuasion: The Politics of Direct Presidential Action*. Princeton, NJ: Princeton University Press, 2003.

Neustadt, Richard E. *Presidential Power and the Modern Presidents*. New York: Free Press, 1990.

Rudalevige, Andrew. *The New Imperial Presidency*. Ann Arbor: University of Michigan Press, 2005.

Schlesinger, Arthur M., Jr. *The Imperial Presidency*. Boston: Houghton Mifflin, 1973.

Skowronek, Stephen. *Presidential Leadership in Political Time*. Lawrence: University Press of Kansas, 2007.

Yoo, John. *Crisis and Command: The History of Executive Power from George Washington to George W. Bush*. New York: Kaplan, 2009.

Critical Thinking

STATEMENT: Constitutionally, the president has more power than Congress.

PROBLEM: How would one go about testing the accuracy of this statement? Where do you start? Are there value neutral ways of measuring power?

CHAPTER 5

The Presidential Job Description in a System of Shared Powers

"The accumulation of all powers legislative, executive, and judiciary in the same hands...may justly be pronounced the very definition of tyranny."

JAMES MADISON, *Federalist Papers*, No. 47

Anyone searching for the paradoxes of the American presidency need look no further than the president's informal as well as formal job description: high expectations, yet limited power; many demands, constrained resources. We expect the president to accomplish great things, yet often tie his hands. Of course, as discussed earlier, the job of the president has changed and enlarged dramatically since 1789. While the constitutional provisions relating to presidential power remain virtually unchanged, the responsibilities and expectations placed on the office have increased significantly.

Further, the president is embedded in a system—the separation of powers. In this three-branch system of government some powers are separated, some shared and blended, but little is given exclusively to the president. As such, on most issues, he must elicit the cooperation of other branches if he is to legitimately act. In the midst of the war against terrorism, this system—as we shall later explore—has come under particularly acute strain.

Historians still debate the motives of the framers of the U.S. Constitution. Whether great advocates of or traitors to robust democracy, it is clear the framers harbored concerns about both mass-based democracy and executive tyranny. These concerns are evident when one examines the inventing of the American Presidency.

To understand what is expected of presidents today, we need to examine the invention of the presidency as well as its evolution over time. Only then can we fully appreciate the many roles and demands placed on the presidency.

For this chapter, Paradox numbers 1, 4, 5, and 6 most directly apply. We want a powerful president, yet the separation of power enchains the office. We like presidents who are above politics, yet dealing with Congress demands great political as well as partisan skill. We expect presidents to unify us, yet our politics are hyper-partisan and divisive; we want visionary policies, yet demand pragmatism and for the president to follow our will.

In establishing a separation of powers system with checks and balances, the framers of the Constitution sought to both empower a presidency with energy *and* limit the reach of the office. They wanted "republican energy" in the new executive, an energy animated by shared and separated powers that *both* the president and Congress exercised, often together.

THE PRESIDENCY AS DEFINED AND DEBATED IN 1787

The presidential job description as outlined in the Constitution was a medley of compromises. The framers wanted a presidency strong enough to do what was asked of it and yet not one that would use governmental authority for selfish ends or contrary to the general welfare. In almost every instance presidential powers were shared powers. Perhaps only the pardon power was a truly imperial grant of power.

Despite the administrative, diplomatic, commander-in-chief, and veto powers granted to them, presidents found they had to act within a set of strong constitutional, political, and social restraints. They had to be sensitive to the dominant elites, the cultural "rules of the game," and, of course, the threat of being impeached or turned out of office at the next election.

The writers of the United States Constitution created, by design, what some call an "anti-leadership" system of government. Their goal was less to provide a system of government than one that would not jeopardize liberty. Freedom was their goal; governmental power their concern. The men who toiled in that hot summer of 1787 in Philadelphia thus created an executive institution, a presidency that had limited powers.

The framers primarily wanted to counteract two fears: the fear of the mob (democracy, or mobocracy) and the fear of the monarchy (centralized, tyrannical executive power). The menacing image of England's King George III, against whom the colonists rebelled and whom Thomas Paine called "the Royal Brute of Britain," served as a powerful reminder of the dangers of a strong executive. To contain power they set up an executive office that was constitutionally rather weak (Congress had, on paper at least, most of the power), based on the rule of law, with a separation of powers, ensuring a system of checks and balances.

To James Madison, the chief architect of the Constitution, a government with too much power could be a dangerous government. A student of history, Madison believed human nature drove people to pursue self-interest, and therefore a system of government designed to have "ambition checked by ambition" set within rather strict limits was the only hope to establish a stable government that did not endanger liberty. Realizing that "enlightened statesmen" would not always guide the nation, Madison embraced a checks-and-balances system of separate with overlapping and shared powers. Madison's concern for a government that controlled and limited powers is seen throughout his writings, yet nowhere is it more vivid than when he wrote in *The Federalist Papers*, No. 51, "You must first enable the government to control the governed; and in the next place, oblige it to control itself."[206]

Yes, government was to have enough power to govern, but no, it could not have enough power to overwhelm freedom. If one branch were empowered to check another, tyranny might be thwarted. There is scant concern in Madison's writings for the needs of a strong government. Thus, the Constitution was both an enabling and a constraining document.

Alexander Hamilton was the convention's chief defender of a powerful executive. An advocate of strong central government, Hamilton promoted a version of executive power quite different from Madison's dispersed and separate powers. Where Madison wanted to check authority, Hamilton wished to enhance authority; where Madison believed that the new government's powers should be "few and defined," Hamilton wanted to infuse the executive with "energy."[207] A feeble executive implies a feeble execution of the government. A feeble execution is but another phrase for a bad execution, and a government ill-executed, whatever it may be in theory, must be, in practice, a bad government.

Hamilton wanted a strong president within a more centralized federal government. Yet such a system would undermine Madison's determination to check government power—the presidency, a unitary office headed by one man, would have no internal check. Thus Madison insisted on the need for strong external checks, that is, a strong Congress. While Madison may have won the day at the Convention, creating a presidency with fairly limited powers, history has generally been on Hamilton's side.

Looming in the background was the influential presence of Thomas Jefferson. Supportive of small government and democracy, Jefferson was suspicious of centralized power. But Jefferson's vision of small government, an agrarian economy, and a robust democracy, was given little attention at the Convention. A Madisonian model emerged.

Like most of the founders, Madison feared government in the hands of the people, yet he likewise feared too much power in the hands of any one person. Thus, the Madisonian model called for both protections against mass democracy and limits on governmental power. This is not to say the founders wanted a weak and ineffective government. Had that been their goal, they could have kept the Articles of Confederation. But they did not want a government that could act too easily. The theory of government that the Madisonian design necessitates is one of consensus, coalition, and cooperation on one hand, and checks, vetoes, and balances on the other.

As a result the presidency is a rather limited institution with few independent powers. The paradox thus created, especially in the modern period, is how can a president bring Hamiltonian energy to this Madisonian system for Jeffersonian ends? The framers did not make it easy for the government to act or for presidents to lead. That was not their intent. They left the powers and contours of the office somewhat vague—expecting Washington to fill in the gaps. This created, in Edward S. Corwin's words, "an invitation to struggle" for control of government.[208] A modern efficiency expert, looking at the framers' design for government, would likely conclude that the system could not work well: too many limits, too many checks, not enough power, and not enough leadership. Yet this is the way the framers wanted it.

What did the framers create? The chief characteristics, the chief mechanisms to control and empower the executive are

Limited Government, a reaction against the arbitrary, expansive powers of the king or state, and a protection of personal liberty;

Rule of Law, only on the basis of legal or constitutional grounds could the government act;

Separation of Powers, the three branches of government divided but sharing in power; and

Checks and Balances, by separating power, each branch could limit or control the powers of the other branches of government.

Constitutionally, the U.S. faces a paradox: the Constitution both empowers and restrains government. In fact, the Constitution does not clearly spell out the power of the presidency. Article I is devoted to the Congress, the first and constitutionally the most powerful branch of government. Article II, the executive article, deals with the presidency. The president's power cupboard is, compared to the Congress, nearly bare or at least vague. Section 1 gives the "executive power" to the president, but does not reveal whether this is a grant of tangible power, or merely a title. Section 2 makes the president commander-in-chief, but reserves the power to declare war for the Congress. Section 2 also gives the president power to grant reprieves and pardons; power to make treaties (with the advise and consent of the Senate); and the power to nominate Ambassadors, Judges, and other public ministers (with the advise and consent of the Senate). Section 3 calls for the president to inform the Congress on the State of the Union and to recommend measures to Congress, grants the power to receive Ambassadors, and imposes on the president the duty to see that the laws are faithfully executed. These powers are significant, yet in and of themselves do not suggest a strong or independent leadership institution.

Thus, the president has two types of power: formal (the ability to command), and informal (the ability to persuade). The president's formal powers are limited and (often) shared. The president's informal powers are a function of skill, situation, and political time. While the formal power of the president remains fairly constant over time, the president's informal powers are variable, dependent on the skill of each individual president. This is not to say a president's formal powers are static—over time presidential power has increased significantly—but the pace of change has been such that it was over one hundred years before the presidency assumed primacy in the U.S. political system.

The structure of government dispersed or fragmented power: there is no recognized, authoritative vital center; power is fluid and floating; no one branch could easily or freely act without the consent of another branch; power was designed to counteract power, ambition to check ambition. It was a structure designed to force a consensus before the government could act. The structure of government created by the framers did not create a leadership institution, but three separate semi-autonomous institutions that shared power. One scholar concluded, "the framers designed a system of shared powers within a system that is purposefully biased against change."[209]

THE PRESIDENCY AS REDEFINED BY WASHINGTON AND HIS SUCCESSORS

The Constitution was the result of bargains and compromises. One area of dispute was the power the new president would be granted. Unable to come to terms with this question, the framers were forced to leave the powers of the president somewhat ambiguous. This was not especially troublesome because they knew who the first president would be: George Washington. The founders held Washington in such high regard that they were confident he would set the proper tone for the office.

George Washington loomed large in the early republic. Washington sailed in uncharted waters and is credited with establishing sound precedents. He lent dignity to this newly invented presidency, developed a version of consensus leadership where possible and executive independence where necessary, was guided by the rule of law and recognized the limits of his power, and generally remained true to the requirements of constitutional government. Above all, he established the legitimacy of the office of president.[210]

Keenly aware that as the first occupant of the presidential office every act of commission and omission would be noticed, scrutinized, and perhaps established as precedent, Washington was careful to establish the independence of the office yet still respect the integrity of the Congress. Shortly after his inauguration he commented that "many things which appear of little importance in themselves...may have great and durable consequences from their having been established at the commencement of a new general government."[211] Washington also imposed his regal persona and his republican sentiments on the new office, and in effect, brought to life what the framers had merely invented.

Following Washington, the power of the presidency rose and fell depending on circumstances, the will of the president, and the demands of the time.[212] Thomas Jefferson (1801–1809) stretched the powers of the presidency, using the nascent political party to aid in achieving his goals.[213] Andrew Jackson (1829–1837) asserted the independence of the presidency and linked his power to the people. Jacksonian democracy represented a broadening of democracy and a connection between the president and the people of which the framers were suspicious. Jackson portrayed himself as the "tribune of the people" and asserted a brand of leadership linked to popularity.[214]

Abraham Lincoln (1861–1865) demonstrated that during a crisis, the powers of the presidency could be expanded. Using a combination of claimed emergency and war powers, Lincoln took bold action during the Civil War. He blockaded Southern ports, called up the militia, arrested persons suspected of disloyalty, and suspended the writ of *habeas corpus*, all without congressional authorization. Lincoln knew he had intruded into areas of congressional authority, yet claimed the doctrine of necessity as his justification.[215]

During the presidency of Theodore Roosevelt (TR; 1901–1909), the United States emerged as a world power, intent on making its mark on the international stage. TR aggressively asserted presidential power both at home and abroad, and reestablished presidential primacy. Roosevelt used the presidency as a "bully pulpit" and contributed to the rise of what is called the "rhetorical presidency,"[216] seeing the president as the "steward of the people." Viewing power expansively, TR asserted that "it was not only his right but his duty to do anything that the needs of the nation demanded unless such action was forbidden by the Constitution or by the laws.... Under this interpretation of executive power I did and caused to be done many things not previously done by the president and the heads of the departments. I did not usurp power, but I did greatly broaden the use of executive power."[217]

The presidency of Woodrow Wilson (1913–1921) further established the United States as a world power and the presidency as a pivotal center or lever of American government. Wilson used powerful rhetorical skills in conjunction with a reliance on party and programmatic leadership to establish the presidency as the guiding force for the nation. When combined with his leadership during World War I, Wilson elevated the office of presidency to one of national and international leadership.[218]

Mixed in between Jefferson, Lincoln, and TR were a series of lesser or even lackluster presidents who often diminished the office. For every Jackson, there was a Tyler; for every Lincoln, a Grant; for every Wilson, a Harding. Yet if there were presidential underachievers along with those who stretched the boundaries of presidential power, clearly the institutional trend was in the direction of growing influence.

THE PRESIDENCY AS REDEFINED BY FDR
AND THE MODERN PRESIDENTS

The institution of the presidency as we know it today was born in the 1930s. The stepchild of depression and war, it was during the Franklin D. Roosevelt (FDR) era (1933–1945) that the presidency became a truly modern institution.

The economic depression of 1929 and the world war a decade later contributed to the presidency-centered nature of our national government, and the leadership style and skill of FDR established the United States (for better or worse) as a presidential nation.

FDR, considered by presidential scholars to be one of the nation's greatest presidents, was a powerful and effective chief executive. Under his leadership the presidency became the prime mover of the American system, and people began to look to the federal government and to the presidency as the nation's problem solver. The federal government had grown, and with it presidential responsibilities, ending the era in which presidents such as Calvin Coolidge could claim that his greatest accomplishment was "minding my own business."

Roosevelt's success transformed both the presidency and public attitudes about it. He created expectations of presidential leadership that would be imposed on his successors. The "heroic" model of the presidency was established as a result of FDR's leadership, and for the next forty years, presidential scholars would often promote the model as good and necessary. FDR's successors would labor in his dominant shadow.[219]

If Roosevelt was an important president, the myth of FDR took on even greater stature. An inflated view of Roosevelt passed for fact in popular and scholarly mythology of the presidency. He was, of course, not as powerful as many remembered him.

Truman assumed the presidency in the final days of World War II. To the surprise of most of his contemporaries, Truman became an effective president, though his popularity could never match FDR, and it would be only much later that some of his contributions were fully appreciated. This created a sense in which people said, "Surely if *he* can do the job, there must be something inherent in the office which brings out greatness in even the most common of men."

When Dwight D. Eisenhower became president in 1953, the Republican lent a bipartisan air to the majesty of the office. While not an activist president, Ike did manage to exert a hidden-hand type of leadership in an era where the public seemed anxious to take a break from the hurly-burly world of politics.[220]

If the FDR legacy seemed to be in limbo during the Eisenhower years, Ike's successor was determined to revive it. John Kennedy proposed an activist administration. Yet try as he might, President Kennedy's legislative proposals often fell prey to unresponsive leaders in Congress. Stymied by an intransigent Congress that took the system of checks and balances quite seriously, the Kennedy legislative record was at best mixed.

A presidency-centered model came to dominate thinking. It was more than an operating style of government, it was also a philosophy of governing. It was an operating style in that it promoted a government in which the president was to direct or lead government from a perch of great power. It was a philosophy of government in that it legitimized a strong central government. This diminished democratic responsibility in the people, and promoted responsibility and power in the leadership class. It also failed to recognize the potential danger of the heroic leadership model.

Lyndon Johnson's remarkable legislative achievements in the aftermath of John Kennedy's assassination confirmed for many the wisdom of the strong presidency model. The FDR legacy was revived. Lyndon Johnson temporarily brought the strong presidency model back to life.

If the public suspended its skepticism about a strong presidency and placed its faith in the heroic presidency model, why did scholars go along? Of course, there were a few voices in the wilderness, warning of the dangers of unchecked presidential power,[221] but in general, scholars, like the public, were generally intrigued by or perhaps seduced by the strong presidency.

Just when the public was lulled into a false sense of security concerning the benevolence of presidential power, however, the war in Vietnam and the reaction against it caused everyone to rethink their assumptions.

U.S. involvement in Vietnam began quietly, escalated incrementally, and led to tragedy. By 1968, the United States was engaged in a war that it could not win, and from which it could not honorably withdraw. It was a "presidential war," and it brought the Johnson administration to its knees.[222]

After important legislative successes, the problem of Vietnam would overwhelm Johnson and the nation. The nation was torn apart. Divisiveness overtook the nation. The strong presidency, so long seen as critically important for the American system, now seemed too powerful, too unchecked, and alas, even a threat. After years of hearing calls for "more power to the president," by the late 1960s the plea was to rein in the overly powerful White House.

If Vietnam led to questions about the power of the presidency, Johnson's successor Richard Nixon would raise new concerns about that power. With the constitutional crisis known as Watergate, Richard Nixon, named an "unindicted co-conspirator" by the grand jury, became the nation's first president to resign from office.

In reaction to the abuses of power by Johnson and Nixon, Congress attempted to reassert its power. The Ford and Carter presidencies, rather than being imperial, seemed imperiled. It was a time of presidents being constrained.

In the 1980s, Ronald Reagan began to resurrect presidential power. Yet his successes were overshadowed by enormous budget deficits and the Iran-Contra scandal.

Claiming a bold mandate and focusing on several key economic items, Reagan managed to get much of his agenda enacted. Yet after an impressive start, Reagan faltered. Success in dealing with Congress gave way to frustration. Reagan had trouble overcoming the system's roadblocks and, unwilling to accept the limits placed on the office, he and members of his administration went beyond the law and abused power in the Iran-Contra scandal.

George H. W. Bush was a manager at a time when the nation needed a visionary leader. Bush was at his best when he had a clear goal to achieve—for example, the Gulf War, a goal imposed on him by events. But when it came time for him to choose, to set priorities, to decide on direction, he floundered.

The Clinton presidency was one of the most paradoxical and fascinating roller-coaster rides in history. Clinton was a brilliant rogue. He was a masterful politician. He was also a man severely character challenged. His serial affairs and dishonesty about them resulted in the most extensive investigations ever launched into the conduct of a president.

He was a gifted empathizer, yet also a national seducer. He brought out the worst in his adversaries even as he tried to bring about the best in the American people. In 1995, after the Republican mid-term electoral landslide, Clinton looked like a lame, if not a dead, duck. But Republican House Speaker Newt Gingrich, led by a slash-and-burn style of politics, stepped in to help orchestrate a government shutdown that made Clinton look good, and granted him victory in the 1996 presidential contest. And during the dark days of impeachment, when Clinton's adversaries had a credible case for impeachment, his enemies stepped in and saved him. Independent Counsel Kenneth Starr and House Republicans leaders offered an alternative that forced the public into the president's corner, saving him from himself.

Clinton's "Third Way" (between the liberal left of the Democratic party and the hard right of the Republicans) often allowed him to "triangulate" himself between two political extremes, and offer voters a moderate alternative to the old style left-right models.

After a hotly disputed election, George W. Bush assumed the presidency. Bush initially had success with tax cuts and education reform. But his presidency changed dramatically after the terrorist attack against the United States on September 11, 2001.

The attack changed the political circumstances under which Bush governed, and created a "crisis presidency." Power shifted to the White House, as the public, Congress, and much of the world community rallied behind the president.

The 9/11 attack gave the administration, at least for awhile, a focus. It also removed many of the normal restraints that impeded presidential authority prior to the attack. The public rallied behind the president. Congress supported Bush. The Democratic opposition gave Bush nearly a free hand to act. Other nations, again, at least for awhile, gave support.

How would Bush use this power? The president already had in place an experienced foreign and defense policy team. They were given a clear goal: stop terrorism. The usually complex world was reduced to a simple equation: terrorists were the enemy, they had to be defeated! It was a single-minded goal and it gave drive and focus to the administration.

Initially, the president's goal was clear: go after the al-Qaeda terror network and overthrow the Taliban government in Afghanistan. An international coalition helped weaken the al-Qaeda network and a short, seemingly successful war in which the Taliban were overthrown gave the president key early victories in the war against terrorism.

But when the president turned his attention to Iraq and Saddam Hussein, a long-time thorn in the side of the United States, things got more complicated. The administration was determined to overthrow Hussein, and when initial efforts to take the case for war to the United Nations failed to generate support for a war in Iraq, the administration cobbled together what it called the "coalition of the willing" (essentially the United States and Great Britain) and launched a war against Iraq.

The war generated vigorous opposition from nations across the globe, including France, Germany, Russia, and others. World opinion, which was strongly supportive of the United States in the year after the 9/11 terrorist attack, turned against the United States.

A Gallup poll taken in January of 2003 asked if respondents had a positive or negative attitude toward U.S. foreign policy. The results were disturbing. In Spain, negative reactions outstripped the positive 57 percent to 9 percent; in Russia, 55 percent to 11 percent; in Argentina, 58 percent to 13 percent; and in Pakistan, 46 percent to 8 percent. Results such as these led British historian Michael Howard to note, "a year after September 11, the United States finds itself more unpopular than perhaps it has ever been in its history."[223]

Amid this wave of opposition to U.S. policy, the administration promoted the use of a "first strike" policy. Stressing preemption over deterrence, military superiority over all possible rivals, and a willingness to use force as a tool of policy, it was a policy that according to a *New York Times* editorial, "bristles with bold assertions of American power."[224]

The president also faced criticism for undermining certain constitutional rights and liberties of U.S. citizens.

In the wake of the war against Iraq, the president was forced to defend himself against claims that he had misled the public, Congress, and the international community in the run-up to war. George W. Bush made the case for war on the basis of claims that Iraq had weapons of mass destruction (WMDs), and was thereby a direct and imminent threat to the United States and our allies. But after the war, when no WMDs were found, it seemed the administration had oversold the case, and in some instances, knowingly fudged the data.[225]

As the Bush presidency limped to a conclusion, a financial crisis hit the United States, then the global economy. A few large corporate institutions crumbled, the stock market plummeted, several banks failed, home foreclosures skyrocketed, and the administration scrambled for a rescue plan. With a plan for massive government intervention, the administration tried to stop the economic bleeding. But the snowball effect was too much to stop and the president left office largely discredited, with approval ratings near the twenty-five percent mark.

THE JOB OF THE MODERN PRESIDENT

Nowadays a president is asked to be countless things that are not spelled out with any clarity in the Constitution. We want him to be a national cheerleader of morale as well as international peacemaker, a moral leader as well as the nation's chief economic manager, a politician in chief, and a unifying representative of all the people.

We want every new president to be everything, at least of virtue, that all our great presidents have been. No matter that the great presidents were not as great as we think they were. Rightly or wrongly, we believe our greatest presidents were men of talent, tenacity, and optimism, men who could clarify the vital issues of the day and mobilize the nation for action. Our great presidents were transforming leaders who could not only move the enterprise forward but could summon the highest kinds of moral commitment from the American people.

Yet, rarely is a president a free agent. He nearly always mirrors the fundamental forces of society: the values, the myths, the quest for order and stability and the vast, inert, and usually conservative forces that maintain the existing balance of interests. Ours is a system decidedly weighted against radical leadership, a system that encourages most presidents, most of the time, to respond to the powerful, organized, and already represented interests at the expense of the unrepresented. Moreover, a president today must preside over a highly specialized and sprawling bureaucracy of his own.

Reality, as well as expectations, has expanded and recast the presidency, organized it around three major interrelated policy areas that we may call subpresidencies:

1. foreign affairs and national security,
2. aggregate economics, and
3. domestic policy, or "quality of life," issues.

The president's time is absorbed by one or another of these competing policy spheres, and his staff and cabinet have come to be organized around these three substantive areas.

THE FOREIGN AFFAIRS PRESIDENCY

Modern presidents concentrate on foreign and national security policy, often at the expense of the other policy areas. This is understandable. Since World War II, the United States has been the hegemonic, or dominant, power of the Western alliance. Since the devolution of the Soviet empire in 1989, the United States has been recognized as the major superpower in the world. U.S. world leadership for the past fifty years has been linked to presidential power: a strong America necessitated, so many believed, a strong presidency. Thus, presidents focused increased attention on a policy domain over which they exercise significant control: foreign affairs.

To be sure, an exclusively foreign, economic, or domestic problem is a rarity, and many issues intersect all three areas. Critical problems such as trade, inflation, energy development, drug abuse, or environmental problems, not to mention war, require planning and policy leadership that cut across the three areas of presidency. Still, a close examination of how presidents have spent their time in the past fifty years suggests that foreign policy matters (often crises) have driven out domestic policy matters. Economic matters usually come in second.

The founders never intended a president to be the dominant agent in national policymaking, yet they did expect the president to be a major influence in the field of foreign affairs. In the eighteenth century, foreign affairs were generally thought to be an executive matter. The first task for a national leader is the nation's survival and national defense. Today, especially in the nuclear age, foreign-policy responsibilities cannot be delegated: they are executive in character and presidential by tradition. After the Bay of Pigs tragedy (1961), President Kennedy vividly emphasized the central importance of foreign policy: "It really is true," he told a visiting Richard Nixon, "that foreign affairs is the only important issue for a President to handle...I mean, who gives a s... if the minimum wage is $1.15 or $1.25, in comparison to something like this [The Bay of Pigs]?"[226] Kennedy frequently said the difference between domestic and foreign policy was the difference between a bill being defeated and the country being wiped out.

White House advisers from all the recent administrations agree that presidents spend at least half of their time on foreign-policy or national security deliberations. In some instances, this emphasis on foreign policy and national security has occurred by choice, most notably for President Nixon, who said, "I've always thought this country could run itself domestically—without a President; all you need is a competent Cabinet to run the country at home. You need a President for foreign policy; no Secretary of State is really important; the President makes foreign policy."[227] President George H. W. Bush also had a much greater personal interest in foreign affairs as opposed to domestic policy. President Johnson, on the other hand, was strongly disposed by experience toward domestic programs, but was unable to prevent his presidency from being consumed by military affairs.

In addition, presidents naturally work hardest where they see both hope of success and leeway for significant personal impact. Former Nixon counsel Leonard Garment pointed to yet another reason when he explained Nixon's preference for foreign policy in this way to Theodore White: "In foreign policy, you get drama, triumph, resolution—crisis and resolution so that in foreign policy Nixon can give the sense of leadership. But in domestic policy, there you have to deal with the whole jungle of human problems."[228]

But presidents cannot focus on foreign affairs at the exclusion of the nation's domestic needs. George H. W. Bush is a case in point. After successfully winning a Persian Gulf War over Iraq, Bush's popularity rose to historically unprecedented levels. Yet between January of 1991 and November of 1992, a slow economy and domestic drift led to electoral defeat.

Most scholars believe that there are significant differences in the institutional balance of power when one compares the realms of domestic to foreign policy. Presidents, it is widely believed, have greater power in the foreign policy arena than they do in domestic and economic policy.

In the 1960s political scientist Aaron Wildavsky argued that since the end of the second world war, presidents have been more successful at attaining their policy goals from Congress in foreign policy than in the domestic arena. Thus, Wildavsky concluded, a president is usually more effective in international affairs and foreign policymaking. Commenting on the power of the presidency in the international area, Wildavsky asserted, "there has not been a single major issue on which Presidents, when they were serious and determined, have failed."[229]

While Wildavsky's "two presidencies" notion may be a bit oversimplified, it does highlight certain patterns. In foreign affairs, presidents can assert their will by being proactive, and force the Congress to be reactive. By setting policy, the president sets in motion events of his choosing. If Congress wishes to intercede, it does so in response to acts already taken. The initiative usually belongs to the president.

"The Constitution is an invitation to struggle for the privilege of directing American foreign policy."[230] In the post-World War II era, it is a struggle largely won by presidents. While the Constitution created a model of shared power, history, precedent, wars, crises, aggressive presidents, and an often supine Congress have tilted the balance of power in a presidential direction.[231]

Constitutionally, the president may be on shaky ground, but in practical terms, it is difficult to stop a strong, assertive president in foreign affairs. Clinton's NATO intervention into Bosnia, George W. Bush's unilateral actions in response to the war against terrorism, and Barack Obama's bombing of Libya are cases in point. While all presidents claim their use of foreign policy power is grounded in the Constitution, such claims of independent authority are debatable. It is the Congress, even in foreign affairs, that has the broadest and clearest constitutional mandate, but its power has atrophied due to lack of use. Even the power to declare war, which is expressly granted to the Congress, has slipped through the hands of the legislature. The *War Powers Act* and the Constitution notwithstanding, it is the president who, by acting, holds primacy in war and foreign affairs.[232]

Much of foreign policy involves diplomatic activities that are generally under the purview of the executive, and in most areas, presidents simply presume authority to act. Likewise, much activity in foreign affairs does not require legislation,[233] and, to make matters worse (or better if you are a president) during a crisis, presidents proceed with considerable authority and few checks.

Perhaps the chief power a president has is the presumption that he or she speaks for and represents the nation to the world. This allows a president the opportunity to act, to make decisions, and to announce policies, thereby preemptively eliminating most potential challengers. By preemptive initiatives, the president may tie the hands of potential rivals on the congressional side. To defy the president on a matter of national security often risks appearing unpatriotic, especially in moments of international crisis. Thus, presidents can both muffle potential critics and force the Congress to submit to their will. Teddy Roosevelt sending the fleet halfway around the world in defiance of congressional budget restrictions, then saying, "I sent the fleet...will they leave them there?"; George H. W. Bush sending U.S. troops to the Middle East following the 1991 Iraqi invasion of Kuwait, preparing for war, building public support, and *then* challenging Congress to issue a vote of support: all serve as examples of how presidents, by acting and forcing the hand of Congress, can get their way.[234]

Over the course of a term, presidents spend more and more time dealing with foreign affairs, perhaps in part because they so often get frustrated being rebuffed in domestic and economic policy. They also, in recent years, have become preoccupied with foreign and defense policy because the United States has troops in and is highly involved in military activities in South Korea, Afghanistan, Kuwait, Iraq, Somalia, Yemen, and elsewhere. Since presidents need to be and be seen as accomplishing things to maintain their reputation as "the leader," they almost naturally gravitate to the area in which their power is greatest. The irony, of course, is that the president has the greatest power in the area where they are probably most (potentially) dangerous and in need of controls and checks and balances, and is most controlled in the least dangerous area most in need of leadership.

When Barack Obama became president his "in-box" was overflowing with problems: two wars, a bone crushing economic recession, and a budget crisis of massive proportions. He campaigned on "hope" and "change," raising expectations, and he promised to change the highly partisan culture in Washington.

In foreign policy, Obama sought to lower the bellicose rhetoric, reengage with allies, reenergize the American "brand" across the globe, move the United States away from unilateralism to a more multilateral approach to policymaking, disengage from the war in Iraq, place greater attention on the war in Afghanistan, close the detention camp in Guantanamo, end torture, and in general develop a more nuanced liberal internationalist approach to foreign affairs. It was a huge "to do" list.[235]

Obama came to the presidency with little real foreign policy experience. He did, however, assemble an experienced and respected team of advisers and cabinet officials.

Obama's early months were, however, more than mere rhetoric and symbolism. He tackled a wide range of important foreign policy issues. He wound down U.S. involvement in Iraq; ratcheted up before easing down the U.S. role in Afghanistan, ordered the Guantanamo detention center closed, reached a nuclear arms deal with Russia, revived America's reputation abroad, and it was under President Obama's leadership that terrorist Osama bin Laden was killed by U.S. Navy Seals, and Libya's Muammar Gaddafi was toppled from power.

But Obama was no miracle worker, and several stubborn problems eluded his grasp. Iran continued to develop its nuclear weapons program, no significant improvement was achieved in the Israeli-Palestinian conflict, Guantanamo remained open, and no progress was made in climate control.[236]

President Obama's response to the 2011 Arab Spring uprisings was uneven, yet firm.

Obama continued to aggressively prosecute the war against terrorists while lowering the rhetoric and confrontational "us versus them" posturing. He dramatically increased the use of unmanned drones to strike at terrorists in Pakistan, Yemen, and Somalia. Some saw continuities between the Bush and Obama anti-terrorist policies, referring to Obama as "Bush lite."[237]

THE ECONOMIC PRESIDENCY

As the economic crisis of 2008 demonstrated, the president is also held responsible for insuring a secure economy. In fact, the second largest portion of presidential policy time is spent on macroeconomic policies: issues of monetary and fiscal policy such as trade and tariff policy, inflation, unemployment, the stability of the dollar, and the health of the stock market. With the subprime collapse of the U.S. housing market and the subsequent stock market crisis, the president was compelled to spring into action in an effort to bring stability to the falling economy. But just how much control does a president have over the economy?

In the early days of the Republic, presidents had less involvement in the development of economic policies. The nation was young, not yet a world power, and Congress was in primary control of determining the budget and setting economic policy. Presidents began to get more involved in setting economic policy with passage of the Budget and Accounting Act of 1921. This law directed the president to formulate a national budget and created a Bureau of the Budget. The Pandora's Box was opened. Beginning with Franklin D. Roosevelt, presidents began to expand their involvement in economic and budgetary matters.

While the expectations of presidential responsibility and control of the economy have grown enormously in the past sixty-five years, the powers given to the president to manage the economy have not risen accordingly, creating yet another presidential paradox. We expect presidents to bring about economic breakthroughs, but rarely give them the power necessary to work miracles.

Historical circumstance, presidential desire, legislative acquiescence, and public expectation have all contributed to the emergence of a powerful, but limited, presidency in economic affairs. While congressional efforts to recapture their constitutional duty over the "power of the purse" are evident (e.g., The Congressional Budget and Impoundment Control Act of 1974), the president remains a central figure in setting economic policy for the nation.

A president can scarcely hide from the hard, visible quantitative economic indicators: unemployment rates, consumer price indexes, the gross domestic product, interest and mortgage rates, commodity prices, oil import price levels, and stock-market and bond-market averages. In the era of instant cable and Internet news, these figures are available to everyone, at any time, and the American people increasingly judge and measure their presidents on whether they can cope aggressively with recession and inflation, can offer effective economic game plans (preferably without tax increases), and can use the nation's budget as an instrument for ensuring a healthy and growing economy. The complex issues of tax reform and income redistribution are always on the agenda of national politics.

But a president's statutory responsibilities for maintaining full employment and pursuing stabilization policies are not matched by political resources or available expertise. In most areas of our economy the consumers are relatively weak or unorganized, but an uneven performance by the economy will call down on a president immediate pressure from wealthy businessmen, unions, and farmers, and from their large delegations of friends in Congress.

A further paradox of the president's role as economist-in-chief of the nation relates to the contradictory demands we place on the government. We want to cut spending, cut taxes, and cut the deficit, but we don't want any of "our" favorite programs cut (and every line in the budget is somebody's favorite). Most people want the government to do more but spend less. In a robust economy, the hard choices become much easier, but in a staggering economy, or one burdened with debt, all the choices become painful—as George W. Bush and Barack Obama found out in recent years.

When the economy crashed in 2008, President Bush, a free market devotee, found himself confronted with a frightening choice: stick to principle and watch as the world sunk into an international depression, or intervene and try to stop the financial bleeding. "America's financial system is at stake," Treasury Secretary Hank Paulson told the president. "Did I," Bush asked himself, "want to be the president overseeing an economic calamity that could be worse than the Great Depression?" Bush decided "to be Roosevelt, not Hoover."[238] He acted, pouring money into the financial system via the Troubled Asset Relief Program. Bush got the federal government actively involved in bailing out Wall Street and American business. It was only a beginning. President Obama would inherit the financial mess.

Perhaps the most intransigent problem President Obama faced on taking office was what to do about the economy. He inherited an economy still in a free fall after the 2008 recession. The housing bubble had burst, the stock market plummeted, unemployment was near 10%, and the economic meltdown threatened to get even worse.

Obama acted swiftly and relatively boldly. He engineered a stimulus package, the American Recovery and Reinvestment Act, putting nearly $800 billion into the economy.[239] He coordinated mortgage relief, a bailout of the auto industry, achieved greater protection for credit card holders, and initiated Wall Street regulations. These policies helped stabilize the economy, yet the recovery proved slow and was a budget buster. [240]

President Obama deserves some credit, along with his predecessor, President Bush, for quickly responding to the economic meltdown. Some credit their actions for pulling the United States out of what otherwise would have been a massive international depression. However, stabilizing the economy was one thing, seeing a rebound in jobs quite another.[241]

THE DOMESTIC PRESIDENCY

Presidents concentrate on those areas in which they think they can make the greatest impact, in which the approval of interest groups and the public can be most easily rallied. Yet involvement in domestic policy is costly, both financially and politically. Moreover, newly elected presidents find that budgets are virtually fixed for the next year and a half if not longer, and that in domestic matters they are dependent on Congress, specialized bureaucracies, professions, and state and local officialdom. Is it surprising, then, that the implementation of domestic policy can become the orphan of presidential attention? Is it possible presidents rationalize that they must concern themselves with foreign and macroeconomic policy as they lose heart with the complicated, hard-to-affect, divisive domestic problems?

From Roosevelt through Obama, recent presidents learned that progress on the domestic front was more difficult than they had imagined it would be. They complain that there are greater limits on their ability to bring about favorable results in the domestic sphere than they had imagined. Clinton's efforts to restructure national health care programs and policy is a notable example. George W. Bush's efforts to "reform" social security is another.

Domestic failures, while not generally as dramatic as failures abroad, can nonetheless undo a president. It was President George W. Bush's tepid response to the Hurricane Katrina devastation of the Gulf region in September of 2005 that significantly cut into Bush's support and his image as a strong leader.

President Bush ultimately recognized the political impact of his unwillingness to move forcefully when confronted with the Katrina crises:

> In a national catastrophe, the easiest person to blame is the president. Katrina presented a political opportunity that some critics exploited for years. The aftermath of Katrina—combined with the collapse of Social Security reform and the drumbeat of violence in Iraq—made the fall of 2005 a damaging period in my presidency. Just a year earlier, I had won reelection with more votes than any candidate in history. By the end of 2005, my of my political capital was gone.[242]

Presidents are usually more successful influencing foreign affairs than domestic policy. In fact, most presidents face major defeats in the domestic arena. Clinton with health care reform and Bush with social security and immigration reform are but two drops in a seemingly endless sea of domestic policy failures. Pitting your reputation on the back of domestic legislation is rarely a winning formula. LBJ's Great Society was the exception; not the rule.[243]

President Obama entered office with an ambitious domestic agenda. This made him a polarizing figure, and Republicans in Congress wasted no time going on the attack. Very early it was clear that candidate Obama's call for a more civil brand of Washington, DC, politics would not come about, and as president, Obama faced a harsh brand of hyperpartisan politics.

In an effort to gain greater control over the domestic agenda, President Obama took the creative but not completely unprecedented step of relying more on policy "czars" than any of his predecessors.[244] Whereas Cabinet officers are required to occasionally testify before Congress, these so called Czars report only to the president. In relying on Czars such as Carol Browner (Climate Change) and Nancy-Ann Parle (Health Care), President Obama tried to centralize more domestic authority under White House control, thereby giving him an upper hand in making policy.[245]

President Obama's domestic agenda was severely restricted by the ongoing deficit crisis: there simply was not enough money—even if the United States went further into debt—to do all Obama wanted. Thus, Obama had to set priorities, and he set health care reform as his top priority.[246]

Obama, perhaps futilely, tried to build a bipartisan coalition in support of his health insurance initiatives, yet the more he tried to reach out and find common ground the more Republicans in Congress decided to oppose him on this matter. Obama was able to get some support from the medical profession, pharmaceutical companies, and groups like Catholic hospitals, yet Republican's didn't budge. And Obama, perhaps wishing to avoid some of the criticism leveled against President Clinton who handed Congress "his" bill in 1993, neglecting to get sufficient Congressional advice or buy-in prior to submitting the legislation, gave Congress an exceptionally high amount of authority to devise their own bill, within some agreed on parameters. It was a long, difficult, and costly struggle, but in the end, health care reform, the Affordable Care Act, was achieved.

No sooner had the ink dried at the bill signing than opposition went on the attack, attempting to get the Courts to override "Obama Care," stoking political opposition that contributed to the rise of the Tea Party movement, and using radio talk shows and cable television to attack health care as budget busting. In the end, health care may have been a policy win for Obama, but it might also have been a political loss.

After his 2010 health care win, Obama's domestic agenda stalled. Political opposition hardened. The Tea Party movement targeted Obama. The 2010 mid-term elections were a disaster for the Democrats as the Republicans gained control of the House. Independent voters, key to Obama's 2008 election, were abandoning the president. The sluggish economy hurt the president. He was on the defensive, facing the 2012 election with some formidable liabilities.

How did this turn around so quickly? In 1992 candidate Bill Clinton kept reminding his campaign of the theme: "It's the economy, stupid." And indeed it was, and is. A weak recovery, sustained high levels of unemployment, fear of the future, and an organized and impassioned opposition all worked against the president.

Obama actually achieved a great deal of what he promised during his campaign. He was one of the most successful presidents in a generation. His significant policy and legislature success, however, did not translate into political success. Just the opposite in fact: the more of his promises he kept, the less the public approved of Obama and his party.[247]

THE MULTIDIMENSIONAL PRESIDENCY

Within each of these presidencies or policy subpresidencies, a president is asked to provide functional leadership in seven activity areas: crisis management, symbolic leadership, priority setting and program design, recruitment of advisers and administrators, legislative and political coalition building, program implementation and evaluation, and oversight of government routines and early warning of problem areas. These are not compartmentalized, unrelated functions, but rather

President Bush comforts and rallies the nation in the immediate aftermath of the 9/11 attack against the United States. AP Photo / Doug Mills.

a dynamic, seamless assortment of tasks and responsibilities. This job description does not exhaust all presidential activity; rather, the examples in Table 5.1 attempt to classify the major functional as well as substantive responsibilities of the office. Of course, political activity solely for personal enhancement (such as reelection) should be acknowledged as a presidential preoccupation, just as staying elected is a prime objective for most legislators. In practice, no president can divide his job into tidy compartments. Instead, a president must see to it that questions are not ignored simply because they fall between or cut across jurisdictional lines. Presidents must act alternately, and often simultaneously, as crisis managers and as symbolic, priority-setting, coalition-building, and managerial leaders. Ultimately, all these responsibilities mix with one another. Being president is a little like being a juggler who is already juggling too many balls and is forever having more balls tossed at them.

Crisis Management

A crisis is a situation that occurs suddenly, heightens tensions, carries a high level of threat to a vital interest, provides only limited time for making decisions, and possesses an atmosphere of uncertainty. Crisis management involves both pre-crisis planning and the handling of the situation during a crisis.

When crises and national emergencies occur, we instinctively turn to the president. Presidents are asked during a time of crisis to provide not only political

TABLE 5.1 The Presidential Job Description

Types of Activity	THE SUBPRESIDENCIES		
	Foreign Policy and National Security (A)	Macro Economics (B)	Domestic Policy and Programs (C)
Crisis Management	Wartime leadership; missile crisis, 1962; Gulf War, 1991	Coping with recessions 1992, 2008	Confronting coal strikes of 1978; L.A. Riots, 1992; L.A. Earthquake, 1992; Health Care Reform, 2010
Symbolic and Morale-building Leadership	Presidential state visit to Middle East or to China	Boosting confidence in the dollar	Visiting disaster victims and morale building among government workers
Priority Setting and Program Design	Balancing pro-Israel policies with need for Arab oil	Choosing means of dealing with inflation, unemployment	Designing a new welfare program, Health Insurance
Recruitment Leadership (advisers, administrators, judges, ambassadors, etc.)	Selection of Secretary of Defense, U.N. Ambassador	Selection of Secretary of Treasury, Federal Reserve Board Governors	Nomination of federal judges
Legislative and Political Coalition Building	Selling Panama or SALT treaties to Senate for approval	Lobbying for energy-legislation package	Winning public support for transportation deregulation
Program Implementation and Evaluation	Encouraging negotiations between Israel and Egypt	Implementing tax cuts or fuel rationing	Improving quality health care, welfare retraining programs
Oversight of Government Routines and Establishment of an Early-Warning System for Future Problem Areas	Overseeing U.S. bases abroad; ensuring that Foreign-aid programs work effectively	Overseeing the IRS or the Small Business Administration	Overseeing National Science Foundation or Environmental Protection Agency

and executive leadership but also the appearance of confidence, responsible control, and the show of a steady hand at the helm. Popular demand and public necessity force presidents nowadays to do what Lincoln and Franklin Roosevelt once did during the national emergencies of their day, namely, to do what is required to protect the union, to safeguard the nation, and to preserve vital American interests.

In normal times, the checks and balances of the U.S. political system can be formidable, severely limiting presidential initiatives. But in a political crisis, most of these checks evaporate, and the president is given wide discretionary leeway in the exercise of executive prerogative or emergency powers. While the Constitution contains no explicit provisions for government during a crisis, in an emergency a president can invoke emergency statutes or merely assume power and become the nation's crisis manager-in-chief (as did Abraham Lincoln in the Civil War, Franklin D. Roosevelt during the Great Depression, and John F. Kennedy during the Cuban Missile Crisis).

The most significant factor in the swelling of the presidential establishment in the post-1939 era has been the accretion of new presidential roles during national emergencies, when Congress and the public have looked to the president for decisive responses. The Constitution neither authorized presidents to meet emergencies nor did it forbid them to do so. All strong presidents have taken advantage of this omission. The Great Depression and World War II in particular caused sizable increases in presidential staffs. After the Russians orbited Sputnik in 1957, President Eisenhower added science advisers; and after the Bay of Pigs in 1961, President Kennedy enlarged his national security staff. The Cold-War commitments as President Kennedy enumerated them in his Inaugural Address, to "pay any price, bear any burden, meet any hardship, support any friend, oppose any foe," and the presence of nuclear weapons fostered the argument that only presidents could move with sufficient quickness and intelligence in national security matters. When major crises occur, Congress traditionally holds debates, but just as predictably delegates authority to the president, charging them to take whatever actions are necessary to restore order or regain control over the situation.

Primary factors underlying the transformation of the presidency of the Constitution to the modern crisis management presidency are the invention of nuclear weapons, the emergence of the Cold War, the permanence of large standing armies, and the interdependent role of the United States in the world economy. Constant crises in national security have dominated American thinking throughout the twentieth century. Such crises include the Japanese bombing of Pearl Harbor in 1941, the North Korean invasion of South Korea in 1950, the Russian launching of Sputnik in 1957, the offensive missiles placed in Cuba by the Russians in 1962, the Viet Cong offensives in South Vietnam in the mid and late 1960s, and the various Middle East wars and incidents over the past generation.

SYMBOLIC, MORALE-BUILDING, AND SHAMANISTIC LEADERSHIP

The American presidency is more than a political or Constitutional institution. It is a focus for intense emotions. The presidency serves our basic need for a visible and representative national symbol to which we can turn with our hopes and aspirations. The president has become an icon who embodies the nation's self-understanding and self-image. Thus, we place our president on a high pedestal yet demand democratic responsiveness. The president is at once our national hero and national scapegoat.

Presidents are the nation's number-one celebrity; almost everything they do is news. Merely by going to a sports event, or a funeral, or in the celebration of a national holiday, or visiting a particular nation, presidents not only command attention, they convey meaning. By their actions presidents can arouse a sense of hope or despair, honor or dishonor.

Although Americans like to view themselves as hardheaded pragmatists, they, like humans everywhere, cannot stand too much reality. People do not live by reason alone. Myths and dreams are an age-old form of escape. People will continue to believe what they want to believe. And people turn to national leaders just as tribesmen turn to shamans—yearning for meaning, healing, empowerment, legitimacy, assurance, and a sense of purpose.

Americans expect many things from their presidents—honesty, credibility, crisis leadership, agenda-setting and administrative abilities, and also certain tribal leader or priestly functions we usually associate with primitive or religious communities. In a way, the president serves as high priest, national leader, and hand-holder-in-chief. A president's personal conduct affects how millions of Americans view their political loyalties and civic responsibilities. Of course, the symbolic influence of presidents is not always evoked in favor of worthy causes, and sometimes presidents do not live up to our expectations of moral leadership. Still, a great many people find comfort in an oversimplified image of presidents as *priests* and *prophets* of our civil religion, and as *defenders* of the *democratic faith* and *evocative spokespeople* of the American Dream.

United in this one institution are multiple roles that are on the surface confusing and conflicting. A president's unifying role as a head of state and symbol-in-chief, especially in times of crisis, often clashes with his advocacy of program initiatives and partisan responsibilities. Further, presidents invariably take advantage and borrow from their legitimacy as representative and symbolic head-of-state to expand their political and partisan influence.

The framers of the U.S. Constitution did not fully anticipate the symbolic and morale-building functions a president would have to perform. Certain magisterial functions such as receiving ambassadors and the granting of pardons were conferred. Yet the job of the presidency demanded symbolic leadership from the very beginning. Washington and his advisors would readily recognize that in leadership at its finest, the leader symbolizes the best in the community, the best in its traditions, values, and purposes. Effective leadership infuses vision and a sense of significant meaning into the enterprise of a nation.

George Washington was one of the few continental figures of his day. He was already a warrior hero. He had commanded with distinction the revolutionary patriots for over eight years. In victory he became a prime symbol of that crusade. His integrity, judgment, lengthy service both in and out of uniform to his country, and his devotion to his troops and his countrymen set him apart from his fellow founders.

Washington wasn't a great philosopher, orator, lawyer, or even organizer. Even his military abilities have been questioned. His mind was keen yet it was slow in operation, being little aided by invention or imagination.

Yet the nation needed a hero. America had no heritage of celebrated public servants, other than those in England, and hence it was essential for national pride to endow our first hero with lavish praise. His countrymen did precisely this. And Washington understood their need and not only accepted it graciously, but he used it as a means of legitimizing both his new office and the new national government he had labored so long to bring into being.[248]

No matter how ably others had explained the Constitution, and especially the provisions for presidential leadership, it was now up to President Washington to carry out the promise of the office, and establish the precedents to be followed as long as the country survived. Washington was fully aware that the process of making the Constitution work had only just begun. He knew that written documents do not implement themselves. He appreciated that a living, real constitution includes customs, traditions, practices, interpretations, and precedent setting to fill out the vagueness of the written provisions.

In some ways Washington became the nation's first secular priest, or societal shaman. In helping his countrymen to transcend their ordinary definitions of reality he helped instill a new nationalism and a new sense of purpose.

VISION, PRIORITY SETTING, AND PROGRAM DESIGN

Presidents, by custom, have become responsible for proposing new initiatives in the areas of foreign policy, economic growth and stability, and the quality of life in America. This was not always the case. But beginning with Woodrow Wilson and particularly since the New Deal, a president is expected to promote peace, prevent depression, and formulate domestic programs to resolve countless social problems.

Reagan presents an interesting case of a president who shaped the national policy agenda because he was a more ideologically committed president than most of his predecessors. Reagan's conservatism helped him develop a vision, a policy agenda, and a program of action. There is a good and bad side to being an ideologue. It can be good in that a committed ideologue can simplify complex problems; on the bad side, many problems do not lend themselves to simple solutions. On the good side, ideology can help get an administration marching in the same direction; on the bad side, people may march like lemmings, over a cliff. On the good side, ideology highlights certain variables in problem solving; on the bad side, it hides or obscures other equally important variables. On the good side, ideology gives passion to purpose; on the bad side it can also degenerate into crusading extremism.

George W. Bush campaigned as a moderate, stressing education and softening some of the hard right stances that alienated centrist voters from the Republican Party. He spoke of "compassionate conservatism" and convincingly presented himself as a non-ideological pragmatist. But in the aftermath of the 9/11 tragedy, and emboldened by popular support and success in the 2002 midterm elections, Bush moved further to the political right, and on issues such as the environment, faith-based programs, taxes, civil liberties, and certain foreign policy issues, Bush emerged more as a conservative than his more pragmatic father.

Because power in the American system is not clearly given to any one branch, a policy entrepreneur can, on certain issues, capture control of the policy agenda. If this can be done, a president may be able to force an otherwise reluctant Congress to at least meet part of his policy goals. And no one is better positioned to attract attention than the president. If presidents are to lead and not merely preside, they must shape and try to influence the agenda.

Presidents are often criticized for not being programmatic enough, for not being passionately committed. The fact is, presidents, by force of habit, almost always want to extend their personal influence, not their ideology, over people and programs. They are generally suspicious of long-range planning. Politicians inherently fear being in advance of their time. They enjoy flexible processes and eschew explicit platforms forever visited on them by well-meaning expert advisers. Presidents are constantly being asked to plan, to forecast, to prevent us from going down the path to policy disasters, yet their instinct is "to leave their options open."

The essence of the modern presidency lies in its potential capability to resolve societal problems.

An effective president will attempt to clarify many of the major issues of the day, define what is possible, and harness the governmental structure so that new initiatives are possible. A president, with the cooperation of Congress, can set national goals and propose legislation.

RECRUITMENT LEADERSHIP

A president's mot strategic formal resource is the ability to recruit people who share the president's convictions to fill high-level positions in both the executive and judicial branches. According to what might be called the "good person theory," a presidency is only as good as its staffs, cabinet, and counselors. Quality and loyalty are what is wanted. In practice, the view that a president dominates the recruitment and appointment process is misleading.

After running for the presidency for several years, the successful candidate often finds that the people courted during the campaign—delegates, press, financial contributors, machine leaders, advance aides, or political strategists—do not have the skills or experience needed to manage the executive branch. Kennedy repeatedly complained, "People, people, people! I don't know any people (for the cabinet and other top posts). I only know voters! How am I going to fill these 1,200 jobs?"[249] Almost half of Kennedy's eventual cabinet appointees were unknown to him.

In the postelection rush many appointments are made on the basis of subjective judgments or ethnic or geographical representation and from too limited a field of candidates. Ironically, at the time when presidents have the largest number of jobs to fill and enjoy their greatest drawing power, they have less time and information to take advantage of this major prerogative than at any other point. Later in the term, presidents have fewer vacancies and usually less prestige; candidates from outside the government are wary about being saddled with troubled programs and recognize that little can be accomplished in the last year or two.

A president sometimes errs in recruiting only like-minded appointees; this can lead to an amiability and conformity in thinking. Social psychologist Irving Janis pointed out that this leads to a dangerous inclination to eek concurrence and groupthink at the expense of critical judgment.[250] The cult of loyalty to President Nixon doubtless encouraged the suspension of critical and objective thinking on the part of some of those involved in the Watergate affair.

Some potential appointees do not want to live or even be near Washington, DC. Others balk at the idea of having to disclose their financial background and income. Others do not care to live in the glare of an intrusive media, or have every detail of their past in print on the front page of the newspapers. Involvement with past administrations or too close an association with past scandals or major industries connected with a new assignment may be enough to occasion congressional hostility to a presidential nomination. Congress is more selective these days to any kind of potential conflict of interest, especially when there is divided government. Both George H. W. Bush and Clinton were forced to withdraw nominees when relatively minor past blemishes were brought to light by the opposition. In 1997, Clinton was forced to withdraw both CIA nominee Tony Lake and William Weld, his nominee for U.S. Ambassador to Mexico. Likewise, Obama was not able to move ahead with his nominations of former U.S. Senator Tom Daschle and Governor Bill Richardson because of perceived legal issues.

Effective presidents shrewdly use their recruitment resource not only as a means of rewarding their campaign supporters and enhancing their ties to Congress but also as a vital form of communicating the priorities and policy directions of their administrations. One student of the appointment process described the importance of this function:

> A President's nominees are the primary link between him and the millions of men and women in the federal bureaucracy. Most of these men and women are located in the executive branch of government and technically they work for the President. But he has little power to hire and fire them, he cannot control their political loyalties, and he lacks the time and resources to supervise their activities. His executive appointees must act as his surrogates in dealing with the federal bureaucracy. The quality and the character of the people he chooses to serve in executive positions will have a major impact on the ability of his transient administration to control the permanent government.[251]

Even when presidents have recruited able and loyal persons to their administration, they run the risk of a high turnover. The average cabinet member has stayed in post for only about two or three years, as we will discuss in chapter 7.

LEGISLATIVE AND POLITICAL COALITION BUILDING

To govern is to build coalitions, to form alliances and power networks. In relatively few areas can a president act unilaterally and not face challenges to his authority. Custom and the design of the U.S. system necessitate coalition building by political leaders.

The centrifugal force of American politics pulls the system apart and encourages independent entrepreneurship. Power is not fused as in parliamentary democracies: presidents and members of Congress are elected relatively independent of one another, and parties do not develop a great deal of cohesion among the branches. Political scientists Benjamin Ginsberg and Martin Shefter agree that since elections fail to provide clear governing coalitions, the president and Congress end up resorting to "politics by other means" to influence policy.[252]

This dilemma highlights the essential difference in what it takes to get elected and what it takes to govern. Getting elected requires the development of an "electoral coalition." Governing requires the development of a "governing coalition." These may be different, even contradictory things.

To get elected, Barack Obama made appeals to a wide variety of traditionally Democratic interest groups, hoping to pull a sufficient number of these groups together to ensure his election. It was a successful electoral strategy. But was it good for governing? As soon as the election was over, all these groups approached Obama demanding he keep his promises and deliver the goods. And President Obama delivered, ending "don't ask, don't tell," passing landmark legislation in several areas, and passing health care reform. This generated an incredible backlash—opposition from the military and fundamentalist religious groups all but paralyzed the administration.

One of the misleading indications of presidential power or success is the so-called presidential box score used by *Congressional Quarterly* to indicate successes and failures in legislative programs. If Congress has approved a majority of a president's legislative program, the *Congressional Quarterly* may headline its story, "Congress Acts Favorably on President X's Requests." The impression often given is that a president is the chief legislator; the Congress is mainly passive and has yielded its legislative authority.

However, box scores should be used with caution. First, they are often deceptive because legislative measures are by no means equal in importance. Moreover, scores fail to distinguish between measures that were central and those that were peripheral to presidential priorities. Further, they are skewed by the high percentage of presidential requests in the areas of defense and foreign policy, which Congress approves somewhat more readily than other matters. They show nothing of these programs a president wanted but, recognizing the overwhelming likelihood of defeat, never requested at all. Much of what the president does not achieve consists of what is never requested rather than of what is proposed but does not get passed. Finally, sometimes a president merely anticipates what is going to pass Congress and adds an endorsement at a late stage in its legislative development.

Another idea in which Congress influences presidential initiatives is in the shaping of legislation. Many scholars conclude nowadays that Congress merely delays and amends and is basically incapable of creating legislation or formulating policy. In fact, however, Congress sometimes plays the dominant role in initiating legislation; the formulation as well as the enactment of virtually all major legislation relating to domestic and economic policy is the result of extensive conversations between the presidency and Congress and between both of the institutions and pivotal interest groups.

Much of the policy presidents supposedly formulate and propose as their own is derived directly from traditional party priorities, from previous presidents, or from Congress. Just as the celebrated New Deal legislation had a fairly well-defined prenatal history extending back several years before its espousal by FDR, so also recent investigations into the origins and enactment of most of the New Frontier and Great Society legislative programs, for example, broader medical-care programs, federal aid to education, and the more activist stance on civil rights indicate they too were the fruition of past recommendations by the Democratic Party.

Presidents have major resources with which they can enhance their political coalition and legislative lobbying roles. First, they can achieve a closer contact with the American public than any other politician in the country. The president can and often does appeal directly to the people for their support. This does not always work, yet when a president can define an issue and rally the public's concern, Congress and other power centers usually will take careful note.

A second resource is the use of patronage. Patronage today refers not only to jobs and favors rendered but also to campaign trips into districts and states, invitations to the White House, and countless considerations that a president can exchange in an effort to win friends and influence votes. The president's congressional liaison office, with a staff of sometimes up to twenty in recent years, works full-time trying to employ these possibilities for maximum advantage.

The third resource is a president's role as a political party leader. Although a president has no formal position in the party structure, a president's influence over national policies and appointments and celebrity status command respect from party leaders. Presidents need the party's support to enact their programs. Presidents find they must bargain and negotiate with party leaders just as they do with other independent party brokers.

POLICY IMPLEMENTATION AND EVALUATION

Implementation, the carrying out and realization of presidential goals, is a crucial, if unappreciated, part of a president's job. The provisions made within the executive office to ensure presidential control over implementation simply do not guarantee this happens. Repeatedly, federal programs fail to accomplish desired goals. When such failures occur, it is relatively easy to blame the original legislation rather than examine what happened after a bill became law. Of course, poorly written legislation can yield poor results. But students of national policymaking now realize even the best legislation can fail owing to problems encountered during implementation. Sometimes these problems can lead to outright failure of a program; more often, however, they mean excessive delay, underachievement of desired goals, or costs far above those originally expected.

Implementation is a process involving a long chain of decision points, all of which need to be cleared before a program can be successfully carried out. At each decision point is a public official or community leader who holds power to advance—or delay—the program. The more decision points a program needs to clear, the greater the chance of failure or delay. Special problems result if the successful implementation of a national program depends on the cooperation of state and local officials. The state or locality may be eager to help; another might be opposed to a program and try to stop it. The advent of new federalism and the vast growth in the number and scope of federal grant-in-aid programs have added to the problem of implementation.

If anything has been learned by students of the presidency, it is that policy-making does not end once a law is passed (or when a court decision or presidential executive order is handed down). The implementation of such laws, especially the development of specific guidelines and regulations, can have just as great an impact on public policy as the law itself. The ultimate responsibility for the implementation of the nation's governmental decisions rests with the president.

Presidential decisions transmitted to the bureaucracy often have a way of getting watered down or ignored. The routines of governmental bureaucracies are geared to maintaining the status quo. That's fine if a president merely wants to maintain the status quo. But most presidents want to change at least some policies. Yet policies persist from one administration to the next remarkably unchanged. Resistance to change is reinforced by several factors, chief of which are (1) inadequate communication and determination by a president, (2) the alliances between bureaucrats and the appropriate special interest and congresspersons, and (3) inadequate information and evaluation processes.

Another major factor minimizing presidential influence in the implementation stage is that executive branch departments are more the creation of Congress than the White House. Special interest groups often effectively capture administrative as well as legislative officials and succeed in fragmenting the organization to their own ends.

Congress, even when it is dominated by the president's party, often does not want to increase presidential discretion within executive agencies. The congressional committee structure in large measure parallels executive-branch organization, and what often appear to be structural absurdities in the executive branch may persist because of long-standing jurisdictional disputes within Congress. Citing their responsibility of administrative review, these committees jealously protect what they consider to be their prerogative to determine how the departments and agencies they oversee are to be restructured. In addition, members of Congress guard those areas in which they have developed expertise and the close relations with government officials and extragovernmental clientele. A committee reorganization could diminish a member's sources of campaign finance or even jeopardize his or her chances for reelection.

Some observers suggest presidents have ignored the managerial side of their responsibilities because of a lack of incentives or rewards in this area. In the words of one public administration expert, "No President has been able to identify any significant political capital that might be made out of efforts to improve management except for the conservative purpose of economizing or reducing costs."[253] Others feel that the way in which our civil-service system is organized encourages bureaucratic reluctance or resistance.[254] Still others remind us that the president frequently lacks authority to issue directions to operating departments.

In sum, the array of formal powers and accumulated "chief executive" prerogatives that we commonly associate with the modern presidency do not, in fact, guarantee the achievement of very much.

OVERSIGHT AND EARLY-WARNING SYSTEMS

Still another part of the job of the modern president is the design of oversight and early-warning systems and putting these to effective use. Often, little presidential time or stamina remains for inquiring into those routine activities that make up the great bulk of federal governmental work. Unfortunately, routine activities that are neglected or improperly monitored and evaluated can escalate to crisis proportion. But, for the most part, presidents must delegate large amounts of discretion to political subordinates and career professionals, and their influence over routine activities is felt only indirectly: through appointees, budgetary examinations, or legislative clearance. Presidents may view these activities as self-executing, or may even attempt to disassociate themselves from them, but much of the administrative and executive burden of the presidency consists of imaginative supervision of program implementation. The functional task of a president in the leadership of federal implementation activities is much more than merely issuing directives to the cabinet. It entails compromise, coalition building, education, and political leadership just as much as does the winning of congressional or public support. The quality of bread-and-butter service and assistance programs is important to the average American; a president, like it or not, is held responsible for the general quality of governmental performance.

Only through the skillful monitoring of routine governmental activities can a president know whether citizens are getting a fair return on their taxes. Only by a more imaginative use of presidential resources in overseeing these activities can the activities be prevented from becoming the sources of crises themselves. To be sure, supervision and reform must come not only from presidents but also from other quarters as well. But how effective a president is in fashioning an executive oversight and review system is crucial. On one hand, presidents must be able to delegate vast responsibilities to talented managers; on the other hand, they must have an early-warning system that alerts them through, among other means, their managers about inadequate government performance, about experimentation that yields negative results, and about progress in research and development that could provide corrective feedback.

An effective organization is a learning organization—a system that ensures governmental activities concerned with implementation and routine would be brought to a president's attention when necessary and as they affected priority-setting and political-leadership tasks instead of only when they become matters of crisis management. Interior and transportation officials, for example, should detect evidence of impending fuel shortages sufficiently in advance to permit a president to commission studies and devise remedial strategies before the crisis occurs. Homeland security officers should be alert to pending terrorist threats.

If one of the purposes of presidential power is to execute federal law faithfully and to help avert costly crises, the presidency must be organized systematically as a learning agency, capable of anticipating and preventing system overload, communication failures, and corruption or ineptness in the operations of the executive branch.

CONCLUSION

Several incentives help shape the performance of the presidential job. As they have operated in the recent past, these incentives ensure that certain responsibilities get special attention, whereas others become neglected. Preoccupation with problems of national security and macroeconomics leaves little time for leadership in the area of domestic policy. Crisis management, symbolic leadership, and priority setting also crowd out the tasks of lobbying and program implementation and supervision. Creative follow-through is seldom adequate; the routines of government often go neglected. Program evaluation and the imaginative recruitment of program managers for appropriate tasks never receive the sustained attention they merit. On balance, White House officials often do what is easy to do or what they perceive as urgent, sometimes to the neglect of doing what is important.

Presidents tend to concentrate on several areas of the presidential job. In part this may be because we have created a nearly impossible presidential job description—we give our presidents too much to do and too little time in which to do it. In part, however, recent presidents have also been, or so it would appear, lulled into responding to those parts of their job that are more glamorous, and more prominent. Presidential activity in symbolic, priority-setting, and crisis contexts can convey an image of strength, vigor, and rigor.

The true measure of presidents' effectiveness is their capacity to integrate multiple responsibilities to avoid having initiatives in one area compound problems in another, or having problems go unattended merely because they defy the usual organizational boundaries. Another challenge of presidential leadership is the intricate balancing of each aspect of the presidential job with the others. A close examination of presidential performance in recent years relative to the whole matrix of the job suggests that presidents are strong in some areas and weak in others, and that the overarching job of synthesis and integration is seldom performed adequately.

Those who devise structural solutions to what are essentially political questions are likely to be disappointed. We shall get improved presidential performances only when we have a clearer idea of what we want to do as a nation and when we understand better the mix of incentives that now shape the way presidents respond to their political and executive duties, and to the times.

FOR DISCUSSION

1. Is the job of being president too much for one person?
2. Do the war against terrorism and the 2008–2010 recession demonstrate the need for greater presidential power, and if so, what checks might be appropriate on executive authority in the modern age?

DEBATE QUESTIONS

1. That the president has too much power in foreign affairs.
2. That the Unitary Executive view of presidential authority is not grounded in the Constitution.

FURTHER READINGS

Adler, David Gray, and Larry N. George, eds. *The Constitution and the Conduct of Foreign Policy*. Lawrence: University Press of Kansas, 1996.

Edwards, George C. *The Strategic Presidency*. Princeton, NJ: Princeton University Press, 2009.

Genovese, Michael A., ed. *Contending Approaches to the American Presidency*. Washington, DC: CQ Press, 2012.

Gergen, David. *Eyewitness to Power*. New York: Simon & Schuster, 2000.

Jones, Charles A. *The Presidency in a Separated System*. Washington, DC: Brookings, 1994.

Rossiter, Clinton. *Constitutional Dictatorship: Crisis Government in the Modern Democracy*. Princeton, NJ: Princeton University Press, 1948.

Critical Thinking

STATEMENT: The separation-of-powers system is the chief reason the U.S. government so often fails or is overly slow to solve problems.

PROBLEM: How do we identify the factors that inhibit sound governmental decision making and problem solving? What keys open the door to the effective use of governmental power? Is the British model (fusion of power) a better system than ours?

CHAPTER 6

Presidents and Congress

Our republic, we know, was designed to be slow-moving and deliberative. Our founding fathers were convinced that power had to be
entrusted to someone, but that no-one could be entirely trusted with
power. They devised a brilliant system of checks and balances... there
could be no rash action, no rush to judgment, no legislative mob rule,
no unrestrained chief executive....

The difficultly with this... in today's cyberspace age is that everyone
is in check, but no-one is in charge.

SENATOR WILLIAM S. COHEN (R-MAINE; LATER SECRETARY OF
DEFENSE), *Washington Post National Weekly Edition*, January
28–February 4, 1996, p. 29.

I n September of 2008, the United States, indeed the entire international financial
system, seemed on the verge of a meltdown. The subprime lending crisis in the
United States led to the collapse of some of the largest banks and financial companies in the nation, and there was the very real threat that this would lead to an
international depression.

The Bush administration called for a $700 billion bailout. But the president
did not—on his own—have the authority to disburse such sums. He had to get
congressional approval.

In a matter of days, the intense, often contentious back-and-forth exchange
between the Administration and members of Congress led to a revised proposal
that authorized the $700 billion bailout, but with added protection for the taxpay-
ers, and added regulations on the financial sector.

On September 29, 2008, the House voted against the bailout 227–206. House
leaders twisted arms and Bush administration officials feverishly called Members
in an attempt to turn 12 votes and save their plan. After defeat in the House, the

bill went to the Senate, where a series of "sweeteners" were added. On October 1, the revised bill passed the Senate 74–25 and the new proposal went back to the House where, on the second go around, it passed on October 3 by a comfortable margin of 263–171.

After a whirlwind of activity, "the system worked." A Republican president and a Democratic Congress, facing a potential crisis, hammered out an agreement intended to lend stability to the teetering markets. It wasn't easy, it wasn't pretty, yet it demonstrated how two separated institutions could come together to solve problems. Yes, it worked, but only for a time. It wasn't long before cooperation degenerated into open conflict.

The relationship between the president and Congress is at the nexus of the separation of powers system. It can animate or debilitate the governing process, and is central to understanding the paradoxes of the presidency. For example, Paradox number 4 posits that we admire the "above politics" bipartisan approach (as both Bush and Obama hoped to bring to Washington politics), yet the presidency is perhaps the most political office in the American system (witness Obama and the strained passage of health care reform in 2010). Likewise Paradox number 5 reminds us that we want a president who can unify us (as Obama tried to do in the 2008 general election), yet the job requires taking firm stands and making controversial decisions that often divide us (again, Obama's health care reforms).

SEPARATE INSTITUTIONS/SHARED POWERS

The principal designer of the nation's capital, Major Pierre L'Enfant, had more than mere space in mind when he located the president and Congress at opposite ends of Pennsylvania Avenue. Congress, he decided, would be housed atop Jenkins Hill, giving it the high ground. The president would be a little over a mile away, at the end of a long street that would serve as a threadlike link connecting these two separated institutions. Not only did the Constitution separate the executive and legislative branches, but geography would as well.[255]

Yet if the U.S. system is to work, both branches must find ways to bridge the gap and join what is separated. The founders saw the separation of powers not as a weakness but as a source of strength, as a way to ensure deliberation and prevent tyranny. Cooperation between the president and Congress was what the framers required if energetic government was to be achieved. But how was a president to develop the collaboration necessary to make the system of separate institutions sharing power work?

The relationship between the president and Congress is the most important one in the American system of government. Only Congress can allocate resources, and presidents who consistently attempt to go around the Congress cannot long succeed. A president may not like it, but sustained cooperation with Congress is a necessity. Presidents may act unilaterally in a few areas, but most of the president's goals require a partnership with Congress.

This is no easy matter. As one long-time presidential adviser noted, "I suspect that there may be nothing about the White House less generally understood than the ease with which a Congress can drive a president quite out of his mind and up the wall."[256]

It is common to see the president as the driving force behind new initiatives, and we often relegate Congress to a supporting role. While this is sometimes true, is does a disservice to the rich and complex give and take that makes up presidential/Congressional relations. Yes the president sometimes leads, but often he takes up ideas already percolating up in Congress. Lawmaking is a "two-way street,"[257] with the president sometimes influencing Congress and at times the Congress influencing the president.

THE PRESIDENT'S CONSTITUTIONAL PLACE

In matters requiring legislative authorization the Congress ultimately has the upper hand. While a president is sometimes seen as leader of the nation, agenda setter, vision builder, and legislator-in-chief, it is the Congress that has the final say. And since there are multiple veto points in Congress, any of which may block a president's proposal, the forces wishing to prevent change usually have the advantage. The American system has many roadblocks, yet few avenues for easy change.

People nowadays expect presidents to lead the Congress. But public expectations notwithstanding, a president's legislative powers are constitutionally (Article II, Section 3) thin. The Constitution grants the Congress "all legislative power" but establishes a relationship of mutual dependence and power sharing. The more ambitious a president's agenda, the more dependent that president is on congressional cooperation. Presidents have the veto power. They report on the state of the union, and extraconstitutionally they may suggest legislation, lobby Congress, help frame the agenda, and build coalitions. Still, overall presidential powers over Congress are limited.

The peculiar paradox is that in a real sense, as many have noted, no one is completely in charge. Responsibility and power are fragmented. This often creates a fascinating blame game with presidents blaming the Congress for the ills of the nation and the Congress blaming the president.

In this the United States stands in contrast to parliamentary systems such as that of Great Britain. Rather than having a separation of powers, parliamentary systems have a *fusion* of power. The prime minister is elected from and by the majority party in the Parliament. Prime ministers are responsible to, yet also have power over, the majority party, and are thereby granted more legislative power than a U.S. president possesses. Fusing the executive and legislative powers together creates more power and greater accountability. If things go well or ill, the voters know who is responsible.

HISTORICAL EVOLUTION

Congress was established as the dominant and constitutionally most powerful branch of government, and the first few presidents were minimally involved in the legislative process. But the founders' vision soon gave way to political reality, and slowly presidents began to pull power into the White House. Congress was often a willing participant in giving additional power to the presidency. The rise of the legislative presidency did not follow a clear unobstructed path. Some of the more ambitious chief executives such as Jefferson used the newly forming political parties to exert influence in Congress. Others such as Jackson exploited popular opinion to gain influence. Still, others such as Lincoln and FDR gained additional powers during crisis.

Sprinkled between these power aggrandizing presidents were less assertive or weaker chief executives. Thus, an institutional ebb and flow characterizes power relations between the president and Congress. Over time, however, this tug of war has moved toward a stronger president in the legislative arena. Today many scholars argue that, "What was designed as a congressionally centered system has evolved into a presidentially centered...system."[258] Still, Congress has a way of frustrating even the most skilled of presidents, especially when there is divided government, with the control of the presidency and Congress in the hands of vying political parties.

While the popular expectation is that the president is a "chief legislator" who "guides Congress in much of its lawmaking activity,"[259] reality is often different. The decentralized nature of power in Congress, the multiple access and veto points within the congressional process, the loosely organized party system, the independent/entrepreneurial mode of the legislators, and the weakness of the legislative leadership all conspire against presidential direction and leadership. This means that presidents often impact Congress only "at the margins," and are more "facilitators" than leaders.[260]

The theory on which the U.S. government is based assumes a reasonable amount of cooperation between the two branches. As Supreme Court Associate Justice Robert Jackson wrote in 1952, "while the Constitution diffuses power the better to secure liberty, it also contemplates that practice will integrate the dispersed powers into a workable government."[261]

In this chapter we look at our system of separate branches and the conflict between the branches. Later in the chapter, we examine some of the measures Congress has taken in recent decades to try and assert its authority in its continuing struggle with the White House.

THE POLITICS OF SHARED POWER

The framers anticipated that the president and Congress would often disagree over policy, for they gave the president veto power over legislation, but gave Congress the power to override that veto. They gave the power to nominate top personnel to the president but gave the Senate power to confirm. They authorized presidents to negotiate treaties but required the Senate's approval by a two-thirds vote before the president could ratify a treaty. The framers also knew from their study of history that heads of government were more prone to going to war than were the people's representatives, so they vested the final authority for war in the legislature.

Constitutional democracy in the United States was designed to be one of both shared powers and division.[262] The framers wanted disagreement as well as cooperation because they assumed that the checks and balances within the government would prevent a president and Congress from "ganging up" against the people's liberties. The framers actually made such disagreements inevitable by providing a president, Senate, and House of Representatives elected by different constituencies and for different lengths of service.

The United States is notable among major world powers because it is neither a parliamentary democracy nor a wholly executive-dominated government. Our Constitution invites both Congress and president to set policy and govern the nation. Leadership and policy change are encouraged only when two, and sometimes all three, branches of government concur on the desirability of new directions.

The politics of shared power has often been stormy, as the Bill Clinton health care proposal, George W. Bush's social security reform attempts, and the Obama climate change initiative illustrate (all failed!). The politics of shared powers is characterized by changing patterns of cooperation and conflict depending on the partisan and ideological makeup of Congress, the popularity and skills of a president, the strength of the political parties, and various events that shape the politics of the times. As we will discuss, the politics of shared powers in an era of divided government can aptly be described as the politics of Congress's varying success at asserting itself in relation to the initiatives and leadership provided by presidents.[263]

Today, divided government has become the rule rather than the exception. Since 1952 there has been a split in partisan control of the presidency and Congress for about two-thirds of the time.

And while even in eras of divided government, presidents and congresses sometime find ways to work together, in recent years *partisanship* has morphed into *hyperpartisanship*,[264] as witnessed in Figure 6.1. Earlier key legislation was grounded a semipartisan crossover voting. But in recent years, major legislation was almost exclusively passed along party lines, with virtually no Republicans crossing over to support Obama.

Even with divided control of the presidency and Congress (see Figure 6.1), the two institutions must and do find ways to work together.[265] Divided government, while sometime leading to gridlock, may also lead to more moderate policies, an increased likelihood of executive–congressional negotiations and bargaining, and it may also keep the executive in check.[266] (See Figures 6.2 and 6.3.)

The opposition party in Congress often mounts its own programs. It will, when possible, defeat a president's policy initiative and substitute its own. This effort becomes all the more troublesome, of course, for a president when Congress is controlled by the opposition party.

Note the contrast between the 111th Congress (2009–2011), where the Democrats controlled the White House and both Houses of Congress, and the 112th Congress (2011–2013), when the Republicans controlled the House of

Figure 6.1. The End of Bipartisanship[1]

REPUBLICANS WHO VOTED FOR . . .

Year	Legislation	House	Senate
2010	Financial regulations	0	3
2010	Health care reform	0	0
2009	Economic stimulus	0	3
1965	Medicare	70	13
1965	Voting Rights Act	111	30
1964	Civil Rights Act	136	27
1935	Social Security	81	16

DEMOCRATS WHO VOTED FOR . . .

Year	Legislation	House	Senate
2001	No Child Left Behind	197	43
2001	Bush tax cuts	28	12
1981	Reagan tax cuts	47	37

[1] Adapted from Bill Schneider, "Republican Revival?," *Inside Politics* Issue 5, June 2010.

Representatives. The 111th was an especially activist Congress, passing a wide range of bills, including the president's $787 billion stimulus package, major health care reform, and the Dodd–Frank law (Wall Street banking regulation); approved a nuclear arms treaty with Russia passed a tax bill compromise and food safety regulations; approved two Supreme Court nominees and new credit card consumer protections; extended homebuyer credits, the student aid program, and the Patriot Act; and more. Indeed initially Obama had an uncommonly successful track record with Congress. In 2009 his success rate on getting legislation passed was a record high of 96.7 percent.[267] It was an impressive volume of activity. (See Figure 6.3.)

However, after the Democrats got trounced in the 2010 midterm election, losing 63 seats (and control) in the House, and 6 in the Senate, the Republicans were able to flex their newfound political muscle and block virtually all of the President's agenda. In this case, divided government meant divisive government and led to a deadlocked government. Approximately $40 billion was spent in the 2010 election, about 40 percent more than in the previous midterm election. Nonparty, outside groups spent four times what they spent in 2006. The Republicans outspent the Democrats by a wide margin.[268] (See Figure 6.4.)

Money mattered, but the Republicans were also aided by the rise of conservatives and libertarian Tea-Party activists who bolstered the ranks of the Republican Party. Intensely anti-Obama, these activists put pressure on the party leaders to oppose virtually all of President Obama's legislative proposals in 2011 and 2012.

The politics of shared power necessitates ongoing efforts to agreement building between a president and Congress. The model, or theory of government, on which the American system was founded, is based on consensus and coalition building. Consensus means agreement about *ends*; coalitions are *means* by which the ends are achieved. Since power is fragmented and dispersed, something (crisis) or someone (usually, a president) had to pull the disparate parts of the system together. [269]

A coalition can be formed if the president has a clear, focused agenda; if the president can forcefully and compellingly communicate a vision; and if the public is ready to embrace that vision. If a president can develop a consensus, he or she can sometimes muster the power to form the coalitions necessary to bring the vision to fruition.

Simply placing a legislative package at the doorstep of Congress is never enough. Presidents must work to build support within and outside Congress. They must build coalitions. Of course, building coalitions is easier said than done. Institutional combat, not collaborative power sharing, characterizes this relationship, as both branches attempt to maximize power and govern independently.

THE PRESIDENT IN THE LEGISLATIVE ARENA

Members of Congress quickly take the measure of the new president. Will the president stand firm? Will the president bend? Will the new president work with us or act independent of Congress? Will the president be highly partisan or bipartisan? Will the president be able to intimidate us, or can we lead the White House? Who will set the tone?

While the separation of powers and divided government are obstacles, they are not insurmountable barriers to cooperation. Presidents and Congress can legislate when the leaders of both institutions engage in bargain and compromise.[270]

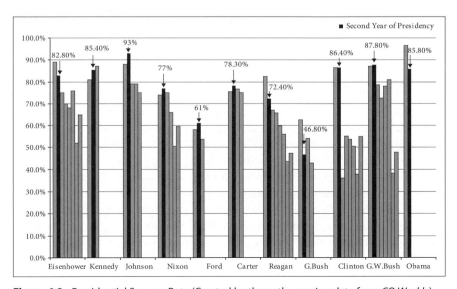

Figure 6.2. Presidential Success Rate (Created by the authors using data from *CQ Weekly*)

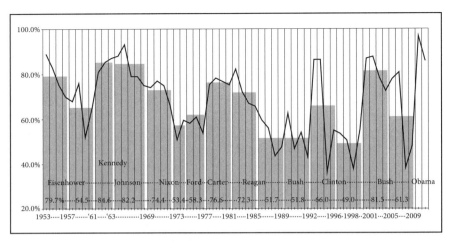

Figure 6.3. Presidential Success with Congress (Created by the authors using data from *CQ Weekly*)

Ever since Richard Neustadt's book *Presidential Power* was first published in 1960, presidency scholars have been arguing over just how much influence a president can exert over Congress. Neustadt famously portrays the president as lacking the power to command Congress to pass his preferred legislation because ours is a system with separated institutions sharing power. Lacking the power to command, presidents are compelled to persuade.

In attempting to persuade Congress, presidents can employ an *inside* or *outside* strategy. The inside strategy—Going Washington—calls for a president to bargain, make deals, compromise, and engage in coalition building. Such face-to-face lobbying, some argue, yields benefits as presidents and members of Congress find some common ground, and presidents cajole, coax, or pressure Congress to act.

The outside strategy—Going Public—argues that the president influences Congress by going over the heads of Congress and making direct appeals to the public.[271] Presidents lobby the people, then, armed with popular rapport, lobby Congress from a stronger political position. Is there empirical support for the going public approach to leadership? Certainly presidents act as if this approach yields results—that is, they repeatedly do go public. Yet, rare is the case when their efforts are rewarded. George Edwards argues that such efforts are usually a waste of time, and may even be counterproductive.[272] Edwards suggests that presidents usually get more mileage by "staying private."

While Edwards makes a powerful case, other scholars see presidents—at times and under certain conditions—successfully employing a going public strategy. These studies[273] assert that the Bully Pulpit can be employed as an agenda setter, and that if properly utilized the public strategy pays dividends. In practice, then, presidents are well advised to sometimes "go Washington" and at other times "go public," while at other times—probably on most major initiatives—they must do both.

Figure 6.4. The Growth of Divided Government, 1928–2008

Election Year	President	House of Representatives	Senate	Divided/Unified
1928	R (Hoover)	R	R	
1930	R (Hoover)	D	R	
1932	D (Roosevelt)	D	D	
1934	D (Roosevelt)	D	D	
1936	D (Roosevelt)	D	D	
1938	D (Roosevelt)	D	D	
1940	D (Roosevelt)	D	D	
1942	D (Roosevelt)	D	D	
1944	D (Roosevelt)	D	D	
1946	D (Truman)	R	R	d
1948	D (Truman)	D	D	d
1950	D (Truman)	D	D	d
1952	R (Eisenhower)	R	R	u
1954	R (Eisenhower)	D	D	d
1956	R (Eisenhower)	D	D	d
1958	R (Eisenhower)	D	D	d
1960	D (Kennedy)	D	D	u
1962	D (Kennedy)	D	D	u
1964	D (Johnson)	D	D	u
1966	D (Johnson)	D	D	u
1968	R (Nixon)	D	D	d
1970	R (Nixon)	D	D	d
1972	R (Nixon)	D	D	d
1974	R (Ford)	D	D	d
1976	D (Carter)	D	D	u
1978	D (Carter)	D	D	u
1980	R (Reagan)	D	R	d
1982	R (Reagan)	D	R	d
1984	R (Reagan)	D	R	d
1986	R (Reagan)	D	D	d
1988	R (G. H. W. Bush)	D	D	d
1990	R (G. H. W. Bush)	D	D	d
1992	D (Clinton)	D	D	u
1994	D (Clinton)	R	R	d
1996	D (Clinton)	R	R	d
1998	D (Clinton)	R	R	d
2000	R (G. W. Bush)	R	D*	d
2002	R (G. W. Bush)	R	R	u
2004	R (G. W. Bush)	R	R	u
2006	R (G. W. Bush)	D	D	d
2008	D (Barack Obama)	D	D	u
2010	D (Barack Obama)	R	D	d

Vital Statistics on American Politics 2011–2012 by Harold W. Stanley; Richard G. Niemi, Copyright 2011. Reproduced with permission of CQ PRESS in the format Republish in a textbook via Copyright Clearance Center.

*Democrats gained control of the Senate after Vermont senator James Jeffords switched from Republican to Independent (voting with the Democrats) in May of 2001, breaking the 50–50 tie left by the 2000 election.

Under what conditions are presidents likely to establish their agenda and get congressional support? When is the Congress most likely to follow a president's lead? And when is it likely that a president will follow the lead of Congress?

While there is no magic key to unlocking the door too cooperation, a number of factors lend themselves to presidential success when dealing with Congress. First, in crisis situations, a president is accorded additional deference, and the Congress usually supports the president. Second, if a president has a clear electoral mandate (when the campaign was issue oriented, a president won by a significant margin, and the president's party has a majority in Congress), the Congress may follow. Third, the president may exert pressure on members of Congress when he won the election by a landslide and ran ahead of the member in his or her own district (this is usually referred to as "presidential coattails").

Fourth, presidential popularity is said to be source of power over Congress. But how easily can presidents translate popularity into power? Many social scientists are skeptical, believing that popularity has only a marginal impact on presidential success within Congress.[274] Others, as we stated in chapter 2, argue that popularity can be converted into power.[275]

Fifth, skill can make a difference, but how much of a difference? As with popularity, scholars disagree: some arguing that skill is of little importance,[276] others that it is important.[277] One scholar warns that

> It is important to depersonalize somewhat the study of presidential leadership and examine it from a broader perspective. In this way there are fewer risks of attributing to various aspects of presidential leadership consequences of factors largely beyond the president's control. Similarly, one is less likely to attribute incorrectly the failure of a president to achieve his goals to his failure to lead properly. Things are rarely so simple.[278]

Skills such as knowledge of the congressional process, appropriate timing, bargaining, deal making, persuasion, and consensus and coalition-building skills; moving the public; setting the agenda; self-dramatization; arm twisting; trading; and consultation and co-optation can all be used to advance the president's goals.

Partisan support in Congress is the sixth (and many believe most important) major factor shaping presidential success with Congress. Parties sometimes serve as a bridge linking the institutional divide between the president and Congress. Lyndon Johnson had such a large majority of party members in Congress (especially from 1965 to 1967) that even if several dozen Democrats abandoned the president, he could still get his majority in Congress.

In the past two decades the two political parties have become more ideologically polarized. This, plus the persistence of divided government, has made bargaining and compromise more necessary *and* more difficult.[279] It has also contributed to the decline of civility in our politics.[280]

Linked to this is the seventh factor: the nature of the opposition in Congress. How many votes do they have? How ideologically committed are they? How cohesive are they as a group? How willing are they to work with the president?

President Obama knew well the turbulence of partisan politics in Congress. His legislative success rate was high in his first two years when Democrats controlled both Houses of Congress. Yet, when Republicans won control of the House in the 2010 midterm election, his success rate dropped.

The eighth factor that shapes presidential success or failure in Congress is the nature of consultation between the branches.[281] One of the lessons every president learns is that a president must consult, not only with the president's own partisans, but with the opposition as well. Attempting to gain cooperation and agreement must be the first step. A president also has to have an effective legislative liaison office that listens and works closely with the leadership on the Hill. Then too, a president needs to appreciate policy values and political needs of the members of Congress. Presidents sometimes need to follow as well as lead, especially when there are better ideas to be found in Congress.[282]

Finally, the size and type of agenda a president pursues may have significant impact. An ambitious agenda is difficult to pass in good times, but in tough times, the tough choices appear to be impossible choices.[283]

Congress can, of course, play a major role in setting and sometimes shaping the national public policy agenda. It may be difficult for a plural institution

Figure 6.5. Success Rate History

Eisenhower		Nixon		Reagan		Clinton	
1953	89.0%	1969	74.0%	1981	82.4%	1993	86.4%
1954	82.8	1970	77.0	1982	72.4	1994	86.4
1955	75.0	1971	75.0	1983	67.1	1995	36.2
1956	70.0	1972	66.0	1984	65.8	1996	55.1
1957	68.0	1973	50.6	1985	59.9	1997	56.62
1958	76.0	1974	59.6	1986	56.1	1998	51
1959	52.0	**Ford**		1987	43.5	1999	37.8
1960	65.0	1974	58.2%	1988	47.4	2000	55
Kennedy		1975	61.0	**G. H. W. Bush**		**G. W. Bush**	
1961	81.0%	1976	53.8	1989	62.6%	2001	87%
1962	85.4	**Carter**		1990	46.8	2002	88
1963	87.1	1977	75.4%	1991	54.2	2003	78.4
Johnson		1978	78.3	1992	43.0	2004	72.6
1964	88.0%	1979	76.8			2005	64.1
1965	93.0	1980	75.0			2006	51.5
1966	79.0					2007	38.3
1967	79.0					2008	47.8
1968	75.0					**Obama**	
						2009	96.7%
						2010	85.8
						2011	57.1

(Created by the authors using data from *Congressional Quarterly*).

to lead, yet Congress sometimes acts as a leadership and lawmaking as well as a representative institution. When is this the case? This happens when a party enjoys strong majorities in both chambers; when a president is vulnerable, such as at the end of a term, or is politically wounded (as Nixon was in 1973 and 1974); and when the Congress has strong leaders, as when Sam Rayburn and Lyndon Johnson exercised impressive leadership toward the end of the Eisenhower presidency. (See Figure 6.5.)

But the central question under consideration here is, Can a president lead Congress? The answer remains: Yes, yet not often, and not usually for long. A mix of skill, circumstances, luck, popularity, party support, timing, and political capital need to converge if effective collaboration of these two highly political branches is to occur.

PARTIES AND PRESIDENTS: AN AWKWARD ALLIANCE

The Constitution deliberately created a separate legislative branch and a separate executive branch. Yet making our Madisonian system of separate powers work effectively requires some help to encourage meaningful cooperation between the branches. One of the devices that often serves this intermediary function is the American political party.

A political party at its best brings like-minded people together, that is, people who share similar policy perspectives. Thus members of Congress and a president who are members of a common party not only can talk more easily across

President Clinton, a Democrat, although popular with voters, was nonetheless *imperiled* by the Republican-controlled Congress. His popularity has risen to over 70 percent approval in recent years and his address at the 2012 Democratic National Convention was widely admired.

the branches, but can devise collaborative mechanisms to produce agreed-on legislation, treaties, budgets, and similar political decisions. One of the paradoxes of the president–party relationship is that while the party can be one of the useful tools of presidential leadership, it is often less developed and less appreciated than should be the case.

It is often said that presidents are leaders of their political parties. In fact, however, a president has no formal position in the party structure. In theory, the supreme authority in our parties is the national presidential convention. More directly in charge of the national party, at least on paper, is the national committee (and each committee has a national chairperson).

In practice, successful presidents control their national committees and, often, their national conventions as well. Although the national committee picks the party chair, nowadays a president almost always lets the committee know whom he or she wants. Modern presidents hire and fire national party staff at will.

Political parties once were a defining source of influence for a president. It used to be said, for example, that our most effective presidents were effective in large part because they had made use of party support and took seriously their party leadership responsibilities. But as our parties have declined in organizational importance, there has been more of an incentive for presidents to "rise above" the party and run alone.

Today, the presidential–party relationship is strained. National party chairpersons come and go. Few party chairpersons of the president's party have enjoyed much influence. Many have been regarded at the White House as little more than clerks or emissaries.

President and party need each other, yet each sometimes becomes frustrated and even annoyed with the other. What has been the role of the president as party leader? What of presidents' use of party as an appeal to Congress for support of their programs?

Our earliest presidents vigorously opposed the development of political parties. They viewed them as factions and divisive—something to be dreaded as the greatest political evil. The Constitution makes no mention of political parties. In his Farewell Address of 1796, George Washington warned against the "spirit of party generally" and said that the nascent parties were "the curse of the country." And James Monroe once wrote to his friend James Madison, saying, "Surely our nation may get along and prosper without the existence of parties." But if the inventors of the presidency bemoaned the emergence of parties, they soon came to accept them as inevitable, and many even attempted to use parties to their advantage.

The president's role as party leader developed over time; it was a role grafted onto the presidency. A president today serves as the party's "most eminent member," titular leader of the national committee, most visible spokesperson for the party, and, as chief architect, he or she initiates the party's program.

But the president is also, in many ways, independent from the party. Today, the party does not control the nomination; it is comparatively weak and relatively undisciplined; there are separate national, state, and local organizations;

presidential involvement can be sporadic; and ordinarily, presidents need support from the opposition to pass their proposals and have them accepted as legitimate.

However, the president needs the party. The legislative grids usually lock if the president, even with help from the party, cannot grease the machinery of government: "To be successful, to be powerful the president needs the lubricating of party. Since Washington, all the presidents considered great or near great were active and powerful party leaders. And failures neglected or failed to adequately use party."[284]

One of the chief reasons presidents seek ways other than legislation to make policy is that they are so often unable to get Congress to pass their proposals. This sometimes leads to the use of administrative tactics, or engaging in *fait accompli* acts, going public, or moving beyond the law. But if the president has a strong party on which to rely (and solid party majorities in Congress), the temptation to achieve results by other means is not as great. Parties can help presidents govern while helping maintain democratic accountability.

The parties enabled officeholders to overcome some of the limitations of our formal constitutional arrangements. Political parties facilitated coordination among the separated branches. President Andrew Jackson especially used his resources to promote partisan control of government. Jackson's achievements as party leader transformed the office, so much so that he is sometimes called the "first modern president."

The president became both the head of the executive branch and the leader of the party. The first six presidents usually acted in a manner that accorded Congress an equality of power. However, starting with Andrew Jackson the president began more and more to assert his role not simply as head of the executive branch but as leader of the government. By the skillful use of his position as head of the party he persuaded Congress to follow his lead, thereby allowing him to assume greater control of the government and to direct and dominate public affairs.[285]

Many scholars believe that the effective presidents have been those who, like Jackson, strengthened their position by becoming strong party leaders. Cooperation and progress can be achieved through party alliances. "Since the office did not come equipped with the necessary powers under the constitution, they had to be added through a historical process by the forceful action of vigorous presidents whose position was strengthened by the rise and development of political parties."[286]

Few presidents have been able to duplicate Jackson's success. Most have found it exceedingly difficult to serve as an activist party builder and party leader while trying to serve also as chief of state and national unifier. President William Howard Taft lamented that the longer he was president, "the less of a party man I seem to become."[287] President William McKinley said he could no longer be president of a party, for "I am now President of the whole people."[288]

Once in office, presidents often try to minimize the partisan appearance of their actions. This is so in part because the public yearns for a "statesman" in the White House, for a president who is above politics. We, the public, don't want presidents to act with their eyes on the next election. And we don't want them to favor any particular group or party.

Herein lies another of the enduring paradoxes of the presidency. On one hand, presidents are expected to be neutral public servants, avoiding political and party considerations. On the other hand, they are supposed to work closely with party leaders. Also, they must build political coalitions and drum up support, especially party support, for what they believe needs to be done.

To take the president out of partisan politics, however, is to assume incorrectly that the president will be so generally right and the leaders and rank and file of their party so generally wrong that the president must be protected from the push and shove of political pressures. But what president has always been right? Having a president constrained and informed by party platforms and party leaders is what was intended when our party system developed.

THE "NO PARTY" PRESIDENCY

Are we moving to a no-party presidency? Parliamentary regimes such as Great Britain have strong disciplined parties, and the prime minister can rely on the party in the Parliament to gain passage of his or her proposals. But in the United States with less disciplined parties, presidential power is more personalized. While parties matter in the United States, they do not matter as much as in Britain or other European democracies.

These factors undermine party in this country:

- An antiparty bias exists in the political culture.
- Our history is generally one of weak parties.
- The nomination process is not in the control of party regulars.
- The party does not run presidential campaigns.
- Office seekers are entrepreneurs first, partisans second.
- Parties are not the prime fund-raisers; individual office seekers are.
- Presidents generally have short coattails.

Presidents encounter a number of disincentives when determining what approach to take toward party leadership. In the nominating and governing processes, it is often more useful to eschew party than embrace party. As political scientist Robert Harmel writes

> The context of presidential politics provides few incentives for presidents to lead their party organizations, and most recent presidents have acted accordingly. While none has totally abandoned his party, it can be said without exaggeration that the record has been one of neglect more than active party leadership.[289]

Given the difficulties presidents have in exerting effective party leadership, it may seem surprising that presidents do spend some of their precious resources on party. But as difficult as party leadership may be, the alternative, to allow the parties to deteriorate, is worse. The demise of party has a number of adverse consequences. If party is of only sporadic use to presidents, it is of some use. In a process where a president's resource cupboard often seems relatively bare, party may serve as an aid in moving the machinery of government. It may not be much, but it is something.

PRESIDENTS AND USE OF PARTY APPEAL IN CONGRESS

Presidential control of party support in Congress varies a lot, in part on whether a president enjoys large working-party majorities in Congress, in part due to whether the president enjoys high popularity, and in part on what time it is in a presidential term. Presidential coattails, once thought to be a significant factor in helping elect members of a president's party to Congress, have had little effect in recent years. Members usually get reelected because of the partisan makeup of their districts and the fact that they can take advantage of incumbency or that they have a large war chest of campaign money, not based on whether they have worked cooperatively with the White House. Congressional races are less affected by national issues or national trends. Time and again, presidents have found in midterm congressional elections, as was the case in 2006 and 2012, that they can do little to help members of their own party who are in trouble. Presidential attempts to unseat or purge disloyal members of Congress in the president's party have not worked. Roosevelt's celebrated "purge" of nonsupportive Democrats in the congressional elections of 1938 was mainly in vain. Anti-New Deal Democrats won reelection or election for the first time in most of the places where he tried to wield his influence.

Presidents today have little retaliatory leverage to apply against uncooperative legislators. Members of Congress, as a result of various congressional reforms, have more and more resources (trips home, large staffs, more research facilities, more home offices and staffs in their districts) to help win reelection. With the dramatic growth of government programs and governmental regulation, members of Congress are in a good position to make themselves seem indispensable to local officials and local business people, who need to have a Washington "friend" to cut through the red tape and expedite government contracts or short-circuit some federal regulation. These kinds of developments have enhanced reelection chances for most members while at the same time making them less dependent on the White House and less fearful of any penalty for ignoring presidential party appeals.

A president's appeal to fellow party members in Congress is effective only some of the time. President George W. Bush won surprising Republican congressional support for his Iraq war policies yet failed to win support for his "reform" initiatives on social security and immigration policies. And a fair number of Republicans wound up actively opposing Bush on such issues as torture, stem cell research, and some of his economic "bailout" initiatives.

Party caucuses may be stronger in Congress, yet legislators know that neither the White House nor fellow members in Congress will penalize them if they can claim that "district necessities" forced them to differ with the party on a certain vote—even a key vote. Presidents doubtless will contrive to encourage party cohesion, but just as clearly, party support will vary on the kinds of measures the president is asking them to support.

THE PRESIDENTIAL VETO

A president can veto a bill by returning it, together with specific objections, to the House in which it originated. Congress, by a two-thirds vote in each chamber, may override the president's veto. Another variation of the veto is known as the pocket veto. In the ordinary course of events, if the president does not sign or veto a bill within ten weekdays after receiving it, it becomes law without the chief executive's signature. But if Congress adjourns within the ten days, the president, by taking no action, can kill the bill. (See Figure 6.6.)

The President's veto strength lies in the usual failure of Congress to get a two-thirds majority of both houses. Historically Congress has overridden less than 7 percent of presidents' vetoes. Yet a Congress that could repeatedly mobilize a two-thirds majority against a president can almost take command of the government. This is a rare situation, yet such was the fate of Andrew Johnson in the 1860s.[290]

Presidents can also use the veto power in a positive way. They can threaten that bills under consideration by Congress will be turned back unless certain changes are made. They can use the threat of vetoes against some bills Congress wants badly in exchange for other bills that the president may want. A presidential veto can also protect a national minority from hasty, unfair legislation passed in the heat of the moment. But the veto is essentially a negative weapon of limited use to a president who is pressing for action.

In short, there is little Congress can do when confronted with a veto. It must either get enough votes to override the veto or modify the legislation and try again. Presidents are able to make the vast majority of their regular vetoes stick.[291]

PRESIDENTS AND CONGRESS IN FOREIGN AFFAIRS

If the constitutional framers expected presidents to play a relatively minor role with respect to domestic policy, they had different expectations with respect to foreign and national security matters. That is why they made the president the agent in making and ratifying treaties, with senatorial consent, and also gave the president considerable control over the military forces.

Although foreign affairs in the eighteenth century were generally thought to be an executive matter, the framers did not want the president to be the only or even the dominant agent. Various powers vested in Congress by the Constitution were explicitly designed to bring the national legislature into the making of foreign and military policy. Indeed, a good part of the Constitution was written to deprive the executive of control over foreign policy and foreign relations, which under the English system was so dramatically vested in the king. Thus the framers

Figure 6.6. Presidential Vetoes, 1789–2008

President	Regular Vetoes	Pocket Vetoes	Total Vetoes	Overridden Vetoes
Washington	2	—	2	—
Madison	5	2	7	—
Monroe	1	—	1	—
Jackson	5	7	12	—
Tyler	6	3	9	1
Polk	2	1	3	—
Pierce	9	—	9	5
Buchanan	4	3	7	—
Lincoln	2	4	6	—
A. Johnson	21	8	29	15
Grant	45	49	94	4
Hayes	12	1	13	1
Arthur	4	8	12	1
Cleveland	304	109	413	2
Harrison	19	25	44	1
Cleveland	43	127	170	5
McKinley	6	36	42	—
T. Roosevelt	42	40	82	1
Taft	30	9	39	1
Wilson	33	11	44	6
Harding	5	1	6	—
Coolidge	20	30	50	4
Hoover	21	16	37	3
F. Roosevelt	372	263	635	9
Truman	180	70	250	12
Eisenhower	73	108	181	2
Kennedy	12	9	21	—
L. Johnson	16	14	30	—
Nixon	24	18	42	6
Ford	53	19	72	12
Carter	13	18	31	2
Reagan	39	39	78	9
Bush, G. H. W.	29	17	46	1
Clinton	37	1	37	2
Bush, G. W.	11	1	12	4
Obama	2	—	2	—
Totals:	1,499	1,065	2,563	110

(Created by the authors using data from the U.S. Senate Historical Office, Senate Library)

gave Congress as a whole the sole power to declare war, and they plainly intended the Senate to serve as a partner in the shaping and making of foreign policy. Constitutional scholar Leonard W. Levy goes even further: "The framers meant, at the most, that the president should be a joint participant in the field of foreign affairs, but not an equal one."[292]

But as the world leadership role of the United States has increased, so also has the foreign policy role and the power of the president. From 1940 onward, "the Oval Office is where foreign policy for better or worse has been made."[293] Policies that have succeeded in recent decades—the Marshall Plan, the Truman Doctrine, the Panama Canal Treaty, the first Iraq War, the Camp David Accords, the North American Free Trade Agreement, the military mission in Libya—have been those in which presidents encouraged careful collaboration and debate in Congress. When presidents involved Congress and the people in the shaping of new foreign policies, those policies have generally won legitimacy and worked. "The policies that have failed have tended to be those adopted by presidents without meaningful debate—Roosevelt's Yalta policy toward Poland, Kennedy's intervention in the Bay of Pigs... Reagan's Iran-contra policy, among others."[294]

BUSH, THE CONGRESS, AND IRAQ

In the war against terrorism, President George W. Bush almost always got his way. This should not be a surprise, as after all: there was a crisis in foreign affairs, the public wanted action, and the Congress was controlled by the president's party. It was a recipe for expanded presidential power.

As a result of the terrorist attack on the United States, the Bush administration argued that a whole new approach to foreign policy was required. The Cold War was over and the president declared an international war against terrorism; the *U.S.A. Patriot Act* was passed, a Department of Homeland Security was established, a war against the Taliban government in Afghanistan took place, the Al Qaeda terrorist network was pursued, and a war against Saddam Hussein in Iraq took place. But perhaps most significantly, the administration developed a new strategic doctrine: preventive First Strike.

In September of 2002, the administration released its national security strategy document that opened thus: "The major institutions of American national security were designed in a different era to meet different requirements. All of them must be transformed."[295]

And transform them he did. This document describes a fundamentally new, even revolutionary approach to the use of power internationally. *Deterrence* and *containment*, the core doctrines of U.S. power for fifty years during the Cold War, were overnight bolstered or replaced with doctrines of preemption and preventive warfare.

President Bush's first strike/preemptive policy, when joined to his "you're either with us or against us" approach and his willingness to "go it alone" led to what is referred to as "unilateralism" in foreign policy. This frustrated our traditional allies, just when the United States most needed their help in the global war against terrorism. A nation can pursue its foreign policy interests unilaterally (alone), bilaterally (between two nations), or multilaterally (involving many nations). The President was signaling a willingness to go it alone where necessary.

The reaction *against* the United States was highly critical, especially when one considers how overwhelming support *for* the United States was in the aftermath of the September 11 attacks. The response from traditional allies was difficult to ignore. A deep vein of global resentment was struck—not just from adversaries but from long-time friends as well.

In what came to be known as the "Bush Doctrine," the United States, while pursuing diplomatic solutions, assumed the right to engage a preemptive strike against presumed threats. Such strikes may—as was the case with Iraq—involve a "coalition of the willing," but the United States would not be bound by international organizations such as the United Nations or NATO, but would—where necessary—act alone. Such unilateralism sparked a firestorm of opposition from traditional allies and led to accusations of "bully" and "imperialism" leveled against the United States.

The Bush doctrine was to speak *loudly* and *use* a big stick. As the most powerful nation in the world, the United States had the means to enforce its will on much of the world, and matched with public support, congressional acquiescence, and Bush's willingness to go-it-alone if necessary, great strains were put on traditional alliances.

At home, the administration cut many constitutional corners undermining the civil rights and liberties of the U.S. citizens in the detention centers, denying them the right to be charged with crimes, denying their rights to an attorney, even incarcerating children without charges. The president and attorney general John Ashcroft, emboldened by popular support and congressional acquiescence, and armed with the U.S.A. Patriot Act, dramatically expanded the government's authority to investigate and retain U.S. citizens. Both at home and abroad, major changes were taking place. And both at home and abroad, decisions would be made by the president and the president alone, without the normal checks and balances supplied by the Congress or the Courts.

This, of course, goes against much of what the founders of the Republic believed about human nature and the potential for power to corrupt. Uncontrolled power is what the framers feared. But in the war against terrorism, it had become U.S. policy. The framers of the U.S. Constitution believed that power in one person's hands would invariably lead to corruption and abuse. The very framework of the government they created—the separation of powers—is testimony to their suspicions about human nature and power in the hands of one person or branch of government. A system of checks and balances would, the framers believed, diminish the chances that one man could assume too much power.

September 11, 2001, opened a door to power. President Bush used this opportunity to recast U.S. foreign policy in new, some would say radical, ways. In doing so, the president was engaged in what critics see as a risky venture, entered into with little debate and in the absence of meaningful consultation with allies or the Congress.

Presidents make choices. During war or crisis, presidents often have the power to turn choice into policy. These choices have consequences. Therefore, during war or crisis, leadership matters. In normal times, presidents face an array of constraints that usually force them to bargain, compromise, settle for less, and make deals. Thus, while presidential leadership is always important, it is most consequential—for good or ill—in time of crisis.

THE "IMPERIAL PRESIDENCY" ARGUMENT

No matter what the circumstances, though, most people expect Congress to fully exercise the system of constitutional checks to rein in the president, and vice versa. Late in the 1960s and in the early 1970s, a number of events made many fear that Congress had become too passive and the presidency too powerful.

In the early 1970s, the Vietnam War was finally winding down, but not without leaving the nation reeling from the protests, civil unrest, and loss of lives associated with that unpopular and largely unsuccessful war. The nation's grief and outrage were fueled, too, by revelations that both Johnson and Nixon had misled Congress and acted in some instances without congressional approval in making and conducting the war. These disconcerting events were compounded by the Watergate scandals and the growing realization that a president of the United States had acted to obstruct justice. These developments led Arthur M. Schlesinger, Jr., a historian and former adviser to John F. Kennedy, to write *The Imperial Presidency*, charging that presidential powers were so abused and expanded by 1972 that they threatened our constitutional democracy.[296]

Schlesinger and other proponents of the "imperial presidency" view contend the problem stems in part from ambiguity concerning the president's power as commander-in-chief; it is a vaguely defined office, not a series of specific functions. Schlesinger and others acknowledged that Johnson and Nixon did not create the imperial presidency; they merely built on some of the questionable practices of their predecessors. But some observers contend there is a distinction between the abuse and the usurpation of power. Abraham Lincoln, Franklin Roosevelt, and Harry Truman temporarily usurped power in wartime. Johnson and Nixon abused power, deceiving Congress, misusing the Central Intelligence Agency, and manipulating public opinion and the electoral process.

Secrecy has often been used to protect and preserve a president's national security power. Nixon, it is said, pushed the doctrine beyond acceptable limits. Before Eisenhower, Congress expected to get the information it sought from the executive branch, and instances of secrecy and executive privilege were the rare exceptions. By the early 1970s, however, these practices had become more common. And a Congress that knows only what the president wants it to know is not an independent body.

After the 9/11 attack against the United States, President George W. Bush assumed expanded powers and circumvented the Congress in a variety of ways, including issuing executive orders as a way of establishing policies without the consent of Congress, claiming powers to intern U.S. citizens without charge or a trial and without access to a attorney, and expanding the use of secrecy in the executive branch. This led to charges of the imposition of a new imperial presidency; yet initially, the public was unmoved by such criticisms.[297]

Schlesinger's views are a useful point of departure for discussing the alleged too-powerful presidency. The chief complaints involve such presidential activities as war making, emergency powers, diplomacy by executive agreement, and government by veto.

PRESIDENTIAL WAR-MAKING POWERS BEFORE 1974

The Constitution delegates to Congress the authority to declare the legal state of war (with the consent of the president), but in practice the commander-in-chief often starts the fighting or initiates actions that lead to war. This power has been used by the chief executive time and again. In 1846, James K. Polk ordered American forces to advance into disputed territory. When Mexico resisted, Polk informed Congress that war existed by act of Mexico, and a formal declaration of war was soon forthcoming. William McKinley's dispatch of a battleship to Havana harbor, where it blew up, helped precipitate war with Spain in 1898. The United States was not formally at war with Germany until late 1941, but prior to the Japanese attack on Pearl Harbor, Franklin Roosevelt ordered the navy to guard convoys to Great Britain and to open fire on submarines threatening the convoys. Since World War II presidents have sent forces without specific congressional authorization to Korea, Berlin, Vietnam, Lebanon, Grenada, Cuba, Libya, Panama, Kuwait, and Haiti—in short, around the world.

From George Washington's time until today, the president, by ordering troops into battle, has often decided when Americans will fight and when they will not. When the cause has had political support, the president's use of this authority has been approved. Abraham Lincoln called up troops, spent money, set up a blockage, and fought the first few months of the Civil War without even calling Congress into session.

Congress was angered when it learned (several years after the fact) that in 1964 President Johnson won approval of his Vietnam initiatives on the basis of misleading information. Under Nixon in 1969 and 1970 a secret air war was waged in Cambodia with no formal congressional knowledge or authorization. The military also operated in Laos under Nixon without formally notifying Congress. It was to prevent just such acts as these that the framers of the Constitution had given Congress the power to declare war; and many members of Congress believed that what happened in Indochina in the 1960s and 1970s was the result of the White House's bypassing the constitutional requirements. They also agree, however, that the presidential excesses came about because Congress either agreed too readily with presidents or did little to stop them.

During hostilities, especially if the military action is not an all-out war with the nation's vital interests clearly at stake, such as World War II, the country and Congress typically rally behind a president. As casualties mount and fighting continues, support usually falls off. In both Korea and Vietnam, presidential failure to end the use of American ground forces led to increased political trouble.

The end of the war in Vietnam, the 1974 impeachment hearings, and the resignation of President Nixon gave Congress new life.[298] It set about to recover its lost authority and discover new ways to participate more fully in making national policy. We now examine Congress's more notable efforts to reassert itself.

THE CONTINUING DEBATE OVER WAR POWERS

The dispute over war powers arises because of some seemingly contradictory passages in the Constitution, which state that Congress has the power to declare war, that the executive power shall be vested in the president, and that the president shall be the commander-in-chief of the army and navy.

In 1973 Congress overrode Richard Nixon's presidential veto and enacted the War Powers Resolution, which declared that henceforth the president can commit the armed forces of the United States only (1) after a declaration of war by Congress; (2) by specific statutory authorization from Congress; or (3) in a national emergency created by an attack on the United States or its armed forces. After committing the armed forces under the third circumstance, the president is required to report to Congress within 48 hours. Unless Congress had declared war, the troop commitment must be ended within 60 days. The president is allowed another 30 days if the chief executive claims the safety of United States forces requires their continued use. A president is also obligated by this resolution to consult Congress "in every possible instance" before committing troops to battle. Moreover, at any time, by concurrent resolution not subject to presidential veto, Congress may direct the president to disengage such troops. A concurrent resolution is passed when both chambers of Congress wish to express the "sense" of their body on some question. Both houses must pass it in the same form. These resolutions are not sent to the president and do not have the force of law. Because of a 1983 court ruling, the question of whether Congress can remove the troops by concurrent resolution or legislative veto is now in doubt.

Few people were satisfied with the War Powers Resolution of 1973.[299] Nixon vetoed it because he said it encroached on presidential powers. Purists in Congress and elsewhere said it was clearly unconstitutional, yet cited reasons different from Nixon's. They said it gives away a constitutional power plainly belonging to Congress, namely, the war-making or war-declaring power, for up to 90 days.[300]

All recent presidents have opposed the War Powers Resolution as unwise and overly restrictive. They claim it gives Congress the right to force them to do what the Constitution says they do not have to do, withdraw American forces at some arbitrary moment. The War Powers Resolution has not really been tested in the courts because it raises political questions judges generally seek to avoid.

For the most part, presidents act as if the War Powers Resolution did not exist. Bill Clinton sent U.S. troops to Somalia, Haiti, and under NATO auspices, to Bosnia. In all cases, American soldiers were placed in danger of attack by adversaries. But President Clinton acted on his own, without direct congressional authorization, although Congress rather grudgingly did pass both supportive and restricting resolutions with respect to Clinton's sending troops on a Bosnian peacekeeping mission.

In 1999 a Republican-led House voted against President Clinton's use of U.S. forces in Kosovo. Again, however, while refusing to authorize the military mission, they did not cut off funding. Such mixed messages send both a partisan and an institutional message. The partisan message is that Republicans are willing to go after a Democratic commander-in-chief, even in the midst of military action. The institutional message is that Congress will, at times, attempt to assert its rights even when confronting a president over acts of war, but will go only so far.

In the early months of the war against terrorism, in 2001 and 2002, President George W. Bush acted unilaterally in a number of areas, including the arrest, without recourse to legal counsel, of U.S. citizens. The congressional response to such usurpations of power was meek. Further, Bush prosecuted the war in Afghanistan with little congressional oversight, and was able to initiate a United Nations resolution against Iraq with little congressional involvement. He claimed to have unilateral authority to invade Iraq, if events warranted it. Such claims, rather than reviving accusations of an imperial presidency, were mostly ignored in Congress.

Candidate Obama criticized the Bush Administration for their claims of independent authority to launch military attacks. Yet as President, Obama did not seriously consult with Congress nor did he seek supporting legislation or start the clock on the 60-day War Powers Resolution for the 2011 bombing of Libya.

Citing a United Nations Security Council resolution as authorization (which has no binding legal authority in the United States), the president argued that the military mission "is narrowly focused on saving lives." In June of 2011, the administration released a report, "Unites States Activities in Libya," arguing that as the air strikes "do not involve sustained fighting or active exchange of fire with hostile forces, nor do they involve the presence of U.S. ground troops...,"[301] the War Powers Resolution does not apply.

Blowback to Obama's bombing in Libya led to an odd coalition of House Democrats and Republicans bringing the legitimacy of the president's actions to a vote. On June 24, the House voted 295–123, with 70 Democrats voting with the majority, refusing to sanction the Libyan bombing missions. Shortly thereafter the House voted 238–180 *not* to cut out funding for the mission.

It was a stunning rebuke of a commander-in-chief in the middle of a military action. And while it was a largely symbolic act—had they truly been serious they would have cut funding—it did send a powerful message. Was this an empty gesture or a serious warning shot?

In 2007, the National War Powers Commissions, chaired by two former secretaries of state, James A. Baker and Warren Christopher, attempted to revisit the question of war powers in the United States. Their report, issued in 2008, called for the repeal of the War Powers Resolution of 1973, hoping to replace it with a proposed War Powers Consultation Act.

A proposed War Powers Consultation Act called for greater consultation between the president and Congress when armed conflict seemed likely, created a new Joint Congressional Consultation Committee to help streamline the process, and required Congress to vote up or down on war within a 30-day time period.

While well intentioned, this proposal was not a real solution. As one political scientist argues, "The proposal merely rearranges the deck chairs on a sinking ship."[302]

So what is to be done? Why not scrap the War Powers Resolution and go back to the framers' understanding of the war powers? Congress has the Constitutional authority to declare war. If a president wants to engage American forces in armed conflict he must, unless he is confronting a direct attack on the United States, go to the Congress and, in effect, ask for permission. Period.

What are the lessons of the War Powers Resolution of 1973? On one hand, Congress tried to reassert itself, and tried to get tough about unilateral presidential war making. On the other hand, presidents have mostly ignored the resolution and viewed it as a nuisance. In the 1990s many members of Congress recognized that the 1973 approach was not effective and perhaps not wise. Those who want to strengthen the resolution and force presidents to comply with it to the letter do not have the votes to get their colleagues to confront the White House. Many Republicans would prefer to scrap the resolution altogether, saying it has not worked and it is not proper for Congress to undermine a president who has to act fast in today's military emergencies, never mind what the Constitution may imply on the matter.[303]

Another group in Congress would like at some point to modify the War Powers Resolution to make it workable. They would have Congress establish a special consultative group of some eighteen congressional leaders who would meet with the president before decisions are made committing American troops to situations where hostilities are probable.

Constitutional and political questions will continue to surround the war-making powers as long as our constitutional democracy survives. The constitutional debate over the precise character of this power continues even as practical accommodations in our constitutional system evolve.[304]

CONFIRMATION POLITICS

The framers regarded the confirmation process and its advice and consent by the Senate as an important check on executive power. Alexander Hamilton viewed it as a way for Congress to prevent the appointment of "unfit characters."

Presidents have never enjoyed exclusive control over hiring and firing in the executive branch. The Constitution leaves the question somewhat ambiguous: "The President...shall nominate, and by and with the Advice and Consent of the Senate, shall appoint Ambassadors, other public Ministers and Consuls, Judges of the Supreme Court, all other officers of the United States." The Senate jealously guards its right to confirm or reject major appointments. During the period of congressional government after the Civil War, presidents had to struggle to keep their power to appoint and dismiss. Presidents in the twentieth century gained a reasonable amount of control over top appointments.[305]

Today the U.S. Senate and the president often struggle over control of top personnel in the executive and judicial branches. Time spent evaluating and screening presidential nominations has increased. Senators are especially concerned about potential conflicts of interest and about related character and integrity concerns.

President Clinton often watched in frustration after several of his nominees for attorney general, CIA director (Tony Lake in 1997), surgeon general, and judges and ambassadors withdrew after their nominations raised stiff opposition in the Senate. Presidents Bush and Obama registered similar frustrations.

The Senate's role in the confirmation process was never intended to eliminate politics but rather to use politics as a safeguard. Some senators in recent years object that the Senate has rejected occasional nominees because of their political beliefs and thus interfered with the executive power of presidents. In such instances, so this complaint goes, the Senate's decision is not a reflection of the fitness of a nominee but rather of the political strength of the president.

The Senate's participation in recent years has become more thorough and more independent. "Unfortunately, the process has also become more tedious, time-consuming, and intrusive for the nominees," according to one study. "For some, this price is too high, particularly in conjunction with the requirements of the Ethics in Government Act of 1978. For others, the process is annoying and distasteful but not enough of a roadblock to prevent them (nominees) from going forward."[306]

Because of the tradition called senatorial courtesy, a president is not likely to secure Senate approval for appointments against the objection of the senators from the state where the appointee is to work, especially if these senators are members of the president's party, even if his party does not control the Senate. Thus, for nearly all district court judgeships and a variety of other positions, senators can exercise what is in fact a veto. This veto can be overridden only with great difficulty. Further, it is usually exercised in secret and is subject to little accountability. But this form of patronage is sufficiently important to senators that senatorial courtesy is likely to continue.

There is a difference between judicial appointments, especially those to the Supreme Court, and administration appointments.[307] The Senate plays a greater role in judicial appointments because of both the life terms judges and justices serve and the fact they constitute an independent and, as we discuss in the chapter 9, vital branch of the government.[308] There is, as noted, an argument that when it comes to cabinet-level positions in the executive branch, a president ought to be able to choose those who share the president's views and will carry out the general views of the White House. In contrast, a president is not expected to have or to enjoy partisan loyalty from those nominated to the bench. Thus Presidents George H. W. Bush and Reagan had more difficulty in winning confirmation for their nominations to the Supreme Court than they had with their cabinet nominations.[309]

The confirmation provisions in the Constitution have fulfilled most of the intentions of the framers. The Senate has been able to use its power to reject unqualified nominees. It has sometimes also been able to prevent those with conflicts of interest from taking office. In addition, senators have been able to use the confirmation process to make their views known to prospective executive officials. Indeed, the very existence of the confirmation process generally deters presidents from appointing weak, questionable, or "unfit characters." Yet, by and large, presidents have still been able to appoint the people they want to important positions.[310]

FUSING WHAT THE FRAMERS SEPARATED

A few reformers believe relations between the president and Congress are so bad that what we have is a "constitutional disorder"[311] and only major reforms can right the wrongs that the framers inflicted on us. The "wrong" in this case is said to be the separation of powers, which fragments and shares political power between the different branches. These commentators see the separation as a weakness that often leads to divided governments, which brings about divisive politics, which ends up in deadlock.

This separation is a structural problem, and the cure is the *fusion* of executive and legislative power. The model is British parliamentary democracy.[312] In *Constitutional Reform and Effective Government*, James L. Sundquist offers a parliamentary critique of American government.

Failed government is the problem for which Sundquist suggests the U.S. system has no real cure. What happens "when a president fails as a leader?": a stalemate. But would a system organized along more parliamentary lines solve this problem? Sundquist believes there is much we can learn from the Canadian and British parliamentary systems, yet warns against wholesale grafting of the parliamentary model onto the U.S. system. He writes that "for most constitutional reformers the parliamentary system represents only a source of ideas for incremental steps that might bring more unity to the American government, each step to be considered on its own merits in terms of its adaptability to American tradition and institutions. Parliamentary democracy is not a model to be adopted in its entirety, supplementing the entire U.S. constitutional structure with something new and alien."[313]

In an effort to promote greater collaboration between the branches, Sundquist offers several proposals, all designed to modify the separation of powers. Among these are such ideas as allowing members of Congress to serve in the president's cabinet, giving cabinet officers a place in the Congress, and, most important of all, strengthening political parties. He notes, "Whatever can be done to strengthen political party organizations will serve to improve cohesion between the executive branch and the President's party in the Congress. The party is still the web that infuses the organs of government with a sense of common purpose."[314] But in the long run, Sundquist laments "proposals for formal institutional linkages between the branches...hold little promise."[315]

James MacGregor Burns, in another provocative study, *The Power to Lead*, takes a similar reformist approach, examining the symptom of failed government and prescribing the cure of a parliamentary alternative. Burns, like Sundquist, sees anti-leadership tendencies intentionally built into the Constitution, and this leads to either deadlock or the overpersonalization of politics.[316]

Mainstream political scientists disagree with the prescriptions put forward by Sundquist and Burns. They say that a president who enjoys both a working majority in Congress and a strong party might be too free to impose his or her own program on the nation. And if the Twenty-Second Amendment were voided, this vigorous president might, over time, be able to dominate the judicial branch as well. Critics also say their schemes are designed almost entirely to strengthen the White House and weaken Congress.

Defenders of our presidential system say it generally serves us well. It is a system, they say, that reflects the cautious temperament of the American people. The vitality of the system depends on new ideas and new people, not on importing parliamentary features. In parliamentary systems the parties are so tightly organized that they often become rigid. The American system was intended to have tension in it. It sometimes swings a bit too far in one or another direction, yet it generally works. It is, moreover, especially well designed to protect the liberties of individuals and minorities and it has succeeded in preventing authoritarianism.

Finally, opponents of the Sundquist–Burns proposals say the principle of separation of power is no less valid today than it was in 1787. The national legislature was designed to prevent tyranny of any one leader and tyranny of the majority. Yes the system is often slow and cautious and hostile to bold leadership initiatives. Yet isn't this appropriate to its responsibilities and primary function? Most Americans, want a certain amount of deadlock and delay on policy initiatives that emerge out of presidential or party brainstorming. The genius of the American Congress, then and now, is its capacity for deliberation, debate, and prudent reflection.

THE CONTINUING STRUGGLE

Congress has not won back much of its allegedly lost powers, and most observers are skeptical of Congress's ability to match the president's advantages in setting the nation's long-term policy direction over the long run. Ronald Reagan demonstrated that a popular president who knew what he wanted could influence the national policy agenda and also win considerable cooperation from the Congress. George W. Bush and his father demonstrated that a president could win public and congressional support for foreign policy and military initiatives, even with Congress controlled by the opposition party.

The American public may be skeptical and critical about its political leaders, yet it has not really lost its belief that presidents matter. Most Americans want presidents to be effective, especially in international and economic leadership. Whether or not people believed in Ronald Reagan's policy priorities, many supported his view that the country needed a strong president who would strengthen the presidency and make the office a more vital center of national policy than it had been in the years immediately following the Watergate scandals. Whether people were critical of Clinton's character or not, Americans generally recognized his leadership efforts to encourage trade, promote new jobs, and advance the cause of civil rights and environmental protection.

A central question during the 1970s was whether, in the wake of a somewhat diminished presidency, Congress could furnish the necessary leadership to govern the country. Most people, including many members of Congress, did not think Congress could play that role. The routine answer in the twenty-first century is that the United States needs a presidency of substantial power if we are to solve the financial, trade, deficit, productivity, and other economic and national security problems. We live in a continuous state of severe challenges, if not emergencies. Terrorism or nuclear warfare could destroy our country. Global competition of almost every sort highlights the need for swift leadership and a certain amount of efficiency in government. Many people realize, too, that weakening the presidency may, as often as not, strengthen the vast federal bureaucracy and its influence over how programs are implemented more than it would strengthen Congress.

Congress is simply not structured for sustained leadership and direction. Power in Congress is too fragmented and dispersed. Congress can, on occasion, provide leadership on various issues, yet it is far less able to adapt to changing demands and national or international crises that arise than is the presidency. The presidency is a more fluid institution and thereby can usually more quickly adjust and adapt.

Congress's efforts to reassert itself were more a groping and often unsystematic, if well-intentioned, attempt to be taken seriously than a concerted effort to weaken the presidency. It did not take long for observers to appreciate that when a president is unable to exercise authority and leadership, no one else can usually supply comparable initiative. Not only did we reaffirm the pre-Watergate view that the presidency is usually an effective instrument for innovation, experimentation, and progress, but a majority of Americans concurred that to the extent the country is governable on a national basis, it must be governed from the White House by a president and top advisers who can figure out a way to gain the cooperation of various coalitions.

FOR DISCUSSION

1. Who should decide when the United States goes to war? Have things changed so much since 1787 that presidents should have this power? Or should Congress still have this crucial responsibility? If so, is Congress prepared to execute this responsibility?

2. Because of congressional delays and roadblocks presidents have increasingly resorted to using executive orders, signing statements, and other forms of unilateral authority. Is this good? Is this inevitable?

DEBATE QUESTIONS

1. We should amend the Constitution to provide for an item-veto authority for presidents.
2. That Congress has ceded and delegated too much of its constitutional authority to the executive branch and must reclaim its lost or stolen powers.

FURTHER READINGS

Beckmann, Matthew N. *Pushing the Agenda: Presidential Leadership in U.S. Lawmaking, 1953–2004.* New York: Cambridge, 2010.

Cameron, Charles M. *Veto Bargaining: Presidents and the Politics of Negative Power.* New York: Cambridge University Press, 2000.

Canes-Wrone, Brandice. *Who Leads Whom? Presidents, Policy, and the Public.* Chicago: University of Chicago Press, 2006.

Howell, William G., and Jon C. Pevehouse. *While Dangers Gather: Congressional Checks on Presidential War Powers.* Princeton, NJ: Princeton University Press, 2007.

Krehbiel, Keith. *Pivotal Politics: A Theory of U.S. Lawmaking.* Chicago: University of Chicago Press, 1998.

Mann, Thomas E., and Norman J. Ornstein, *It's Even Worse Than It Looks: How the American Constitutional System Collided With the New Politics of Extremism.* New York: Basic Books, 2012.

Mayhew, David. *Divided We Govern.* New Haven, CT: Yale University Press, 1991.

Rudalevige, Andrew. *Managing the President's Program: Presidential Leadership and Legislative Policy Formulation.* Princeton, NJ: Princeton University Press, 2002.

Critical Thinking

STATEMENT: The rise in presidential power can be attributed to a failure of Congress to defend its institutional powers.

PROBLEM: What are the causes of the rise of presidential power from 1787 to today? What role has Congress played? And if Congress is to blame, how might we get Congress to better perform its check and balance duties?

CHAPTER 7

Presidents as Chief Executives: Challenges and Resources

> Many of the embarrassing blunders that have done the most damage to
> recent presidencies were not the result of external "enemies" sabotag-
> ing the president but resulted from the actions of loyal subordinates
> in the White House.... [Presidents] should be aware of the major ele-
> ments of administration proposals, they should make major staff deci-
> sions, and they should be aware of what their immediate staff aides are
> doing in their names.
>
> JAMES P. PFIFFNER, ed., *The Managerial Presidency,* 2nd ed. (College
> Station: Texas A & M University Press, 1991), p. 7

The U.S. Constitution put the president in charge of the day-to-day operation of the federal departments and agencies. Article II, Section I opens with "The executive power shall be vested in a President of the United States of America." The Constitution further gives the president the power to require the opinion of the principle office in the departments "upon any subject relating to the duties of their respective offices." Presidents are also charged "to take care that the laws be faithfully executed." Being put-in-charge, however, is a far cry from making the executive branch work efficiently and effectively.

In the beginning presidents didn't have much administrative help. Newly elected President George Washington for a while had just one aide, his nephew, who Washington paid for out of his own pocket. Today a president has a White House staff of 400 to 500, 15 cabinet secretaries with nearly as many advisers with cabinet status, thousands of Executive Office of the President staffers, and few million others scattered in the civilian and military services of the executive branch.

But every president learns that though they may be atop this now sprawling executive branch they are not always in charge of everything. Hurricanes, oil spills, terrorist attacks, and the like can occur without warning. Moreover, some agencies and officials seem to have plans or even policies and priorities of their own. President John Kennedy, for example, was inadequately informed about the "Bay of Pigs" CIA operation that imploded on him in his early months at the White House—which he eventually had to halt and take the responsibility for its failure. Other presidents apparently neither knew about nor supported prisoner abuse scandals that happened on their watch. A few presidents have had to fire military commanders for actions in conflict with White House priorities.

"The plain fact is" writes public management scholar Peri E. Arnold, "that no modern president has fully managed the executive branch."[317] Most presidents are indifferent as managers. Some, like Harry Truman or Barack Obama, had little executive experience. Presidents also lack the time to become full time executives-in-chief.

We recruit politicians, not managerial wizards. Moreover, presidents with so many competing responsibilities in national security and in dealing with Congress are reluctant to expend much of their personal capital on administrative matters.

Sometimes presidents lack the skill to manage effectively. Yet inattention to matters of personnel and implementation cause considerable problems. Indeed, many of the mistakes or blunders of recent presidencies can be traced to lack of attention to the administrative responsibilities that are critically important to a successful presidency.[318]

This chapter will examine how both the cabinet and an extensive administrative presidency consisting of an Executive Office of the President have developed to help presidents become better managers. We treat both the frustrations presidents face and the various strategies or tools presidents try to use to influence executive branch performance.

The paradox of the presidency–executive branch relations is that presidents are thought to be atop and "in charge" of the federal bureaucracy. But, in practice, a president sometimes finds bureaucratic resistance, gets in conflict with an occasional cabinet member, and must regularly contend with congressional and interest group lobbying within the scores of federal agencies. Then, too, some civilian and military federal employees have their own ideological views to the right or the left of a particular White House. Further, federal employees, as we will discuss, often feel more of an allegiance to the Congress and to the law, as they perceive it, than to the wishes of a president or White House aides. In short, presidents have to work very hard to lead, inspire, manage, and regularly negotiate with countless members of their own branch of government.

An Executive Office of the President is the institutional home for the White House staff and about two dozen agencies and staff established to help presidents coordinate with the cabinet and the operation of the executive branch.

Let's first examine the long and often complex political history of presidents and their cabinets.

TABLE 7.1

The Institutional Presidency

President

The Cabinet

State
Treasury
Defense
Justice
Health and Human Services
Labor
Commerce
Transportation
Energy
Housing and Urban Development
Veterans Affairs
Agriculture
Interior
Education
Homeland Security

Others with Cabinet Rank

U.N. Ambassador
CIA Director
Environmental Protection Agency Administrator
Director, Office of Management and Budget
U.S. Trade Representative
Chair, Council of Economic Advisors

White House Staff

Chief of Staff
Press Secretary
Legislative Affairs
Political Affairs
Public Liaison
Communications Director
White House Counsel
Intergovernmental Affairs
Policy Planning and Development
Cabinet Liaison
Domestic and Economic Affairs
Science and Technology Policy
National Security Affairs

Executive Office of the President

Council of Economic Advisers
Office of Management and Budget
Office of National Drug Control Policy
United States Trade Representative
Council on Environmental Quality
National Security Council
Domestic Policy Council
National Economic Council
Office of Administration
Office of Science and Technology Policy
President's Foreign Intelligence Advisory Board
Privacy and Civil Liberties Oversight Board
White House Military Office
Office of the First Lady
White House Office of Health Reform

PRESIDENTS AND THE CABINET

The presidential cabinet in America is a misunderstood political institution. This is in part because the cabinet in some parliamentary systems has more influence as a policymaking group. This is not the case in the United States.

The American cabinet is too big and too diverse a group to function effectively in policymaking. Some cabinet members are appointed as much for their representativeness as for their policy or managerial expertise. Then, too, there is usually a lot of turnover in the cabinet, so much so that cabinet secretaries rarely form a cohesive policymaking team.[319] George W. Bush, for example, had only one of his cabinet members stay for his full two terms. He had three Attorneys General, and three Secretaries of Treasury, Agriculture, HUD, and Veterans Affairs. Cabinet members serve mainly as presidential emissaries to a department and as policy advisers to the president singly or occasionally as part of a selective team, for example, as a member of the national security or economic policy team.

President Jimmy Carter, an engineer and more of a manager than most presidents, acknowledged that he used his cabinet less and less as his four years wore on. "After a few months, the cabinet meetings became less necessary," Carter wrote. "As a result, in the first year we had thirty-six sessions with the full cabinet, then, during the three succeeding years, twenty-three, nine and six such meetings respectively."[320]

Most recent presidents have held fewer cabinet meetings the longer they were in office. President Obama infrequently met with his cabinet.

The framers discussed at length the possibility of creating some form of executive council that would comprise the president, heads of the departments, and the chief justice of the Supreme Court, yet decided to leave things flexible. Indeed, the

The president is one person but the presidency is an institution. Here President Obama addresses his Cabinet. AP Photo/Susan Walsh.

U.S. Constitution makes no provision for a cabinet. It merely states there are to be principal offices of the executive departments. The first Congress passed statutes that provided for the creation of three departments: State, War, and Treasury. An attorney general was also authorized, yet this would be a part-time adviser, not the head of a department.

From the outset President George Washington regarded his officers as assistants and advisers. "He began the practice of assembling his principal officers in council. And this practice became in the course of time a settled custom. The simple truth is, however, that the cabinet is a customary, not a statutory body."[321] The term *cabinet* was probably first used in 1793, but mention of it in statutory language did not occur until 1907.

President Andrew Jackson did not even convene his cabinet as a group during his first two years in office, often relying instead on a "kitchen cabinet" of staffers and newspaper friends. President James Polk held at least 350 cabinet sessions during his four years. Lyndon Johnson told his cabinet secretary that the thing that bothered him most about cabinet meetings was they were so dull; he said, "I just don't want them falling asleep at the damned [cabinet] table."[322]

SELECTING CABINET ADVISERS

Few acts of presidential leadership are as important as the appointment of cabinet members and senior advisers. Presidents are thought to have a free hand in choosing their cabinet members, yet this is not exactly the way it works. In addition to administrative competence and experience, loyalty and collegiality are basic considerations in selections. Other factors are at work as well. Party rivals often have to be placated either with an appointment to the cabinet or selection as the vice presidential running mate.

Regional, ethnic, gender, and geographical considerations are almost always important. Thus the Agriculture post is traditionally given to a Midwesterner, and the Secretary of the Interior is almost always a Westerner. After capturing the presidency, a president usually goes about selecting the cabinet in such a way as to try to win the confidence of major sections and sectors of the nation.

Each cabinet member of the now 15 official cabinet departments has to be confirmed by a majority in the U.S. Senate. Nominees are examined carefully at both ends of Pennsylvania Avenue and by interest groups and the media. This precludes those who will not submit to this process. Some are unwilling to sacrifice their privacy and much higher salaries. Still others sometimes pose conditions under which they would accept nomination, and the conditions are not acceptable to the president. Others are put off by the conflict-of-interest regulations and the Ethics in Government Act and the lengthy vetting process that recent presidents such as Obama have insisted on.[323]

It has also become harder to attract many talented individuals to cabinet-level positions due to the media culture of "gotcha" politics in Washington, DC. Both recent and past mistakes get spotlight attention, and top administrative appointees are attractive targets.

A president has to select certain cabinet officers because of the needed expertise they will bring to the administration and the policy needs of certain departments. Typically, for example, the secretary of defense is someone who has worked closely with that department in some previous capacity. A treasury secretary is traditionally viewed as, at least in part, the financial community's representative in the cabinet. In selecting a treasury secretary a president-elect usually wants someone who can simultaneously serve as a "spokesperson" to the financial world and as a "spokesperson" for those interests.

Generalists are often appointed to head up some of the domestic departments such as commerce, transportation, and HUD, while politicians especially close to clientele groups are often appointed head of agriculture and interior.

Cabinet picking invariably entails guesswork. It's about future performance. "You try to improve your odds," says former presidential adviser Stephen Hess. "You ask people you respect and trust to propose names or comment on candidates, you interview finalists and ask the right questions, you turn to experienced vetters to review the file."[324] Yet most presidents become aware after a while that some of their cabinet choices as well as some of their top White House aides were a mistake. Jimmy Carter and George W. Bush both wound up firing at least a handful of their cabinet members. Obama nudged out several aides.

President Clinton's first labor secretary, Robert B. Reich, shared this view about staffing a new administration:

> No other democracy does it this way. No private corporation would think of operating like this. Every time a new president is elected, America assembles a new government of 3,000 or so amateurs who only sometimes know the policies they're about to administer, rarely have experience managing large government bureaucracies, and almost never know the particular piece of it they're going to run. These people are appointed quickly by a president-elect who is thoroughly exhausted from a year and a half of campaigning. And they remain in office, on average, under two years—barely enough time to find the nearest bathroom. It's a miracle we don't screw it up worse than we do.[325]

THE JOB OF A CABINET MEMBER

Defining the job of a cabinet member depends on one's vantage point. Members of Congress believe a cabinet officer should communicate often and well with Congress and be responsive to legislators' requests. Reporters want a cabinet officer to be accessible, to make news; they applaud style and flair as well as substance. Interest groups want a cabinet member who can speak out for their interests and carry their messages to the White House and Congress. Civil servants in a department are generally looking for a cabinet leader who will boost departmental morale and appropriations. White House aides are concerned about a cabinet officer's loyalty to the president in addition to their ability. Presidents want a cabinet member who will conserve their freedom of action and enhance their administration's reputation without embarrassing or overshadowing them.[326]

There is little or no training for new cabinet secretaries. They are thrown into the fire and expected to serve many masters. Robert Reich noted the feelings of isolation of a new secretary when he wrote, "I'm on my own from here on. There's no training manual, no course, no test drive for a cabinet secretary. I'll have to follow my instincts, and rely on whomever I can find to depend on along the way. I'll have to listen carefully and watch out for dangers. But mostly I'll have to stay honest with myself and keep perspective. Avoid grandiosity. This is a glamorous temp job."[327]

Presidents and senior White House aides expect cabinet officers and related agency heads to creatively manage their bureaucracies and to be responsive yet not overly responsive to their departments' natural client interest groups. White House staffers are well aware of the "iron triangles" that form enduring issue networks involving outside interest groups, likeminded members of Congress and their staffs, and veteran career federal employees. These networks are well known as being able to block presidential priorities or to merely promote their own alternative public policy initiatives. These triangular interests preexist every new presidential administration and, in most instances, they will be there when that administration retires.

Presidents and their aides repeatedly say the last thing they want to see is a cabinet member who has become a special pleader at the White House for some of the special-interest groups. "The cabinet officer must certainly be attentive to his departmental business, and he should seek to ensure that the president has timely notice of the impact of policies on his department's specific interests," a former White House aide writes. "But a Secretary should never choose his departmental interest as against the wider interest of the Presidency."[328]

The greatest test of cabinet members arises from the fact that they become tied almost as closely to Congress as they are to a president. Indeed, cabinet officers are legally obligated to obey Congress and the courts as well as the president—even though the various branches may hold contradictory views. In the perpetual tug-of-war between the branches, the cabinet officer is often like the knot in the rope. "His or her appointment is subject to Senate confirmation. Every power a cabinet officer exercises is derived from some Act of Congress; every penny he or she expends must be appropriated by the Congress; every new statutory change the cabinet officer desires must be submitted to the Congress and defended there," writes Bradley Patterson. "A cabinet officer's every act is subject to oversight by one or more regular or special congressional committees, much of his or her time is accordingly spent at the Capitol and, with few exceptions, most of the documents in his or her whole department are subject to being produced at congressional request."[329]

When a president makes a decision a cabinet officer is expected to carry it out. In fact, however, it is inevitable that after a person has been in the cabinet for a time and has become enmeshed in the activities and interests of a department, he or she develops certain independent policy views. A certain hardening of view may set in as the cabinet secretary gets pushed by subordinates, interest-group leaders, or others in a direction that makes it likely that he or she will at least occasionally come into conflict with the president. When this happens, the White House typically complains that the cabinet member has "gone native"—he or she has been captured by the interests native to that department. Often, the cabinet officer wants to extract more money out of the president's budget for the department. A budget director once complained, "cabinet members are vice presidents in charge of spending, and as such they are the natural enemies of the presidents."[330]

THE WEST WING WANTS LOYALTY
ALONG WITH COMPETENCE

Firing cabinet members is the last thing presidents like to do. When it is done it is usually only after it is "overdue." And they do it at the risk of political backlash. President Andrew Johnson's removal of Secretary of War Stanton contributed to Johnson's impeachment. President Nixon's removal of special prosecutor Archibald Cox and the related resignations of Attorney General Elliot Richardson and Deputy Attorney General William Ruckelshaus badly damaged what remained of Nixon's credibility. Ronald Reagan fired Secretary of State Alexander Haig, White House Chief of Staff Donald Regan, and Secretary of Health and Human Services Margaret Heckler and encouraged some others, such as Labor Secretary Raymond Donovan, to resign.

Nixon fired Interior Secretary Walter Hickel after a celebrated "personal letter" from Hickel to the president was leaked to the press. Hickel was especially frustrated because he only saw the president once or twice for policy discussions. His letter included these pointed sentences: "Permit me to suggest that you consider meeting, on an individual and conversational basis, with members of your cabinet. Perhaps," continued Hickel, "through such conversations we can gain greater insight into the problems confronting us all, and most important, into solutions of these problems."[331] Hickel's resignation was soon arranged.

From the perspective of the West Wing, these are the questions asked about cabinet members: Have they managed the department well? Do they recruit talented officials to the department? Are they loyal to the president? Can they "handle" the interest groups associated with that department? Have they brought prestige to the department and to the administration? Have they come up with fresh and innovative ideas? Have they been able to implement the administration's programs in their department? This is a lot to ask, and it explains why White House–cabinet relations can often lead to so much frustration.

THE ROLE OF THE CABINET IN POLICYMAKING

A romantic view of the mythical American cabinet is encouraged in part by presidents themselves. Reagan, Clinton, and Obama all emphasized the importance of the cabinet when they picked their original teams. Reagan, early in 1981, told his cabinet nominees that he intended the cabinet to function much like a board of directors in a corporation, the president deliberating with them and seeking their input prior to decisions.

A consistent pattern seems to characterize president–cabinet relations over time. Just as a president enjoys a distinctive honeymoon with the press and partisan officeholders, White House–cabinet ties are usually the most cooperative during the first year of an administration. A newly staffed executive branch, busily recasting the political agenda, seems to bubble over with new possibilities, proposals, ideas, and imminent breakthroughs. Ironically, White House staff, who soon will outstrip most of the cabinet in power and influence, receive somewhat less publicity at this time. In the immediate postinaugural months, the Washington political community, and the executive branch in particular, becomes a merry-go-round of cheerful open doors for the new team of cabinet leaders.

But this ends soon. Little over a year in office, Reagan's White House aides developed a distrust for many of their departmental secretaries, saying they had generally become advocates of their own constituencies. "Cabinet government is a myth," said a Reagan staffer. "I'm not sure it has dawned on the [cabinet] members yet that they have been cut out of the decision making process."[332] Obama cabinet and agency heads complained the president and his staff quickly became isolated and developed a hard to penetrate "fortress." Some cabinet people blamed the brilliant yet domineering Rahm Emanuel, Obama's initial chief of staff. According to many sources, Emanuel thought the cabinet was useless, didn't involve many of them, and mainly called them to complain when things went wrong. He was replaced by Bill Daley, who had been a Secretary of Commerce under Bill Clinton. One of Daley's top assignments from Obama was to repair White House-cabinet relations, but Daley left less than a year later.[333]

Domestic crises and critical international developments begin to monopolize the presidential schedule. As a president has less time for personal contacts, cabinet members become disinclined to exhaust their personal political credit with him. A president's program becomes fixed as priorities are set, and budget ceilings produce some new rules of the game. Ambitious, expansionist cabinet officers become painfully familiar with various refrains from executive office staff, usually to the effect that there just isn't any more money available for programs of that magnitude; or that budget projections for the next few years require more spending cuts; and, perhaps harshest of all, that a proposal is excellent but will just have to wait.

A top White House staffer under Nixon aptly captures the complex entanglements of time, presidential priorities, and interactions of people:

> Everything depends on what you do in program formulation during the first six or seven months. I have watched three presidencies and I am increasingly convinced of that. Time goes by so fast. During the first six months or so, the White House staff is not hated by the cabinet, there is a period of friendship and cooperation and excitement. There is some animal energy going for you in those first six to eight months, especially if people perceive things in the same light. If that exists and so long as that exists you can get a lot done. You only have a year at the

most for new initiatives, a time when you can establish some programs as your own, in contrast to what has gone on before. After that, after priorities are set, and after a president finds he doesn't have time to talk with cabinet members, that's when the problems set in, and the White House aides close off access to cabinet members and others.[334]

After the first year or so, presidents become increasingly concerned with leaks from their administration. They worry about saying things or having key decisions made in large groups. They also, in President Carter's words, believe their time is "too precious to waste on many bull sessions among those who have little to contribute...."[335] So what do they do? They begin to hold fewer cabinet meetings and hold smaller sessions with the inner cabinet and with their own White House inner circle.

President Kennedy, who regarded the idea of the cabinet as a collective consultative body largely as an anachronism, once asked: "Just what the hell good does the cabinet do, anyway?" The nature of a problem, he thought, should determine the group with which he met.

In short, presidents have found it neither comfortable nor efficient to meet frequently with their cabinets as a whole. When they have, it seems to have been as much for purposes of theater, symbolic reassurance, or appearance of activity as for substantive debate or learning.

Why are more spirited and substantive discussions absent from the modern-day cabinet? The number of people attending cabinet sessions is too large. Recent presidents have often had nearly thirty people crowded in their cabinet meetings—this includes the president, vice president, the fifteen regular cabinet members, and a dozen key advisers like CIA director, UN ambassador, and top budget, economic, and political advisers. Most cabinet members are unlikely to talk about their troubles or highly sensitive topics in a group that large. Thus both presidents and cabinet members become disillusioned with government by cabinet meeting. But the alternatives cause problems, too. "Of course, if you don't have cabinet government, you have government by a White House staff that has not been confirmed by the Senate," says former Attorney General Griffin Bell. "So you lose one of the checks and balances in our system."[336]

One of the president's dilemmas is that a fundamental separation of policy formulation and its implementation often develops. Whereas most major policy decisions are made by the president and a smaller number of personal aides, responsibility for enacting these programs rests, for the most part, with the cabinet officers and their departments. The gap between these two functions of the executive branch has been widening, a result of the transference of power from the somewhat more public institution of the cabinet to the relatively hidden offices of the White House staff.

The very character of the cabinet—a body with no constitutional standing, members with no independent political base of their own and no requirement that the president seek or follow their advice—helps contribute to its lack of influence as a collective body. Ultimately, the influence of the cabinet rests entirely on the role a president desires for it. Recent presidents have made that role a limited one.

A CABINET OF UNEQUALS

Cabinet roles and influence with the White House differ markedly according to personalities, the department, and the times. Each cabinet usually has one or two members who become the dominant personalities. Herbert Hoover's performance as secretary of commerce under Harding and Coolidge was of this type. Robert McNamara enjoyed especially close ties with both Kennedy and Johnson. And James Baker, George Shultz, and Edwin Meese all carried special weight with Ronald Reagan. Donald Rumsfeld and Dick Cheney became the major players in the George W. Bush administration, at least for the first six years. Hillary Clinton, Bob Gates and Treasury Secretary Geithner served these inner cabinet roles for Obama.

Certain departments and their cabinet officers have gained prominence in recent decades because every president has been deeply involved with their priorities and missions—Defense and State in the Cold War as well as in the war on terrorism, for example. Other departments may become important temporarily in the president's eyes, sometimes because of a prominent cabinet secretary who

TABLE 7.2 Ways of Looking at the Traditional Executive Departments

Seniority	Expenditures	Personnel	Inner & Outer Cabinet
1. State	1. Defense	1. Defense	*Inner:*
2. Treasury	2. Treasury	2. Veterans' Affairs	1. State
3. War/Defense	3. HHS	3. Homeland Security	2. Defense
4. Interior	4. Agriculture	4. Justice	3. Treasury
5. Justice	5. Veteran's Affairs	5. Treasury	4. Justice*
6. Agriculture	6. Labor	6. Agriculture	*Outer:*
7. Commerce	7. Transportation	7. Interior	5. Agriculture
8. Labor	8. Education	8. HHS	6. Interior
9. HHS[†]	9. HUD	9. Transportation	7. Transportation
10. HUD[‡]	10. Energy	10. Commerce	8. HHS
11. Transportation	11. Homeland Security	11. Labor	9. HUD
12. Energy	12. Justice	12. Energy	10. Labor
13. Education	13. Interior	13. State	11. Commerce
14. Veterans' Affairs	14. State	14. HUD	12. Energy
15. Homeland Security	15. Commerce	15. Education	13. Education
			14. Veteran's Affairs
			15. Homeland Security

Source: www.whitehouse.gov/omb/budget/fy2012 and Statistical Abstract of the United States, 2012.
Note: Some expenditures, such as for wars, are not easily traced to certain departmental outlays.
*Sometimes inner, sometimes outer: "Inner" and "Outer" cabinet is our classification done according to the counseling-advocacy departments and based on our research interviews.
[†]HHS, Health and Human Services.
[‡]HUD, Housing and Urban Development.

is working in an area in which the president wants to effect breakthroughs: for example, John Kennedy's Justice Department headed by his brother Robert. The Treasury Department has become a central player in exacting economic times, such as the Bush and Obama eras.

Vast differences exist in the scope and importance of cabinet-level departments. The huge Defense Department and the smaller departments of Labor, Housing and Urban Development, and Education are not at all similar. Certain agencies not of cabinet rank—the Central Intelligence Agency, for example—may be more important, especially in a post-9/11 world, than certain cabinet-level departments. Conventional rankings of the departments are based on their longevity, annual expenditures, and number of personnel. Rankings according to these indicators can be seen in the first three columns of Table 7.2. Even a casual comparison of these columns reveals unexpected characteristics. Thus, although the State Department is over two hundred years older than some of the newer departments, its expenditures are among the lowest. On the other hand, the much younger Department of Human Services, ranks rather high in expenditures.

The contemporary cabinet can be differentiated also into "inner" and "outer" cabinets, as shown in the fourth column in Table 7.2. This classification, derived from interviews, indicates how White House aides and cabinet officers view the departments and their access to the president. The occupants of the inner cabinet generally have maintained a role as counselor to the president; the departments all include broad-ranging, multiple interests. The explicitly domestic policy departments, with the exception of Justice, comprise the outer cabinet. By custom, if not by designation, many of these cabinet officers assume a relatively straightforward advocacy orientation that overshadows their counseling role.

THE INNER CABINET

A pattern in recent administrations suggests strongly that the inner, or counseling, cabinet positions are vested with high-priority responsibilities that usually bring their occupants into collaborative relationships with presidents and their top staff. Certain White House staff counselors also have been included in the inner cabinet with increasing frequency. The secretary of defense was one of the most prominent cabinet officers during recent administrations, for each president recognized the centrality of national security issues. The defense budget and DOD priorities makes it imperative for presidents to work closely with defense and top military chiefs. Despite the inclination of some presidents to serve as "their own secretary of state," the top people at the Department of State have nevertheless had a direct and continuous relationship with contemporary presidents. Recent treasury secretaries also have played impressive roles in presidential deliberations on financial, business, and economic policy. The position of attorney general often, though not always, has been influential as well.

The Inner Cabinet, as discussed here, corresponds to George Washington's original foursome. The status accorded these cabinet roles is, of course, subject to ebb and flow, for the status is rooted in a cabinet officer's performance and relationship with the president as well as in the crises and the fashions of the day.

Members of the so-called Inner Cabinet as well as trusted confidential aides to a president may enjoy access and proximity, yet these don't guarantee job security. Take the George W. Bush presidency as an example. Over time, Bush, in effect, fired Secretary of Treasury Paul O'Neill, Secretary of State Colin Powell, Secretary of Defense Donald Rumsfeld, Attorney General Alberto Gonzales, and CIA Director George Tenet. This may tell us more about Bush than these officials, yet it highlights the temporary nature of even presidential Inner-Cabinet relationships.[337]

A NATIONAL SECURITY CABINET

The seemingly endless series of international crises—Indochina, Central America, South Africa, the Middle East, Bosnia, Afghanistan, Pakistan, and Iraq; and the tensions with the Russia, North Korea, and Iran—have made it mandatory for recent presidents to maintain close relations with the two national security cabinet heads. Just as George Washington met almost every day with his four cabinet members during the French crisis of 1793, so also have all of our recent presidents been likely to meet at least weekly and be in daily telephone communication with their inner cabinet of national security advisers.

Throughout recent administrations, presidents and their staffs have complained about the operational lethargy of the State Department. Although the secretary of state is customarily considered by the White House to be a member of the president's inner cabinet, the department itself is often regarded as difficult to deal with. White House staffers invariably cite the State Department to illustrate White House–department conflicts. They scorn the narrowness and timidity of the foreign service and complain of the custodial conservatism reflected in State Department working papers. In State, more than in the other departments, the method and style of personnel, the special selection and promotion processes, and the protocol consciousness all seem farther removed from the political thinking at the White House. State Department personnel invariably become stereotyped by White House aides as preoccupied, cautious, and traditional.

ATTORNEYS GENERAL

The Justice Department is often identified as a counseling department, and its chiefs usually are associated with the inner circle of presidential advisers. That Kennedy appointed his brother, Nixon appointed his trusted campaign manager and law partner, Carter appointed a personal friend, and Reagan appointed his personal attorney and later one of his campaign managers to be attorneys general indicates the importance of this position, although extensive politicization of the department has a long history. The Justice Department traditionally serves as the president's attorney and law office, a special obligation that brings about continuous and close relations between White House domestic policy lawyers and Justice Department lawyers. The White House depends heavily and constantly on the department's lawyers for counsel on civil-rights developments, presidential veto procedures, tax prosecutions, antitrust controversies, routine presidential pardons, the overseeing of regulatory agencies, and separation-of-power questions. It's Office of Legal Counsel has close ties to the White House.

Obama appointed a former Bill Clinton Justice Department Official, Eric Holder, as his Attorney General. Holder had been a campaign adviser to Obama and had become something of a close confidant. Obama, wanting to project the image of not letting politics interfere with legal matters, delegated considerable discretion to Holder for dealing with terrorist suspects and a variety of other sensitive matters. But after several embarrassing political missteps by Holder or his Department, the Obama White House became less deferential to Holder. Some aides just felt he had too much of a "political tin ear" and thus recentralized some of his decision-making authority to the White House.

TREASURY SECRETARY

The secretary of the treasury is a critical presidential adviser on both domestic and international fiscal and monetary policy, but this person also plays somewhat of an advocate's role as an interpreter of the nation's leading financial interests. Treasury has become a department with major institutional authority and responsibility for income and corporate tax administration, currency control, public borrowing, and counseling of the president on such questions as the price of gold and the balance of payments, the federal debt, and international trade, development, and monetary matters. In addition, the treasury's special clientele of major and central bankers has unusual influence. Also, the treasury secretary is typically a pivotal figure in crucial negotiations with Congress on tax and trade matters.

The importance of the treasury secretary as a presidential counselor derives in part from the intelligence and personality of the incumbent. Some were influential in great part because of their self-assuredness and personal magnetism. President Eisenhower liked his Treasury Secretary George M. Humphrey: "In Cabinet meetings, I always wait for George Humphrey to speak. I sit back and listen to the others talk while he doesn't say anything. But I allow that when he speaks, he will say just what I was thinking."[338]

Reagan's second-term treasury secretary, James A. Baker, was regarded as one of the most important individuals in government for several reasons. He had the confidence of the president, he enjoyed a reputation for competence, and he was nearly always a central player in policy decisions concerning the dollar, trade and tariff legislation, tax reform, and our economic relations with key allies. Clinton's Secretary of Treasury, Robert Rubin, was given credit for the economic strategies that helped boost the economy and win Clinton his 1996 reelection.[339]

THE OUTER CABINET

The outer-cabinet positions deal with strongly organized and more particularistic clientele, an involvement that helps to produce an advocate relationship with the White House. These departments—health and human services, HUD, labor, commerce, interior, agriculture, transportation, energy, education, and veterans' affairs—are considered the outer-cabinet departments. The newer department of homeland security is harder to locate because of its many diverse responsibilities. Because most of the president's controllable expenditures, with the exception of defense, lie in their jurisdictions, they take part in the most intensive and competitive exchanges with the White House and the OMB. These departments experience heavy and often conflicting pressures from clientele groups, from congressional interests, and from state and local governments. These pressures sometimes run counter to presidential priorities. Whereas three of the four inner-cabinet departments preside over policies that usually, though often wrongly, are perceived to be largely nonpartisan or bipartisan—national security, foreign policy, and the economy—the domestic departments almost always are subject to intense crossfire between partisan and domestic interest groups.

White House aides and inner-cabinet members may be selected primarily on the basis of personal loyalty to the president; outer-cabinet members often are selected, as mentioned, to achieve a better political, geographical, gender, ethnic, or racial balance. In addition to owing loyalty to their president, these people must develop close relationships with the congressional committees that approved them and finance their programs.

OUTER-CABINET ISOLATION

As tensions build around whether, or to what extent, domestic policy leadership rests with the departments, with the OMB, or with the White House, and as staff and line distinctions become blurred, the estrangement between the domestic department heads and the White House staff deepens. White House aides often grow to believe they possess the more objective understanding of what the president wants to accomplish. At the same time the cabinet heads, day in and day out, must live with the responsibilities for managing their programs, with the carrying out of laws delegated to them by Congress, and with the multiple claims of interest groups.

John Ehrlichman, one of President Nixon's senior West Wing aides, wrote that Nixon viewed many of his domestic cabinet officers as "crybabies" and would often threaten to fire them or transfer them to some more remote position. Nixon, says Ehrlichman, disliked meeting with them, disliked their demands on his time, and disliked their constant efforts to increase their budgets.

Joseph Califano, a former senior White House aide under LBJ who served as Health, Education and Welfare (HEW) cabinet head under President Jimmy Carter, says Carter's White House aides were generally both incompetent and hostile. They were constantly leaking negative comments about him and other cabinet members. White House operatives pressured cabinet members to do political chores and make campaign stops, and sometimes they opposed vigorous enforcement of the laws. In Califano's case this meant they would have liked him to ease up on his antismoking campaign and university desegregation efforts. Califano contends he had good relations with Carter. But White House staffers under Carter, with one or two exceptions, rarely answered his phone calls and seldom took an interest in his work. Califano, for his part, had a big ego and wanted more independence. Mutual resentment was the result. Eventually Carter fired Califano.

The size of the bureaucracy, distrust, and a penchant for the convenience of secrecy lead presidents to rely heavily on senior White House staffers and in more recent administrations, White House policy czars. The White House and executive office aides increasingly become involved not only in gathering legislative ideas but also in getting those ideas translated into laws or executive orders and then into programs. Program coordination and supervision, although often ill managed, also become primary White House interests. To an extent, these additional responsibilities transform the West Wing and the nearby Eisenhower Executive Office Building into an administrative rather than a staff agency. Outer-cabinet departments, understandably, begin to lose the capacity to shape their programs, and the department heads feel uneasy about the lack of close working relations with the president.

Rather than try to strengthen departmental capacities to come up with broader, more innovative proposals, recent presidents, impatient for action, instead have relied on a wide array of advisory boards, commissions, task forces, policy czars, or special envoys.

President Obama, perhaps reflecting his limited administration experience or possibly his distrust of the bureaucracy, appointed nearly a dozen White House level policy czars in his first term to help him coordinate or implement his priorities. He initially had them for economic recovery, for the Middle East, for Afghanistan–Pakistan, for health care reform, for regulatory reform, for energy and climate change, for terrorism, and he even had a "car czar" to help oversee the bailout and recovery of GM and Chrysler.

Three years later most of these policy czars had quit or had faded away. Moreover, Obama's White House staff experienced considerable turnover and sometimes an image of being dysfunctional. White House relations with many cabinet members were strained.[340] Top Obama advisers, however, praised him for his way of asking them to come up with what they believed were the right policies, such as on economic recovery, and for them to leave the politics and political strategy to him. These advisers understandably admired him for this.

Obama's White House staff turnover is hard to explain. The tough economic times were probably part of it. Part of it may also have been his paradoxical or contradictory personality. He campaigned as a transformational leader but, in large part because of the institution, he governed much more as a transactional politician. He could be an inspiring speaker, yet he could also be stoic, insular, and instinctively deliberative. He campaigned advocating a major overhaul of how government and politics in Washington worked, yet excepting on health care and his various economic stimulus measures, he often became preoccupied with incrementalism and trying to find common ground.[341]

Obama's many difficulties also came from having too many underdefined policy czars. These czars invariably confused the chain of command and raised questions in everyone's mind of who was really in charge, and who was accountable. These ad hoc czars are often resented by cabinet heads who fear their authority is being diluted.

"White House czars can act authoritatively," writes James Pfiffner, "when they directly represent the president's wishes, but presidents do not have time to continually back up individual czars on a regular basis." Further, adds Pfiffner, these czars can often be frustrated because of their uncertain status and their uncertain budgets.[342]

THE RISE OF THE ADMINISTRATIVE PRESIDENCY

As presidents fail to get Congress to respond favorably to their legislative proposals, ways are sometimes found to "go around" Congress. Frustrated by congressional delays and nay-saying, presidents look for ways to achieve their policy goals without going through the difficult and cumbersome legislative arena. One strategic approach popular with recent presidents is to use various unilateral powers to slow or accelerate the implementation of laws.

Every president has relied on certain administrative discretionary authority they believe is appropriately theirs. Thomas Jefferson purchased the Louisiana territory this way. Lincoln issued his famous Emancipation Proclamation this way. Kennedy created the Peace Corps by Executive Order. But not all executive decision making goes uncontested. Thus FDR's internment in World War II of thousands of Japanese-Americans, even though it initially won support from a majority in the Supreme Court, was later viewed as a mistake. Some of George Bush's early post-9/11 decisions on warrantless wiretapping and treatment of enemy combatants were overruled by the courts or Congress or both.

Presidents always encounter a fair amount of bureaucratic as well as congressional resistance. But presidents employ a variety of administrative tools to influence how government works.

Among these resources or devices are

- ➡ Executive orders
- ➡ Executive agreements
- ➡ National Security agreements
- ➡ Reorganizations or restructurings
- ➡ New personnel decisions, recess appointments, and firings
- ➡ Signing statements attached to their veto messages

➡ Presidential memorandums to agency heads
➡ Presidential proclamations

An *executive order* is a directive a president issues to provide guidance that laws are faithfully and properly executed. It is an implied power, not specifically described in the Constitution, yet deemed essential for the functioning of government. Over the years presidents have used executive orders and similar administrative devices to exercise their influence in the way the bureaucracy performs. President Reagan issued 381 executive orders; President Clinton issued 364. In most instances, Congress and the courts go along with the use of these mechanisms, but their increased use, and occasional misuse, have invited increased scrutiny.[343]

Executive agreements are a pact, or informal treaty, made by a president with a foreign government. The ability to use this instrument is generally derivative from some broader treaty or general congressional delegation of power to a president; yet unlike treaties, they do not require the advice and consent of the U.S. Senate.

A *National Security Directive,* or action memorandum, is a formal notification to a department or agency head clarifying a presidential decision in national security policy and generally requiring a follow-up by the agencies involved. They are similar to executive orders, but many of them are treated as "classified" and are not immediately shared with the public or even with the Congress.

These and similar devices, strategically deployed, can enhance the power of a president. Using executive orders, memoranda, signing statements, recess appointments, and a variety of other administrative devices, presidents have been able to make policy without legislative approval and sometimes even against the will of Congress. The Supreme Court has held that executive orders have, under most circumstances, the full force of law (see *Jenkins v. Collard*, 1891).

Originally, the executive order was intended for rather minor administrative and rule-making functions, to help the nation's chief administrative officer administer the laws more efficiently and effectively. Gradually, however, the executive order has become an important and sometimes controversial tool for a president to make policy.[344]

As the nation's chief executive, the president has significant administrative and managerial responsibilities. To do the job, a president needs the power and authority to issue administrative orders and instructions. The executive order, like executive agreements and National Security Directives, is an "implied" power, not specifically mentioned in the Constitution, but deemed essential for the functioning of government.

George Washington issued the first executive order on June 8, 1789. It instructed heads of departments (cabinet officers) to make a "clear account" of their departments. Under the National Administrative Procedure Act of 1946, all executive orders must be published in the *Federal Register*. Congress, if it wishes, can overturn an executive order. Executive orders can also be challenged in court on the grounds that they may violate the Constitution.

Over time, presidents have gone beyond the use of executive orders for merely administrative matters and have begun to use orders to "make law" on more substantive and controversial matters. Such efforts bypass Congress and sometimes overstep the bounds of what is an appropriate use of the administrative tools of the office. Presidents have been accused, with some justification, of "going around Congress" and "legislating" independent of Congress.[345]

Signing statements were issued by presidents citing reasons why they were signing and not vetoing legislation submitted to them by Congress. But occasionally a president would note their differences with the legislation, indicating some portion of it, in their view, may be unconstitutional. In effect, a signing statement can express a president's unwillingness to implement a part of a bill.

President Ronald Reagan issued dozens of signing statements noting his objections to contrarian opinions in legislation he signed. George W. Bush issued 161 signing statements challenging over a thousand statutory provisions. Barack Obama, even though he had criticized this practice, continued it on a lesser scale.

Critics call its excessive use a serious threat to the rule of law since presidents seem to be encouraging executive branch administrators to ignore policies enacted into law by the legislative branch.

The much-debated question here is, when a president indicates the executive branch will not enforce a provision of a law because that president regards it as unconstitutional, is it the same as a veto or item veto? Some scholars contend it is a necessary and justifiable presidential prerogative, while others say it is only appropriate in rare instances when the clear constitutional authority of a president is being challenged.[346]

Presidents will continue to use as many administrative tools that they can put to use to try to achieve and implement their priorities. Congress, the courts, and the public will inevitably push back or object to presidential misuse or excessive use of these implied or unilateral powers. Congress and the judiciary have rarely challenged most of the so called "unitary executive" tools used by recent presidents, partly because there have been so many precedents and partly given the press of other business on their busy calendars. How one stands on these debates often depends on how much one believes in the constitutional principles of separation of powers as well as on one's partisan support or lack thereof for the president who is using these devices.

THE EXECUTIVE OFFICE OF THE PRESIDENT, CONTINUED

An Executive Office of the President (EOP) was created in 1939, as noted earlier, to provide a president more help in running the continually expanding federal departments and agencies. This *EOP* today contains the Office of the First Lady, the White House Office, the Office of Management and Budget, the Council of Economic Advisers, the National Security Council, the Office of the Vice President (though there is also a vice president's office in the U.S. Capitol), and at least a dozen additional policy and advisory boards.

We'll examine just a few of these offices here. We devote a separate chapter, chapter 8, to the origin and workings of the vice presidency.

THE PRESIDENT'S SPOUSE

Presidential spouses have a long history of behind-the-scenes influence. They certainly enjoy great proximity.[347] The notable paradox about first ladies is that the greater their perceived political and policy influence, the more they are criticized because of their unelected and unconfirmed (by Congress) status. Edith Wilson, Eleanor Roosevelt, Nancy Reagan, Hillary Clinton, and Michelle Obama sometimes became feared or resented because they were thought to wield influence that had no basis in constitutional provisions.

While the Constitution may be vague concerning some of the precise powers of the presidency, it is wholly silent on the role of the president's spouse. The first lady or first spouse's public position has evolved from a ceremonial hostess role to that of close and sometimes influential policy adviser.[348]

Initially there was confusion over how to address the president's wife. A nation accustomed to royalty and unschooled in the language of democratic politics understandably had a difficult time coming to grips with this new position. Martha Washington was often referred to as Lady Washington, and some even called the president's wife "Presidentress" or "Mrs. President." Over time the lack of (and some would say the desire for) royalty led to a reemergence of regal address, and it wasn't long before the president's wife was regularly referred to as "First Lady." Many have disliked the title First Lady. Jackie Kennedy so loathed it that for a time she forbade her staff to use the term. "The one thing I do not want to be called is first lady," she said. "It sounds like a saddle horse."[349]

The gradual evolution of the first lady's role from ceremonial/hostess to symbol, surrogate, issue highlighter, campaign worker, and political adviser reflects the impact of certain activist first ladies, the changing role of women in American society, increased power in the executive branch, and the increased public and press attention focused on the White House.

The first openly influential first lady may have been Edith Wilson. When in 1919 her husband had a stroke, Mrs. Wilson became, or so some believe, de facto president, prompting Massachusetts Senator Lodge to comment, "a regency was not contemplated in the Constitution."[350]

The outspoken Eleanor Roosevelt stretched the limits of her role as first lady. The active and independent Mrs. Roosevelt often served as the eyes and ears of FDR. She vigorously championed civil rights, social justice, and peace initiatives such as the creation of the United Nations and the human rights commission. Her four sons were in the military services even before the Japanese attack on Pearl Harbor, and in many ways Eleanor Roosevelt performed as "first mother" during World War II. For twelve-and-a-half years, she traveled the country and the world; volunteered on countless committees and boards; wrote a newspaper column; and played the role of lobbyist, counselor, and sounding board for FDR. Her actions and engagement had a focus. In the words of a sympathetic biographer, Eleanor Roosevelt always "believed that human welfare and social justice should be encouraged and protected under the auspices of an enlightened, caring government."[351]

Since the 1960s, first ladies have played an even greater public and political role than their predecessors. Jackie Kennedy was a valuable partner with her husband along the campaign trail. Her style and beauty contributed to the Camelot mystique that surrounded the Kennedys. Rosalyn Carter attended some cabinet meetings, used her position as a platform from which to advance women's issues, and was active in the field of mental health education. Betty Ford, unlike her husband President Ford, openly supported the feminist Equal Rights Amendment to the U.S. Constitution and controversial pro-choice Supreme Court decision *Roe v. Wade*. Nancy Reagan was also influential. When her husband went through cancer surgery, Mrs. Reagan somewhat downplayed the vice president's role and announced herself as "the President's stand-in."[352] Mrs. Reagan seemed to hold veto power over her husband's schedule, sometimes consulted an astrologer as a guide to her husband's actions, influenced the hiring and firing of key personnel, and, along with spinmeister Michael Deaver, worried a lot about her husband's image and place in history. Some people believed that, in the aftermath of the Iran-Contra scandal, Mrs. Reagan encouraged her husband to negotiate an effective arms deal with the Soviet Union to advance his reputation.

Hillary Clinton was the Clinton administration's unofficial leader on health care reform in 1993 and 1994, regularly attended policy strategy meetings, was an influential adviser to her husband, and was a spokesperson for the administration. Her political influence was not, by historical standards, unusual, but her openness about it was. In recognition of the political role of first ladies, a 1993 U.S. Court of Appeals decision, *Association of American Physicians and Surgeons v. Hillary Rodham Clinton,* concluded that the first lady was "a full-time employee of the government," despite the fact first ladies don't get paid. Hillary Clinton championed political and women's rights on an international stage during the Bill Clinton presidency.[353]

Laura Bush visited 76 countries, often spotlighting the Bush administration's efforts to fight malaria and AIDS. She also became an outspoken supporter of Myanmar's Nobel Prize-winning democratic activist Aung San Sun Kyi.

A president's spouse is often in a no-win situation. Expected to promote worthy causes, she can also be subject to criticism if she has too much influence; asked to serve as first hostess and presidential partner, she cannot make the president appear weak or "unmasculine"; expected to support traditional values, she also likely has strong interests of her own. Tensions are inevitable.

Michelle Obama, a Princeton University and Harvard Law School graduate, came to the White House with career experience in practicing law, working at Chicago's City Hall, and serving as an administrator at the University of Chicago

Medical Center. She initially displayed some reluctance about her husband's career and even about moving to Washington. In addition to raising her young daughters, she later devoted herself to championing the cause of helping military families and advocating nutritional and fitness programs.

She, like some of her predecessors, became something of a fashion setter, and like most first ladies, became a stalwart champion of her husband's political initiatives. Michelle Obama tried to refrain from being explicitly involved in West Wing policy debates, yet she occasionally expressed disappointment with some of her husband's advisers.[354] Her popularity, like a few of her predecessors, was greater than her husband's.

In sum, presidential spouses have performed a wide variety of roles, and no one doubts that a number of them have been influential and important to presidential policy. Some, like Eleanor Roosevelt and Hillary Clinton, became independent and consequential political figures. Some were more inclined to perform family and social responsibilities. No formal job description can exist; the role of presidential spouse will be shaped by the individuals who come as presidential partners.

THE WHITE HOUSE STAFF

The post-World War II era has witnessed a rise in the size, importance, and power of the president's White House and Executive Office staff and a corresponding decline in the importance and power of most of the cabinet. As discussed, many functions once performed by the cabinet are now the responsibility of White House advisers.

Part of the reason for this can be traced to the failure of the cabinet and bureaucracy to supply presidents with the help they believe they need. As noted earlier, presidents come to question the loyalty of some cabinet officials, and the bureaucracy is often a creature of habit where the president may want creatures of politics or at least political responsiveness. Then, too, bureaucracies move at a slower pace than most presidents prefer. The White House staff has emerged to fill this vacuum.

The way a president organizes his staff depends on *personality, experience,* and *circumstances.* Bill Clinton liked to engage with his staff. This led to an open, unstructured staff arrangement. In Clinton's case, it may have been too unstructured. In contrast, the George W. Bush White House was more structured, hierarchical, and disciplined.

Experience also plays a big role in the choice of staffing structure. Eisenhower, accustomed to a hierarchical and formal command structure from his career in the military, chose a formal staffing system for his presidency. There is no one perfect staffing structure for all seasons. In a crisis, for example, presidents often abandon the more formal or customary staff system and rely on a select few close advisers, as Kennedy did during the Cuban missile crisis, and as Bush I did during the Gulf War.

Presidents must also decide how to organize their staff. There are a variety of different possible models: FDR's competitive approach, which set some staff members against other staff members in a dynamic tension; JFK's collegial style, which sought a cooperative, bonding approach; Nixon's hierarchical model, with a closed, rigid pyramid of access and line of authority; and Reagan's delegating style, which shared power and authority with a few senior West Wing aides.

Each style of staff organization has costs and benefits. The key is for presidents to know themselves, their strengths and weaknesses, and to model the staff in such a way as to take advantage of their strengths while ensuring that their weaknesses do not lead to serious mistakes.[355]

"One of the dangers in the White House" said Barack Obama, "is that it gets wrapped up in groupthink and everybody agrees with everything and there are no dissenting views." Obama vowed to counter this, saying, "So I'm going to be welcoming a vigorous debate inside the White House."[356] Still, Obama knew well that there is a time to discuss and listen, and a time to decide, and that, as Harry Truman made clear, "the buck stops here."

The Obama White House operation sometimes suffered from both his inexperience in managerial matters and having a lot of big egos who regularly clashed with one another. His economic and budget advisers clashed with one another about how best to deal with the especially challenging economic crisis they faced. One account suggests it became more dysfunctional than helpful for the president.[357] Obama also ran through several chiefs of staff and experienced several departures in key positions. Several cabinet members, as expected, also retired in 2013.

Perhaps the most visible and often most important members of the White House staffs in recent presidencies are the *chief of staff, the national security adviser*, the *chief political adviser* (or counselor as they are sometimes called), and the *White House Press Secretary*. Let's look at the central White House positions:

WHITE HOUSE CHIEF OF STAFF

It is now widely agreed that each president has to have an effective and trusted senior adviser to oversee the much larger White House and executive office staffs. That same person typically also becomes the chief gatekeeper through whom cabinet members must go to have access to a president.

One of the first questions presidents must decide when putting together their administration is how strong a chief-of-staff they will have. James P. Pfiffner, a student of presidential management, says there are "two firm lessons of White House organization that can be ignored by Presidents only at their own peril: No. 1, a chief of staff is essential in the modern White House; No. 2, a domineering chief of staff will almost certainly lead to trouble" (e.g., Sherman Adams under Eisenhower, H. R. Haldeman for Nixon, Donald Regan for Reagan, and John Sununu for Bush). Sununu, instead of catching lightning for President George H. W. Bush, created it, and was eventually forced out. Pfiffner concludes that "the preferred role for a chief of staff is that of a facilitator, coordinator, and a neutral broker."[358]

A president's chief of staff, unlike cabinet members, needs no confirmation by the U.S. Senate. Yet, in many ways, the chief of staff becomes more consequential than most of the cabinet.

Chiefs of staff, in effect, manage White House operations. Other key operatives such as national security and domestic and economic staffers report through the chief of staff to a president. Several recent chiefs of staffs have required cabinet officials and similar advisory staff organizations to prepare weekly reports for the president, but this must come to the chief of staff.

Chiefs of staff in recent presidencies have usually become deeply involved in helping presidents shape policy priorities, political and legislation strategies, and public relations approaches. It is an exceptionally challenging position and several chiefs of staff have become embroiled in controversial clashes with cabinet members, with first ladies, and with the laws.

President Eisenhower's major chief of staff, former New Hampshire governor Sherman Adams, had to resign in a scandal over gifts he had received. President Nixon's chief of staff, H. R. Haldeman, had to depart because of Watergate scandal cover-ups. One of Ronald Reagan's chiefs of staff was eased out in part because First Lady Nancy Reagan didn't like him.

Jimmy Carter and Bill Clinton had largely ineffective chiefs of staff. Barack Obama's initial chief of staff, the talented but mercurial Rahm Emanuel, may have helped Obama to achieve some initial policy victories, yet he and his oversized ego proved to be disruptive.

Effective chiefs of staff help a president gain control over the White House staff and cabinet. They manage, at least to some extent, the avalanche of intelligence and information that pours into the White House. They try to protect the president's time and strive to serve as both a part of the president's political brain trust and an honest broker so that alternative views receive attention.

Past presidential advisers caution that nothing is more important for chiefs of staff to remember than that their power derives only from the president they serve. "One who forgets this precept, who acts as if he were president, will get into trouble sooner than later."[359]

The challenges, and perhaps the paradox, of serving as a president's chief of staff is that one has to have an enormously strong ego and a strong sense of self-confidence as well as emotional security, yet not let this evolve into an intoxicating swollen ego or narcissistic personality disorder. A few, such as Reagan's first chief of staff James Baker, have served effectively and balanced all these tensions, but several others have failed for a variety of reasons.

NATIONAL SECURITY ADVISER

Every president in recent decades has recruited experienced foreign policy veterans to head up their national security teams and coordinate the national security council (NSC). These councils have grown to include cabinet officers from the state and defense departments, the intelligence agencies, and others, usually including the vice president.

Today's national security assistants often have a staff of up to a hundred or more. Henry Kissinger served, and in many ways defined this position, in the Nixon presidency. He gradually became Nixon's most senior foreign policy strategist and often, both because of proximity and skill, more of the administration's Secretary of State than the real Secretary of State. It was Kissinger who, on Nixon's behalf, helped navigate the end to the Vietnam War and helped reopen relations with China.

National security staffers try to forge coherent presidential foreign policies through the NSC staff and council meeting process.

THE CHIEF WHITE HOUSE POLITICAL COUNSELOR

This is sometimes the least defined role in recent White Houses. But every president since JFK has had one or a few political operatives who concentrated on legislative and election campaigns. JFK had Larry O'Brien, Kenneth O'Donnell, and his brother Robert Kennedy, who had been with him since his political ascendancy in Massachusetts.

George W. Bush had the talented and sometimes controversial Karl Rove play his Rasputin and Svengali roles in ways to maximize Republican victories. Barack Obama, like many of his predecessors, brought several message managers and speechwriters to his staff who had successfully navigated him through the dozens of caucus and primary states and then through the general election of 2008.

Obama's initial chief political guru at the White House, as he had been in the 2007–2008 campaign, was David Axelrod. Axelrod had worked as a news reporter and political columnist for the *Chicago Tribune* for about eight years before becoming a political consultant, specializing in media relations. He worked on behalf of a variety of both political reformers and Daley machine types in the rough and tumble politics of Illinois. He helped a number of flawed politicians get elected, but he was mesmerized with Obama when Obama was an Illinois state senator. Axelrod helped Obama get elected to the U.S. Senate and served as his major strategist and "message manager" in his race for the White House.

Axelrod's two years in the White House proved frustrating and, in many ways, is a case study of the challenge of being the top political guru in any White House. Governing proved to be much more complicated and, in many ways, harder than campaigning. Axelrod at the White House worked with the national party leaders, helped oversee media relations, polling, and was Obama's key aide in translating the president's campaign promises into programs. He also became Obama's main envoy to Sunday morning television talk shows and similar media outlets.

But as the economy went from bad to worse and an ugly polarization set in in response to Obama's proposed health care initiative, the president's popularity dropped—almost twenty points. Axelrod never lost his devotion to Obama but he became somewhat of a scapegoat for Obama's failure to frame a coherent and convincing message. Axelrod looked like a political genius in 2008. But by 2010 he found the media, and a few of his colleagues, pointing to him as a flawed message maven. He, in turn, soured on Washington, DC.[360]

What happened to Axelrod? Obama's political honeymoon came and went quickly. The White House staff and many of its czars and advisory units were poorly organized. And the White House had to deal with two unpopular wars and an even more unpopular and devastating recession. The Obama administration pressed ahead with a number of controversial decisions—and all this plus fierce partisanship made life highly unpleasant for the person in charge of promoting Obama's narrative.

Axelrod went home to Chicago to help coordinate the Obama reelection campaign. Axelrod, Jim Messina, and David Plouffe engineered Obama's masterful 2012 reelection.

WHITE HOUSE PRESS SECRETARY

"I have always thought that the job of the White House press secretary is the toughest position after the presidency itself," writes long-time White House correspondent Helen Thomas. "In fact, an *impossible job* might be a better description because the press secretary is caught between two worlds—an administration that wants to paint a rosy picture, no matter what the facts, and a skeptical perhaps cynical press corps that is seeking truthful answers."[361]

Both Bill Clinton and George W. Bush ran through four press secretaries. The job burns people out for the obvious reasons. Obama's first Press Secretary Robert Gibbs knew it was an all-consuming job and that, after a while, Obama's media coverage would become harsher than what he received in his campaign. And that is just what happened. "Known in Washington shorthand as 'the podium job,' it has achieved a certain iconic stature—or thanklessness—in the ritual kabuki of Washington," writes *New York Times* writer Mark Leibovich. "White House press secretaries get a daily blistering from the press, mighty ridicule from comedians and are subject to the widespread belief that they are unhelpful, obfuscating puppets—which, of course, they sometimes are."[362]

Presidents, not surprisingly, like getting favorable media stories, especially about the priorities they are promoting and the leadership they believe they are providing. Media covering the White House, on the other hand, are always on the outlook for things that are going, or could go, wrong, at the White House: conflict among aides, or between the White House and a cabinet member, campaign promises being broken, hypocrisy, scandals, and gaffes.

All presidents and their media advisers market and "spin" their side of the story. But "presidents who sell themselves and their policies through less than honest marketing often face an eventual day of reckoning."[363] Bush's "Mission Accomplished" speech on the USS Lincoln backfired on him, as did his administration's paying several conservative columnists more than $250,000 to write favorable stories about some of their domestic policy programs.

Many presidents have deceived the public, and the media know this, and that's why they often perform "watchdog" or even "attack dog" duties; this is what Americans want. In the process, however, the credibility of both presidents and the media typically suffer.

ADVOCACY CONFLICTS

Effective presidents have to have the organizational and leadership ability to hear and balance the policy views of both their cabinet members and their White House political advisers. Political scientist Fred Greenstein writes that a "president's capacity as an organizer includes his ability to forge a team and get the most out of it, minimizing the tendency of subordinates to tell their boss what they sense he wants to hear."[364]

Political scientist Alexander L. George encouraged presidents to develop a multiple advocacy advising process that allows contrary and minority viewpoints to be weighed alongside conventional advice. His suggestions do not attempt to diminish partisanship, parochial viewpoints, and bargaining in the presidential advisory process. Instead, this system would seek to strengthen the analytical and rational components of advisory networks.[365] Multiple-advocacy systems that would enhance the constructive advice he might get cannot be imposed on a president. A president must find it compatible with his or her style.

DEALING WITH THE BUREAUCRACY

As the nation's chief executive officer, presidents are supposed to sit at the top of the bureaucracy and control its actions. But their control is incomplete at best. A president operates under a four-year time restraint; the bureaucracy has no such time constraint. The old saying, "Presidents come and go yet bureaucrats stay and stay," speaks volumes. The president is the temporary occupant of the White House; the bureaucracy is, at least in relative terms, the permanent government.

Cabinet members are temporary and often frustrated presiders over huge federal departments. Dr. Steven Chu, Obama's Secretary of Energy, worried about the "glacial pace" of his department and wryly noted that Newton's first law of physics, that a body in motion tends to stay in motion, "does not apply" in Washington. Here "if you start something in motion, it either stops or gets derailed. You have to keep applying force."[366]

The federal bureaucracy, greatly swollen by New Deal and Cold War agencies, as well as by the Great Society and Homeland Security programs, can be one of the most visible "brakes" on a president. Indeed, presidents are quick to fault the bureaucracy for the many problems that beset the implementation and evaluation of presidential programs. Presidents and their aides begin to believe there are a lot of bureaucrats out there who function like those in Dilbert cartoons.

The problem of how to inspire, motivate, and manage the bureaucracy has become a major preoccupation for presidents. Even persons who championed the New Deal grew to recognize that the executive bureaucracy can be a presidential curse. Concern about taming the bureaucracy comes from the right, the left, as well as from moderates. It is a constant theme in presidential campaigns as we saw again in 2012.

Gaining control over existing bureaucracies and making them work with and for the White House is an enormous challenge for presidents. They constantly delegate, they must be most precise about what they delegate, and they must know whether and for what reasons the agencies to which they are delegating share their general outlook. They must be sensitive to bureaucratic politics, to the incentives that motivate bureaucrats, and to the intricacies of their standard operating procedures. They must have some assurance (and hence an adequate intelligence system) that what they are delegating will be carried out properly.

Recent presidents and their aides have sometimes misunderstood the workings of bureaucracy. They sometimes are too impatient for bureaucrats' considerable concern about organizational essence, organizational morale, and organizational integrity. Presidents and many of their aides mistakenly yet frequently look on the executive branch as a monolith, and they are especially offended when senior bureaucrats differ with them or otherwise refuse to cooperate. Presidents too often become defensive and critical of the bureaucracy. They fear, sometimes with reason, that their pet programs will get buried in inert custodial hands. Thus they have often sought shortcuts by setting up new agencies for each of their pet projects and relying increasingly on separate advisory and staff units within the executive office. However, the creation of a new agency does not guarantee presidential control.

Bureau chiefs and career civil servants sometimes do avoid taking risks and responsibility, opting instead for routine and security. The bureaucracy has its own way of doing things, perhaps more conservative or more liberal than what the president wants. But that bureaucratic and presidential interests often differ does not mean that the permanent employees of the federal executive branch constitute an active enemy force. Bureaucratic organizations generally act in rational ways to enhance their influence, budget, and autonomy. And they generally believe that in doing so they act in the nation's interest.

Of course, this sometimes means that bureaucrats will define the national interest differently from the way it is defined in the White House. But a close examination of the two definitions may reveal that both are valid views of what is desirable. Properly understood, the bureaucratic instinct for competition, survival, and autonomy can be creatively harnessed by the White House both to educate itself and to develop cooperative alliances.

How entrenched and sometimes contentious White House–bureaucracy relations may become can be inferred from the fact that whereas tenure on the White House staff averages less than three years, the bureau chiefs, senior members of

Congress, senior staff in Congress, and veteran Washington lobbyists often endure in their posts for fifteen years or more. Former Secretary of Health, Education, and Welfare John W. Gardner once told the Senate Government Operations Committee

> As everyone in this room knows but few people outside of Washington understand, questions of public policy nominally lodged with the Secretary are often decided far beyond the Secretary's reach by a trinity consisting of (1) representatives of an outside body, (2) middle level bureaucrats, and (3) selected members of Congress, particularly those concerned with appropriations. In a given field these people may have collaborated for years. They have a durable alliance that cranks out legislation and appropriations in behalf of their special interest. Participants in such durable alliances do not want the Department Secretaries strengthened. The outside special interests are particularly resistant to such change. It took them years to dig their particular tunnel into the public vault, and they don't want the vault moved.[367]

Practically any new presidential initiative, therefore, faces a strategically placed potential veto group with major allies within the executive branch itself: a social services bureaucracy to resist privatization of social security, a Department of Education to resist educational vouchers, a labor establishment skeptical about "free trade" agreements, and so forth.

The professionalization of many sections of the federal government has created another potentially powerful constraint on presidential action. Professionals in government—for example, senior engineers and physicists in the National Aeronautics and Space Administration or the Department of Defense, physicians and biologists at the National Institutes of Health, and economists throughout the government—are at least equally committed to the values of their profession as to the political fortunes of presidents.

If presidents rarely control the bureaucracy, they still need the bureaucracy to implement their policies. But they are not helpless. Different presidents use different methods to move the bureaucracy. Some presidents do it by placing loyal followers in key positions, others assign a top White House aide envoy to ride herd; some try to circumvent an unresponsive agency, others create new agencies staffed by their hand-picked administrators. Other presidents devote their own time and effort to either persuade, bully, or negotiate with an unresponsive bureaucrat. Still others utilize the unilateral or unitary tools we discussed earlier to influence bureaucracy to comply with their priorities.

Bureaucrats can frustrate a president's wishes in a variety of ways. Orders are never self-executing, and it may not be clear exactly what a president wants. Also, some members of the permanent government may disagree with the president's directives and may intentionally sabotage an order by ignoring it, altering it in its execution, or failing to pass it on to the operational level. Delay is a common form of bureaucratic resistance.

CONCLUSION

Presidents are understandably expected to be good administrators—to see that the laws of the land are properly implemented. Traditional public administration ideas held that Congress would make the laws and that the president, with collaboration of the cabinet heads, would impartially administer the laws. In practice, of course, presidents and their advisers promote a number of their own new policies and regularly push to get these adopted. Moreover, laws are often subject to interpretation as they are implemented, so presidents and executive branch officials are also regularly involved in policymaking even as they administer the laws.

One of the biggest changes in the American presidency over the years has been the growth in the size of the national government, and the scope of its activities. The cabinet has grown from four to fifteen and the staff in and around the White House and Executive Office have grown from a handful to a few thousand.

Presidents often come to office believing that their main challenge will be dealing with Congress. While this is true, they also soon discover that dealing with the highly complex federal bureaucracy is often just as much of a challenge, and takes as much if not more of their time.

A president's ability to nominate the cabinet, subject to Senate confirmation, and appoint up to four thousand other officials to key executive branch positions, is obviously one of their primary assets in trying to influence the executive branch. Other resources for what is now called the administrative presidency include internal review of agency budgets, executive orders, national security directives, White House interpretation of new laws through signing statements, and various personnel and restructuring initiatives.

Presidents nowadays are often challenged by clashing priorities as well as clashing personalities that develop within their own administrations. Thus, even as modern presidents have been given numerous advisory and policy intelligence resources, presidents are paradoxically often constrained, if not overwhelmed, by what we perhaps mistakenly assume is their own branch of government.

New presidents have to quickly become savvy entrepreneurs building effective managerial and innovative organizational cultures right in their executive office of the presidency as well as in the much larger executive branch. This can be a consuming challenge and few presidents have excelled at this.

FOR DISCUSSION

1. To what extent, in your view, should a president's cabinet shape public policy at cabinet meetings?
2. How have recent presidents used administrative or "unitary executive" devices to advance their priorities and influence the bureaucracy?

DEBATE QUESTIONS

1. That the "swelling of the presidency," especially in and around the White House, has concentrated too much political power in one place.
2. That the U.S. Attorney General should be a separately elected official, as it is in the states, to serve as yet another independent check and balance on presidents and the executive branch.

FURTHER READINGS

Howell, William. *Power without Persuasion: The Politics of Direct Presidential Action.* Princeton, NJ: Princeton University Press, 2003.

Kumar, Martha J. and Terry Sullivan, eds., *The White House World.* College Station: Texas A&M Press, 2003.

Mayer, Kenneth R. *With the Stroke of a Pen: Executive Orders and Presidential Power.* Princeton, NJ: Princeton University Press, 2001.

Patterson, Bradley H. *To Serve the President: Continuity and Innovation in the White House Staff.* Washington, DC: Brookings Institution, 2008.

Pfiffner, James P. *Organizing the Presidency*, 2nd ed. Washington, DC: Brookings Institution, 2002.

Suskind, Ron: *Confidence Men: Wall Street, Washington, and the Education of a President.* New York: Harper, 2011.

Thurber, James A., ed. *Obama in Office.* Boulder, CO: Paradigm, 2011.

Critical Thinking

STATEMENT: As we have described, presidents are asked to preside over and lead an effective and efficient executive branch. But this often proves a major challenge.

PROBLEM: What advice would you have for presidents and cabinet members? How could they be more effective? Do presidents need additional new resources to be more effective chief executives? If so, what? And, consider also, to what extent should federal employees serve the president, as opposed to Congress or their own conception of the national interest. (If you come up with bold, innovative suggestions, e-mail them to the White House at www.whitehouse.gov/contact).

CHAPTER 8

The American Vice Presidency

The job [of vice president] doesn't lend itself to high profile and decision making. It lends itself to loyally supporting the president..., giving him your best judgment, and then when the president reaches a decision, supporting it.

GEORGE H. W. BUSH, quoted in Michael Duffy and Dan Goodgame, *Marching in Place* (Simon & Schuster, 1992).

During our country's first 150 years, vice presidents served mainly as the presiding officer and president of the U.S. Senate. The post was often seen as a semiretirement job for party stalwarts, as a resting place for mediocrities or "runners-up." Its occupants typically found themselves in a frustrating spectator role. In most administrations a vice president was a ceremonial ribbon cutter, at best a kind of fifth wheel and at worst a political rival who sometimes connived against the president.

Daniel Webster reportedly turned down an invitation to be vice president in 1848, saying, "I do not propose to be buried until I am dead." Thomas Marshall, Woodrow Wilson's vice president, quipped that "once there were two brothers. One ran away to sea, the other became vice president of the United States, and nothing was heard of either of them again."

Americans, until relatively recently, were more inclined to joke about the office than to think about it. For a variety of reasons, especially with recent experiences, presidents nowadays take the vice presidency more seriously, and its responsibilities, while still mainly ad hoc, have expanded. As Paul C. Light has noted, "After two hundred years as errand-boys, political hitmen, professional mourners, and incidental White House commissioners, Vice Presidents can now lay claim to regular access to the President and the opportunity to give advice on major decisions." [368]

Vice President Biden was feisty and animated during the debate with GOP vice presidential candidate Paul Ryan. AP Photo/David Goldman.

To the founding fathers it was mostly an afterthought. To some scholars it is one of our conspicuous constitutional mistakes. To some modern-day presidents it sometimes appears to be more of a headache or a threat than an asset. To some vice presidents it is often a confusing and unhappy experience. Lyndon B. Johnson said that much of the unhappiness in the office stems from knowing you are on "a perpetual death watch." Vice President Hubert Humphrey once said it was "like being naked in the middle of a blizzard, with no one to even offer you a match to keep you warm.... You are trapped, vulnerable and alone."

John Adams, our first vice president, rightly understood the paradoxical nature of the job, saying "I am nothing, but I may be everything."

Paradoxes abound. Dick Cheney was doubtless George W. Bush's most influential adviser in his first term, yet was less important in the last years of Bush's troubled presidency. In fact, Cheney's prominence along with his strong views may have become, in George W. Bush's eyes, something of a liability.

A vice president's chief importance still consists of the fact, as Adams noted, that he or she may be elevated to the presidency. We yearn for someone to fill the post who has the competence and judgment to be president, yet it is typically an advisory and waiting post.

A prime paradox is how we select vice presidents. At least in modern times we select our presidential nominees by a process of intense democratic exposure and deliberation that is long and grueling. But we leave the designation of the vice presidential running mate almost entirely to the judgment of the presidential nominee, a judgment sometimes made hastily, or for politically expedient reasons, sometimes resulting in an inadequately vetted candidate who ends up embarrassing the presidential nominee.[369]

The main purpose of having such a position is to have a competent leader who generally shares the president's views available if an accident befalls the president. In the past, however, there has sometimes been a temptation of selecting a vice presidential nominee who might balance the ticket to help win electoral college votes. The selection of Richard Nixon in 1952, LBJ in 1960, and Lloyd Bentsen in 1988 were examples of this. These two needs, competence and electoral utility, need not be incompatible, yet they sometimes are. The question also used to arise: How can we get vice presidents of presidential quality if once in office they may have little to do? Some presidents have primarily shared "dirty work," such as press bashing, attacking the opposition party, and funeral duty responsibilities, with their vice presidents. Some did not share much at all for fear of being upstaged. Others have understandably refused to delegate responsibilities.

One student of the office concludes there really can be no deputy or alternate president because of the "indivisibility of presidential leadership and the lack of place for tandem governance for two."[370]

Because vice presidents are always "a heartbeat away" from becoming president, there is often a strain in relations between vice presidents and their bosses. Henry Kissinger wrote that the "relationship between the president and any vice president is never easy; it is, after all, disconcerting to have at one's side a man whose life's ambition will be achieved by one's death."[371] Lyndon Johnson wrote of his vice presidential days, "Every time I came into John Kennedy's presence, I felt like a goddam raven hovering over his shoulder."[372]

Another paradox of the vice presidency is that it is a constitutional hybrid of an office: historically—and still—part legislative yet increasingly now part executive in character. A vice president is, as the Constitution instructs, explicitly president of the U.S. Senate, yet the person in that office has now come to be viewed primarily as "standby equipment" if something happens to a president, and a presidential adviser and troubleshooter.[373]

To the extent that the office was debated in the founding period, it was to argue that the vice president would be a "responsible" tiebreaker when the senate was deadlocked. Yet for a couple of generations now, vice presidents have minimized their senate duties and have made their home a mile and two-tenths down Pennsylvania Avenue at the White House—generally as senior White House advisers.[374]

What it takes to be an effective vice president is different from what it takes to be president. Foremost among the attributes of an effective president are independence and strength of character and skills as a national agenda setter and national unifier. A vice president, on the other hand, even while acting as an "understudy" for the president, must be loyal and self-effacing while trying to avoid being obsequious. A vice president is well aware that the office and its importance are at least 90 percent dependent on the preferences, and even the whims, of the president. A president can bestow assignments to a veep yet can remove these same assignments at will.

Originally the person who received the second highest vote in the presidential election became vice president. This was changed after a bitter dispute and intrigue over the election in 1800, when Thomas Jefferson and his presumed running mate, Aaron Burr, received equal votes. With the Twelfth Amendment to the Constitution (1804), the president and vice president are elected on separate ballots. Nowadays, however, presidents essentially dictate their choice of their running mates and successors. Thus Roosevelt, Kennedy, Nixon, Reagan, Bush, Clinton, and Obama have picked their own presumed successors, a notion the framers did not intend. Some people believe the practice of leaving this vital choice of future national leadership to the discretion of a single individual, the presidential candidate or the president, is unacceptable in a nation that professes to be a constitutional democracy. More on this later.

Support exists for devising better ways to pick vice presidential nominees. This search is important because eight presidents have died in office, four by assassination, four by natural death, and one (Nixon) resigned. One-third of our presidents were once vice presidents, including seven of our last nineteen presidents. And many a vice presidential nominee, an eleventh-hour pick, proved underwhelming.

The vice presidency has been significantly affected by two post-World War II constitutional amendments. The Twenty-Second, ratified in 1951, imposes a two-term limit for the presidency, which means vice presidents have a somewhat better chance of moving up to the presidency. The Twenty-Fifth, ratified in 1967, confirms prior practice that, on the death or resignation of a president, the vice president becomes president, not just acting president.[375] The Twenty-Fifth amendment also provides a procedure, still somewhat ambiguous, to determine whether an incumbent president is unable to discharge the powers and duties of the office. Thus the amendment allows an incapacitated president to lay aside temporarily the powers and duties of the office without forfeiting them permanently, as Reagan did for a few hours in 1985 during a cancer operation.

The Twenty-Fifth amendment also creates a mechanism through which a vice president, together with a majority of the cabinet, may declare a president incapacitated and thus serve as acting president until the president recovers. This procedure answers several problems, yet also, as will be discussed, raises questions.

In addition, the Twenty-Fifth Amendment established procedures to fill a vacancy in the vice presidency (a procedure used when Richard Nixon selected Gerald Ford and when Ford selected Nelson Rockefeller). In the event of such a vacancy, the president nominates a vice president, who takes office upon confirmation by a majority vote of both houses of Congress. This procedure should normally ensure the appointment of a vice president in whom the president has confidence. If the vice president, under these circumstances, has to take over the presidency, he or she can usually be expected to reflect most of the policies of the person the people had originally elected.

This chapter briefly looks first at the traditional challenges of the office. Then it appraises some recent vice presidencies. Finally, it treats questions of vice presidential selection and succession.

TRADITIONAL PROBLEMS

The office, as noted, is often condemned as a non-job. Benjamin Franklin ridiculed the position at the Constitutional Convention of 1787 by proposing the occupant be called "Your Superfluous Highness." "I am not in a leadership position," said Vice President Nelson Rockefeller in 1975. "The President has the responsibility and the power.... The Vice President has no responsibility and no power."[376]

Few offices have been so lampooned. Our first vice president, John Adams, wrote to his wife in 1793 that "My country has in its wisdom contrived for me the most insignificant office that ever the invention of man contrived or his imagination conceived." The great legislator Henry Clay is said to have spurned the job twice. John Nance Garner, FDR's first vice president, said the job "isn't worth a pitcher of warm piss."

American voters send 537 elected officials to Washington. Of these, all but one has a reasonably clear idea of their role and functions. Vice presidents, on the other hand, can never be exactly sure whether their functions will change from week to week. Over time, however, the jobs of the vice president have grown. On paper they look somewhat impressive:

- President of the U.S. Senate
- Member of the National Security Council
- Chair of several national advisory councils
- Diplomatic representative of the president and United States abroad
- Senior presidential adviser
- Liaison with Congress
- Crisis coordinator
- Overseer of temporary coordinating councils
- Presider over cabinet meetings in absence of the president
- Deputy leader of the party and key party fund-raiser
- President-in-waiting and possible future presidential candidate

Vice presidents have done all of these things. Several vice presidents have served their president and their nation well. Sometimes, however, political, psychological, and structural obstacles stand in the way of the constructive use of vice presidents.

PRESIDENT OF THE SENATE

Until about 1940, most presidents and most Americans viewed the vice presidency almost exclusively as a legislative job. Vice presidents were to serve as president of the Senate, preside there, and cast an occasional tie-breaking vote. Article I in the Constitution stipulates "the vice president... shall be president of the Senate, but shall have no vote, unless they be equally divided."

Originally the Senate comprised a small number of elder statesmen; twenty-six men plus the vice president. Tie votes were frequent: John Adams cast twenty-nine tiebreaking votes. John Calhoun cast twenty-nine. Today, however, mainly because the Senate has grown to one hundred members, tie votes occur less than once a year. LBJ and Dan Quayle didn't even get to cast a single tiebreaking vote in their VP years. Dick Cheney cast eight tiebreaking votes in his eight years as vice president.

The Senate was designed in many ways as an ideal place for a vice president to learn the business of government and to serve along with many of the nation's leading lawmakers. The Senate was intended to pass laws, shape national policy, confirm major presidential appointees, oversee the approval of treaties, and, more generally, counsel presidents, particularly in foreign affairs. Over time, the Senate has delegated some of its powers to the president, cabinet, and even to Executive Office advisers, so much so that the Senate is now increasingly indistinguishable from the House of Representatives—neither a council of state nor the prime presidential counseling body.

Members of Congress now look on a vice president as a member of the executive branch. The limits of vice presidential influence in the Senate are illustrated by one of Vice President Spiro Agnew's transgressions of political convention. Early in his tenure, Agnew tried to interest himself in mastering Senate rules as well as learning the Senate's informal folkways: "But he violated protocol by lobbying on the Senate floor in behalf of the tax surcharge extension supported by the administration. 'Do we have your vote?' he asked Senator Len Jordan of Idaho, a Republican. The senator replied, 'You did have until now.'" Thus was established Jordan's rule: "When the Vice President lobbies on the Senate floor for a bill, vote the other way."[377] Thereafter, Agnew seemed to lose interest in trying to become a presidential emissary on Capitol Hill. More recently, some vice presidents have effectively lobbied their friends in Congress, yet they do so with appropriate caution and respect for the independence of the branches.

Some say a vice president should be wholly relieved of traditional Senate functions and freed to participate more directly in executive branch responsibilities. James F. Byrnes of South Carolina, a former senator, associate justice of the Supreme Court, as well as secretary of state once suggested that

> If a motion (in the Senate) does not receive a majority vote, it should be considered lost. It is not wise that the Vice President, a representative of the executive branch of government, should affect the will of the legislators by casting a decisive vote. In short, participation by the Vice President in Senate voting, either in support of his own views or the President's, constitutes a violation of the spirit of the fundamental provision of the Constitution that the three branches of our government shall forever be separated.[378]

Constitutional scholar Joseph Kallenbach also favored such a change, contending that the vice president could then become a sort of "minister without portfolio," subject to executive assignments as a president may direct. "This would not only insure he would function in a subordinate administrative capacity to the President and not be tempted to become a rival," it would also provide assignments over a period of time that would enable him to acquire a wider knowledge of the operations of government as a whole. "In this way," adds Kallenbach, "he could be given a better opportunity than at present to prepare himself for the responsibility of serving as chief executive in case fate should thrust the role upon him."[379]

This suggestion has been ignored, yet most vice presidents now view their Senate "job" as largely symbolic if not mostly irrelevant. Vice presidents show up on certain ceremonial occasions, such as on opening day and when the president addresses a joint session of Congress, yet the job of presiding over the Senate is low on the vice president's priority list.

VICE PRESIDENTS AS "ASSISTANT PRESIDENTS"

George Washington conferred on occasion with Vice President John Adams, but Adams acted in his official executive capacity only once, when he attended a cabinet meeting in 1791. Washington was away and wanted his department heads to get together in his absence, and he requested Adams to join them. Thomas Jefferson, when he served as vice president, declined President John Adam's invitation to attend cabinet meetings. Other vice presidents for the next 120 years generally stayed away from the cabinet sessions—either by personal or by presidential desire, usually both. Then in 1918 Thomas R. Marshall substituted for Woodrow Wilson when Wilson was in Europe. President Warren Harding invited his vice president, Calvin Coolidge, to regularly attend cabinet meetings.

FDR's second vice president, Henry Wallace, an experienced administrator who had already served two terms as secretary of agriculture, was the first vice president to be assigned major administrative duties. Roosevelt made Wallace chairman, successively, of the Economic Defense Board, the Supply Priorities and Allocations Board, the War Productions Board, and the Board of Economic Warfare. In the latter post Wallace became an aggressive administrator and an outspoken advocate.

Reformers sometime urge that vice presidents be assigned specific cabinet responsibilities, such as secretary of defense or attorney general. This might answer the criticism that the vice presidency is an inadequate executive training ground. Critics of this suggestion say, however, that the existing presidentially nominated and senatorially confirmed cabinet members are already hard enough to "keep in line." As an elected department official, a vice president who served as a cabinet secretary/department head would be even tougher to "control" or to "fire." A vice president as department head would also surely be compromised by the narrow clientele constituencies of a single agency. Such a precedent, if established, might also affect the kinds of people a president would pick for vice president. Picking someone who might be a good department head might unwisely subordinate breadth, political talent, or general leadership ability to managerial experience.

Finally, it is not wholly evident that a departmental secretary position provides presidential training. Under some circumstances it might; under others it clearly would not. How many recent department heads come readily to mind as especially promising presidential candidates? To be sure, Jefferson and Madison served as cabinet members prior to their presidencies, but so too did James Buchanan and Herbert Hoover.

One misguided proposal suggests that what we really need to do is to separate the presidency into two functions: the head of state and the chief executive. "What we can do, perhaps, is establish a head of state to greet foreign dignitaries and to visit them abroad, to officiate on occasions when a personification of the nation is required, to become the central figure even at the inauguration of the chief executives, and to live at the White House. The chief executive, who would be elected every four years as at present, would live as cabinet members live."[380] Beguiling as this proposal might be to some people, it has been rejected as naive. It smacks too much, most people think, of importing the royalty feature from Great Britain. Because of this alone it will never gain popularity. Most experts contend, too, that the chief executive office would be significantly weakened if the chief-of-state functions were taken away. Presidents such as the Roosevelts, Reagan, Clinton, and Obama clearly mixed the two and strengthened themselves by doing so.

PSYCHOLOGICAL PROBLEMS OR THE "THROTTLEBOTTOM COMPLEX"

Tensions between a president and a vice president are natural; after all, the vice president is the only officer who works closely with a president who cannot be fired by him.

"Alexander Throttlebottom" was a character in an entertaining 1931 Pulitzer Prize winning Broadway musical satire, "Of Thee I Sing," by George S. Kaufman and Morrie Ryskind. Throttlebottom was a stumbling, mumbling caricature of a decidedly underemployed vice president. Neglected by his president, John P. Wintergreen, Throttlebottom is artfully drawn as an unknown and improbable national leader who had to join a guided tour to get into the White House. Not only did he not want to be vice president or know what was expected of him, he was even refused the right to resign. The unhappy Throttlebottom sat around in the parks and fed the pigeons, took walks, and went to the movies. The character of Throttlebottom provided splendid satire, yet the mocking portrait lingers on.

The estrangement of vice presidents from presidents began with Adams and Washington. Relations between the first president and first vice president were civil but scarcely friendly. Then, during his tenure as vice president under President Adams, Thomas Jefferson refused certain diplomatic assignments. Jefferson said of Aaron Burr, his first vice president, that he was a "crooked man whose aim or shot you could never be sure of."[381] Time and again relations between presidents and vice presidents have been strained, occasionally to the point of open hostility. These examples underscore the mutual frustration.

Roosevelt and John Nance Garner:

The once cordial relations between the two men had long since turned sour. They had little contact except at cabinet meetings, where Garner, red and glowering, occasionally took issue with the President in a truculent manner. Roosevelt hinted he would desert the Democratic cause before he would vote for the Texan for President (in 1940). By early 1940 even official relations between the two men had almost ceased; Roosevelt was hoping that the Vice President would not show up for cabinet meetings. The President was gleeful about Garner's tribulations as a presidential candidate.[382]

Richard M. Nixon and Spiro Agnew:

Nixon barely knew Agnew when he selected him in Miami Beach in 1968. Nixon, himself, had been humiliated in the vice presidential job, a job he called a hollow shell, the most ill-conceived and poorly defined position in the American political system. He proceeded nonetheless to visit an even greater humiliation on Agnew. By most accounts Agnew was scorned by the White House staff and given little of importance to do.[383]

Richard Nixon had at best a cool relationship with President Eisenhower. Vice president Lyndon Johnson was an active vice president yet often felt snubbed and sometimes even humiliated by the JFK White House. Dan Quayle (1989–1993), it is said, spent much of his vice presidency worrying about his image and whether he was going to be dumped. Al Gore enjoyed a closer yet pragmatic relationship with President Clinton, yet it deteriorated in their final year. Dick Cheney's relationship with George W. Bush was complicated. Bush respected the older, more experienced Cheney and regularly included him in policymaking meetings. And, as we will discuss, Cheney became the most influential vice president to date.

Why does the "Throttlebottom complex" persist? Is there something congenitally or structurally deficient in the relationship between the presidency and the vice presidency? Does the relationship have to be hollow, hostile, and counterproductive? "Mistrust is inherent in the relationship," wrote Arthur Schlesinger, Jr., because vice presidents are inevitable "reminders of their president's own mortality."[384] This mistrust is not without historical foundation. Some previous vice presidents have turned against their presidents, mobilizing opposition in the Congress, proposing alternative legislative programs, and preparing to run for the presidency against the president they were then serving. Vice President John Calhoun, more rival than ally, did all these things and more to a much disgruntled President Andrew Jackson. In his fourth year, Calhoun gladly resigned and won an appointment to the U.S. Senate from his state of South Carolina.

Tensions exist for a number of reasons, yet at least one factor is that both the president and the vice president are, or should be, astute politicians, and as Harry Truman once suggested, this often means neither will take the other completely into his confidence.

The following from a "Conversation with Vice President Hubert H. Humphrey" illustrates how one vice president seemingly subordinated his own personal ambitions and vowed nearly feudal homage to his president:

> I did not become vice president with President Johnson to cause him trouble. I feel a deep sense of loyalty and fidelity. I believe that if you can't have that you have no right to accept the office. Because today it is so important that a president and his vice president be on the same wave length.... I'd hate to have the president be worried about me, that I may do something that would cause him embarrassment or that would injure his administration.... There are no Humphrey people, there are no Humphrey policies, there are no Humphrey programs. Whatever we have we should try to contribute, if it's wanted, to the president and his administration. You can't have two leaders of the executive branch at one time.[385]

In spite of this subservient "leaning over backward," Humphrey was never really trusted by LBJ. Humphrey frequently sought more substantive assignments, only to be disregarded. Johnson would occasionally exclude Humphrey from his team of insiders whenever the vice president sought independence or tried to promote his own policy views. This was especially true in the case of certain policy differences he had with Johnson over the Vietnam War.

When is loyalty to a president carried too far? Vice Presidents sometimes became such apologists for their administrations that they cannot help but diminish their credibility.

Gerald Ford saw tensions and jealousies develop between his own five hundred-person White House staff and Nelson Rockefeller's vice presidential staff of seventy aides and assistants. Ford claims he and Rockefeller got along very well. "Nelson was absolutely loyal to me, and he would do anything I asked him to do," writes Ford in his memoir.[386] But Ford, despite saying Rockefeller was eminently qualified to "step into my shoes" if tragedy struck, went along with his political advisers' campaign to dump Rockefeller as a running mate for the 1976 election. Ford was motivated, almost exclusively, by political considerations. Republican conservatives disliked Rockefeller and Ford gave in. He later regretted it.[387]

Despite these traditional problems, the office has endured, and in many ways prospered. The problems have been diminished somewhat by reducing the physical distance between president and vice president and by providing more staff and perquisites. Over the past fifty years, vice presidents have acquired a White House office, impressive staffs (estimates range in the 80 to 90 range), a vice presidential mansion, an Air Force Two, larger Secret Service details, and more.

THE MONDALE EXPERIENCE

The vice presidency "has its frustrations...," said Walter Mondale. "But I went into it with my eyes wide open. I know there is only one president; there is not an assistant president. I'm his adviser."[388] Most students of the vice presidency agree that Mondale enjoyed a close relationship with his boss. Much of the credit was due to President Jimmy Carter. Carter not only said he would give his vice president more to do; he tried in earnest to make the vice president as close as one can get to a full working partner. Mondale enjoyed a standing invitation to participate in any of the president's meetings. He had access to reports and cables. Mondale also had a regularly scheduled weekly luncheon date with Carter.

Mondale came to the job with several assets. He was well known and well liked on Capitol Hill. He knew how Congress and Washington operated. He had earlier been a popular and effective attorney general in his home state of Minnesota. He was, in some ways, also a protégé of the much respected Hubert Humphrey.

Mondale also understood the vulnerable "tender nature" of the vice presidency. Nearly everything contributing to his effectiveness, he knew, depended on a personal relationship with the president. He knew presidential powers are not divisible. He knew he could not long be effective as chief lobbyist or as chief of staff at the White House—two jobs that Carter and his staff sometimes tried to give him. Mondale rejected the chief-of-staff post because he knew if he had taken that assignment it would have consumed him.

Mondale and Carter overcame some of the traditional problems of the vice presidency by treating Mondale's staff as part of the White House staff. Some senior members of the Mondale staff were assigned high-level White House responsibilities, often with supervisory authority over some White House aides. Mondale's staff won high marks for professionalism.

Vice President Mondale is credited with being perhaps the first in that job who regularly exercised substantive policy influence. "What the President needs is not more information, although that is helpful," Mondale reflected; "he needs a few people who can honestly appraise and evaluate his performance.... He needs to hear voices that speak from a national perspective. He has no limit to the number of people who want to talk to him, but that does not assure him of the confidentiality he needs to speak freely."[389]

As his term drew to a close Mondale told his successor, George H. W. Bush, there were some lessons he wanted to pass along. Among Mondale's chief recommendations

- ➡ Advise the president confidentially. The only reasons to state publicly what you have told the president is to take credit for his success and try to escape blame for failure. Either way there is no quicker way to undermine your relationship with the president and lose your effectiveness.
- ➡ Don't wear a president down.... Give your advice once and give it well. You have a right to be heard, not obeyed. A president must decide when the debates must end....
- ➡ Avoid line authority assignments. If such an assignment is important, it will then cut across the responsibilities of one or two cabinet officers or others and

embroil you in a bureaucratic fight that would be disastrous. If it is meaning-less or trivial, it will undermine your reputation and squander your time.[390]

THE GEORGE H. W. BUSH EXPERIENCE

Most observers believe that George H. W. Bush enjoyed almost, yet not quite, as good a relationship with Ronald Reagan as Walter Mondale had enjoyed with Jimmy Carter. Bush started out in a more compromised position. He had cam-paigned vigorously against Reagan in the Republican primaries of 1980. His criti-cisms of Reagan and his proposals had hurt Reagan personally and it is known that for this and perhaps other reasons Bush was not Reagan's first choice for vice president. But Bush was selected, and the Reagan–Bush ticket was victorious in 1980 and again in 1984.

Bush benefited from the model established by Carter–Mondale. He inherited the "Mondale office" in the White House. He was given access to the president's daily briefing papers and other important paper flow in the White House itself. Bush's stock rose when he acted professionally during the time of Reagan's assassi-nation attempt and subsequent hospitalization early in the first term. It rose even more as he became an ardent campaigner for Reagan's economic programs. Bush performed countless partisan chores with effectiveness.

A personal trust between Reagan and Bush developed. At the time of the second inaugural, Reagan enthusiastically toasted his vice president as "the best Vice President this Republic has ever had." Bush, for his part, became about as supportive about his president as any vice president ever. "I can't think of anything that the president has left undone that he might have done to make me feel more comfortable in my job," he said. "And I guess the best example of that is that I am free to walk three doors down the hall to the Oval Office and walk in there. And I don't have any inhibitions doing that."[391]

Like those before him, however, George H. W. Bush was unable to escape some of the ridicule that comes with the job. Thus, during the campaign of 1984, Bush was sometimes portrayed as a man without any ideas of his own. He had become such a "cheerleader-in chief" that he seemed to have compromised some of his own views. The cartoon strip "Doonesbury" portrayed him as having "put his political manhood in a blind trust."

A public opinion survey on Bush and his performance as vice president, seven years into his vice presidency, underscored the liabilities of service as vice president. Roughly half of those polled in a *New York Times*/CBS survey said that "they did not regard the vice presidency as a job that prepared someone to be president." Bush's vice presidency, paradoxically, was both his greatest advan-tage and his greatest liability. Those surveyed obviously knew him because of his visibility and generally (59 percent) viewed him as honest. Yet only 35 per-cent of registered voters held a favorable opinion of him. Finally, few people thought Bush said what he really believed when he did have differences with President Reagan.[392]

THE GORE EXPERIENCE

President Clinton continued the trend of using his vice president for a variety of serious assignments. Al Gore was influential in such policy areas as the environment, emerging technology, and a "reinventing government" bureaucracy reform campaign. In foreign affairs Gore was involved on issues such as U.S. policy toward Russia, South Africa, the Middle East, and nuclear nonproliferation. Al Gore debated Ross Perot on national television over the North American Free Trade Agreement—with great success. He debated rival vice presidential candidate Jack Kemp in the 1996 campaign—again with success.

Gore was seen by White House staffers, the cabinet, and Washington journalists as a force within the administration, a view President Clinton generally reinforced. President Clinton seemed less threatened by Gore than many other president–vice president pairings. Clinton generally viewed Gore as a resource, and he effectively used Gore's skills. But, as noted, their relationship, though highly professional, was always more pragmatic than a close friendship.

The Gore–Clinton relationship became more awkward, however, when Gore began to run for the presidency in 1999 and 2000. Gore's reputation was obviously tarnished in Clinton's second term because of Clinton's Monica Lewinsky scandal, Clinton's subsequent impeachment, and various policy setbacks. Gore had rigorously defended Clinton before Clinton admitted lying to the public. Gore understandably tried to become more independent and put more distance between himself and the politically weakened yet still popular Clinton. Clinton, for his part, occasionally disparaged Gore's campaigning abilities, and this further eroded their now strained friendship. By the summer of 2000 the two were hardly speaking with one another.[393]

Gore went on to win the popular vote for president yet very narrowly lost the electoral college election. That later vote led to a challenge in the Supreme Court where Gore lost in a 5–4 decision favorable to George Bush. Gore did, however, go on to co-win an Academy Award for his documentary film, "An Inconvenient Truth," and later a Nobel Prize for his work on global warming. Gore privately blamed his 2000 loss, at least in part, on Clinton's affair, lying, and impeachment. Clinton was privately hurt that Gore never called on him for explicit campaign help. Not surprisingly, their post presidency relationship was frosty.

THE DICK CHENEY VICE PRESIDENCY

Dick Cheney was probably the most consequential vice president in American history. He, with Bush's apparent consent, further transformed an office that, as we have seen, was often an insignificant office to what many people concluded was a virtual shadow presidency and at times perhaps nearly a co-presidency. He had a greater legislative and administrative experience than his boss, George W. Bush, who was one of the least experienced of modern presidents. Cheney had served in Congress for ten years, rising to a key party leadership position in the House of Representatives. He had served as White House chief of staff under President Ford, and Secretary of Defense under President George H. W. Bush.

George W. Bush trusted the older Cheney in part because of his vastly greater Washington experience, and also because Cheney made it clear to everyone that he had no intention of running for president.

Cheney, with Bush's encouragement, played a crucial role in recruiting dozens of cabinet, subcabinet, and Executive Office of the President personnel—including his one-time mentor, Donald Rumsfeld, to serve as Secretary of Defense.

Cheney brought with him a clearly honed view, essentially a theory, of presidential leadership. He had watched how Congress had reasserted itself during the Ford and Carter presidencies. He believed in a vigorous Congress yet believed even more strongly that America needs a robust and assertive presidency, especially in foreign policy and national security matters.

Indeed Cheney was a veritable crusader, well before his vice presidency, for restoring or expanding presidential power. "He hoped to enlarge the zone of secrecy around the executive branch, to reduce the power of Congress to restrict presidential action, to undermine international treaties, to nominate judges who favored a stronger presidency, and to impose greater White House control over the permanent workings of government."[394] For Cheney this was a philosophical commitment: This is the way it should be, regardless of who was president or which party controlled the White House. In this he may have differed from many traditional conservatives, yet he was not alone. He believed Congress was too unwieldy, leak prone, and risk adverse to provide strategic and responsible national security leadership.[395]

Eight months into the Bush–Cheney presidency, the 9/11 terrorist attacks redoubled Cheney's attitude about the need for a strengthened executive and the need for more secrecy and centralization. George W. Bush, for a variety of reasons, needed practical counsel during those dramatic days, and Dick Cheney was more than willing to offer it. He played a central advocacy role in decisions involving preemptive war in Iraq and the overall conduct of U.S. anti-terrorism policies. Cheney was given an especially wide-ranging portfolio for intelligence policies. Research indicates that Cheney was an even a more aggressive "hawk" in these matters than his boss. Moreover, Cheney's footprints were all over the policy landscape, from energy and environmental matters to tax and budgetary policy, as well on judicial nominations.[396]

Cheney, with a large staff of several dozen, played a key and often effective role in congressional relations and party fund-raising. He regularly traveled abroad, and few people doubted he spoke for George Bush. There were times early in the Bush presidency that Cheney almost seemed the dominant partner, prompting satire about Cheney pulling the levers behind the curtain or serving as Bush's ventriloquist. Both Bush and Cheney worked hard to counter these depictions.

Dick Cheney gradually became a polarizing figure and earned the dubious distinction of being the most disapproved vice president since regular polling began in the 1940s. He was polarizing not only because he took strong positions on

TABLE 8.1 Rating Vice President Cheney

Q. "How would you rate the job Vice President Dick Cheney is doing?	Excellent/ Pretty Good	Only Fair/ Poor
June 2002	55%	34%
June 2005	38	56
June 2006	31	65
June 2008	18	74

SOURCE: The Harris Poll.
NOTE: N = typically 1,000 adults nationwide.

constitutional issues of separation of powers but also because he was unapologetically pro-business, pro-military, anti-UN, and a vigorous champion of American Exceptionalism. Despite stalwart efforts to be a "behind the scenes" low-profile operative, his influence became increasingly apparent.

Cheney inevitably became a lightning rod for the administration. When Bush's popularity declined in his second term, Cheney's declined even lower, often more than 10 percentage points lower than his boss's (see Table 8.1).

Cheney was blamed, rightly or wrongly, for misleading intelligence and "cheerleading" advice leading to the war in Iraq. He was faulted as well for the way the U.S. treated detainees and prisoners of war. He was accused of divisive partisanship:

> The man who held decisive authority in the White House during the Bush years has so far remained unaccountable for the aggrandizement and abuse of executive power; for the imposition of repressive laws whose contents were barely known by the legislature that passed them; for the instigation of domestic spying without disclosure or oversight; for the dissemination of false evidence to take the country into war; for the design and conduct of what the constitutional framers would have called . . . a government within a government.[397]

Nobody can fault Cheney's commitment to fighting terrorism. Strength and resolve were his mantras. "Any would-be terrorist out there needs to know that if you're going to attack [the United States]," he said in probably 2001, "you'll be hit very hard and very quick. It's not the time for diplomacy. It's time for action."[398]

Cheney argued that the Bush White House had been justified in expanding executive authority over a broad range of matters. We had, Cheney contended, ample precedent:

> If you think about what Abraham Lincoln did during the Civil War, what FDR did during WWII. They went far beyond anything we've done in a global war on terror. . . . But we have exercised, I think, the legitimate authority of the president under Article II of the Constitution as commander in chief in order to put in place policies and programs that have successfully defended the nation.[399]

Cheney earned a long list of satirical nicknames, such as "Dark Side," "Big Time," and "Darth Vader" for both his and his staff's willingness to confront politicians, administration rivals and the media for his "do whatever it takes" philosophy to protect America and defeat terrorists. "We also have to work...sort of the dark side, if you will. We've got to spend time in the shadows in the intelligence world," said Cheney after 9/11. "A lot of what needs to be done here will have to be done quietly without any discussion, using sources and methods that are available to our intelligence agencies.... That's the world [terrorists] operate in, and so it's going to be vital for us to use any means at our disposal, basically, to achieve our objectives."[400]

Why was Cheney so influential? His friends, critics, and biographers generally agree on the following:

➡ Cheney had an uncanny understanding of how Capitol Hill, the White House, the national media, and the sprawling executive bureaucracy operated.

➡ By the time he became vice president he was not only independently wealthy, he also had been a leader in corporate America, Congress, the cabinet, and the Republican Party.

➡ He had astutely recruited and helped staff dozens of key positions with Cheney protégés or allies in the Bush administration. He often exercised a veto over potential prospective appointments he didn't like.

➡ He had a well-developed vision about most policy priorities and how our Madisonian separated powers system should function.

➡ He knew also that George W. Bush hated the reputation that his father had earned as a "flip-flopper" and even as a "wimp"; and that he, the son, wanted to have a clear vision, be consistent, have resolve, and most assuredly win reelection to the presidency, which his father had failed to do.

➡ Finally, Cheney had extrapolitical clout that most earlier vice presidents didn't have in that he was not making calculating decisions with an eye on succeeding Bush. As a result, he could intimidate rivals and engage in policy "shakedowns" with cabinet members or members of Congress with little or no fear of their impact on his political fortunes.

Cheney's vice presidency set a benchmark for its influence and for the degree to which he was praised, criticized, caricatured, and investigated.[401]

George W. Bush agreed that Cheney "was very influential." Yet Bush held that Cheney was no more influential than Secretary of State Condi Rice, Secretary of Defense Bob Gates, or National Security Adviser Steve Hadley.[402] Here Bush may have wanted to set the record straight, at least from his standpoint, that Cheney was merely one among many top advisers, and not the domineering "co-equal" partner with a feckless president who some believed was inexperienced. Bush didn't always take Cheney's advice, especially in the last few years of the Bush presidency. Thus, for one example, Bush fired Defense Secretary Rumsfeld over the objections of Cheney. Cheney also argued on occasion for different foreign policy approaches in dealing with Iran and North Korea. He also wanted a full presidential pardon for one of his top aides.

Bush, in a Fox television conversation, alluded to Cheney's deeply rooted, firm, and perhaps even stubborn worldview. "And the thing about Vice President Cheney... [and] his recommendations... [they] are based upon a core set of principles that are deeply rooted in his very being. And he is predictable in many ways because he brings a set of beliefs—and uh, they're firm beliefs."[403]

The Cheney vice presidency was historic, influential, controversial, and consequential. It will be debated for years to come. In his memoir, Cheney chides his fellow cabinet members Colin Powell and Condoleezza Rice for not being tough enough on Iraq, Iran, North Korea, and Syria. He even faults President Bush on certain issues. Critics, including some of his former Bush administration colleagues, believe Cheney will be remembered for his contempt for diplomacy, transparency, and for the rights of enemy combatants. He will be remembered as the "driving force behind interrogation policy" and torture techniques used in the Bush years.[404]

As at least a few Bush advisers concluded, while unilateralism and secrecy are sometimes necessary at the height of a crisis, Cheneyism might have been effective in the short run, it proved disastrous over the long term.[405] Political analysts and scholars will debate the Cheney vice presidency for a long time to come, but his influence and controversial tenure are unlikely to be matched soon.

THE BIDEN VICE PRESIDENCY

Senator Joseph F. Biden, Jr., when he was campaigning for the Democratic Party's presidential nomination in 2007 said he did not think Senator Barack Obama "was ready to be president." A few months later, after his own campaign failed miserably, he backed candidate Obama.

Obama considered naming Senator Hillary Clinton as his vice presidential running mate. But he eventually settled on Biden. Obama and his political advisers wanted someone who would both help the ticket politically as well as be someone who could help him as an effective vice president.

Biden had more than three decades of service in the U.S. Senate including leadership positions on both the Senate Judiciary and Foreign Relations Committees. He had some blue-collar political appeal and was generally well liked by both Democrats and Republicans in Congress. He had also handled himself well in the 2007 primary debate performances.

Obama and his aides worried that Biden was prone to making gaffes and had been dogged by plagiarism charges. "He was also known," wrote Obama campaign manager David Plouffe, "to test even the Senate's standard for windiness, taking an hour to say something that required ten minutes."[406] He was known, rightly or wrongly, as someone who had trouble keeping his thoughts to himself. Less charitably, George W. Bush said, "If bullshit was currency, Joe Biden would be a billionaire."[407]

But Obama went with Biden. Biden turned out to be an effective campaigner both in 2008 and again in 2012.

Biden, in his vice-presidential debate with Governor Palin, claimed Dick Cheney had been "the most dangerous vice president in history." Cheney, to his credit, swallowed this verdict and gracefully telephoned Biden after the Obama–Biden ticket won, congratulated him, and offered to do what he could do to ease his transition into office. Cheney and his wife hosted the Bidens at the vice presidential mansion as part of this post-election graciousness.

Biden played important roles in the Obama White House, yet his advisory roles were neither as consequential nor as controversial as Cheney's role had been in the G.W. Bush White House. This was, in part, because Obama and Biden shared, with few exceptions, the same policy and political views. They were ideologically mostly "on the same page," whereas Cheney's views sometimes sharply differed with more than a few cabinet and White House aides. Biden did hold somewhat different positions than Obama on the increase of U.S. troops in the Afghanistan war in 2010. But, reports say, Biden's verbosity, lack of staff expertise, and perhaps also a lack of focus hurt his case at the time.

Biden was an unfailingly frank adviser yet also an unwaveringly loyal champion of Obama initiatives on the public stage. And Obama trusted Biden with some of the most critical assignments such as promoting a $787 billion Recovery Act, federal debt negotiations, and critical transition discussions in Iraq and Afghanistan. As one top Obama aide said, "This is one shotgun wedding that works."

Joe Biden, the nation's 47th vice president, loves a stage, and he proudly represented the Obama administration in Iraq and Afghanistan as well as at national parks or Democratic Party fund-raising dinners.

Biden was viewed as a classic pragmatist who mostly avoided White House and cabinet infighting that had sometimes characterized the Cheney vice presidency and sometimes plagued the Obama executive office staff.[408] Biden's public opinion poll numbers were much higher than Cheney's had been, and more in line with his president's.[409]

But Biden, despite all his charm and political expertise, was unable to help lessen the partisan gridlock that handicapped the Obama presidency. Perhaps no vice president could alter intense polarization over budget deficit and tax matters. Obama called Biden "the greatest vice president you could ever want."

SELECTION

As noted, apart from the problem of what to do with vice presidents, there is the enduring problem of how best to recruit people to the office and to fill it when vacancies occur. For years the vice presidential nomination process has tempted the fates. It's a pig-in-a-poke system, critics say.[410]

The process invariably begins with a search for someone who will strengthen the presidential ticket, yet it often ends with a search for someone who will not weaken the ticket. The search for someone who will "balance the ticket" causes problems. Sometimes it means choosing party workhorses whose chief virtue is that they have antagonized nobody. Sometimes it means choosing persons mainly because they come from a politically crucial region of the nation. Sometimes this practice means nominating someone from a rival political wing of the party. Sometimes it involves a "unite the party by picking the person who came in second" approach. And then there is always the gamble or "bold stroke" approach of selecting someone who will be a big surprise and put everyone off balance, such as Nixon's choice of Spiro Agnew in 1968, Mondale's choice of Geraldine Ferraro as a 1984 running mate, and John McCain's selection of Alaska Governor Sarah Palin in 2008.

In recent decades the identity of the presidential nominee has been determined in advance of the party convention. Not so the vice president. Some are last-minute choices (Sargent Shriver in 1972), some are surprises (Quayle in 1988 and Sarah Palin in 2008).

Presidents are free to choose whomever they wish as vice presidential running mates. In practice, however, presidential nominees choose someone they believe will (a) help them get elected, (b) help them govern successfully, and (c) share their views so they can help implement the president's agenda should something happen to the president.

Pressure exists to subordinate considerations of proven leadership ability to those of vote-getting power. (Ticket balancing allowed Andrew Johnson, Arthur, Truman, Nixon, and Agnew to rise from relative political obscurity to become vice presidents.) A problem with nearly all of the approaches mentioned previously is that after the excitement fades, the presidential candidate must live with the choice, and the country sometimes gets that person as the next president.[411]

Is it right to entrust the selection of the vice president to the presidential nominee? How many vice presidents have been merely an afterthought at or just prior to the national convention? The initial 1972 selection of Senator Thomas Eagleton of Missouri by George McGovern and the 1968 Governor Spiro Agnew of Maryland selection by Richard Nixon prompted reappraisals, as did the Dan Quayle and Sarah Palin selections in 1988 and 2008.

In 1973 the Democratic Party created a Commission on Vice Presidential Selection, chaired by former Vice President Hubert Humphrey. That Commission made several suggestions, including these: The convention could be extended for a day, permitting a forty-eight-hour interval between the nominatiosns of the presidential and vice presidential candidates. Alternately, the selection of the vice president could be put off for three weeks and the nominee could then be ratified by the party's national committee in a mini-convention (a procedure used in 1972 when McGovern's choice, Thomas Eagleton, withdrew and Sargent Shriver was approved as the vice presidential nominee).[412]

Other reformers suggest that presidential nominees might pick their vice presidential nominees about a month or so before the party's national convention. At the convention, the two would run as a ticket. This method might, proponents say, allow the vice presidential choice to emerge with more stature.

Still another proposal urges that national conventions nominate only the presidential nominee. Then the November election winner would announce a choice of a vice president in December, and the new Congress meeting in January would consider the choice before inauguration day. If the first name was not approved, the new president would submit another. This proposal might not require a constitutional amendment, since the president would in essence be following procedures provided in the Twenty-Fifth Amendment. A problem here, however, is that there will be times when the Congress is controlled by the opposition.

A more radical proposal would require a constitutional amendment: abolishing the vice presidency altogether. Suggestions for abolishing the office have been proposed since the beginning of the Republic. This measure was embraced by a dozen writers in the mid-1970s in the wake of Watergate and at times when we had a vacancy in the vice presidency. Frustrated by various abuses and misuses of the office, critics said, let's get rid of the office before it sinks us. If a president dies or becomes disabled or resigns, let a designated cabinet member (secretary of state or defense or treasury) take over for one hundred days and meanwhile let's conduct a special election for a new democratically elected resident. Historian Arthur M. Schlesinger, Jr., a proponent of this plan, concluded that the multiple problems that surround the modern vice presidency could be eliminated simply by eliminating the office itself:

> There is no escape...from the conclusion that the Vice Presidency is not only a pointless but even a dangerous office. A politician is nominated for Vice President for reasons unconnected with his presidential qualities and elected to the Vice Presidency as part of a tie-in sale. Once carried to the Vice Presidency not on his own but as second rider on the presidential horse, where is he? If he is a first-rate man, his nerve and confidence will be shaken, his talents wasted and soured, even as his publicity urges him on toward the ultimate office for which, the longer he serves in the second place, the less ready he may be. If he is not a first-rate man he should not be in a position to inherit or claim the presidency. Why not therefore abolish this mischievous office and work out a more sensible mode of succession?[413]

Eliminating the vice presidency would reaffirm a basic principle of constitutional democracy, namely, that presidents should be elected by the people. If that principle is accepted, "the principle that if a president vanishes, it is better for the people to elect a new president than endure a vice president who was never voted for that office, who became vice president for reasons other than his presidential qualifications and who may very well have been badly damaged by his vice presidential experience—the problem is one of working out the mechanics of the intermediate election. This is not easy but far from impossible."[414]

At the heart of the matter is whether or not we want to be a government of and by the people. Clearly, we sometimes choose vice presidents for the wrong reasons. It is equally clear, however, that today the vice presidency has become a stepping stone either to the presidency directly or at least to presidential nomination. Nearly 25 percent of our presidents do not serve out their terms. And, as noted, nearly a third of the presidents were vice presidents first (Table 8.2).

The issues at stake here are issues of democratic procedure and political legitimacy. Many people believe the nation could not afford a special election after a presidential death, as in 1945 or in 1963, but other Western nations do so regularly. Others say intermediate elections violate the tradition of quadrennial elections. But what is so compelling or virtuous about waiting until that fourth year if what is at question is the quality and character of the nation's leadership? Moreover, the special election would merely be to fill out the remainder of the departed president's term. What could be more sensible for a self-governing constitutional democracy than that our president must, except for the briefest periods, be a person elected to that office by the American people?

There are, to be sure, some disadvantages to this idea of abolishing the vice presidency and conducting a special election to fill a presidential vacancy. First, it might invite instability during the succession period.

Second, it is doubtful that a sixty- or ninety-day campaign in a nation this large would allow for the full clarification of the challenging and competing issues of the day. It is one thing for Canada or France to conduct a short campaign, but the United States is substantially larger and has weaker political parties, and it usually takes longer here for issues to get sharpened—though it is not entirely apparent that our nearly two-year campaigns do this well. Finally, most people, rightly or wrongly, are not especially displeased by the existing system. Neither are they notably displeased by those who have become vice presidents through the current arrangements. On the contrary, Teddy Roosevelt and Harry Truman are now two of our favorite past presidents.

Overall, the vice presidential nomination process has had a mixed history. We have had nine examples of what happens when a vice president is forced by necessity to become president. Some became respected presidents. Some were major disappointments. Disturbing, however, is the list of those who mercifully did not become president, which includes an alcoholic, a senile veep, the unpredictable and controversial Aaron Burr, and the obviously corrupt Spiro Agnew.

Most people are resigned to living with the existing system.

Presidential nominees will (understandably) choose their running mates with their probable impact on the electoral outcomes in mind. As Barry Goldwater once put it bluntly, we select vice presidents "to win votes." Nor is this concern for political considerations unreasonable. "A party facing an election of such great consequence as the race for the White House would be irrational not to weigh heavily the probable political impact of prospective running mates," wrote Joel Goldstein. He added, "A two-party system provides many advantages to a democracy. It simplifies voter choice, promotes consensus, adds stability to a society, and allows majorities to form. But every virtue has its costs. Compromise is part of the price. The use of the vice presidential nomination to placate disgruntled factions is part of the mortar that holds the political system together."[415]

Mitt Romney doubtless had many of these balancing as well as practical considerations in mind when he picked Paul Ryan of Wisconsin to be his vice presidential running mate in 2012. Ryan added youth, extensive congressional

TABLE 8.2 Vice Presidents Who Became Presidents

Year	Vice President	President Served	Reason for Obtaining Office
1797	John Adams	George Washington	Elected to office
1801	Thomas Jefferson	John Adams	Elected to office
1837	Marlin Van Buren	Andrew Jackson	Elected to office
1841	John Tyler	William Henry Harrison	Harrison died
1850	Millard Fillmore	Zachary Taylor	Taylor died
1865	Andrew Johnson	Abraham Lincoln	Lincoln killed
1881	Chester A. Arthur	James A. Garfield	Garfield killed
1901	Theodore Roosevelt	William McKinley	McKinley killed
1923	Calvin Coolidge	William G. Harding	Harding died
1945	Harry S Truman	Franklin D. Roosevelt	Roosevelt died
1963	Lyndon B. Johnson	John F. Kennedy	Kennedy killed
1968	Richard M. Nixon	Dwight D. Eisenhower	Elected to office
1974	Gerald R. Ford	Richard M. Nixon	Nixon resigned
1989	George H. W. Bush	Ronald Reagan	Elected to office

experience, a mid-western and Catholic background, and strong conservative credentials to their ticket. If that wasn't enough, Ryan was also serious mountain climbing hunter who liked listening to heavy metal music and read libertarian novelist Ayn Rand. His choice was especially pleasing to the Tea Party and *The Wall Street Journal*. Ryan, in the end, did not help much.

SUCCESSION

Despite the other problems associated with the vice presidency, the office eventually did one thing reasonably well—solving our succession problem. Many nations have faltered or even been torn apart by disruptive upheavals because they failed to provide for a prompt, orderly means of transition. Our citizens, like most people, long for system stability and for a sense of continuity.

It is nowadays assumed that the presidential succession process was clearly spelled out when the U.S. Constitution was written. "But in fact, almost uniquely," wrote Jay Winik, "it is here that the Constitution is riddled with vexing ambiguities at best, fraught with astonishing omission, and, at times, downright confusing."[416] Indeed, most people assumed the founders believed that in the event of a presidential death in office, a special election would be conducted to elect a new president.

Then, on April 4, 1841, President William Henry Harrison died, just after one month in office. This caused considerable confusion and speculation. Harrison's cabinet believed the cabinet should govern and make collective decisions with John Tyler having just one vote. This would presumably be some form of cabinet rather than presidential government. Others thought Tyler should serve merely as an acting president or regent. But Tyler, with help from Secretary of State Daniel

Webster and others, stubbornly interpreted, or reinterpreted, the Constitution as making him fully the president. Winik writes, "recognizing that possession was nine-tenths of the law, Tyler set about waging an energetic two-month crusade to secure for himself, at the very least, de facto recognition as president."[417]

Tyler's bold demands established the precedent so that when Zachary Tyler died in July of 1850, everyone accepted that Vice President Millard Fillmore would be president. Similarly, in April 1865, Andrew Johnson, despite his questionable qualifications, was accepted quickly as the legitimate new president.

Our vice presidential succession process may be imperfect, but one of its virtues is the stability it brings to our arrangements. Trauma and instability are avoided, as people know in advance that there is a plan—a legitimate plan—that will be put into effect.

The framers provided that the vice president should be first in the order of succession, but they left it up to Congress to establish the rest of the order of succession. Three statutes and one constitutional amendment speak to this matter. In the first presidential succession act, passed in 1792, the president pro tempore of the U.S. Senate (by custom the senior member of the majority party in the Senate) was named first in line behind the vice president, followed by the speaker of the House of Representatives. If a double vacancy occurred (that is, if something happened to both the president and vice president), this same 1792 act provided that the president pro tempore of the Senate would become acting president "until a president be elected." Hence an immediate special election of some kind would have been called to elect a new president, unless the vacancy occurred in the last months of the presidential term.

This first statute was superseded in 1886 when the heads of the cabinet departments, beginning with the secretary of state, were named as the line of succession. This may have been done to avoid violating the principle of separation of powers. Many people, however, believe an elected official should stand first in line to fill the presidency. Harry Truman, while serving out FDR's fourth term, urged a return to succession by elected congressional officials. In 1947, Congress approved this change, placing the speaker of the House first behind the vice president, followed by the Senate's president pro tempore, followed by the cabinet officers in terms of the departmental seniority—secretary of state and so on.

Some people understandably question the wisdom of having the Senate's president pro tempore, usually the senior and often the oldest member of the Senate's majority party, in this line of succession. This, a few years ago, put Senators Strom Thurmond of South Carolina and Robert Byrd of West Virginia as third in line to serve as president. They were, to put it politely, well past their prime.

Some constitutional scholars criticize the Presidential Successor's Act of 1947 as either unconstitutional or unwise policy. First, Congress, it is thought, should name a cabinet officer not a member of Congress to be in line after a president and vice president are no longer available. This would keep the branches separate. Second, whoever takes over should be from the president's own party. Here, too, it

TABLE 8.3 Line of Succession for President*

Vice President
Speaker of the U.S. House of Representatives
President pro tempore of the U.S. Senate (senior member of Senate's majority party)
Secretary of State
Secretary of Treasury
Secretary of Defense
Attorney General
Secretary of Interior
Secretary of Agriculture
Secretary of Commerce
Secretary of Labor
Secretary of Health and Human Services
Secretary of Housing and Urban Development
Secretary of Transportation
Secretary of Energy
Secretary of Education
Secretary of Veteran's Affairs
Secretary of Homeland Security

*Note that to be eligible, the person has to be a natural-born American citizen.

would make sense for a cabinet officer rather than congressional leader to be next in line to take over the presidency.[418]

Before the Twenty-Fifth Amendment to the Constitution, the vice presidency had been vacant eighteen times for a total of about forty years. Fortunately, during these periods there had been no need to go down the line of presidential succession. Section 2 of the Twenty-Fifth Amendment, ratified in 1967, now provides that "whenever there is a vacancy in the office of the vice president, the president shall nominate a vice president who shall take office upon confirmation by a majority vote of both Houses of Congress."

Some critics of this provision say it gives too much power to the president. Defenders of the provision counter the criticisms as follows:

> In giving the President a dominant role in filling a vacancy in the vice presidency, the proposed amendment is consistent with present practice whereby the presidential candidate selects his own running mate who must be approved by the people through their representatives. It is practical because it recognizes the fact that a vice president's effectiveness in our government depends on his rapport with the president. If he is of the same party and of compatible temperament and views, all of which would be likely under the proposed amendment, his chances of becoming fully informed and adequately prepared to assume presidential power, if called upon, are excellent.[419]

A few critics say that this provision is overly vague on certain points. Thus some would amend it to add deadlines against stalling by either the White House or Congress. Others wondered what would happen if a president resigned or died while his nomination of a vice president was still pending. Would the nominee still stand? Or would the speaker of the House, who had just become president, have the right to nominate his or her choice? Would Congress have the right to choose between the two nominees? That there are remaining questions about presidential succession is, of course, unfortunate, for there are few things more concerning to a constitutional democracy than doubts about who has the legitimate right to govern.

Section 3 of the Twenty-Fifth Amendment provides for presidents to delegate presidential powers and duties to the vice president for a specified period. Debates had long raged over questions of presidential inability or disability. Many presidents had been temporarily unable to fulfill their responsibilities, and two presidents had serious disabilities: Garfield for two and a half months as he was dying, and Wilson for about a year with severe disability before retiring. In each case their vice presidents did not assume presidential duties, in part because they wished to avoid usurping the powers of that office. Now a president can temporarily step aside. Section 3 reads

> Whenever the President transmits to the President pro tempore of the Senate and the Speaker of the House of Representatives his written declaration that he is unable to discharge the powers and duties of his office, and until he transmits to them a written declaration to the contrary, such powers and duties shall be discharged by the Vice President as Acting President.

There is some uncertainty about when a vice president is formally put in the position of discharging the powers and duties of the presidency. Is it when the White House staff telephones the vice president? Is it when a president signs the required letters to congressional leaders? Is it when those leaders receive the letters?

Less than eight hours after a 1985 surgery, Ronald Reagan signed a letter to the congressional leaders reclaiming his responsibilities. Bush was presumably also notified at the same time. Nowadays these notifications should doubtless be sent via fax or e-mail, not by letter. White House aides inevitably will play the intermediary role in most of these circumstances, but this first test suggests that there are additional procedures to be ironed out.

Confusion arose, too, when in 1991 President George H. W. Bush announced that, in the event that his irregular heartbeat required electric shock therapy, power would be turned over to Vice President Quayle. While such a transfer of power was never required, the process once again raised questions.

What if there is contention about whether the president is disabled or fit? Section 4 of the Twenty-Fifth Amendment speaks to this, though here again, the provisions invite ambiguous interpretation. The beginning of this section reads

> Whenever the vice President and a majority of either the principal officers of the executive departments or of such other body as Congress may by law provide, transmit to the President pro tempore of the Senate and the Speaker of the House of Representatives their written declaration that the President is unable to

discharge the powers and duties of his office, the Vice President shall immediately assume the powers and duties of the office as Acting President.

The "principal officers of the executive departments" refers implicitly to the members of the cabinet. However, nowhere in the Constitution or anywhere else is there a formal definition of who is in the cabinet. It varies not only from president to president but from season to season, depending on whom a president wishes to include.

Another problem in this section that may raise uncertainty in the future involves the provision of how a president may regain his or her powers. A president, so the amendment provides, can inform the leaders of Congress that no inability exists and ask to resume the powers, but the vice president, together with a majority of the cabinet, can contest the president's assertion. What then? Well, says the provision, Congress has to decide quickly whether the president is able or unable. Complications can plainly arise in the vague wording. Presidents could conceivably keep insisting they are able to continue. Meanwhile, as Congress debates the issue, two persons could both be attempting to exercise presidential powers.

Most of these problems can be cleared up without resorting to any changes in the Twenty-Fifth Amendment. Informal agreements and unambiguous precedents will diminish the confusion. The amendment is plainly a compromise of many different proposals, none of which is entirely satisfactory. Constitution writing is always difficult; accommodating every conceivable problem is impracticable.[420]

CONCLUSION

What of the vice presidency? Ambiguous and fragile though it may be, this office is here to stay, paradoxes, uncertainties, tensions and all. The office "solves" our nation's succession problems and can be made into a relatively useful learning advisory and troubleshooting position. The job will remain attractive to many aspiring politicians precisely because it is one of the major paths to the presidency, and it can also these days be an attractive capstone to a distinguished political career.

Vice presidents will continue to have, and perhaps should have, a more or less undefined set of troubleshooting and advisory functions. Different incumbents will bring different skills and strengths to the office. Some will be astute policymakers. Some will be better at diplomacy. Some will be gifted political negotiators or coalition builders. Flexibility is needed.

Every president, together with his or her vice president, will define for themselves their practical, personal, and political relationships. The Constitution will—and should—continue to be silent on what those are. The Mondale, Gore, Cheney, and Biden precedents have transformed the office, yet these precedents, while not necessarily binding on future presidents, will nonetheless frame how vice presidential–president relations will take place for some time to come.

Efforts in the past several presidencies to make the office function more effectively should continue. The most obvious way of upgrading the vice presidency is to enhance the quality of the vice presidential selection process. Given all its problems and all the ambiguities of the position, a case can be made to abolish it or to relegate it to its historic Senate responsibilities. Yet this is highly unlikely. Our tradition and political tendencies all point toward retaining the office.

In the end, although the office may remain puzzling, the person holding the office is usually important, and the presidential–vice presidential partnership can be a critical one in the overall success of a presidency. Still, a central paradox remains: nearly all the credit for a successful presidency goes to the president. Vice presidents almost always lose their independence and sometimes even their identity, if not their integrity. The most damning and illustrative example of this was when President Dwight Eisenhower was asked toward the end of his presidency to cite an example of a major idea that Vice President Nixon had contributed to the Eisenhower presidency. Eisenhower responded with the embarrassing, "If you give me a week, I might think of one. I don't remember." Eisenhower's remark haunted Nixon in his 1960 presidential campaign as well as in subsequent campaigns.[421] As this anecdote suggests, the vice presidency can be both an effective training and a frustratingly maiming experience.

FOR DISCUSSION

1. Compare the vice presidencies of Al Gore, Dick Cheney, and Joe Biden.
2. In what ways can a vice president influence presidents and public policy?

DEBATE QUESTIONS

1. That the office of vice president be abolished.
2. That vice presidents should not have the right to cast votes in the U.S. Senate when there are tie votes.

FURTHER READINGS

Baumgartner, Jody C. *The American Vice Presidency Reconsidered*. Westport, CT: Praeger, 2006.
Cheney, Dick. *In My Time: A Personal and Political Memoir*. New York: Threshold, 2011.
Gellman, Barton. *Angler: The Cheney Vice Presidency*. New York: Penguin, 2008.
Goldstein, Joel. *The Modern American Vice Presidency*. Princeton, NJ: Princeton University Press, 1982.
Light, Paul C. *Vice Presidential Power*. Baltimore: Johns Hopkins Press, 1984.
Warshaw, Shirley Anne. *The Co-Presidency of Bush and Cheney*. Stanford: Stanford Politics and Policy, 2009.

Critical Thinking

STATEMENT: The language in the U.S. Constitution does not allow a president to fire a vice president.

PROBLEM: Should this option be available since the stakes are so high? This could prevent a vice president who for whatever reason has fallen out with the president from succeeding to the presidency.

CHAPTER 9

Presidents and the Court

> For most practical purposes the president may act as if the Supreme Court did not exist.... The fact is that the court has done more over the years to expand than contract the authority of the presidency.... In the nature of things judicial and political, the court can be expected to go on rationalizing most pretensions of most presidents. It is clearly one of the least reliable restraints on presidential activity.
>
> CLINTON ROSSITER, *The American Presidency* (New York: Harcourt, Brace and World, Inc., 1960), p. 56, pp. 58–59.

The history of presidential-Supreme Court relations is generally one of the nation's highest court encouraging an expansive view of presidential power. Although the Supreme Court has occasionally halted presidential action or declared a presidential act unconstitutional, the Court has more frequently legitimized the growth of presidential power.

The framers of the Constitution intended the Court to serve, along with the presidency, as a check on the anticipated or at least potential excesses of the national legislature. The Court, they hoped, would comprise wise, virtuous, and well-educated statesmen who would preserve the Constitution, especially from legislative encroachment. Most framers believed the Court would work hand-in-hand with the executive. Some even viewed it as part of the executive department or at least engaged in the similar functions, namely, executing, interpreting, and applying the laws.

Both the president and the Court have a national constituency. But where the president serves many masters, the court serves only one: the Constitution.

Presidents and the Court have had their share of clashes. This is to be expected. The Constitution stands as the supreme law of the land in a nation governed by laws, not men. The rule of law has a key limiting and empowering function for our government. Yet the Constitution is sometimes ambiguous, sometimes silent on grave matters of concern; the law is flexible and changing, open to interpretation. Differences of opinion, interest, and interpretation are inevitable. In most, yet by no means all, encounters between presidents and courts, presidents emerge victorious. The exceptions are notable. Jefferson was told by the Marshall Court that he had acted wrongly. Lincoln, after his death, was rebuffed for using military courts in areas where they were not justified. FDR saw several early New Deal initiatives struck down by the Court as unconstitutional. Truman was ordered by the Court to release steel mills from federal control. Richard Nixon's policy and political intentions were overturned by the federal courts on at least seventy-five occasions, most famously in the summer of 1974 when the Supreme Court directed him to release White House tapes for use in criminal investigations. Bill Clinton, in areas such as executive privilege and executive immunity, often found himself rebuked by the courts.[422] George W. Bush suffered a series of judicial rebuffs in the war against terrorism.

Here are some basic characteristics of two hundred and twenty-five years of presidential-Supreme Court relations.

- There is no getting politics out of a nomination to the Supreme Court. Picking justices is a political act. Presidents usually want to "pack" or at least shape the Court, but they possess no special legal or constitutional right to impose their views on a whole branch for a generation. The Constitution entitles a president only to try, not necessarily to succeed.[423]

- Presidents nominate Supreme Court justices and their nominees are usually confirmed by the U.S. Senate. Most justices conform to the general intentions of the presidents appointing them. However, about 20 percent of the justices deviate and become "wayward justices." That is, they vote and write decisions contrary to the views and values of those who appointed them. Several factors encourage justices, once on the bench, to grow independent from the presidents who nominated them.

- The Supreme Court is generally a friend of the presidency and supports the use of presidential power, especially in wartime or in the conduct of foreign affairs. Indeed the judiciary has played a significant role in the trend toward executive primacy in foreign policymaking.

- The justices can thwart presidential initiatives and are most likely to do so if evidence exists that Congress would agree with the Court, and if there is clear absence of any authority for the presidential action either in the Constitution or in congressional statutes. They are also likely to weigh in against a president when a president's public approval is low, at the end of his term, or after the president has left office or died.

- Presidents take an oath of office, typically administered by the Chief Justice, pledging to uphold the Constitution and not necessarily what the Supreme Court says about the Constitution. Presidents reserve the right to interpret the Constitution for themselves. They may, as they usually do, defer to the judgment of the Court, yet they do not have to accept or agree with the judicial reasoning.

This chapter explores these realities and seeks to answer the following questions and paradoxes. How do presidents select nominees for the Supreme Court? Why do some nominees get rejected? Why do some justices grow independent once on the Court? What were the Lincoln and FDR experiences with the Court and why did Roosevelt try to "pack the Court?" When, and in what circumstances, has the Court acted to expand the prerogatives of the chief executive, and when has the Court restrained the presidency? Can we expect the judiciary to constrain a powerful and popular president bent on exercising his or her will? Finally, do national security considerations justify virtually any means, constitutional or otherwise, a president wishes to adopt to ensure U.S. security?

For this chapter, Paradox number 1 is especially germane: we demand a powerful leader, yet are suspicious of the potential to abuse power. We want our presidents to govern effectively and solve problems, yet do not give them sufficient constitutional authority to meet these demands. And often, it is the Court that must seek to reign in a too powerful, abusive president.

PRESIDENTIAL NOMINATIONS TO THE COURT

At the Federal Convention of 1787 in Philadelphia many delegates believed the national legislature should appoint the justices. The important Virginian Plan had suggested this method. But it was opposed as impractical. It had not worked well in the states. The legislature would be too large to make such personnel decisions.

"Do Over": In the oath-taking on January 20, 2009, Chief Justice John Roberts misplaced "faithfully" in the oath, requiring a do-over at the White House on January 21. Pete Souza/ Getty Images.

And there were other objections. Yet strong opposition to legislative appointment was met with equally strong opposition to appointment by the chief executive.

Alexander Hamilton, in an effort to break the deadlock, proposed that all major officials be nominated by the president with the Senate having the right to approve or reject them. Although Hamilton's proposal was an ingenious compromise, delegates rejected the concept of two-branch participation in the appointment process twice before approving it only in the last month of their deliberations.

In modern times, presidents have had to look at the judicial selection process as a partnership venture between the White House and the Senate.[424] A judicial nominee must win a majority confirmation in the Senate. Presidents usually get their way with cabinet and top executive department nominations. The widely accepted view is that presidents are entitled to the assistance in the executive branch of people they respect and trust and whose views are compatible with their own. The Supreme Court, however, is different. It's a separate branch and most members of the Senate nowadays think they have a co-equal responsibility for who should sit on the nation's highest court.[425]

The U.S. Constitution is silent as to the criteria that should guide a president in selecting a Supreme Court nominee. As Terry Eastland, a former Reagan and Bush administration aide, writes, "This is a matter clearly within the president's discretion." However, "the considerations that have decisively influenced presidents in judicial selection have included political patronage, geographical balance, judicial philosophy, and—especially in recent years—race and gender."[426] Judicial values and judicial philosophy are plainly now the dominant criteria.

Most presidents understandably seek to nominate to the bench persons who share their partisan and policy preferences.[427] In effect, presidents make predictions about the likely future performance and policy opinions of their potential nominees. If a president can nominate two or three members to the Court, that president's political philosophy can extend beyond his or her term in office. Thus presidents pay a great deal of attention to who they shall nominate. In many instances this has led to nomination of friends, advisers, and loyal partisans. Yet party label alone is not enough. President Theodore Roosevelt wrote to his friend Henry Cabot Lodge and outlined some of his views about what was important as he considered the Massachusetts Chief Justice Oliver Wendell Holmes, Jr., as a Supreme Court nominee. To Lodge he wrote, "I should like to know that Judge Holmes was in entire sympathy with our views, that is, with your views and mine...before I would feel justified in appointing him."[428]

In recent decades, presidents have been slightly more partisan in judicial selection (see Table 9.1). Jimmy Carter did not get the opportunity to nominate any Justices to the Supreme Court, but Ronald Reagan was able to nominate three: Sandra Day O'Connor, Antonin Scalia, and Anthony Kennedy. Reagan also elevated William Rehnquist to Chief Justice in 1986. George H. W. Bush nominated David Souter and Clarence Thomas. Bill Clinton nominated two justices to the Court: Ruth Bader Ginsburg and Stephen G. Breyer. George W. Bush nominated John Roberts as Chief and Samuel Alito as an associate justice. And Obama

TABLE 9.1 Party Affiliation of District Judges and Court of Appeals Judges Appointed by Presidents

President	Party	Appointees from Same Party
Roosevelt	Democrat	97%
Truman	Democrat	92%
Eisenhower	Republican	95%
Kennedy	Democrat	92%
Johnson	Democrat	96%
Nixon	Republican	93%
Ford	Republican	81%
Carter	Democrat	90%
Reagan	Republican	94%
Bush, G. W. H.	Republican	89%
Clinton	Democrat	88%
Bush, G. W.	Republican	87%
Obama	Democrat	93%

SOURCES: Sheldon Goldman, "Judicial Selection Under Clinton: A Midterm Explanation," *Judicature* (May/June 1995): 280; Sheldon Goldman and Elliot Slotnick, "Clinton's Second Term Judiciary: Selection Under Fire," *Judicature* (May/June 1999). See also the Alliance for Justice, Judicial Selection Project, at www.afj.org/jsp.home.html

nominated Sonia Sotomayor and Elena Kagan to the court. All these justices came from the nominating president's party. (See Table 9.2.)

The appointment of federal judges also reflects the partisan interests of the president and his party (see Table 9.1). Only 13 of over 100 members of the Supreme Court came from a party other than the president's. Republican presidents tend to appoint more white men to the bench than do Democrats who appoint a higher percentage of women and minorities to federal judgeships.

President Obama had a comparatively easy time getting his two Supreme Court nominees confirmed by the Senate. In 2009, he nominated Sonia Sotomayor to replace retired Justice David Souter. The first Hispanic nominated to the Court, Sotomayor came from humble beginnings, received an A.B. from Princeton University, and a J.D. from Yale Law School. At the time of her nomination, Sotomayor was a Judge of the Court of Appeals for the Second Circuit. She was confirmed by a 68–31 vote in the Senate.

In 2010, Obama nominated Elena Kagan to replace John Paul Stevens. Kagan, the fourth female to serve on the Court, served as Solicitor General in 2009–2010; before that she was Dean of the Harvard Law School. She was confirmed by a 63–37 Senate vote (see Table 9.3).

Presidents have been influenced by a variety of factors when searching for potential Supreme Court nominees. First is finding someone who shares their ideological and philosophical views. Second, presidents are politicians and they naturally want praise and political credit for their appointments. Reagan's first nominee, Sandra Day O'Connor, conveniently satisfied both these standards. She

TABLE 9.2 Supreme Court Appointments, 1975–2012

Name	Year of Appointment	Prior Law School	Appointing President	Prior Judicial Experience	Government Experience
Antonin Scalia	1986	Harvard	Reagan	U.S. Court of Appeals	Assistant Attorney General: Office of Legal Counsel
Anthony M. Kennedy	1988	Harvard	Reagan	U.S. Court of Appeals	—
Clarence Thomas	1991	Yale	Bush, G. H. W.	U.S. Court of Appeals	Chair, Equal Employment Opportunity Commission
Ruth Bader Ginsburg	1993	Columbia	Clinton	U.S. Court of Appeals	—
Stephen G. Breyer	1994	Harvard	Clinton	U.S. Court of Appeals	U.S. Senate Committee on the Judiciary
John Roberts	2005	Harvard	Bush, G. W.	U.S. Court of Appeals	Department of Justice, Office of Legal Counsel
Samuel Alito	2006	Yale	Bush, G. W.	U.S. Court of Appeals	U.S. Senate Aide
Sonia Sotomayor	2009	Yale	Obama	U.S. Court Of Appeals	Assistant District Attorney
Elena Kagan	2010	Harvard	Obama	N/A	Solicitor General

was a strong Reagan supporter and her appointment won enormous praise for the president, especially from women's groups.

Still other factors are at work. Nominees have to be confirmed by a majority of the U.S. Senate. Presidents or their aides consult leading senators, especially those from a prospective nominee's home state. They also often consult with members of the Senate Judiciary Committee, the committee responsible for confirmation hearings and initial screening. Presidents also generally take into account the wishes of public and private sector leaders and interest groups who have a known interest in the nomination.

Who gets nominated and confirmed? They have all been lawyers, and in recent years most have been graduates of distinguished law schools. Almost all have been active in politics in some way or another. Some have served in local or state elective office. Some have been party leaders. Some were actively involved in presidential campaigns. A few even ran for the presidency themselves (Taft,

TABLE 9.3 Supreme Court Nominations: Senate Confirmation in the Modern Era

President and Party	Nominee	Year of Senate Vote	Vote Count	Confirmation
Obama (D)	Elena Kagan	2010	63–37	Yes
	Sonia Sotomayor	2009	68–31	Yes
G.W. Bush (R)	Samuel Alito	2006	58–42	Yes
	John Roberts	2005	78–22	Yes
	Harriet Miers	(Withdrawn)	N/A	**No**
Clinton (D)	Stephen Breyer	1994	87–9	Yes
	Ruth Bader Ginsburg	1994	96–3	Yes
G. H. W. Bush (R)	Clarence Thomas	1991	52–48	Yes
	David Souter	1990	90–9	Yes
Reagan (R)	Anthony Kennedy	1988	97–0	Yes
	Robert Bork	1987	42–58	**No**
	Antonin Scalia	1986	98–0	Yes
	Sandra Day O'Connor	1981	99–0	Yes
Ford (R)	John Paul Stevens	1975	98–0	Yes
Nixon (R)	William Rehnquist	1971	68–26	Yes
	Lewis Franklin Powell Jr.	1972	89–1	Yes
	Harry Blackmun	1970	94–0	Yes
	G. Harrold Carswell	1970	45–51	**No**
	Clement Haynsworth	1969	45–55	**No**
	Warren E. Burger	1969	74–3	Yes

Hughes, and Earl Warren). Almost a third served as executive branch officials in the national government before their appointment to the Court, as was the case with both George W. Bush's nominees. Nine were attorneys general, four were solicitors general, at least eighteen held cabinet-level posts, and over a dozen held various other Department of Justice positions.

Perhaps the most common background in the recent past has been some experience serving as a state or federal judge. Why? In part because it was believed this was ideal training for service on the nation's highest court. Presidents also recognized it was easier to discern the predictable future responses of a potential Court member if their decisions could be studied.

The Constitution nowhere stipulates that Court members be lawyers. Nor is there any congressional statute insisting on judicial experience. Yet no one disputes the need for *legal* experience. The desirability of *judicial* experience, however, is less clear. Several distinguished justices did not have prior judicial experience, including John Marshall, Earl Warren, Louis Brandeis, Robert Jackson, and Lewis F. Powell. Intelligence and temperament, as well as being well read, would seem to be just as important as lower court experience. However, most future court nominees are likely to come from the lower federal courts.

Future presidents will probably consider these political factors:

(1) whether their choice will render them more popular among influential interest groups; (2) whether the nominee has been a loyal member of the President's
party; (3) whether the nominee favors presidential programs and policies; (4)
whether the nominee is acceptable (or at least not "personally obnoxious") to the
home-state Senators; (5) whether the nominee's judicial record, if any, meets the
Presidential criteria of constitutional construction; (6) whether the President is
indebted to the nominee for past political services; and (7) whether the President
feels "good" or "comfortable" about his choice.[429]

Issues of race and gender will also doubtlessly play a role in presidential Court
nomination decisions.

CONFIRMATION BATTLES

Article II, Section 2, provides the president shall have power, "by and with the
advice and consent of the Senate," to appoint Supreme Court justices. If a president
decides simply to assert his power to pack the court with good friends or unqualified or extremist persons, senators from the opposition party, or even from the
president's own party, will try to use their constitutional power to defeat him. Over
the history of the Republic, the senate has rejected twenty-six presidential nominees to the Court (see Table 9.4). This amounts to 15 percent of those nominated.
This rejection rate increases about 25 percent for presidents in their last year in
office and when the Senate is controlled by the opposition party. More important,
this check on presidential power has forced presidents not to appoint persons who
would fail to win Senate approval. In yet other instances some potential nominees
have taken themselves out of consideration precisely because they feared grueling
confirmation hearings.[430]

Why are some nominees rejected? Sometimes it is because a president is
highly unpopular in the country and in the Senate. President Andrew Johnson's
stock in the Senate was so low he probably could not have had any nominee of his
confirmed; his one nominee fell victim to Senate rejection.

On occasion a practice known as "senatorial courtesy" contributes to the rejection of a nominee. This occurs when the senators or a senator from a nominee's
home state indicate to the White House that they strongly oppose the proposed
Court appointment. This practice is more common in cases of federal district
judge appointments, yet it has in times past undercut a presidential Supreme
Court appointment.

The political and philosophical views of a nominee can sometimes stir up
the opposition of major interest groups and the opposition party, as was the case
in Reagan's 1987 nomination of Robert Bork. This can especially doom a candidacy when the opposition party controls the U.S. Senate, as it did when Nixon,
for example, tried to appoint Clement Hayworth in 1969. Many senators, especially Democrats, viewed Hayworth as too conservative. The senate rejected
another of Nixon's nominees, Florida Judge G. Harrold Carswell, mainly on the

TABLE 9.4 Supreme Court Nominations Rejected, Postponed, or Withdrawn Due to Senate Opposition

Nominee	Year Nominated	Nominated by	Actions
William Paterson[a]	1773	Washington	Withdrawn
John Rutledge[b]	1795	Washington	Rejected
Alexander Wolcott	1811	Madison	Rejected
John J. Crittenden	1828	J.Q. Adams	Postponed
Roger B. Taney[c]	1835	Jackson	Postponed
John C. Spencer	1844	Tyler	Rejected
Reuben H. Walworth	1844	Tyler	Withdrawn
Edward King	1844	Tyler	Postponed
Edward King[d]	1844	Tyler	Withdrawn
John M. Read	1845	Tyler	No action
George W. Woodward	1845	Polk	Rejected
Edward A. Bradford	1852	Fillmore	No action
George E. Badger	1853	Fillmore	Postponed
William C. Micou	1853	Fillmore	No action
Jeremiah S. Black	1861	Buchanan	Rejected
Henry Stanbery	1866	Johnson	No action
Ebenezer R. Hoar	1869	Grant	Rejected
George H. Williams[b]	1873	Grant	Withdrawn
Caleb Cushing[b]	1874	Grant	Withdrawn
Stanley Matthews[a]	1881	Hayes	No action
William B. Hornblower	1893	Cleveland	Rejected
Wheeler H. Beckham	1894	Cleveland	Rejected
John J. Parker	1930	Hoover	Rejected
Abe Fortas[e]	1968	Johnson	Withdrawn
Homer Thornberry	1968	Johnson	No action
Clement F. Haynsworth, Jr.	1969	Nixon	Rejected
G. Harrold Carswell	1970	Nixon	Rejected
Robert H. Bork	1987	Reagan	Rejected
Douglas H. Ginsburg	1987	Reagan	Withdrawn
Harriet Miers	2005	Bush, G. W.	Withdrawn

Source: Updated from David M. O'Brien, *Storm Center: The Supreme Court in American Politics*, 3rd ed. (New York: Norton, 1993), p. 75.
[a] = Reappointed and confirmed.
[b] = Nominated for chief justice.
[c] = Taney was reappointed and confirmed as chief justice.
[d] = Second appointment.
[e] = Associate justice nominated for chief justice.

basis of inadequate professional competence. Opposition to Carswell came fast and strong. One respected law school dean suggested this nominee presents more slender credentials than any other nominee for the Supreme Court put forth in the twentieth century, and after the confirmation hearings were completed, most senators agreed with this verdict.

Sometimes the Senate rejects a nominee to signal its opposition to the policy or recent record of the incumbent Supreme Court. Sometimes senators are unsure of the political reliability of a nominee. And sometimes the Senate merely makes a mistake, as some observers believe it did when it rejected President Herbert Hoover's 1930 nomination of Judge John J. Parker of North Carolina.

The Senate usually takes its constitutional responsibility seriously. As noted, senators view an appointee to the Court as more consequential than most members of a president's cabinet. Court nominees are seen as more important because of their longer tenure, their independence from the White House, and their impact over a whole range of public policy issues. The Senate Judiciary Committee and then the senate itself closely scrutinize these nominees. Poor selections such as Madison's choice of Alexander Wolcott, Grant's choice of George Williams, and Nixon's choice of G. Harrold Carswell, have been rejected often enough to set reasonable standards. Although the Senate rejected only four nominees in the twentieth century, presidents and White House advisors with any sense of history are aware that the Senate jealously prizes this shared power of appointment.

Only recently has the confirmation process turned into a more openly partisan conflict. As the stakes for various interest groups grew, so too did partisan bickering, "gotcha politics," and televised hearings as theater.[431] Early public hearings were a rarity. The first truly public hearing occurred in 1916 for nominee Louis Brandeis, and Brandeis didn't even show up for that. The first nominee to testify before the Senate Judiciary Committee was Harlan Fiske Stone in 1935, and it wasn't until the 1960s that it became customary for nominees to testify. Every nominee since then has testified before the Senate.

In late 1987, Reagan's nomination of Robert H. Bork incited sharp differences of opinion about how much the Senate should take into account the philosophical views of a nominee. Some Democrats in the Senate, such as Ted Kennedy and Joe Biden, proclaimed that the framers had intended the broadest role for the senate in choosing members of the Court and hence they had wide authority in checking into a nominee's constitutional views and values. At least one Republican senator disagreed, saying that for the Senate to require that judicial candidates pledge allegiance to the political and ideological views of particular senators or interest groups could lead to paralyzing the Senate in a gridlock of competing interest groups, each hawking its own agenda. A New York Times/CBS News public opinion survey at the time found that Americans believed senators should attach importance to nominee's positions on constitutional issues when judging the nominee's fitness in the confirmation process.

The George H. W. Bush nomination fight over Clarence Thomas in 1991 was one of the most notable in U.S. history. Thomas barely won confirmation by a 52 to 48 vote, but both his nomination and especially his confirmation battle triggered a major political backlash for George H. W. Bush and to some extent for the U.S. Senate.[432]

During the Clinton years, confirmation politics often were deeply partisan events. While partisanship has always played a part in the process, an intense partisanship affected confirmation politics in the 1990s. "The Republicans rewrote the rules when Clinton was in office," said judicial scholar Sheldon Goldman. The process has broken down, he added; "The partisanship has gotten out of hand. The 'advise and consent' process has turned into 'obstruct and delay.'"[433]

Republicans blocked many Clinton nominees, delaying the holding of hearings on others, and refused to even deal with still others. It was a strategy designed to prevent the president from filling seats on the bench. And when George W. Bush became president in 2001, and the Democrats controlled the Senate, they did much the same.

This led a frustrated Bush to propose process changes in the confirmation system, setting specific deadlines for the president and Senate to act on judicial nominations.[434] But such efforts went to the back burner when Republicans regained control of the Senate in 2003, and Bush's judicial nominees fared somewhat better with their partisans in control of the process.

In 2005, President Bush nominated Harriet Miers to the Supreme Court to replace Sandra Day O'Connor. Miers came under fire from both the left (who accused her of being underqualified and too much the Bush loyalist) and right (who found her insufficiently conservative). When it became clear Miers could not muster enough votes for confirmation, the President awkwardly withdrew the nomination. Since 1968, six nominees failed to be confirmed, a clear indication of the contentiousness of Court nominations and the seriousness of the Senate role in confirmation struggles.[435]

WAYWARD JUSTICES

Once confirmed, new members of the Court are in no way obliged to the president who appointed them. Indeed, there is an element of unpredictability in how justices will vote in future years. Loyalty to the president who appointed them is not considered a proper reason for judgment on the Court. Even justices who have "pleased" their sponsoring president acknowledge that they think and act differently once they join the Court. Such was the case in 2012 when Chief Justice John Roberts angered some Republicans when he cast the tie-breaking vote that upheld the constitutionality of "Obamacare."

Justice William H. Rehnquist said any president who attempts to leave a lasting ideological stamp in the Court will typically fail. Unexpected legal developments, the Court's time-honored tradition of independence, the role of precedent, the influence of eight colleagues already there, and other factors diminish a president's efforts to leave a mark on the Court.

How often do presidents fail to get what they want in the people they appoint to the Supreme Court? One student of the judiciary found at least 20 percent of the justices have "deviated" from the expectations presidents held for them. In some instances, such as the Earl Warren case, we can relate judicial performance to presidential expectations with considerable precision. More often assumptions have to be made based on the general political views of the presidents and on the situations in which they operated. In still other cases of short tenure, it is near impossible to discern the "loyalty" or "deviation" of a justice. Political scientist Robert Scigliano examined the fit or lack of fit between justices and presidents and concluded:

…that about three-fourths of those justices for whom an evaluation could be made conformed to the expectations of the Presidents who appointed them to the Supreme Court.…

Our conclusion is an important one in that it indicates limitations upon the ability of Presidents to influence the policies of the court through appointments and assures us, retrospectively at least, of a certain, but crucial, measure of judicial independence from Presidential attempts to bring the Court closely into line with the executive branch of government.[436]

Why have so many justices disappointed the presidents who appointed them? Sometimes it is because the presidents and their advisors failed to examine closely the already known views of the prospective nominee. Woodrow Wilson apparently overlooked some of the doctrinal conservatism of McReynolds. Eisenhower apparently engaged in some wishful thinking in his selection of Earl Warren. Ike was also in debt to Warren politically for his help at the last stages of the 1952 presidential nomination battle. Warren had not done a lot, but what he did do, Eisenhower greatly appreciated.

The constitutional obligations of the court are different from those of being a friend or advisor to a president. The Court is not supposed to be a rubber stamp for anyone, and most of the justices come to view themselves as virtually a sovereign in their own right. The Court, moreover, decides when violations of the law, including violations by the executive branch, occur. The Court, further, is charged with keeping the president and others in the executive branch in their constitutional place. The *Marbury v. Madison* (1803), *Ex parte Milligan* (1866), *Youngstown Sheet and Tube Co. v. Sawyer* (1952), and *U.S. v. Nixon* (1974) tradition is important to the Court, and its new justices become defenders of this tradition.[437]

Life tenure adds an incentive to think, act, and decide independently. The framers knew that what Alexander Hamilton called "the least dangerous branch" would need to be at least somewhat free from the influences of ambition and interest if they were to perform their responsibility. This gives justices "high honor, high responsibility, and guaranteed tenure and salary, so that they need neither seek higher office nor worry about retaining the one they have. These conditions, at once emancipating and greatly demanding, result in judicial behavior which may not conform either to presidential expectations or to the views that the justices expressed before joining the Court."[438]

Once a justice is on the Court, a president cannot effectively threaten, intimidate, or retaliate against a wayward or contrarian justice. There may be times and circumstances when presidential "jawboning" would sway a decision but, as the following examples suggest, they would be the exception to the rule. Jefferson tried in vain to have a justice impeached. FDR tried to reorganize or pack the Court. Nixon, in a crucial case involving him, hinted he might not comply with the Court's decision. These presidential intrigues failed.

Thus, there is, as there should be, a certain amount of unpredictability in the judicial appointment process. Presidents can never be certain their nominees will be approved by the Senate. Nor can a president ever be sure a justice will not "grow" or change when he or she dons the judicial robes. Chief Justice John Robert's deciding vote in favor of the president in the Obama Health Care Case, surprised many court-watchers, and yet, such "side-switching" is not at all unprecedented. A Yale law professor put it well: "You shoot an arrow into a far distant future when you appoint a Justice and not the man himself can tell you what he will think about some of the problems that he will face."[439]

THE TEMPTATION TO MOVE BEYOND THE LAW

Given the many roadblocks and agents that have a veto that may block the president's path, it is not surprising that the more ambitious presidents get frustrated as others block their way. Well-organized opposition in Congress, demanding special interests, an uncooperative business community, an adversarial press, and others can at times seem to gang up on the White House.

When faced with these multiple opposing forces, most presidents feel trapped. The choice may appear to be either to accept defeat or take bold action on behalf of what presidents claim is the national interest. Making the complex separation of powers work is difficult under the best of circumstances; in normal times it may seem impossible to get the system moving. Thus, rather than accept defeat, some presidents are tempted to cut corners, act unilaterally, move beyond the law, even stretch the constitutional limits a bit.

Knowing they will be judged on how much they are able to accomplish, presidents, when faced with potential gridlock, look for ways to get around Congress. Sometimes presidents can exert unilateral authority, and at other times, they may stretch the envelope and venture into areas of questionable legitimacy.

Presidents may see the system itself as the problem and thus feel justified in going beyond the law. Richard Nixon with Watergate[440] and Ronald Reagan with the Iran-Contra scandal are two pronounced examples.[441] Clinton and George W. Bush in some of their antiterrorism initiatives also illustrate this.

Some presidents get away with it (e.g. Reagan); some do not (Nixon). But when the choice seems to be stay within the law and fail (Ford, Carter) or go beyond the law and maybe you will succeed and maybe you won't get caught, the temptation is great, too great for some leaders to resist.

An attitude of arrogance may overtake the president and his top staff. "We know best" and "they are blocking progress" leads to the belief that the "slight" abuse of power is being done for the greater good. But such an attitude leads to the Imperial Presidency, and to further abuses of power.[442]

President Reagan was convinced that communism was an evil that had to be fought at all costs; that the Marxist government in Nicaragua was a serious and direct threat to the United States; that the Congress was soft on communism; and that public opinion, which opposed U.S. intervention, was uninformed in spite of Herculean efforts by the administration. Therefore, Reagan was faced with the difficult choice of either accepting the will of Congress, the voice of the people, and the law, or acting on what he believed to be in the national interest. He acted. Likewise, George W. Bush engaged in domestic surveillance that was clearly illegal. He believed the law interfered with his responsibility as Commander-in-Chief, so he moved beyond the law.

Putting aside for a moment the question of whether Reagan and Bush were correct about the threat Nicaragua and terrorists posed, one thing is clear: they decided that the law was wrong and that they would not be bound by law. This was one of the chief reasons why the framers insisted on checks and balances: to control abuses of power.[443]

Must a president, in all circumstances and at all times, obey the law? And whose interpretation of the law must a president obey? May a president disregard a decision of the Supreme Court he finds legally objectionable? Some of our most famous presidents—Jackson, Lincoln, and Franklin Roosevelt—clashed with Congress and the Court. Did they cross a line in doing so? Is the president entitled to claim that his understanding of the Constitution should supersede that of Congress or decisions and precedents of the Courts?

No man is above the law. And yet, who—if anyone—has the "final word" on what the law means or how it is to be applied to the separate branches?

Conventional wisdom as well as constitutional design suggest that Congress *makes* laws, the Executive branch *implements* laws, and Courts *interpret* laws. But in practice these distinctions blur. There is a separation of powers, but there is also a blending or sharing of powers. Presidents, through the veto power, are a part of the legislative process. And as executives, presidents must interpret the laws they are to implement. If the lines of distinction are blurred, so too are the lines of authority. In practice, presidents execute, interpret, make, and implement the law. But just how independent and absolute is a president's authority to apply his or her understanding of the law to events?

There is no one, central authoritative center of power in the American system. There are three branches, three centers vying for political control.

All three branches have a vested interest (a self-interest) in determining what is and is not constitutional. And when and why should one branch willingly cede this important power to a rival branch? Thus, the president will assert a claim in determining precisely what the Constitution means, and because power can be bendable and fluid, the president's stake in establishing a constitutional territorial claim can have enormous consequences.

To the question, "should a president obey the law?," the presumptive answer must, of course, be "yes." After all, the president takes an oath to do so. And yet, must a president obey a law he deems unconstitutional or immoral? Can such laws be binding? And precisely whose view of law shall a president obey? The Constitution? Statutes passed by Congress? Interpretations of the Supreme Court? Does the separation-of-power logic allow presidents room to dispute or even violate laws of the congress and precedents of the Court?[444]

A president is no mere passive observer in this power struggle. A president has a constitutional stake in the outcome. And if the separation of powers divides, it also commingles. While each branch has a specific area of authority, no branch is completely autonomous of the other branches, or "wholly unconnected with each other."[445] Because of this, conflict will arise. Each branch must attempt to protect its powers from the others, and there will be times when clashing interests lead to political conflict.[446]

Increasingly, presidents have asserted a broad power to disregard laws they believe to be infringements of their institutional authority, that they see as unconstitutional, or that they believe inhibit the ability of the government to respond to the needs of national security. This control over the interpretation of the law is a part of the rising influence of an administrative strategy presidents employ to gain leverage over policy.

THE PRESIDENT'S EMERGENCY POWER

Is a president ever justified in stretching the Constitution? And if so, who decides? While the word *emergency* does not appear in the Constitution, the founders envisioned the possibility of a president exercising "supraconstitutional powers" in time of national emergencies.[447]

During a crisis, presidents often assume extraconstitutional powers. The branches, which under normal circumstances, check and balance a president, will usually defer to the president in times of national crisis. A president's institutional position offers a vantage point from which he can more easily exert crisis leadership; and the Congress, Court, and public usually accept the president's judgments.

The idea that there might be a different set of legal and constitutional standards for normal conditions than for emergency conditions raises some unsettling questions regarding democratic governments and constitutional systems. Can democratic regimes function in any but prosperous, peaceful circumstances? Or must the U.S. constantly rely on the strength of a despot or "constitutional dictatorship" to save it from disaster? Are constitutional governments incapable of meeting the demands of crisis?[448]

Nowhere in the Constitution is it specified that a president will have additional powers in times of crisis. History, however, has shown us that in times of national emergency the powers of a president have greatly expanded, and while former Justice Abe Fortas writes that, "Under the Constitution, the president has no implied powers which enable him to make or disregard laws,"[449] we can see that this is precisely what American presidents have done.

The consequence of this view of an enlarged reservoir of presidential power in emergencies was characterized by constitutional scholar Edward S. Corwin as "constitutional relativity."[450] By this Corwin envisioned a constitution broad and flexible enough to meet the needs of an emergency situation as defined and measured by the Constitution. The Constitution can be adapted, in short, to meet the needs of the times. If the times call for quasi-dictatorial action by the executive, the Court could find this acceptable.

PRESIDENTIAL ACTION IN TIMES OF EMERGENCY

In practice a president's emergency power has been great in comparison to powers under normal circumstances. When faced with a crisis situation, presidents have made exaggerated claims of power, have acted on these claims, and generally have gotten away with these excessive, and often extralegal, uses of power. History provides us with clear examples of the enormous power of a president in an emergency situation.[451]

Presidents on occasion act with little regard for the wishes and dictates of the other branches. The necessity for quick, decisive, often extraconstitutional actions, which the crisis may demand, places a heavy burden on the president. Being the only leader able to move quickly, the president must shoulder the burden of meeting the crisis. According to Richard Longaker, "In time of crisis constitutional limitations bend to other needs."[452]

For the crisis presidency to be seen as legitimate

1. The president must face a genuine and a widely recognized emergency;
2. Congress and the public must, more or less, accept that the president should exercise supraconstitutional powers;
3. Congress may, if it chooses, override presidential acts;
4. the president's acts must be public so as to allow Congress and the public to judge them;
5. there must be no suspension of the next election; and
6. the president should consult with Congress where possible.

Lincoln and Roosevelt met (more or less) these requirements; Nixon and Reagan often did not. Clinton's was a mixed case.[453]

Even when the preceding requirements are met, however, one should not be casual about presidential usurpations of power. Presidents must be held to account. As the Supreme Court reminded us in *Ex parte Milligan* (1866), "wicked men, ambitious of power, with a hatred of liberty and contempt of law, may fill the place once occupied by Washington and Lincoln."

After the terrorism of 9/11, the public rallied behind George W. Bush in support of his efforts to battle the terrorist network responsible for the attack on the United States. While the president generally pursued his goals with reason and proportionality, some of the administration's actions proved controversial. The attorney general questioned the patriotism of anyone who objected to administration actions, and ordered the detention, without being charged with a crime, without access to an attorney, and without recourse to judicial appeal, of several American citizens and numerous non-nationals.[454]

Bush was able to get the Congress to quickly pass the U.S. Patriot Act into law. He orchestrated a war against Afghanistan, whose Taliban government had been harboring the terrorists of Al Qaeda. All of this was done either with the near rubber stamp approval of Congress or on the president's own claimed authority, independent of congressional authorization.

But Bush's actions raised concern when in late 2002, the administration announced a major shift in U.S. strategic policy when they released "The National Security Strategy of the United States of America." This report announced the replacement of deterrence with a new policy of preemption. This was a presidential directive, with little or no congressional involvement or authorization. It was a major transformation of U.S. strategic policy, was solely a presidential policy, and paved the way for a preemptive strike on Iraq.

COURT DECISIONS AND PRESIDENTIAL POWER

The Supreme Court rarely rules against a President. The two circumstances when the Court is most likely to decide against a sitting president are during times of intense political conflict and change (i.e., the Depression) or when partisan holdover majorities control the Court (i.e., in the Jefferson administration when the president faced a Court made up entirely of Justices appointed by Federalist presidents).

Five types of Supreme Court decisions are possible when presidential powers come into question (see Table 9.5). Most of the time, as noted, the Court approves or *expands* presidential authority. It often also *legitimizes* presidential power. The Court can also duck the question on the grounds that it is a political matter to be settled by Congress and the president. On rare occasions, a *two-sided decision* is possible, when the Court may restrict an individual president but add to the power of the office. The Nixon tapes decision in 1974 is illustrative of a two-sided ruling. The Court ordered Nixon to yield his tapes. The Court also, and for the first time, recognized executive privilege as having constitutional standing. Sometimes, of course, in a clash of views, the Supreme Court *restricts* or curbs a president and presidential powers.

How often do we see the Supreme Court handing down these kinds of decisions? The two-sided rulings are rare. The Court, over its history, has often avoided questions affecting presidential power. Justices, for example, rarely want to deal with questions about the legality of a war such as in Vietnam.

When sensitive issues of national security arise the Court often invokes what is commonly called the doctrine of "political questions" to avoid head-on collisions with the president. The doctrine rests on the separation of powers theory, namely, that the Supreme Court exercises the judicial power and leaves policy or political questions to the president and Congress. Chief Justice John Marshall invented the "political question" doctrine as early as 1803 when he said that matters in their nature political are not for this Court to resolve. He affirmed this later, as in 1829, when he refused to rule on a boundary dispute between the U.S. and Spain. The judiciary shall not, said Marshall, decide foreign policy. Questions such as foreign boundaries, he added, are more political than legal.

Expanding and legitimizing decisions are common. They are much more likely than restricting decisions. Nearly every analyst of Court–presidency relations emphasizes the Court's role in the expansion of presidential powers. Most

TABLE 9.5 Types of Court Decisions Regarding Presidential Power

Type of Decision	Definition	Example
Expanding:	Decision adding power to presidency.	*U.S. v. Curtiss-Wright Export Corp* (1936). Recognizes it as necessary for presidents to have more power in foreign than in domestic affairs.
Legitimizing:	Decision giving Court approval for presidential activities that were questioned.	*Korematsu v. U.S.* (1944). Approved FDR and executive powers to intern Japanese-American citizens in World War II.
Avoiding:	Decisions the Court decided "not to decide"; avoids getting involved.	*Massachusetts v. Laird* (1970). Denied to hear a case that questioned the president's broad power in the Vietnam War, thus avoiding a decision on the war.
Two-Sided:	Decisions going against a president yet adding power to institution of the presidency.	*U.S. v. Nixon* (1974). Nixon told to yield tapes, yet court recognizes "executive privilege" as valid in serious national security situations.
Restricting:	Decisions curbing or even diminishing presidential power.	*Youngstown Sheet and Tube Co. v. Sawyer* (1952). Truman and his Secretary of Commerce told they had exceeded their power in seizing the nation's steel mills to prevent a strike. Truman based his action on general powers of his office. Court held he could take no such action without express authorization from Congress.

of the time, the Supreme Court has supported the vigorous actions of our strong presidents. Although his sweeping verdict exaggerated the case, many students of presidential-judicial relations modify this judgment only slightly today.[455]

The Supreme Court has been and will likely continue to be a supportive ally in most potential showdowns, especially in the case of emergency or national security contexts.[456]

Many of the cases cited here are cases in which the highest court essentially gave or approved of power that had been previously undefined or undetermined. The issue at stake is whether presidents are able to cite a law or precise wording in the Constitution, or whether their broad and vague "executive power" allow them to conduct certain activities.

The Prize Cases (1863) were not the first dealing with presidential power to come before the Court, yet they are the first dealing with extraordinary, independent actions taken during a crisis. The Supreme Court ruled 5–4 that Lincoln could wage war with the South, under his authority as commander-in-chief, without congressional declaration. Presidential discretion was deemed sufficient for exercising this power. Indeed it was deemed to be within the broad grant of executive power found in Article II of the Constitution. The maxim that "There are two Constitutions, one for peace, the other for war" has its roots in these Civil War decisions.[457]

Before 1863, under international law, ships could be legally taken as prizes only when a conflict had been recognized as a war between two belligerent powers. Thus, if the Supreme Court said the South did not have belligerent status, it appeared the justices would have had to rule the blockade as illegal. They decided instead to give primacy to executive discretion.

Another pro-presidency landmark case, *In re Neagle* (1890)[458], dealt not with foreign affairs but rather with the domestic task of effectively carrying out the functions of government. David Neagle, deputy U.S. marshal in the San Francisco region, was assigned to travel with Supreme Court Justice Stephen J. Field. Field's life had been threatened by a Californian, whom Field had sentenced to prison. The U.S. Attorney General assigned Neagle to help protect Field. In implementing his assignment Neagle had to shoot, fatally it turned out, the man who in fact did try to attack Field.

The central question involved in this case was whether a president has either the constitutional or the prerogative sources of power to execute orders of the kind assigning Neagle to his duties. Is a president limited to enforcing only acts of Congress?

Here again the Supreme Court ruled the president had been granted broad executive powers that he must be able to use at his discretion to administer properly the laws of the land. The Court openly acknowledged it was interpreting the word *law* in a liberal manner, the only conceivable manner that would serve the interests of justice in this instance. The president's executive order was clearly constitutional under the "faithfully execute" clause of the Constitution. The president's duty to fulfill this clause is consequently not limited to the enforcement of acts of Congress, according to their express terms, "but includes also the rights, duties and obligations growing out of the Constitution itself, our international relations, and all the protection implied by the nature of the government under the Constitution."

This decision strengthened and expanded the powers of the presidency. This broad interpretation was underlined a few years later in a subsequent Court case that legitimized President Grover Cleveland's sending troops into the Chicago area to deal with a railroad strike. Workers at the Pullman railroad company in 1894 had gone out on strike over certain wage reductions. The American Railway Union carried out a secondary boycott against the Pullman company, a boycott that eventually threatened violence. A federal court issued an order seeking to halt the boycott on the grounds the strike crippled interstate commerce. Union President Eugene V. Debs and his aides ignored the court order, were arrested, convicted of contempt, and sentenced to prison. President Grover Cleveland had dispatched federal troops to Chicago and ordered the U.S. Attorney in Chicago to halt the strike. Debs not only ignored these federal initiatives but petitioned the

Supreme Court for a writ of habeas corpus, challenging his detention as illegal. Writing for the Court in this famous *In re Debs* (1895) case, Justice David J. Brewer affirmed sweeping executive emergency powers.

In a 1926 landmark decision, *Myers v. The United States*, the Court in a 6-3 decision granted a president, and presumably the presidency, with further administrative power, authorizing presidents to remove governmental officials without obtaining the consent of Congress. Frank Myers, postmaster for Portland, Oregon, was removed by President Woodrow Wilson without Wilson's securing Senate consent. Myers brought suit for salary for the remainder of his term. Back in 1876 Congress had passed a law providing for Senate participation in the removal of postmasters. Thus the question now, in the 1920's, was this: May Congress limit a president's removal power?

Here is a rare instance in which the Supreme Court went against the wishes of Congress, at least as represented by the old statute under which Myers claimed to have his job protected. As we have seen, the Court usually defers to congressional judgment when Congress has specifically addressed the issue at hand, yet in this case the Court did not. The majority in this case believed a strict separation of powers is necessary if the executive is to function effectively. Perhaps the next major expansion of presidential power came in a case previously discussed in the section on Franklin Roosevelt. In the *United States v. Curtiss-Wright Export Corporation* (1936), the Court, in a 7–1 decision, chose to affirm and expound at length on the broad foreign powers held by the president. The executive, the Court said, was the sole spokesman of the nation, not of the Constitution, of the national government, or of Congress. To many observers this expansive decision came close to saying the president was "the sovereign." Congress could delegate, or so it seemed, virtually any foreign policy authority to the White House.[459]

A year later, in *United States v. Belmont* (1937), a near unanimous Court ruled the national executive has the sole right to enter into executive agreements with other nations. State laws or policies do not supersede presidentially arranged international agreements even if they are not precisely in treaty form requiring Senate approval. Implicitly, if not explicitly, the Court ruled executive agreements had the binding force of treaties. Although an international compact is not always a treaty, the federal government has sole claim to "external affairs" and the external powers of the United States are to be exercised without regard to state policies or laws.[460]

In 1944, an even more decisive delegation of authority was added to the long list of pro-presidency precedents. The Court, in the already noted *Korematsu* and related cases, gave the president national security powers even when those powers extended primarily to domestic public policy considerations. On February 19, 1942, President Roosevelt issued an executive order empowering the secretary of war to clear the three West Coast states and parts of Arizona of all persons of Japanese descent, 70,000 of whom were American citizens, and place them in detention centers.

Fred T. Korematsu, an American-born citizen of Japanese descent, violated the civilian exclusion order, a part of the implementation of FDR's general order, and was given a suspended sentence of five years of probation by the federal court. He appealed his case and the Court began to consider his and similar cases in May 1943.

Lawyers for Mr. Korematsu in 1943 (and in later years when his conviction was overturned) said Roosevelt in effect was using his commander-in-chief authority to condemn a race to imprisonment. No charge had been issued; no trial conducted. With his action, FDR called into question several constitutional rights for all American citizens: personal security, the right to move about freely, and the right not to be deprived of those rights except on an individual basis after trial by jury. All these traditional rights were imperiled. The force of the Fifth Amendment that guaranteed equal treatment under the law and due process was weakened. The character of U.S. citizenship and the wartime powers of the military over citizenry were also called into question.

On December 18, 1944, the U.S. Supreme Court ruled against Korematsu, effectively legitimizing FDR's actions as constitutional. During the trial, no claim was made that Korematsu was a disloyal citizen. His "crime" consisted solely of refusing to leave the restricted West Coast region, in the state where he was a citizen near the house where he was born.

Korematsu is an example of the Supreme Court's reluctance to question and its readiness to affirm a president's determination of necessity under the conditions of wartime. In dissent, Justice Frank Murphy said the judicial test of whether the executive, on a plea of military necessity, can validly deprive an individual of his rights must be reasonably related to a public danger that is so immediate as not to admit of delay and not to permit the intervention of ordinary constitutional processes to alleviate the danger. He obviously thought the situation did not warrant the conviction.

Scholars now regard the *Korematsu* decision as one of the Court's dismal blunders. Racism, hysteria, and misleading military judgments were at work. One legal scholar concludes

> Given the tensions of the period after Pearl Harbor, one might charitably advance the excuse of wartime hysteria for the harried members of Congress and the executive branch who made the initial decisions. No such excuse can be entertained for the justices of the Supreme Court who abandoned their most sacred principles at the first whiff of grapeshot.[461]

One of the ironic expansions came about as a result of the *U.S. v. Nixon* case in 1974. The case involved an appeal made by the Nixon Administration to vacate an order by federal district court Judge John Sirica requiring Nixon to release tapes and transcripts of sixty-four White House conversations that had been subpoenaed by Watergate Special Prosecutor Leon Jaworski. The executive branch claimed the president had the right under the doctrine or custom of "executive privilege" to withhold the tapes. It was essential, it claimed, for presidents to be able to speak freely with their advisors without fear that such conversations would be available for public consumption.

Although the Court, speaking through Chief Justice Warren Burger, held Nixon's claims erroneous, it also believed it was their duty to define executive privilege. The Court seemed to say national security considerations would weigh heavily in balancing executive privilege against a competing constitutional claim. In the case at hand, in the summer of 1974, national security was not being threatened, this was a criminal case, and hence Nixon had to yield the tapes. To be sure, then, the Court limited President Nixon's claims of executive privilege, yet only after acknowledging for the first time the constitutionality of executive privilege.

A divided Supreme Court in June of 1982 ruled 5–4 that a president enjoys absolute immunity from civil damage suits for official actions exercised while on duty in the White House. Toward the end of 1995, President Clinton, however, found himself facing charges of sexual harassment. Paula Corbin Jones accused the President of improperly approaching her while Clinton was governor of Arkansas. She was a state employee at the time. In 1997, the Supreme Court ruled unanimously that a sitting president is not immune from civil suits of this type, and the Paula Jones case was allowed to proceed. Eventually, a settlement was reached between the parties.

Several post 9/11 actions by President George W. Bush and Attorney General John Ashcroft headed for the courts. The actions taken by this administration in response to the terrorist attack against the United States have some precedent in history, as do court decisions challenging the constitutionality of such acts. The courts are asked to adjudicate on a vexing set of concerns: does the *rule of law* apply in a crisis? What are the proper limits on a president acting without the consent of the Congress during a crisis? Must the United States, to defend itself, undermine the Constitution?[462]

Although FDR suffered some initial setbacks, he eventually got most of what he wanted from the Court and indeed shaped, with nine appointments, a decidedly pro-national government and pro-presidency Court. Nixon also suffered several setbacks. He lost a number of cases both in the Supreme Court and in lower federal courts. During the Clinton and George W. Bush years, the courts decided several cases against the president.

PRESIDENTIAL LOSSES BEFORE THE SUPREME COURT

Presidents do occasionally lose key Court decisions. The Court has taken decisive stands against presidents after the Civil War, during the first New Deal, briefly near the end of the Korean War, during the Watergate affair, in the second Clinton term, and against President Bush in the war against terrorism. Moreover, these anti-presidency stands were often tempered by the fact that they generally were not direct, independent, or confrontational challenges to a president. Thus the Court stood up to Lincoln only after his assassination. The Court backed off after its brief though significant foray against the early New Deal legislation, and reacted to Watergate only after the press, the public, and Congress were already "up in arms."[463] The Court, then, has not been a very secure protector of rights and freedoms during times of crisis.

Still, when presidents have acted against provisions of the Constitution or an explicit congressional directive, or both, the Court has been inclined to stop them from treading further. The Court, understandably enough, is usually a bit bolder in these assertions of its role when a president has suffered notable declines in public approval.

Because we have treated some of these cases earlier, especially in the discussions of Lincoln and FDR, and because the major pattern in the Court-presidency relationship has been in expanding presidential power, we shall just briefly discuss these restraining decisions. Note, however, that these counterpoint decisions are no less important; they are merely the exceptions to the pattern.

The first significant case arose in Jefferson's term when Chief Justice John Marshall, Jefferson's antagonist, explicated the doctrine of judicial review. The *Marbury v. Madison* (1803)[464] decision, while cleverly avoiding a direct confrontation with the president, gave the Court the means for serving as the primary interpreter of what laws or executive action conform to the U.S. Constitution. In the process of handing down this decision John Marshall also said President Jefferson and his Secretary of State James Madison acted improperly. More important, however, was the establishment of the Court and its authority to serve as a vital branch if not exactly a coequal branch with the other two branches of government.

A year later, the Court in a unanimous decision instructed executive branch officials to pay for damages in the seizure of the Danish vessel, a seizure the Court said took place because of improper or invalid presidential instructions. The *Little v. Bareme* case involved the following question: whether a naval captain could be found civilly liable for following what the Court found to be an executive order that went beyond what Congress had authorized.[465]

Chief Justice John Marshall confessed that initially he believed that although President John Adams's instructions of 1799 could not give a right for the seizure, they might yet excuse the navy captain, Captain Little, from paying damages. He added, however, "I was mistaken." The instructions were invalid and therefore furnished no protection for the navy captain, who obeyed his president at his peril, because the congressional legislation in question authorized only the seizure of vessels proceeding to French ports. Executive instructions cannot, the Court ruled, ever change the nature of an administrative transaction or legalize an Act that would have been a plain trespass. If the Congress had been silent on the matter, the president's general authority as commander-in-chief would probably have been sufficient, but once Congress had prescribed the manner in which the law was to be carried out, the president and all other executive officials were obliged to respect the limitations imposed by congressional statute.

Another major case again arose during a military emergency (just as nearly all limiting or presidency-constraining decisions arose during unusual circumstances), the Civil War, during which Lincoln had suspended the writ of habeas corpus. Chief Justice Taney, acting in his additional role as a circuit court judge, ruled Lincoln had no constitutional power to suspend the writ. Lincoln never complied with this order, and a major lesson was learned. Rarely again would the Court attempt to stop a presidential action while it was taking place. Presidents can seldom if ever be enjoined from taking an action, only reprimanded once they have taken it. Still, *Ex parte Merryman* (1861) was important in that a Supreme Court justice recognized limits to presidential power, even in wartime.

In *Ex parte Milligan* (1866), the Court did place clear limitations on the emergency powers of the president, limiting his military authority. Yet this happened after the fact, after the war was over, and after Lincoln had died. In the *Korematsu* case of 1944, when the danger to the Union was arguably nonexistent, a different Court ignored this *Milligan* Civil War precedent and granted to the chief executive all the powers Lincoln had assumed and more. Thus, in many respects, these two Civil War limitations can be said to be insignificant in the overall definition of presidential power, even as they are important because they were among the first weak attempts by the Supreme Court to recognize that individual rights deserve to be considered as important as a strong national executive.

Other clashes between the Court and the presidency arose once again in emergency circumstances, during the height of the Depression. Here again, the Court believed the president lacked the constitutional authority to act alone in "saving the Union." Roosevelt's multiple plans to shore up the economy or regulate economic behavior met with Court disfavor. The Court's several rulings about the unconstitutionality of the early New Deal measures have already been discussed. Congress, in one sense, had erred by giving Roosevelt too general a mandate. Had FDR been carrying out specific congressional plans, he would have probably won the Court's approval in most instances (although it is doubtful Congress could have agreed on specific plans for him to administer). These anti-New Deal Court rulings represented a distinction the Supreme Court has always made between foreign and domestic affairs. In foreign affairs, a president hardly needs even a general mandate from Congress. But domestic and economic affairs have usually required more detailed statutes from Congress.

This maxim was proved true once again in the 1935 case of *Humphrey's Executor v. United States*.[466] In this case, a congressional prescription for removing a Federal Trade Commission commissioner was violated by Franklin Roosevelt. The Court responded by narrowing and in some ways overturning the *Myers* decision it had made just nine years earlier. In this 1935 ruling, the Court acknowledged that Congress, in creating agencies to carry out judicial and legislative duties, could restrict a president's removal power in specified cases, and thus it overruled FDR. *Humphrey* became one of only a handful or so of the actual major precedents serving to limit presidential powers.[467]

Another case in which a president was limited came during what most people might consider less than a national crisis, although President Truman apparently thought otherwise. This was the *Youngstown Sheet and Tube Co. v. Sawyer* (1952) case. Sawyer was Truman's secretary of commerce who was instructed by Truman to seize and operate certain steel mills that otherwise would have been shut down by union strikes (or, depending on your outlook, by the failure of the steel mill companies to improve pay and benefits).

The Korean War was dragging on and on. The pending shutdown of the steel mills so concerned Truman that he appealed to both sides, but to no avail. Steel supplies were low already and some Pentagon officials believed a major Chinese offensive was in the making. The United States Steel Corporation was willing to meet the United Steel Workers terms, but only if it could get some relief from the wartime price controls the Truman administration was exercising over the steel industry. Truman refused this. He also refused to invoke provisions of the Taft-Hartley Act, recently passed by Congress over his veto, that might have permitted yet another way out of the impasse.

Truman seized, through his secretary of commerce, all the steel mills affected by the strike. This accounted for eighty-six companies, over two hundred steel mills, 600,000 workers, and 95 percent of the nations steel production.

The seizure was implemented without much administrative trouble. Executive order number 10340 was issued, and all employees of these mills now worked for the U.S. government and did so at the same wages as before. Every company was ordered to fly the American flag above its mills. Everyone complied. Yet the steel companies didn't like it and filed suit in federal district court. The district court agreed with the steel mills and issued a preliminary injunction against the seizure. Hours later, the court of appeals issued a stay of the preliminary injunction and the seizure was allowed to continue until the Supreme Court could be brought into the matter.

Meanwhile Truman, his popularity already low, was attacked for being a bully, a usurper, a lawbreaker, and an architect of a labor dictatorship. "Newspapers, magazines, steel executives, business organizations, and Republicans [exceeded] their own performances of the Roosevelt years. They attacked Truman as a Caesar, an American Hitler or Mussolini, an author of evil...."[468] Within days the Supreme Court responded and heard the case. The steel companies hammered away at the unconstitutionality of Truman's actions. He had, they said, acted without congressional approval and without constitutional justification.

Truman's Justice Department countered with every plausible precedent, especially from the Lincoln and FDR eras. It didn't work. Justice Hugo Black, speaking for a 6–3 majority, agreed with the steel companies. No clause in the Constitution justified Truman's action, nor had it been authorized by Congress.

The Court ruled that the Korean crisis was not a full-scale emergency justifying the full invocation and exercise of presidential war powers. This case obviously had serious political ramifications. Truman was furious about this decision, and also bitter toward his appointee and former Attorney General Tom Clark, who voted against him.[469]

Other notable cases limiting executive power involve Nixon. Richard Nixon several times tested the limits of the office, sometimes succeeding in gaining power for the office and sometimes having his authority curbed. In the Pentagon Papers case, or *New York Times Co. v. United States* (1971),[470] the Supreme Court acted for the first time under wartime conditions since it had done so belatedly during the Civil War to protect institutional liberties against inroads from the executive branch. Vietnam was, however, an undeclared war, being waged with diminishing public or congressional support and by a somewhat unpopular president.

The Nixon administration attempted to halt publication in the *New York Times* and the *Washington Post* of a collection of classified but leaked essays and documents entitled "History of U.S. Decision-Making Process on Vietnam Policy." The real question, the only question on which, ultimately, this decision is based, is whether publication of these articles and documents would have yielded "direct, immediate, and irreparable damage to our nation and its people."

Nixon and the Justice Department said the publication of the so-called "Pentagon Papers" assaulted the principle of government control over classified documents. There are other parts of the Constitution that grant power and responsibilities to the president, they claimed, and the First Amendment was never intended to make it impossible for the president to function or to protect the security of the nation.

The Court was not persuaded. They ruled 6–3 in favor of the *New York Times* and permitted publication. The reasoning of the justices, however, is not simple to explain. There were six separate opinions for the majority and one for the three dissenters. The common bond linking the six majority judges was that the executive branch had simply failed to prove that the publication of these documents posed a major threat: "Any system of prior restraint of expression comes to this Court bearing a heavy presumption against its constitutional validity," the Court said. "The Government thus carries a heavy burden of showing justification for the enforcement of such a restraint."[471]

While the Supreme Court in this important case did not allow the Nixon Administration to run roughshod over the First Amendment, it left the door open for executive discretion. Several justices acknowledged that had the publication of the Pentagon Papers truly threatened national security, they might have allowed for prior restraint. The Court still would not put an absolute limit on executive authority.

A second decision that somewhat limited presidential power was a unanimous one in *U.S. v. U.S. District Court* in 1972[472]. Here the Supreme Court ruled that domestic surveillances required a warrant from the courts. And in fact, a lower court extended this decision to foreign wiretaps (made for national security purposes).

Critics of Nixon's and of the growing expansion of presidential power especially welcomed this decision. Clear limits, they believed, were placed on the executive through this opinion. Consequently the FBI had to disconnect several wiretaps.

There are indications, however, that the executive branch's compliance with this Court ruling has undermined its spirit. In practice, the executive branch wins regular approval through convenient procedures the Judiciary and the Justice Department subsequently established, for example, making it easier for a president to gain Foreign Intelligence Surveillance Act (FISA) approvals.

All three branches were ensnared and forced to confront issues and resolve disputes that, in more temperate times, likely would have been resolved by more informal means. But requests from both Congress and the independent counsel for information—for notes, memos, diaries, e-mail communications, and files— were met with executive refusal. Resistance replaced accommodation, acrimony trumped goodwill, and entrenchment dictated the use of subpoenas, grand juries, and courtroom trials. Thus it was that law and politics, public opinion and political wrangling, and person posturing and constitutional maneuvering propelled the three branches into a dispute over presidential power and independence.

In the end, the courts shrank the powers of the presidency in some key areas. In the Paula Jones lawsuit, the president's lawyers sought immunity from the suit while the president was in office, asking that the case be postponed until after Clinton left office. The Supreme Court eventually decided that the president enjoys no immunity, even temporary, from civil suits for unofficial acts.[473] This makes future presidents more open to court challenges and gives presidents somewhat less protection from lawsuits, frivolous and otherwise.

Presidents have long claimed that discussions with aides were privileged and could be kept from Congress. In past conflicts over such information, presidents usually struck a compromise with Congress. But during the Clinton years, all sides took an all-or-nothing approach. Thus, the courts were called to intervene. And in the end, the Court sided with Congress, leaving Clinton and future presidents more vulnerable and less protected. On the other hand, when the same courts were asked, in the early days of the presidency of George W. Bush, to force Vice President Dick Cheney to reveal with whom he had discussed a controversial energy policy, the courts sided with Cheney and against the Government Accountability Office, the investigatory arm of Congress.

In the aftermath of the September 11, 2001, terrorist attack against the United States, President Bush's power increased. A rally-'round-the-flag' effect lifted his popularity, the public demanded action, the Congress deferred to the president, and the courts waited silently in the wings. Unshy about using this power, Bush launched a war against terrorism and challenged the rule of law.

Many of these things were done solely on the orders of the President.[474] But did the President—acting alone, on his own claimed authority—truly have such discretionary powers? Had the United States come full circle from a revolution against the tyrannical power of a British King only to edge toward an elective version of monarchical authority in the president?

If Bush initially had a free hand, over time the president's policies, one by one, began to backfire and opposition began to build.

Surprisingly, one of the first and most forceful rebuffs of the President and his policies came from the Republican-dominated Supreme Court. In a series of critical decisions, the Court—after standing alone in opposition to the President— rejected some of the key claims of an independent authority that animated presidential actions, and trimmed the power sails of the presidency.

In 2004, in *Rasul v. Bush*[475] the Court, in a 6–3 decision, ruled that those detained in Guantanamo Bay had a right to challenge their imprisonment in an American court. The Bush administration had maintained that these detainees had no such rights. The President was forced to back down, and established a three-person military parcel to review the status of detainees.

Also in 2004, in *Hamdi v. Rumsfeld*[476] the Court reversed the dismissal of a *habeas corpus* petition brought by a U.S. citizen, Yaser Esam Hamdi, held as an "illegal enemy combatant." In this 8–1 decision, Justice Sandra Day O'Connor, writing for a plurality of four Justices, denied the President powers to hold U.S. citizens without legal process, writing that "A state of war is not a blank check for the President," and that the commander-in-chief clause is not a license to "turn our system of checks and balances on its head."

In June 2006, in *Hamdan v. Rumsfeld*[477] the Court held that the military commissions set up by the Bush administration to try detainees should be halted because they violated the Uniform Code of Military Justice as well as four Geneva Conventions signed in 1949 by the United States. In a 5–3 ruling, the Court said the President did not have the inherent authority, absent the approval of Congress, to set up special military trials. Bush then went to the Congress, which authorized such trials and stripped detainees of certain rights and appeals.

But in 2008, in *Boumediene v. Bush*,[478] the Court, in a 5–4 ruling, held that foreign prisoners held at Guantanamo Bay did have a right to a hearing before a federal Judge. Writing for the majority, Justice Anthony Kennedy noted that "the laws and Constitution are designed to survive, and remain in force, in extraordinary times. Liberty and security can be reconciled; and in our system they are reconciled within the framework of the law."

In sum, Bush's overreaching claims of inherent, independent powers in wartime were modified by the Supreme Court. The Bush-Cheney quest for unilateral power met a Supreme Court intent on constitutionalizing the president's wartime powers. The rule of law and the separation of powers, battered, bruised, and challenged, emerged, viable, if not fully intact.[479]

CONCLUSION

Supreme Court justices tend to share with presidents a similar national perspective and a common outlook about the national interest. However, they have different obligations and responsibilities and operate in a different political forum. More often than not, the Supreme Court and the lower federal courts have sided with presidents as new demands and emergencies encouraged presidents to stretch the formal powers of the office. This trend or pattern is now well established and rooted in Sutherland's famed, if controversial, 1936 *Curtiss-Wright* decision. This judicial deference exists especially in wartime and when presidents enjoy high popularity. But such deference is not without its limits, as several recent presidents discovered.

The Court appreciates that only the president is elected by the nation. Still it is a paramount function of the Court to insist that presidents do not go beyond what is necessary or to try to singularly embody the nation's sovereignty. No president should be allowed to make the law or disregard for long the general commands of the U.S. Constitution.

Strong presidents invariably look for ways to expand their prerogatives and authority. Often, of course, this may be due to the emergencies confronting the nation. Their public approval ratings can have an important bearing on whether they win victories in clashes with the Court. Strong presidents try to nominate new justices who will advance their policies and values. For several generations now it has become common practice for presidents to appoint justices with a sympathy to their policy leanings, and this will continue.

One of the strengths of the Supreme Court is its ability to function as an independent and at least a somewhat unpredictable institution. No president can shape it for long. As noted, members of the Court develop their own independent constitutional philosophies, the more so the longer they remain on the Court.

Courts are most likely to take on presidents who boldly make claims of independent power: Lincoln during the Civil War, FDR during the Great Depression, and George W. Bush during the war against terrorism, for example. Even when these presidents are popular, presidents who push the envelope on presidential power too far may well face a Court willing to push back. Courts are more likely to defer to presidents in foreign affairs rather than domestic, during times of war or crisis rather than in normal times, and when the partisan majority on the Court is controlled by the president's party.

We cannot expect the Supreme Court to be the sole or even main accountability check on presidents. Our system functions best when Congress, the president, and the Court each energetically promote their own independent vision of good government. Preferring a strong presidency should not lead one to want a corresponding weakness in the other two branches, but rather a corresponding strength and assertiveness.

FOR DISCUSSION

1. What prevents the Court from challenging claims of presidential power?
2. Should the nomination of Supreme Court Justices be taken out of the hands of presidents and given to an independent, nonpartisan commission?

DEBATE QUESTIONS

1. That Presidents have the right to determine what the Constitution means with regard to operations within the executive branch.
2. That the Courts have been too deferential to claims of inherent presidential authority.

FURTHER READINGS

Abraham, Henry J. *Justices, Presidents and Senators,* 5th ed. Lanham, MD: Rowman & Littlefield, 2008.

Adler, David Gray, and Michael A. Genovese, eds. *The Presidency and the Law: The Clinton Legacy.* Lawrence: University Press of Kansas, 2002.

Binder, Sarah and Forrest Maltzman. *Advice & Dissent: The Struggle to Shape the Federal Judiciary.* Washington, DC: Brookings Institution, 2009.

Nemacheck, Christine L. *Strategic Selection: Presidential Nomination of Supreme Court Justices from Herbert Hoover Through George W. Bush.* Charlottesville: University of Virginia Press, 2007.

Sollenberger, Mitchel A. *Judicial Appointments and Democratic Controls.* Durham: Carolina Academic Press, 2011.

Critical Thinking

STATEMENT: We cannot expect the Courts to check the excesses of presidential power.

PROBLEM: Why might this be so? Historically, is this statement accurate? What tools or resources do presidents and Courts have in this potential conflict?

CHAPTER 10

The Future of the American Presidency

> A strong president is a bad President, a curse upon the land, unless his means are constitutional and his ends democratic, unless he acts in ways that are fair, dignified, and familiar, and pursues policies to which a "persistent and undoubted" majority of the people has given support. We honor the great Presidents of the past, not for their strength, but for the fact that they used it wisely to build a better America.
>
> CLINTON ROSSITER, *The American Presidency*
> (New York: Harcourt, Brace, 1956), p. 257.

The presidency changes from season to season, occupant to occupant, issue to issue. We may never unravel many of the paradoxes of the American presidency. Yet there are things the American people and presidents can do to encourage effective presidential performance.

We want to be led, yet we cherish our independence and freedom. We want a "take charge" leader in the White House, yet demand accountable and responsive leadership. We want a fearless leader for these fearful times, yet we don't want a fearlessness that turns into recklessness. Many Americans are now less content to hold presidents to account only every four years when they go to the polls: they yearn for more regular accountability. With few exceptions, voters regularly punish the president's party in midterm elections, and, as discussed earlier, the public generally diminishes its approval for presidents the longer they are there. Our system is built on distrust of powerful leaders and the need for their accountability.

Popular conceptions of the presidency have changed dramatically over time. During the Depression and World War II we demanded a powerful, heroic presidency. During the Cold War we wanted a powerful foreign affairs presidency to thwart the rising threat of communism's spread. Yet abuses of power, the war in Vietnam, and Watergate led to accusations of an imperial presidency, and we sought to clip the wings of the president. Today, in an age of terrorism and economic challenge, we again seek a president who can fix what is broken.

We want the presidency to be there always, ready at three a.m., or whenever emergencies threaten, to rise when the demand grows and step back in less pressing times. We want a presidency with the potential to be heroic when we need it, but constrained and limited at other times.

This chapter examines the need for and challenge of both empowering and holding presidents accountable, and discusses some existing and proposed checks on the president.

YESTERDAY, TODAY, AND TOMORROW

We need a president grounded in the fundamental truths of the framers, yet an office that can meet the challenge of the modern era and is prepared to lead effectively in the twenty-first century.

We believe that the baroque system of checks and balances works best when presidential leadership animates and drives the system, but not just any type of presidential leadership. At its best, the president can be a leader, a teacher, a guide, and a mobilizer. Yet, the office that nourishes responsible leadership is also capable of great abuse.

How do we (a) transform our eighteenth-century Constitution into a guiding document capable of serving a twenty-first-century superpower and (b) support presidential power and leadership yet control and ensure its constitutionality? Can the presidency be made both powerful *and* accountable? Will this require major surgery, or merely political improvisation?

The United States *needs* presidential leadership. The only way to reduce the need for a strong presidency is to reduce America's role in the world, retreat from global leadership, reduce the size of government, and free the economy of regulations and controls. This will not happen any time soon.

The presidency is thus necessary, yet always potentially dangerous. We can't live without it, yet living with it may threaten constitutionalism and our traditional notions of a republic. How do we resolve this dilemma?

HOLDING PRESIDENTS TO ACCOUNT

Any discussion of presidential leadership and accountability must take into account the ever-present paradoxes of the presidency. Some part of us wants a larger-than-life, two-gun, charismatic Mount Rushmore leader. Harrison Ford in the movie *Air Force One* (1997), and President Whitmore, along with his buddy Will Smith in *Independence Day* (1996), vivified this yearning. Still, there is also our remarkably enduring antigovernment, anti-leadership, chronic-complainer syndrome. We want strong, gutsy leadership to operate on alternate days with a "national city manager." We want presidents to have a wealth of power to solve our problems, yet not so much they can do lasting damage.

Accountability implies not only responsiveness to majority desires and answerability for actions but also taking the Constitution, plus the people and their views, into account. It also implies a performance guided by integrity and character. Accountability implies as well that important decisions could be explained to the people to allow them the opportunity to appraise how well a president is handling the responsibilities of the office.

To whom is accountability owed? No president, it would seem, can be more than partially accountable to the people, for each president will listen to some people and some points of view more than to others. If we have learned anything in recent years, however, it is that any notion of presidential infallibility has been rejected. Arbitrary rule by powerful executives has always been rejected here. But what should be done when there are sharp differences between experts or when expert opinion differs sharply from the preponderance of public opinion? How much accountability, and what kind, is desirable? Is it not possible that the quest for ultimate accountability will result in a presidency without the prerogatives and independent discretion necessary for creative leadership?

As Michael Lind reminds us, "presidential democracy is not democracy."[480] A too-strong presidency jeopardizes freedom. A too-weak president jeopardizes stability. An imperial presidency is not democracy, yet an imperiled presidency is equally troubling. The overriding challenge for any democracy is both to empower and to control those who govern.

The modern presidency, in fact, may be unaccountable because it is too strong and independent in certain areas and too weak and dependent in others. One of the perplexing circumstances characterizing the state of the modern presidency is that considerable restraints sometimes exist where restraints are least desirable and inadequate restraints are available where they are most needed. Also, presidential strength is no guarantee that a president will be responsive or answerable. Indeed, significant independent strength may encourage low answerability when it suits a president's short-term personal power goals.

THE PRESIDENCY AND DEMOCRATIC THEORY

How do you grant yet control power? Can the presidency be empowered yet also democratized?

These are classic questions our framers faced and these have been central to debates in democratic political theory. Leadership implies influence; accountability implies limits. Contradictions aside, accountability is a fundamental piece of the democratic puzzle. In essence it denotes that public officials must be answerable for their actions. But to whom? Within what limits? Through what means?

There are essentially three types of accountability: *ultimate accountability* (which the United States has via the impeachment process), *periodic accountability* (provided for by presidential as well as midterm elections and occasional landmark Supreme Court decisions), and *daily accountability* (somewhat contained in the separation of powers).[481] James Madison believed elections provided the "primary check on government" along with the separation of powers ("ambition will be made to counteract ambition"), plus "auxiliary precautions" should take care of the rest.[482] Others believe that public opinion is the main check on presidents, and in the long run, how a president will be judged by historians.

There *are* times when presidents abuse power or behave corruptly. But even in two of the more notable bouts with presidential abuses—Watergate and the Iran-Contra scandal—the president was stopped by the countervailing forces of a free press, an independent Congress, an independent judiciary, and eventually an aroused public.

We may hold presidents accountable, but can they be made responsible? That is, can they muster enough power to govern? One means for improving accountability and also empowering leadership is to strengthen the party system in America. Our parties are, at least by European standards, relatively weak, and quite decentralized. A stronger party system might possibly mobilize citizens, diminish the fragmentation of the separation of powers, and lessen the atomization of our citizenry—yet this seems unlikely and might well create its own set of problems.

All presidents work to be successful, yet what does it mean to be a success? High, favorable popularity? Achieving policy goals? A high congressional box score for getting legislative priorities adopted into law? Peace and prosperity? Enhanced liberty and greater opportunity for all?

If success is measured merely by getting one's way, then many bullies would be judged successful. But success means more than getting what one wants. In determining success, we must always ask, "power for what *ends*," because power divorced from purpose is potentially dangerous and democratically undesirable.

Presidential politics should be concerned with central issues and values. Candidates who run for the White House and thereby seek the power to influence the lives of millions of Americans ought to do so because they have a vision of building a better and more just America. If this is not the case, those candidates who are merely seeking power for its own sake should be smoked out in the election process.

If we look on government as the enemy, and politics as a corrupt profession, our anger turns to apathy and power (but not responsibility) slips through our hands. We often look at politics not as a means to achieve public good, but as an evil; we see elections as the choice between the lesser of two evils; we presume our democratic responsibilities are satisfied merely by the act of voting every so often, or we abandon politics altogether.

This is why politics and elections matter. People who give up on politics in effect abdicate the possibility of implementing cherished policy ideas. People who give up on politics and parties are essentially giving others power over their lives. You can't hate politics and politicians and love representative democracy.

In a democracy, a successful president pursues and uses power, not for self-serving ends, not to aggrandize his or her own narcissistic status, but to help solve problems and help citizens enjoy the blessings of freedom and opportunity.

The best of democratic leaders are teachers who both understand and educate us about the promise and mission of America. They move the government in pursuit of the consensus generated from the values of the nation. They appeal to the best in citizens and attempt to lead the nation toward its better self.

Franklin Roosevelt suggested that the presidency "is preeminently a place of moral leadership." Thus, presidents should use their office to appeal to our better instincts, and lead democratically. It was through politics and government that the nation's progressive social movements helped move us toward greater racial and gender equality, devised policies to expand education and opportunities to a wider segment of the population, and attempted to protect and expand the rights of citizens. These battles are far from over. As a nation, we have a long way to go before we can truly grant the blessings of liberty and prosperity to all citizens, yet it is through politics—and only through politics—that we can achieve these goals.

Politics, to us, is the name for that complex process of talking, bargaining, conflict managing, and agreement building that makes it possible for us to live together in a civilized way. It is in this sense that politics is much more than a necessary evil—it can be a liberating activity and a necessary good.

Politics is the art of trying to bring about the possible, the achievable, and the most desirable elements of our mutually shared aspirations. But politics is a two-way street. Presidents should help set priorities, inspire vision, and motivate us; yet if we want government to succeed, citizens, through political parties, interest groups, the Internet, and other means, need to guide and encourage responsible presidential leadership and if necessary rebuff irresponsible presidential activities.

Presidents may and have also used the powers of the presidency to promote economic stability and growth in America. The Roosevelts, Wilson, Kennedy, Reagan, Clinton, and Obama all strove to stimulate the economy and promote favorable trade programs that in turn created jobs and economic security. Presidents generally know what is expected of them as promoters of economic development, yet here again they are likely to respond to the yearnings and lobbying of those who become actively engaged in the political process and party politics.

The ends power serves are important, but in presidential terms, virtue is not enough. A successful president must have *character* and *competence*. Character without competence (resources, skill, power) gives us noble yet ineffective leaders; competence without character may lead to government by demagogues or rogues.

Presidents who lead in the democratic spirit can encourage leaders, foster citizen responsibility, and inspire others to assume leadership responsibilities in their communities. Democratic leaders share a purposeful vision about mutually shared aspirations and also challenge, engage, and educate citizens.

The United States needs a strong presidency and a democratically accountable presidency, and this in turn necessitates a robust civic culture. Political scientist Benjamin R. Barber notes the difficulty inherent in such a quest:

At the heart of democratic theory lies a profound dilemma that has afflicted democratic practice at least since the eighteenth century. Democracy requires both effective leadership and vigorous citizenship: yet the conditions and consequences of leadership often seem to undermine civic vigor. Although it cries for both, democracy must customarily make do either with strong leadership or with strong citizens. For the most part, depending on devices of representation in large-scale societies, democracy in the West has settled for strong leaders and correspondingly weak citizens.[483]

As discussed earlier, the American presidency operates within a system of shared power, one in which the claims of many groups constantly compete. Presidential struggles with other governmental and extragovernmental centers of power stem from the larger societal conflicts over values and the allocation of wealth and opportunity. As a result, the presidency becomes a place in which few truly bold decisions are made; most of its domestic policies are exploratory, remedial, or experimental modifications of past practices.

Limitations on a president's freedom of action are, to be sure, often desirable. Many of the checks and balances that are still at work today were deliberately designed by the framers of the Constitution. In some measure, presidents should be the agents of their campaign commitments, their party platforms and principles, and their announced programs. They should be responsive most of the time to the views of the majority of the American people. Presidential behavior should be informed by the Constitution, existing laws, and the generally understood values that define democratic procedure. The notion that party programs, spelled out in campaigns, allow the public some control over policy through the election process is a valuable brake, one that needs, if anything, to be revitalized. Other brakes that limit presidential discretion may be viewed as positive or negative, depending on an individual's political and economic views. The constraining of a president by the bureaucracy and by special interests is implicitly, if not explicitly, a kind of accountability, even if they are not exactly the kind we necessarily want as our prime constitutional safeguard against the abuse of power.

The nation's founders would have been pleased to see how the system of checks and balances has thwarted executive tyranny. But they might, we believe, be less pleased with the alternating conditions of presidential unilateralism followed by the gridlock that often characterizes relations between the president and Congress.

Is the separation-of-powers model *the* problem? Was it Madison's curse or blessing to us? Does it create dysfunctional deadlock and paralysis? To presidents, there must be times when it seems so. Woodrow Wilson, writing in 1884 (long before he became president), saw the separation as creating a massive political escape clause for blame and responsibility. Wrote Wilson

> Power and strict accountability for its use are the essential constituents of good government.... It is, therefore, manifestly a radical defect in our federal system that it parcels out power and confuses responsibility as it does. The main purpose of the Convention of 1787 seems to have been to accomplish this grievous

mistake.... Were it possible to call together again the members of that wonderful Convention... they would be the first to admit that the only fruit of dividing power had been to make it irresponsible.[484]

On reflection we are reminded of the positive benefit of separating, sharing, and overlapping power. If one values, as we do, deliberation, discussion, and debate, and if we accept a model of democratic governing based on consensus and cooperation, then the reform agenda will be short. But some see the separation as the likely suspect in the crime of stalemate and gridlock.

Americans are great fixers. Americans have proposed hundreds of amendments to our Constitution in the hopes of improving our republic. The presidency is the subject of many such proposed reforms. We now discuss some of them. Most of these proposals, we believe, are undesirable and would probably make things worse. We must be sure that in searching for a quick-fix panacea, reform does not de-form.[485]

"VOTES OF NO CONFIDENCE?"

One of the responses to Watergate and the abuse of power by Richard Nixon was a proposed constitutional amendment providing for a vote by Congress of no confidence in a president.[486] The effect would be similar to the recall now provided for in about sixteen states.

How would a no-confidence amendment work? A three-fifths vote of the members of each House present and voting would be necessary. Such a resolution would take priority over any other pending issue before Congress. If adopted, Congress would fix a date, between 90 and 110 days, for a special election for the president and vice president as well as for members of Congress. If it occurs near the regular congressional election date, that date would be used. Note that under most such proposals, the incumbent president is eligible to stand for reelection even though he or she was the target of the no-confidence vote.

A reason put forward in defense of the no-confidence proposal is that the presidency in modern times has grown too powerful, especially in crisis contexts and in foreign affairs. Presidential power, it is argued, has risen above the level where the system of checks and balances can be effective in countering presidential actions. More bluntly, however, advocates of the no-confidence or similar national recall proposals believe that the four-year fixed term is a liability if and when we have incompetent presidents who lose the confidence of the nation. Incompetence, they point out, is not an impeachable offense. A "no-confidence" vote might also be a way to replace a hopelessly failed administration.

A goal of the proposed vote of no confidence is to make future presidents more accountable to Congress, as well as more accountable to the American people. But aren't modern presidents already accountable to Congress? Because Congress sometimes fails to do its constitutional job of keeping presidents accountable does not mean that the power is missing. A president, it is assumed, would realize that he or she is accountable for their actions, proposed programs, negotiations, policies, and decisions and would have to face up to criticisms by Congress. The commission of high crimes or felonies would no longer be needed to justify a president's dismissal. Maintaining the confidence of Congress and the general public would be an ongoing necessity. Matters such as Vietnam or Iraq policy, for example, would have to be discussed in greater detail with congressional leaders to ensure that a president had the support of Congress. The vote of no confidence would be a means of retaliation against a president who too often worked behind the scenes or otherwise manipulated the spirit of checks and balances. Advocates reason that major decisions would have to be made by consultation, instead of by one person or a White House cabal. To some extent, then, this constitutional amendment would introduce a certain amount of plural or shared decision making in our national government. The fundamental dangers of decisions by a Lone Ranger president would be thereby reduced.

In a nutshell, the arguments in favor of the vote of no confidence are these:

- Impeachment is an inefficient check. At best it protects against gross criminal violations of the public trust but not against presidential incompetence.
- The president would be more disposed to working with Congress, explaining policies, and educating Congress and the general public about plans and conduct in office.
- This proposal would force more presidential consultation with Congress and the leaders of the major parties and should lessen the secrecy surrounding presidential policymaking.
- The proposal does not take power away from the president; it only makes presidents more responsible for how they use their powers.

Critics view this reform as a prime example of "good intentions, bad policy." Congress, they point out, has plenty of resources with which to check a president if only they would use them. Further, even though presidents have become paramount in the conduct of foreign affairs, Congress has numerous means at its disposal to oversee this exercise of power.

In certain situations it would seem that a vote of no confidence would give Congress the power to continually frustrate a president with whom it disagreed. The alternatives are a government of continuous presidential elections and overall paralysis or a government in which president and Congress are so close as to defeat the basic concept of the separation of powers so fundamental to our system.

Moreover, the elections that would be the result of a vote of no confidence might well produce governmental instability and make the development and implementation of long-term programs very uncertain. A vote-of-no-confidence arrangement might lead presidents to avoid making significant changes in policy that would antagonize Congress. Innovative leadership could be thwarted, as presidents might gear most of their actions to public opinion polls, to the wishes of the majority at the expense of minority rights, and to the short term at the expense of the longer term public interest. The proposal might lead a president to concentrate on short-term or immediately popular initiatives to "create" favorable public approval at the expense of long-term planning.

Our view is that this proposed cure is worse than the occasional ailment. The vote-of-no-confidence procedure would not necessarily improve the quality of presidential leadership, nor would it enhance accountability in any significant way. Presidents do not intentionally make poor decisions. What could result might be far worse than the rare arrogant president we have had to endure. This measure might make presidents too dependent on Congress, or conform too closely to popular opinion. This measure might even give us an endless line of unsuccessful short-term presidents and result in a paralyzed nation.

WHAT ABOUT A "PRESIDENT'S QUESTION HOUR IN CONGRESS"?

During his 2008 campaign for president, Senator John McCain of Arizona proposed that, if he was elected, he would be willing regularly to go to Congress and, like British and Australian prime ministers, answer detailed questions about his initiatives and his conduct in office.

Some of you may have seen on C-SPAN English prime ministers such as Gordon Brown, Tony Blair, and David Cameron face tough questions from their own party's members of parliament as well as from opposition members. It can be quite theatrical as prime ministers defend their positions and speculate about hypotheticals. This "show" is, of course, televised in England and it serves several functions. It is one means to keep a government accountable. It can often be a lively educational debate or forum from which citizens can learn about what is going on in their country. And it plainly gives some legitimacy to the "loyal opposition" or dissenters.

Those who favor this idea for the United States contend that it would encourage needed transparency and help elevate the debate over an administration's priorities. It could be done without a constitutional amendment and it could even be done as an experiment for a year or two, or even for an administration.

A U.S. version might presumably take place just once a month and therefore not place unreasonable demands on a president's valuable time. And indeed, a president already has to prepare for similar give-and-take exchanges with unelected media representatives on a fairly regular basis. So why not hold similar dialogues with the people's representatives?

Critics of this proposal point out that our presidential system differs from a parliamentary system: ours is a system of separate branches. This proposal confuses that separation.

Further, presidential cabinet as well as chief military and intelligence officers already participate in frequent congressional committee hearings and these administration officials are as well if not better informed on detailed policy matters than most presidents are.

Finally, presidents regularly meet with party leaders—both their own and opposition leaders—at the White House, and these exchanges are likely to be more productive and less likely to be grandstanding than the theater of a "President's Question Hour."

This reform is unlikely for political reasons. Presidents are unlikely to risk their independence and lessen their "bully pulpit" clout (such as it is) by submitting to what could be some heated and acrimonious cross-examinations by opposition party leaders. Presidents and their media and message advisers are unlikely to give their opponents such a prominent and recognized public forum. Would such a proposed innovation encourage a more democratic and constitutional presidency? Perhaps a little. Yet, as noted, it is unlikely.

A THIRD PARTY TO THE RESCUE?

Critics and reformers from almost every viewpoint regularly propose that a creative, vital new third party might be just what is needed to infuse more common sense and energy into our sometimes creaky political system.

"We usually have two parties bankrupting the country," says political scientist Larry Diamond. Indeed, "our two-party party system is ossified, it lacks integrity and creativity and any sense of courage or high aspiration in confronting our problems."[487]

Others agree, saying we have been poorly served by an existing two-party duopoly. We need, writes Tom Friedman, a rigorous third party that would propose serious education reform without worrying about the teachers unions; "financial reform without worrying about losing donations from Wall Street; corporate tax reductions to stimulate jobs without worrying about offending the left; energy and climate reform without worrying about offending the far right and coal-state Democrats; and proper health care reform without worrying about offending insurers and drug companies."[488]

The point is, the critics say, that the two main traditional parties are so tied to well-organized, well-financed vested stakeholders that a paralyzing gridlock has made for a timid and virtually do-nothing government. It has also led to unreasonable and dangerous partisan brinkmanship.

Third-party movements are hardly new. Teddy Roosevelt's Bull Moose Party transformed the 1912 election even though it came in second. Illinois Congressman John Anderson preached pragmatic centrist fiscal reform in 1980 when he challenged President Carter and Governor Ronald Reagan. Texas businessman Ross Perot won nearly 19 percent of the popular vote in 1992 as he tried then, and again in 1996, to build a new third party dedicated to balancing the budget. He called his party the Reform Party. Consumer advocate Ralph Nader tried on several occasions to build a third party comprised of environmental and anti-globalization activists. Libertarians of the Ron Paul stripe have regularly run. Such parties raise instructive issues and occasionally force the two main parties to explain their policies.

Our entrenched two major parties and our election laws have made it diffi-cult for a third party to become a major party. The last time a third party won the presidency was in 1860 when the nation was pulverized by the looming Civil War and huge national division. State requirements for third-party candidates to get on the ballot are often very restrictive. Plus our Electoral College system, as currently implemented, means that even if a new party can win millions of votes in scores of states, you still might wind up with few if any of the 270 electoral votes needed to win the presidency.

Americans may be frustrated with our two existing parties, yet more than 60 percent of us are registered or loosely affiliated with these parties. And another 20 percent or more regularly vote with the party they "lean" toward. Many, if not most, of the so-called "independents" are really not that independent.

The Democrats and the Republicans are usually joined by the media in pre-dicting that a vote for a third party is either a wasted vote or one, such as a vote for Ralph Nader in 2000, that probably was a "spoiler" vote, winding up hurting your second choice candidate.

"Like fast-food giants McDonald's and Burger King, the GOP and the Democratic Party are," writes political scientist Ross K. Baker, "a known quan-tity and somewhat reassuring for their very familiarity. A third party is a mystery burger."[489]

The political reality is that third parties have limited prospects in the near term. When third parties occasionally generate popular and constructive ideas, one of the major parties almost always modifies and adopts these ideas into their own platforms. Nixon did this with some of George Wallace's ideas. Republicans and Democrats did this with a few of Ross Perot's ideas.

Our two-party system needs to be challenged. And a vigorous multiparty sys-tem in America might well stir people to participle more in the political process. If we so value competition in the marketplace, maybe it would also be good for our seemingly sclerotic political system.

Still, the two-party system has served this sprawling, decentralized country reasonably well. The history of the last three or four generations suggests that presidents are relatively successful in either enacting their policy goals or at least helping to advance their ideas so that at a later time they will be embraced. The Marshall Plan, the GI Bill, the Interstate Highway System, Civil and Voting Rights, Environmental Protection, Free Trade Agreements, Tax Reform, Economic Stimulus Initiatives, and Affordable Care Health Insurance reform along with much more, has been achieved even if these accomplishments often took years of collaborative and multibranch negotiations. Ours is an often slow and messy sys-tem, yet it is representative and deliberative even if privileged interests admittedly have the loudest voice.

We have witnessed in recent years some new groups including one called "No Labels" who have tried to challenge the existing party system. But they won little support in part because there is not much unity among independents. Independents are independent for a whole lot of reasons. "Non-partisanship" can work at the school board level but less so in national politics. Partisanship is politics. "People have different political sensibilities; they cluster and the clusters are called parties" writes columnist George Will. "They have distinctive understandings of the meaning and relative importance of liberty, equality, and other matters."[490] Politics arises from the actions of activists who are partisans with contending perspectives.

It is unlikely, we believe, that a magical third party is the answer to our modern day political problems, yet the threat of possible third parties and especially their creative proposals is certainly a healthy situation.

Third parties are, we think, less the answer than lessening some of the pernicious effects of money in politics and finding incentives for politicians in both our main parties to collaborate on vital national interests.

SHOULD WE REPEAL THE TWENTY-SECOND (TWO-TERM LIMIT) AMENDMENT?

One of the frequently debated reforms of the American presidency is whether the Twenty-Second Amendment weakens or strengthens the office and whether it weakens or strengthens constitutionalism.[491]

Congress proposed the Twenty-Second Amendment in 1947, and with 70 percent of those voting in Congress supporting it, it sailed through both houses and won ratification in 1951.

Advocates of repeal say this two-term limit violates the American citizen's right to decide who will be their leader. If the people want to vote for someone, especially an experienced veteran in the White House, there should be no rule telling them they don't have that choice. "It bespeaks a shocking lack of faith in the common sense and good judgment of the people,"[492] wrote political historian Clinton Rossiter.

Every president's sun now begins to set the day the second term begins—the "lame duck" syndrome.[493] We have, critics say, dealt the modern presidency a major blow by depriving second-term presidents the political weapon of their availability for another term, which keeps both supporters and rivals guessing.

Proponents of a strong presidency fear that the Twenty-Second Amendment limitation weakens presidential independence and shifts the balance of power back too much in the direction of the Congress—a branch they fear is too unwieldy, risk averse, and "leaky" to provide the type of leadership we need in the twenty-first century.

The "fact remains that those who take pride in [this] amendment are Whigs, men who fear the presidency and put their final trust in Congress, and that those who propose to repeal it are Jacksonians, men who respect Congress but look for leadership to the presidency."[494]

Advocates of retaining the Twenty-Second Amendment say eight years is plenty. The notion of rotation in office is healthy and desirable, especially in a robust constitutional democracy. Most presidents burn out in their second terms. Eight years should be ample time to introduce one's own and one's party's best ideas and to try to bring about necessary policy changes. If such changes are valid and valued, they will doubtless be continued by the next administration. Moreover, most Americans reject the idea that any political leader is indispensable.

The two-term limit is invariably healthy in our two-party system. It helps prevent political stagnation. The two parties benefit and are rejuvenated by the challenge of recruiting and nominating a new team of leaders.

We oppose repealing the Twenty-Second Amendment for a number of reasons. A long-term presidency would be able to pack the Supreme Court as well as the whole judiciary. A long-term executive was precisely what we fought the Revolution to rid ourselves of. Finally, for a variety of understandable reasons, the presidency has become a far more powerful branch than ever imagined by the framers of our Constitution. Most of this cannot be reversed. Thus the Twenty-Second Amendment is a practical new "auxiliary precaution" in Madison's sense of checks and balances.

A truly indispensable person could be kept on as a key presidential adviser or cabinet member to see us through some crisis. But surely in a nation 100 times larger than we were in 1788, we should have plenty of talented would-be effective presidents.

In short, Americans want an effective presidency, yet, as we have noted several times, they fear the arbitrary abuse of power and the potential of presidents who someday may delude themselves into believing they are indispensable.

The two-term limit allows an honored citizen to serve eight years in one of the world's most consequential positions, yet it protects the country from potential excesses of power that could come from prolonged tenure. On balance, although the Twenty-Second Amendment has its drawbacks, it is, we believe, an imperfect yet acceptable compromise. We don't believe it weakens effective, responsible presidents, and it helps guarantee that a presidential dictatorship will not take root in this Republic.

SHOULD PRESIDENTS BE GRANTED AN ITEM VETO?

The proposed item veto—sometimes called "the line-item veto"—would allow a president to veto, delete, or send back to Congress any subsection or portion of an appropriations bill passed by Congress. Proposed item veto measures typically provide for a process by which Congress could override, by a two-thirds vote in both houses, a presidential item veto.

Congress enacted a statutory provision giving presidents this type of veto, but the U.S. Supreme Court (in *Clinton v. City of New York,* 1998), rejected this delegation of power to presidents, saying it was a violation of the Constitution's Presentment Clause, as the power allowed the president to, in effect, rewrite legislation presented to him by Congress. The Court's majority opinion made it clear this type of power could only be given to a president through the amendment procedures set forth in Article V of the Constitution.

Still, several presidents and many reformers advocate this idea as a means of giving presidents needed responsibility for controlling deficits and eliminating wasteful, so-called earmarked spending. An item veto proposal was favorably approved by a bipartisan vote in the U.S. House of Representatives of 254 to 173 in 2012.

Here, in brief, are the reasons advocates urge giving item veto authority to presidents:

→ The item veto would help eliminate waste and "pork" in the federal budget.

→ The president's general veto has been subverted by various congressional practices of huge "overstuffed" appropriations, tax benefits, or bailouts presented to the White House—and the item veto would restore the intended objectives of the presidential veto power.

→ Most state governors have an item veto authority, and they like it because it gives them a tool for reminding legislators that economy in the public interest is just as important as spending in local district interests. Polls regularly show that majorities of business executives as well as the American public support this "reform."

The item veto proposal has a certain amount of appeal and deserves periodic debates, yet we believe it illustrates once again journalist H. L. Mencken's theorem that for every difficult and complex problem, there is an obvious solution that is simple, easy, and wrong. In our view, the item veto authority would provide more power than an effective president needs, and more than a misguided or imperial president should have. The marginal benefits of trimming some "fat" from congressional spending and tax benefit measures would be outweighed, we think, by weakening of a Congress too inclined in recent generations to delegate away its constitutional power. Passing the buck to presidents along with much of Congress's legislating authority is ill-conceived and a constitutionally counterproductive idea.[495]

Here are the major reasons to oppose amending the Constitution to provide presidents with item veto authority:

→ It would shift additional power away from Congress and doubtless expand the power of unelected aides at the White House and in the Office of Management and Budget.

→ It could encourage further irresponsibility in congressional spending behavior and thereby weaken Congress as an institution for collective policymaking.

→ The item veto could strengthen a president's hand in dealing with individual members of Congress, pressuring them to support presidential priorities or risk having their special projects item vetoed. In the hands of a big-spending president this might have the ironic effect of encouraging greater rather than smaller deficits.

→ Both presidents and members of Congress already have procedures available to them to eliminate pork; they just have to have the willpower to vote them down, or veto them down. George W. Bush, for example, who ran as a conservative opposed to big government, rarely used his veto authority to force Congress to address issues of waste. Why not insist that Congress and presidents use the authority they already have?

→ Studies show the item veto has had a limited effect on spending level in those states that provide for it. It mainly changes the composition of the spending, often substituting a governor's priorities for those of state legislators.

→ Most economists believe the proposed item veto along with the proposed mandatory "Balance the Budget" amendment would be unwanted and unwarranted straightjackets, especially during economic or national security crises.

→ One Reagan Administration economist faulted George W. Bush's call for an item veto "as little more than smoke-and-mirrors—an effort to show that he is serious about out-of-control spending without actually doing anything to cut spending or even restrain its growth." Bruce Bartlett adds, "But no one should delude themselves into thinking that the lack of a presidential line-item veto is all that stands between us and a balanced budget."[496]

In recent years, lawmakers have fashioned what many are calling a modified item veto. This new proposal, called "expedited rescission," tries to get around the Supreme Court's ruling that said only a president may sign or veto a bill. Under this new modification—or limited item veto—Congress would pass an appropriations bill, send it to the White House, then a president could sign the bill but send one or two packages of wasteful spending items back to Congress. Congress would then vote on these in both chambers within a specified time, as much as 45 days, with no amendments or, in the Senate, no filibuster allowed.

Most presidents would welcome this as a tool to go after wasteful "earmarking." But some critics think that even this watered down presidential item veto weakens Congress and is yet another example of delegating legislation authority to the White House.

"It's a disgusting idea," said Louis Fisher, a respected scholar of Congress and constitutionalism. "It's a cheap and easy thing for members to do. But it weakens Congress. And to have this very romantic view of the president as better guardian of the Treasury, I just don't think that's the case."[497]

The most compelling reason to resist the item veto is that it would encourage yet another additional transfer of power from Congress to the presidency—a grant of authority that, yes, would strengthen the president's hand, yet at the price of diminishing the capacity of Congress to function as a separate and centrally vital branch of government.

As we have noted, a strong presidency is desirable, yet constitutionally we also want a strong Congress and a strong federal judiciary as well as a strong presidency. And, in the long run—the framers were right—the public and national interests will be best served when each of our branches are able and willing to exercise fully these individual as well as shared prerogatives.

LIMITING THE PRESIDENT'S WAR POWERS

"Today I authorized the armed forces of the United States to begin a limited military action in Libya," said President Obama in 2011. I authorized? Shouldn't it be "we" (Congress) authorized?

The Constitution explicitly gives to the Congress the power to declare war. However, over the past decades presidents have largely usurped this power. James Madison called war "among the greatest of national calamities,"[498] and he and virtually all the other framers believed that only the representation of the collective wisdom of society—the Congress—should take the nation into war.[499]

Madison feared a replay of the imperial prerogatives of a king, where one man could take the nation into war. "The Constitution supposes," he wrote, "what the History of all Govts demonstrates, that the Ex[ecutive] is the branch of power most interested in war, and most prone to it. It has accordingly with studied care, vest the question of war in the Legisl[ative]."[500]

In the modern world, where the United States is the globe's only superpower, can the war power be tamed and brought back under congressional control? Should it? Given the importance of the decision to go to war, it makes good constitutional sense to put presidential decisions under closer scrutiny and tighter controls.

And yet, Congress *already has* all the constitutional authority it needs to tame the presidency in war. Strengthening or rewriting the War Powers Resolution might help some, but there is no constitutional or statutory way to instill more backbone into the Congress. If Congress wishes to "chain the dog of war," it already has all the necessary tools at its disposal.

Over a decade after 9/11, the public—in spite of the failure in the Iraq War— still seems comfortable allowing presidents to exercise broad national security and war-making powers. And if the public does not insist that Congress reclaim its war-declaring authority, it is unlikely Congress will do so on its own.

THE ULTIMATE CHECK: IMPEACHMENT
AND REMOVAL

Impeachment is obviously one of the most potent checks against the abuse of executive power, yet over the nation's history it has been the least used check. For practical purposes, it is a political action, phrased in legal terminology, against an official of the federal government. The Constitution deals with the subject of impeachment and conviction in six places, but the scope of the power is outlined in Article II, Section 4:

> The President, Vice President and all civil officers of the United States, shall be removed from Office on Impeachment for, and Conviction of, Treason, Bribery, or other high Crimes and Misdemeanors.

In the impeachment processing, the House of Representatives acts as the prosecutor and the Senate serves as the judge and jury. Any member of the

House may initiate impeachment proceedings by introducing a resolution to that effect in the House. The House Judiciary Committee may conduct hearings and investigations. The committee then decides either in favor of or against an impeachment verdict and sends its conclusions on to the full House. A majority vote in the House is needed to impeach. Select members of the House, if an impeachment is enacted, would then try the case before the U.S. Senate. In the Senate a two-thirds vote of those members present is needed for conviction and removal.

Only a dozen or so of national officials have been impeached by the House since 1789. Of these, only four were convicted, although one resigned before the Senate took action. Nine of these cases involved federal judges, one involved a senator, one a secretary of war, and two presidents, Andrew Johnson and Bill Clinton. Both Johnson and Clinton were impeached but not convicted.

The impeachment and removal of a president has been a much misunderstood and an obviously cumbersome means of accountability. Its use is fraught with emotion and hazardous side effects, and it necessarily remains a device to be used only as a last resort.

Impeachment is a time-consuming and highly traumatic instrument to deploy. Yet there is no reason to suppose in most instances that impeachment would be any more traumatic than having a person such as Richard Nixon continue in office for another two years when he had long since lost the ability to govern effectively. The impeachment and removal powers may well be an elaborate and difficult-to-use means to hold presidents to account, but as the Andrew Johnson and Richard Nixon cases attest, each in its own way, it can be used. Even though it can be abused, as in the Clinton case, [501] its availability is a reminder to presidents that their power must be exercised in an accountable manner.

An option short of impeachment that was discussed but not utilized during the Clinton impeachment effort was to *censure* the president. While nowhere provided in the Constitution, censure is a means by which Congress—short of impeachment—disapproves acts of a president as unacceptable. The Congress censured Andrew Jackson (though it later rescinded the censure), and there is no reason why it could not revive the practice, applying it to today. There is no formal penalty attached to censure, yet it would be a significant embarrassment to a president on the receiving end of a censure.

CAMPAIGN FINANCE REFORM—AGAIN

As discussed in chapter 3, running for president is a costly enterprise. In 2008, Barack Obama, who opted out of the public financing for the general election, was able personally and through his party to raise over a billion dollars. In 2012, Romney raised even higher sums. This astonishing amount may give the impression that the presidency is for sale to the highest bidder. Candidates must raise vast sums of money, and the sheer magnitude of this fund-raising poses serious questions for democratic accountability and integrity. The dependence of candidates on the largess of big donors raises the appearance, if not the reality, of undue influence if not corruption.

While there is sporadic public support for tightening the campaign finance laws, a combination of recent candidates' great success at raising funds "outside" the system, and the Supreme Court's *Citizen's United* decision allowing for massive undisclosed "independent" campaign spending, dooms efforts to limit the impact of money in our political process—at least for now.

Our political process is awash in money, and it is likely to remain so for quite some time. And yet there are probably few reforms that might have a greater positive impact (for the "public interest") than to regulate the amount and sources of campaign money—as almost every other advanced democracy in the world does.[502]

We may be tilting at windmills, but some form of strict public funding of elections is imperative if we are to give back control of the government to citizens and not special or wealthy interests. Since television is the costliest campaign expenditure, one way to accomplish our goal is to require television and cable stations to—as a condition of getting a broadcast license—give free air time to candidates who rise above a threshold of public support.

Other steps we might take include requiring full disclosure of all money— even Super PACs—that is spent in the political process; or giving each voter a voucher with "x" dollars that citizens could give to any candidate(s) they wished, but only voucher money could be used in a campaign.

While we are concerned with protecting speech, we believe money to be property, not speech, and unless one is guided by the golden rule, "whoever has the gold makes the rule," We can have free speech, a healthy debate, and competitive elections without putting democracy up for sale to the highest bidder.

ACCOUNTABILITY IN AN AGE OF TERRORISM

Immediately after the 9/11 attacks, citizens demanded a strong presidency. For a time, the public reacted favorably to the robust, even unilateral presidency. But as time passed, and problems, especially in Iraq and Afghanistan, persisted, they grew skeptical of a powerful executive. From the libertarian right[503] and idealistic left,[504] critics pointed to the dangers inherent in a strong presidency. Does the presidency pose a threat to constitutional government and democracy in America?

Presidents in the past have greatly aggrandized power sometimes in clearly unconstitutional ways, but the powerful chief executives of yesteryear took great pains to ground their power grabs in the patina of constitutionalism, always acknowledging that the Constitution was king. Lincoln during the Civil War, Wilson in World War I, and FDR in World War II used extraconstitutional authority to see the nation through crises, and acknowledged that while their actions may have exceeded normal practice, they were nonetheless bound to respect constitutional limits, especially as applied by Congress.

After World War II, with the coming of the Cold War, presidents began to claim inherent, independent power, either grounded (mistakenly) in the Constitution or in the claimed authority of precedents from past presidents. During the Korean conflict in the 1950s, President Truman claimed independent authority (as commander-in-chief) to commit U.S. troops to combat. This, of course, violated both the spirit and the letter of the Constitution, but in the atmosphere of Cold War hysteria, few had the political courage to challenge the president. And yet, it is in just such times that the Constitution needs all the defenders it can muster.

From that point presidents began to make grander claims of independent power, all of which led to the emergence of what in the 1970s historian Arthur M. Schlesinger, Jr., described as an *Imperial Presidency*. In effect, there has been a three-stage process in the aggrandizement of presidential war and foreign policy power: In Stage 1, presidents sometimes acted unilaterally but always took great pains to pay deference to the constitutional limitations and role of Congress (even as they bypassed both); in Stage 2, beginning with the Cold War and the Truman presidency, presidents began to claim—and the Congress and public were enablers in this—that they had constitutional powers as commander-in-chief, to send troops into war; in Stage 3, the G. W. Bush administration claimed that not only does the president have constitutional authority to commit the nation to war, but that such a power is *nonreviewable* by the other branches, a claim that, if true, places the presidency on the same plane as the English King we overthrew over two hundred and thirty years ago. Today, amid a "permanent war" against terrorism, the Constitution faces strains as some people favor presidential powers that go beyond what most of us believe is constitutional.

Have we come full circle? Has the American presidency invented in 1787 by men intent on rejecting the divine right of kings and rule by one man, who established a system with a *limited government*, under the *rule of law*, based on a *Constitution* that *separated power* within a regime of *checks and balances* in which the president was to *preside* as but *one of three* separate but connected branches...has that presidency devolved into a *presidential government* that resembles the *imperial* government the framers rejected and overthrew? In short, have we come, at least in some ways full circle from a hereditary monarchy to an elected monarchy with a presidency of imperial proportions?[505]

In an age of terrorism we doubtless need an effective and influential presidency, and we will need one who occasionally bends, but does not break, the Constitution. But we most assuredly don't want one disembodied from the system of checks and balances that has served us so well for so many years. We need a *powerful* presidency that is also a *constitutional* presidency.

"The answer to the runaway presidency," Arthur Schlesinger, Jr., reminded us, "is not the messenger-boy presidency."[506] We have gone to one extreme of presidential power; we need not shift to the other extreme of presidential weakness.

Are there "rules" that should guide us in our effort to attain a strong but accountable presidency in an age of terrorism? While no firm, set rules can be stringently imposed, there are several features of accountability that must apply:

1. In a war or crisis, presidential power *should* expand to meet the demands of the times.
2. Added presidential power does not amount to a blank check for the president.
3. All presidential acts during an emergency are reviewable by the Congress and the Courts.
4. Constitutional rights shall be enforced.
5. Where presidents believe they need to move beyond the law, they must consult with and get congressional approval (perhaps by a joint special committee of both Houses) prior to acting (except in response to an attack against the United States).

THE NECESSITY FOR POLITICS AND DEMOCRATIC ACCOUNTABILITY

A basic question facing our country is not whether government by the people is possible or even desirable in the modern world but rather how the political system and the relationship between the leadership and the citizens can be transformed so that they will approach more closely the ideals of constitutional democracy. This argument has explicitly rejected the view that things must remain as they are because that is the way underlying forces make them. We see the need for a strong yet also a lean and accountable presidency, a presidency that could achieve peace, economic prosperity, and the reforms and innovative changes that would broaden the economic and political opportunities of every American.

We reject the impractical and simplistic notion that returning to the drawing boards and coming up with a new constitution will provide the needed solutions.[507] A new constitutional convention is not needed. Solving major policy problems and keeping presidents honest and responsible are more likely to be accomplished by political than any additional *constitutional* means. No single institutional innovation we have ever heard of could guarantee a commitment to truth, compassion, and justice. Formal constitutional provisions to guard against presidential isolation, such as instituting congressional votes of confidence or repealing the two-term presidential limit, are not the sensible way to increase accountability.

That the American political system and leaders are asked to undertake much of what the rest of society refuses to do is a continual challenge in this nation. But the attempt to reconstitute any single institution in a large, complex society may be rather futile if the fundamental purpose of that institution is to represent and respond to the dominant values of the society. There is little doubt that this society's values are rooted in a strong faith in political and social gradualism, in a deep fear of revolutionary change, and in a steadfast devotion to most of what constitutes the existing order. Political controls, however, do need to be sharpened and strengthened to ensure a continual public and congressional scrutiny of presidential activity. Openness and candor often have been lacking. Presidents and their aides sometimes supply disappointingly little information to the press, to Congress, or to the public on matters of executive agreements, vetoes, executive orders, complex arms sales, pardons, and how they raise campaign contributions.[508] In the seemingly endless attempt to accentuate the positive, White House spin controllers too often have distorted news and thereby aggravated difficulties in credibility by claiming too much credit for fortuitous events or for policy initiatives that may or may not achieve sustained or desirable ends and by projecting the appearance of boldness, usually at the expense of candid discussions of the complexity of problems, the modesty of proposed solutions, and the realities of who must pay and how much.

A free society must mean a society based explicitly on free competition, most particularly competition in ideas and opinions, and by frank discussions of alternative national purposes and goals. Elected leaders and a vigorous media must attack ignorance, apathy, mindless nationalism, and xenophobia—the classic enemies of democracy. Citizens must resist sentimental patriotism that espouses everything as a matter for top priority but in practice avoids the tough political decisions and sacrifices that must be implemented—especially to implement energy independence and downsizing the national debt, to cite just two examples. Needed is a far more thoughtful way of looking at the presidency, leadership, and at citizen responsibilities.

Congress, the press, and the public must use existing political options as a means to check and occasionally empower presidents. Promoting opportunities for the nation's disadvantaged minorities will always remain major presidential responsibilities and an essential part of the legitimacy of the modern presidency.

We may want to change the presidency, yet *we* also must change. We must make the presidency work, but we must also strengthen Congress, modify unrealistic public expectations and demands, and strengthen the party system. The interconnectedness of the American system—not the health of one branch, but the health of the American governmental system—should be the goal. And while ours is primarily a presidentially driven system, it is also a system that requires cooperation and engagement between the separate institutions that share power.

A precondition of making the separation of powers work better is the need to develop a pragmatic *consensus* around particular governing ideas. This does not mean that all Americans must march in lockstep behind the will of the majority; nor does it mean that we must, or even can, come together on such issues as abortion, same-sex marriage, welfare, or immigration; yet it does point to the need for a people joined together in common pursuit of the common good—a nation, not merely an aggregation of individuals. The division between Congress and president reflects not merely the intuitional battles between two branches of government but often also reflects deeper conflicts and divisions that divide the nation and its people.

Ideal conditions for presidential accountability are difficult to spell out, but the public should know what a president's priorities are, how they will be financed, who will gain and who will lose, and what the alternatives are. The public and its representatives in normal circumstances should be given a chance to evaluate presidential priorities and give their views. Where strong majorities exist, Congress should be able to compete with a president in shaping the nation's policy agenda. Debate exists, however, over the extent to which public opinion should shape or dictate presidential choices. Government by public opinion, however it is devised, can never guarantee justice or wisdom.

No one proposes that a president's decisions should merely reflect majority opinion. The structure of the office in part reflects the desire of its designers to prevent presidents from being threatened or rushed into action by the shifting gusts of public passion. The definition of acceptable limits for presidential accountability will vary over time. If the standards for presidential accountability tilt too far in the direction either of public opinion or of independence and isolation, a president is less able to provide those subtle accommodating and mediating elements of leadership that are essential for effective democratic government. No task defines the essence of presidential leadership in a pluralistic society better than that of devising a workable and purposeful accommodation of the conflicting views of experts, powerful stakeholders, and the people as a whole.

With the proliferation of public opinion polls, presidents are barraged with nearly minute-by-minute CNN, Fox, and MSNBC reports on everything from "How is the president doing?" to the most trivial of minutiae about the White House dog or what's on the president's iPod. The time frame for presidential decision making and problem solving has been shortened. There seems to be less time for reflection, for issues to percolate up or ripen; less time for problems to be debated, discussed, and analyzed. Our instant-gratification culture, or so it often seems, impatiently wants immediate answers.

Although certain presidents have tried on occasion to govern without the benefit of public and partisan support, they seldom succeed. Presidents are in fact usually heavily influenced by their anticipation not only of the next election but also of tomorrow's headlines and editorials, next week's Gallup poll, next month's congressional hearings, and possible reprisals against their programs by Congress, the Supreme Court, the opposition party, and other institutions. In what other nation can a chief executive be overruled in the courts? A judicial check on a chief executive seldom exists in parliamentary systems if the leader retains his party's backing. In what other countries do the legions of newspapers, pamphleteers, tabloids, talk radio, and bulletin-board chat groups flourish with such tolerance and even encouragement?

One of the more confusing aspects of presidential accountability is the way the American people find it convenient to blame presidents for a whole range of problems, regardless of whether the problems have been subject to presidential control. We generally withhold our applause when a president's work is good, yet we seldom fail to hiss presidential blunders. As noted, no matter what presidents do, their popularity is likely to decline. When news is good, a president's popularity goes down or stays about the same; when news is bad, it merely goes down faster. Decline in approval of a president is in large part a function of the inability and unlikelihood of a president to live up to the buildup received during the presidential honeymoon.

Ultimately, however, being paradoxical does not make the presidency incomprehensible. Can we rid the presidency of all paradoxes? We couldn't, even if we wanted to do so. Nothing is wrong with some ambiguity. It is in embracing the paradoxical nature of the American presidency that we may be able to arrive at understanding. And with understanding may come enlightened or constructive criticism. This is the basis for citizen democracy.

The American presidency is a dynamic, not a static, institution. While there are standard role expectations and responsibilities faced by all occupants of the office, such uniformity must be seen as the other side of the coin of the rich diversity each president brings to the office. Each president brings a unique set of skills, experiences, goals, and styles to the presidency, yet the office and the requirements of the times place certain demands on the president. Each new president has to both emulate the master performances of Washington, Lincoln, and FDR, and yet invent his or her own approach that will help build a better America. It is this mix of the unique and the expected that makes the presidency such a fascinating institution.

In the end, presidents will be kept in line only if the people, according to their own personal views, exercise their rights and their political responsibilities. If the people insist both at and between elections that there be more respect for the doctrine of self-restraint, which all branches, including presidents, violate on occasion, it will happen.

James Madison was right. A constitutional democracy must insist on the effectiveness of our "auxiliary precautions"—Congress, parties, the courts, the media, the Bill of Rights, concerned citizen groups—if we are to have acceptable presidential leadership and preserve our constitutional democracy.

FOR DISCUSSION

1. Draft a Constitution of the United States (especially Articles I and II) that fits the contemporary needs of the nation.
2. Is strong presidential leadership compatible with political democracy? Does a strong presidency make for a weak people?
3. What change in the presidency would you most like to see and why?

DEBATE QUESTIONS

1. That the Constitution in our post 9/11 world must be rewritten to grant presidents greater power to protect national security.
2. That the Twenty-Second Amendment (the two-term limitation) be repealed.
3. That to make presidents more effective, more fiscally responsible, and accountable, we should amend the U.S. Constitution and grant presidents the power to item veto.

FURTHER READINGS

Edwards, George C., and William G. Howell, eds. *Oxford Handbook of the American Presidency*. New York: Oxford University Press, 2009.

Ellis, Richard J., and Michael Nelson, eds. *Debating the Presidency*, 2nd ed. Washington, DC: CQ Press, 2010.

Ellis, Richard J. *The Development of the American Presidency*. New York: Routledge, 2012.

Genovese, Michael A. *A Presidential Nation: Causes, Consequences, and Cures*. (Boulder, CO: Westview Press, 2013).

Genovese, Michael A., and Iwan W. Morgan, eds. *Watergate Remembered: The Legacy for American Politics*. New York: Palgrave Macmillan, 2012.

Levinson, Sanford. *Our Undemocratic Constitution*. New York: Oxford University Press, 2006.

Miroff, Bruce. *Icons of Democracy*. New York: Basic Books, 1993.

Pious, Richard M. *Why Presidents Fail: White House Decision Making from Eisenhower to Bush II*. Lanham, MD: Rowman & Littlefield, 2008.

Sabato, Larry J. *A More Perfect Constitution*. New York: Walker, 2008.

Critical Thinking

STATEMENT: The U.S. Constitution, written for a simpler age, no longer serves the interests of a twenty-first-century superpower world leader.

PROBLEM: What are the elements in the Constitution that might empower or limit the president's ability to lead a superpower in a dangerous world? How might presidents overcome these roadblocks? And if you were to design a new Constitution, one better suited to the twenty-first-century, what would it be?

INTERNET LINKS

Presidency

www.whitehouse.gov

www.americanpresident.org

www.americanpresident.org/presidentialresources.htm

www.presidency.ucsb.edu

http://fedbbs.access.gpo.gov

www.columbia.edu/acis/bartleby/inaugural/index.html

www.millercenter.org/academic/americanpresident

www.cstl-cls.emo.edu/renka/PresidencyLinks.htm

Congress

www.senate.gov

www.house.gov

www.cbo.gov

www.govspot.com/must/congress.htm

www.congressweb.com

http://thomas.loc.gov

www.cq.com

www.hillnews.com

http://www.loc.gov

Courts

www.supremecourtus.gov

http://supct.law.cornell.edu/supct

http://usgovinfo.about.com/libraryweekly/aa081400a.htm?once=true&

http://jurist.law.pitt.edu/currentawareness/ussupremes.php

www.lawguru.com/ilawlib/index.html

www.law.cornell.edu
www.findlaw.com

National Opinion

Public Opinion Archives	http://roperweb.ropercenter.uconn.edu
Gallup Poll	www.gallup.com
PEW Research Center	http://people-press.org

Presidential Libraries

	www.archives.gov/presidential-libraries
George W. Bush	http://www.georgewbushlibrary.gov
Bill Clinton	http://www.clintonpresidentialcenter.org
	http://searchclinton.archives.gov
George H. W. Bush	http://bushlibrary.tamu.edu
Ronald Reagan	www.reagan.utexas.edu
Jimmy Carter	www.jimmycarterlibrary.gov/library
Gerald Ford	www.fordlibrarymuseum.gov
Richard Nixon	www.archives.gov/nixon
Lyndon Johnson	www.lbjlib.utexas.edu
John F. Kennedy	www.jfklibrary.org
Dwight D. Eisenhower	www.eisenhower.archives.gov
Harry S. Truman	www.trumanlibrary.org

Departments and Agencies

Department of State	www.state.gov
Department of Defense	www.defenselink.mil
Department of Homeland Security	www.dhs.gov/dhspublic
Department of Justice	www.usdoj.gov
Secretary of Treasury	www.ustreas.gov
Secretary of Commerce	www.doc.gov
Department of Agriculture	www.usda.gov
Department of Labor	www.dol.gov
Department of Energy	www.energy.gov
Central Intelligence Agency	www.cia.gov
National Security Agency	www.nsa.gov
Federal Bureau of Investigation	www.fbi.gov
Agency for International Development	www.usaid.gov

Independent Agencies

Peace Corps	www.peacecorps.gov
Federal Reserve Board	www.federalreserve.gov
Environmental Protection Agency	www.epa.gov

International Trade Commission	www.usitc.gov
Export-Import Bank	www.exim.gov
Overseas Private Investment Corporation	www.opic.gov
Trade and Development Agency	www.tda.gov
NASA	www.nasa.gov

Parties

Democratic National Committee	www.democrats.org
Republican National Committee	www.rnc.org
Constitution Party	www.constitutionparty.com
Democratic Socialists of America	www.dsausa.org
Green Party of the United States	www.greenpartyus.org
Greens/Green Party USA	www.greenparty.org _
Libertarian Party	www.lp.org
Natural Law Party	www.natural-law.org
The New Party	www.newparty.org
Reform Party	http://reformpa.web.aplus.net
Socialist Party USA	http://sp-usa.org
Communist Party USA	www.cpusa.org
Third parties in general	www.politics1.com

Television

ABC	http://abcnews.go.com/
CBS	www.cbsnews.com/
FOX	www.foxnews.com
NBC	www.msnbc.msn.com/id/3032619
CNN	www.cnn.com
PBS	www.pbs.org/news
C-Span	www.c-span.org
MSNBC	www.msnbc.com

Radio

BBC News	http://news.bbc.co.uk
NPR	www.npr.org
Voice of America	www.voanews.com

Useful Blogs

Drudge Report	www.drudgereport.com
Truthdig	www.truthdig.com
Watching America	http://watchingamerica.com
Truthout	www.truthout.org
TomPaine	www.tompaine.com

Common Dreams	www.commondreams.org
The Huffington Post	www.huffingtonpost.com
Daily Kos	www.dailykos.com
TPM: Talking Points Memo	www.talkingpointsmemo.com
Hullabaloo	http://digbysblog.blogspot.com
My DD	http://mydd.com
Open Left	www.openleft.com
Washington DeCoded	www.washingtondecoded.com
MoJoBlog	www.motherjones.com
Salon	www.salon.com
White House Watch	www.washingtonpost.com
The Dreyfuss Report	http://robertdreyfuss.com/blog/
Lapham's Online	http://laphamsquarterly.org
History News Network	http://hnn.us
Foreign Policy in Focus	www.fpif.org
Media Channel	www.mediachannel.org
Human Rights Watch	www.hrw.org
LobbyWatch	http://projects.publicintegrity.org/lobby/
Project Vote Smart	www.vote-smart.org
OpenSecrets	www.opensecrets.org
Right Web	http://rightweb.irc-online.org
Political Money Line	http://moneyline.cq.com
National Security Archive	www.gwu.edu/~nsarchiv/
Real Clear Politics	www.realclearpolitics.com
Portside	www.portside.com
National Priorities Project	www.nationalpriorities.org
Project Gutenberg	www.gutenberg.org
Internet Archive	www.archive.org
Folkstreams	www.folkstreams.net

SELECTED BIBLIOGRAPHY

Reference Works on the Presidency

Edwards, George C., and William G. Howell, eds. *The Oxford Handbook of the American Presidency.* New York: Oxford University Press, 2009.

Genovese, Michael A. *The Encyclopedia of the American Presidency.* 2nd ed. New York: Facts-on-File, 2009.

Goldsmith, William M. *The Growth of Presidential Power: A Documented History.* 3 vols. New York: Chelsea House, 1974.

Graff, Henry F., ed. *The Presidents: A Reference History.* New York: Scribner's, 1984.

Levy, Leonard W., and Louis Fisher, eds. *Encyclopedia of the American Presidency.* 4 vols. New York: Simon & Schuster, 1994.

Milkis, Sidney M., and Michael Nelson. *The American Presidency: Origins and Development.* 5th ed. Washington, DC: CQ Press, 2007.

Nelson, Michael, ed. *Guide to the Presidency.* Washington, DC: CQ Press, 1989.

Shane, Peter M., and Harold H. Bruff, eds. *The Law of Presidential Power: Cases and Materials.* Durham, NC: Carolina Academic Press, 1988.

Warshaw, Shirley Anne. *CQ Press Guide to the White House Staff.* Washington, DC: CQ Press, 2012.

Important Works

Abraham, Henry J. *Justices, Presidents and Senators.* 5th ed. Lanham, MD: Rowman & Littlefield, 2008.

Abrams, Herbert L. *"The President Has Been Shot": Confusion, Disability and the 25th Amendment.* Stanford: Stanford University Press, 1994.

Adler, David Gray, and Larry N. George, eds. *The Constitution and the Conduct of Foreign Policy.* Lawrence: University Press of Kansas, 1996.

———, and Michael A. Genovese, eds. *The Presidency and the Law: The Clinton Legacy.* Lawrence: University Press of Kansas, 2002.

Alter, Jonathan. *The Promise: President Obama's First Year.* New York: Simon and Schuster, 2010.

Alterman, Eric. *When Presidents Lie: A History of Official Deception and Its Consequences.* New York: Viking, 2004.

Arnold, Peri. E. *Making the Managerial Presidency*. Princeton, NJ: Princeton University Press, 1986.

Baker, Nancy V. *Conflicting Loyalties: Law and Politics in the Attorney General's Office. 1789–1990*. Lawrence: University Press of Kansas, 1992.

———. *General Ashcroft: Attorney at War*. Lawrence: University Press of Kansas, 2007.

Barber, James David. *The Presidential Character: Predicting Performance in the White House*. 4th ed. Englewood Cliffs, NJ: Prentice-Hall, 1992.

Baumgartner, Jody C. *The American Vice Presidency Reconsidered*. Westport, CT: Praeger, 2006.

Beckmann, Matthew N. *Pushing The Agenda: Presidential Leadership in U.S. Lawmaking, 1953–2004*. New York: Cambridge, 2010.

Bessette, Joseph M., and Jeffrey Tulis, eds. *The Presidency in the Constitutional Order*. Baton Rouge: Louisiana State University Press, 1984.

Best, Judith A., et al. *The Choice of the People? Debating the Electoral College*. Lanham, MD: Rowman & Littlefield, 1996.

Binder, Sarah, and Forrest Maltzman. *Advice and Dissent: The Struggle to Shape the Judiciary*. Washington, DC: Brookings Institution, 2009.

Borrelli, MaryAnne. *The President's Cabinet: Gender, Power, and Representation*. Boulder, CO: Lynne Rienner, 2002.

Brace, Paul, and Barbara Hinckley. *Follow the Leader: Opinion Polls and the Modern Presidents*. New York: Basic Books, 1992.

Brown, Lara M. *Jockeying for the American Presidency: The Political Opportunism of Presidents*. Amherst, NY: Cambridge Press, 2010.

Burke, John P. *The Institutional Presidency*. Baltimore: Johns Hopkins University Press, 1992.

Burns, James MacGregor. *Roosevelt: The Lion and the Fox*. New York: Harcourt, 1956.

———. *Deadlock of Democracy*. Englewood Cliffs, NJ: Prentice-Hall, 1963.

———. *Presidential Government: The Crucible of Leadership*. Boston: Houghton Mifflin, 1965.

———. *Roosevelt: Soldier of Freedom*. New York: Harcourt Brace, Jovanovich, 1970.

———. *Leadership*. New York: HarperCollins, 1978.

———. *The Power to Lead: The Crisis of the American Presidency*. New York: Simon & Schuster, 1984.

Bush, George W. *Decision Points*. New York: Crown, 2010.

Calabresi, Steven G., and Christopher S. Yoo. *The Unitary Executive: Presidential Power From Washington to Bush*. New Haven: Yale University Press, 2008.

Cameron, Charles M. *Veto Bargaining: Presidents and the Politics of Negative Power*. New York: Cambridge University Press, 2000.

Canes-Wrone, Brandice. *Who Leads Whom? Presidents, Policy and the Public*. Chicago: University of Chicago Press, 2006.

Cannon, Lou. *President Reagan: The Role of a Lifetime*. New York: Touchstone 1991.

Carey, John M., and Matthew Soberg Shugart. *Executive Decree Authority*. Cambridge: Cambridge University Press, 1998.

Carter, Jimmy. *Keeping Faith: Memoirs of a President*. New York: Bantam Books, 1982.

Carter, Stephen L. *The Confirmation Mess: Cleaning Up the Federal Appointments Process*. New York: Basic Books, 1994.

Ceasar, James W. *Presidential Selection*. Princeton, NJ: Princeton University Press, 1979.

Cheney, Dick. *In My Time: A Personal and Political Memoir*. New York: Threshold Editions, 2011.

Clinton, Bill. *My Life*. New York: Knopf, 2004.

Clinton, Hillary. *Living History*. New York: Simon & Schuster, 2003.

Cole, David, and James X. Dempsey. *Terrorism and the Constitution*, 3rd ed. New York: New Press, 2006.

Conley, Patricia H. *Presidential Mandates: How Elections Shape the National Agenda*. Chicago: University of Chicago Press, 2001.

Cooper, Philip J. *By Order of the President: The Use and Abuse of Executive Direct Action*. Lawrence: University Press of Kansas, 2002.

Corwin, Edward S. *The President: Office and Powers, 1978–1984*. 5th ed. New York: New York University Press, 1984.

———. *Total War and the Constitution*. Westminster, MD: Knopf, 1947.

Covington, Cary R., and Lester G. Seligman. *The Coalition Presidency*. Chicago: Dorsey Press, 1989.

Crabb, Cecil V. *Invitation to Struggle: Congress, the President, and Foreign Policy*. 4th ed. Washington, DC: CQ Press, 1992.

Cramer, Richard Ben. *What It Takes: The Way to the White House*. New York: Random House, 1992.

Crenson, Matthew, and Benjamin Ginsberg. *Presidential Power: Unchecked and Unbalanced*. New York: Norton, 2007.

Cronin, Thomas E., and Sanford Greenberg, eds. *The Presidential Advisory System*. New York: Harper & Row, 1969.

———, and Rexford Tugwell, eds. *The Presidency Reappraised*. New York: Praeger, 1977.

———, *The State of the Presidency*. 2nd ed. Boston: Little, Brown, 1980.

———, ed. *Inventing the American Presidency*. Lawrence: University Press of Kansas, 1989.

———, *On the Presidency*. Boulder, CO: Paradigm, 2009.

———, and Michael A. Genovese. *Leadership Matters: Unleashing the Power of Paradox*. Boulder, CO: Paradigm, 2012.

Crouch, Jeffrey. *The Presidential Pardon Power*. Lawrence, KS: University Press of Kansas, 2009.

Dallek, Robert. *Hail to the Chief: The Making and Unmaking of American Presidents*. New York: Hyperion Books, 1996.

———. *An Unfinished Life: John F. Kennedy, 1917–1963*. Boston: Little, Brown and Co., 2003.

Doherty, Brendan J. *The Rise of the President's Permanent Campaign*. Lawrence: University Press of Kansas, 2012.

Donald, David H. *Lincoln*. New York: Simon & Schuster, 1995.

Draper, Robert. *Dead Certain: The Presidency of George W. Bush*. New York: Free Press, 2007.

Draper, Theodore. *A Very Thin Line: The Iran-Contra Affair*. New York: Touchstone Books, 1991.

Dubose, Lou, Jan Reid, and Carl M. Cannon. *Boy Genius: Karl Rove, the Brains Behind the Remarkable Political Triumph of George W. Bush*. New York: Public Affairs, 2003.

Eastland, Terry. *Energy in the Executive: The Case for the Strong Presidency*. New York: Free Press, 1992.

Edwards, George C. *At the Margins: Presidential Leadership in Congress*. New Haven, CT: Yale, 1989.

———, John H. Kessel, and Bert A. Rockman, eds. *Researching the Presidency: Vital Questions, New Approaches*. Pittsburgh: University of Pittsburgh Press, 1993.

———. *On Deaf Ears: The Limits of the Bully Pulpit.* New Haven, CT: Yale, 2003.

———. *Overreach: Leadership in the Obama Presidency.* Princeton, NJ: Princeton University Press, 2012

———. *The Strategic Presidency.* Princeton, NJ: Princeton University Press, 2009.

———. *Why the Electoral College Is Bad for America.* New Haven, CT: Yale, 2004.

Eland, Ivan. *Recarving Rushmore: Ranking the Presidents on Peace, Prosperity, and Liberty.* Oakland, CA: The Independent Institute, 2009.

Ellis, Richard, and Aaron Wildavsky. *Dilemmas of Presidential Leadership.* New Brunswick, NJ: Transaction Publishers, 1989.

———, and Michael Nelson. *The Presidency Debated.* 2nd ed. Washington, DC: CQ Press, 2010.

Farnsworth, Stephen J. *Spinner in Chief: How Presidents Sell Their Policies and Themselves.* Boulder, CO: Paradigm Publishers, 2009.

———, and S. Robert Lichter. *The Nightly News Nightmare: Media Coverage of U.S. Presidential Elections 1988–2008.* Lanham, MD: Roman & Littlefield, 2010.

Farrier, Jasmine. *Passing the Buck: Congress, the Budget, and Deficits.* Lexington: University Press of Kentucky, 2004.

Felzenberg, Alvin S. *The Leaders We Deserve.* New York: Basic Books, 2008.

Fiorina, Morris, et. al. *Culture War? The Myth of a Polarized America.* 3rd ed. Boston: Longman, 2011.

Fisher, Louis. *The Constitution Between Friends.* New York: St. Martin's Press, 1978.

———. *Presidential War Power.* Lawrence: University Press of Kansas, 1995.

———. *The Politics of Shared Power: Congress and the Executive.* 4th ed. College Station: Texas A&M University Press, 1998.

———. *Constitutional Conflicts between Congress and the President.* 5th ed. Lawrence: University Press of Kansas, 2007.

———. *The Constitution and 9/11: Recurring Threats to America's Freedoms.* Lawrence: University Press of Kansas, 2008.

Foner, Eric. *The Fiery Trial: Abraham Lincoln and Slavery.* New York: Norton, 2010.

Fox, Richard L., and Jennifer M. Ramos. *iPolitics: Citizens, Governing, and Governing in the New Media Era.* New York: Cambridge University Press, 2012.

Gardner, John W. *On Leadership.* New York: Free Press, 1990.

Gellman, Barton. *Angler: The Cheney Vice Presidency.* New York: Penguin, 2008.

Gelman, Andrew. *Red State, Blue State, Rich State, Poor State.* Princeton, NJ: Princeton University Press, 2010.

Genovese, Michael A. *The Supreme Court, the Constitution, and Presidential Power.* Landham, MD: University Press of America, 1980.

———. *Contending Approaches to the American Presidency.* Washington, DC: CQ Press, 2012.

———. *The Nixon Presidency: Power and Politics in Turbulent Times.* Westport, CT: Greenwood Press, 1990.

———. *The Presidency in an Age of Limits.* Westport, CT: Greenwood Press, 1993.

———. *The Power of the American Presidency, 1789–2000.* New York: Oxford University Press, 2001.

———. *The Presidential Dilemma: Leadership in the American System.* 2nd ed. New York: Longman, 2002.

———. *Memo to a New President: The Art and Science of Presidential Leadership.* New York: Oxford University Press, 2008.

——, and Iwan W. Morgan, eds. *Watergate Remembered: The Legacy for Presidential Politics*. New York: Palgrave, 2012.

Gergen, David. *Eyewitness to Power*. New York: Simon & Schuster, 2000.

Gerhardt, Michael J. *The Federal Appointment Process: A Constitutional History*. Durham, NC: Duke University Press, 2003.

Gierzynski, Anthony. *Money Rules*. Boulder, CO: Westview, 2000.

Goldsmith, Jack. *The Terror Presidency: Law and Judgment in the Bush Administration*. New York: W. W. Norton, 2007.

Goldstein, Joel K. *The Modern American Vice Presidency: The Transformation of a Political Institution*. Princeton, NJ: Princeton University Press, 1982.

Goodwin, Doris Kearns. *Team of Rivals*. New York: Simon & Schuster, 2005.

Gould, Lewis L. *The Modern American Presidency*. Lawrence: University Press of Kansas, 2003.

Greenstein, Fred. *The Hidden-Hand Presidency: Eisenhower and Leader*. New York: Free Press, 2004.

——. *The Presidential Difference: Leadership Style from FDR to Barack Obama*. Princeton, NJ: Princeton University Press, 2009.

——. *Inventing the Job of President: Leadership Style from George Washington to Andrew Jackson*. Princeton, NJ: Princeton University Press, 2009.

Gregg, Gary L II. *The Presidential Republic: Executive Representation and Deliberative Democracy*. Lanham, MD: Rowman & Littlefield, 1997.

Gutmann, Amy and Dennis Thompson, *The Spirit of Compromise*. Princeton, NJ: Princeton University Press, 2012.

Hamilton, Alexander, James Madison, and John Jay. *Federalist Papers*. New York: New American Library, 1961.

Han, Lori Cox. *Governing from Center Stage: White House Communication Strategies During the Television Age of Politics*. Cresskill, NJ: Hampton Press, 2001.

——. *New Directions in the American Presidency*. New York: Routledge, 2011.

——, and Caroline Heldman, eds. *Rethinking Madam President: Are We Ready for a Woman in the White House?* Boulder, CO: Lynne & Rienner, 2007.

Hargrove, Erwin C. *The President as Leader: Appealing to the Better Angels of Our Nature*. Lawrence: University Press of Kansas, 1998.

——. *The Effective Presidency*. Boulder, CO: Paradigm, 2008.

Harriger, Katy J. *Independent Justice: The Federal Special Prosecutor in American Politics*. Lawrence: University Press of Kansas, 1998.

Healy, Gene. *The Cult of the Presidency: America's Dangerous Devotion to Executive Power*. Washington, DC: Cato Institute, 2008.

Heilemann, John, and Mark Halperin. *Game Change*. New York: Harper Collins, 2010.

Henderson, Ryan C. *The Clinton Wars: The Constitution, Congress and War Powers*. Nashville, TN: Vanderbilt University Press, 2002.

Hess, Stephen. *Organizing the Presidency*. Washington, DC: Brookings Institution, 1976.

——. *What Do We Do Now? A Workbook for the President Elect*. Washington, DC: Brookings Institution, 2008.

Howell, William G. *Power Without Persuasion: The Politics of Direct Presidential Action*. Princeton, NJ: Princeton University Press, 2003.

——, and Jon C. Pevehouse. *While Dangers Gather: Congressional Checks on Presidential War Powers*. Princeton, NJ: Princeton University Press, 2007.

Hyman, Sidney. *The American President*. New York: Harper & Brothers, 1954.

Jacobson, Gary C. *A Divider Not a Uniter*. New York: Pearson, 2007.

Jamieson, Kathleen Hall. *Packaging the Presidency: A History and Criticism of Presidential Campaign Advertising*. New York: Oxford University Press, 1996.

Johnson, Loch K. *U.S. Intelligence Agencies in a Hostile World*. New Haven, CT: Yale, 1996.

——. *Bombs, Bugs, Drugs and Thugs: Intelligence and America's Search for Security*. New York: New York University Press, 2002.

——. *Fateful Decisions: Inside the National Security Council*. New York: Oxford University Press, 2003.

Jones, Charles A. *The Presidency in a Separated System*. Washington, DC: Brookings Institution, 1994.

Kallenbach, Joseph E. *The American Chief Executive*. New York: Harper & Row, 1966.

Kennedy, John F. *Profiles in Courage*. New York: Harper & Brothers, 1956.

Kernell, Samuel M. *Going Public: New Strategies of Presidential Leadership*. 4th ed. Washington, DC: CQ Press, 2006.

——, and Samuel Popkin, eds. *Chief of Staff*. Berkeley: University of California Press, 1986.

Kessel, John H. *Presidents, the Presidency and the Political Environment*. Washington, DC: CQ Press, 2001.

King, Gary, and Lyn Ragsdale. *The Elusive Executive: Discovering Statistical Patterns in the Presidency*. Washington, DC: CQ Press, 1988.

Klein, Joe. *The Natural: The Misunderstood Presidency of Bill Clinton*. New York: Doubleday, 2002.

Kleinerman, Benjamin A. *The Discretionary President: The Promise and Peril of Executive Power*. Lawrence: University Press of Kansas, 2009.

Koenig, Louis W. *The Chief Executive*. 9th ed. San Diego: Harcourt Brace Jovanovich, 1995.

Korzi, Michael J. *Presidential Term Limits in American History*. College Station: Texas A&M Press, 2011.

Krehbiel, Keith. *Pivotal Politics: A Theory of U.S. Lawmaking*. Chicago: University of Chicago Press, 1998.

Kumar, Martha Joynt. *Managing the President's Message: The White House Communications Operation*. Baltimore, MD: Johns Hopkins, 2007.

——, and Terry Sullivan, eds. *The White House World: Transitions, Organizations, and Office Operations*. College Station: Texas A&M, 2003.

Lammers, William W. *Presidential Politics: Patterns and Prospects*. New York: HarperCollins, 1976.

——, and Michael A. Genovese. *The Presidency and Domestic Policy*. Washington, DC: CQ Press, 2000.

Landy, Marc, and Sidney M. Milkis. *Presidential Greatness*. Lawrence: University Press of Kansas, 2001.

Laracey, Mel. *Presidents and the People: The Partisan Story of Going Public*. College Station: Texas A&M University Press, 2002.

Larocca, Roger T. *The Presidential Agenda: Sources of Executive Influence in Congress*. Columbus: Ohio State University Press, 2006.

Laski, Harold. *The American Presidency: An Interpretation*. New York: Harper & Brothers, 1940.

Latimer, Matt. *Speech-less: Tales of a White House Survivor*. New York: Three Rivers Press, 2009.

Lehrer, Jonah. *How We Decide*. Boston: Mariner Books, 2009.

Leuchtenburg, William E. *In the Shadow of FDR: From Harry Truman to Ronald Reagan.* Ithaca, NY: Cornell University Press, 1983.

Lewis, David E. *The Politics of Presidential Appointments: Political Control and Bureaucratic Performance.* Princeton, NJ: Princeton University Press, 2008.

Light, Paul C. *Vice Presidential Power: Advice and Influence in the White House.* Baltimore: Johns Hopkins University Press, 1984.

———. *The President's Agenda.* 3rd ed. Baltimore, MD: Johns Hopkins University Press, 1998.

Loevy, Robert D. *The Flawed Path to the Presidency.* Albany: State University of New York Press, 1995.

Longley, Lawrence D., and Neal R. Peirce. *The Electoral College Primer 2000.* New Haven, CT: Yale University Press, 1999.

Lowi, Theodore J. *The Personal President: Power Invested, Promise Unfulfilled.* Ithaca, NY: Cornell University Press, 1985.

Mackenzie, G. Calvin, ed. *Innocent Until Nominated: The Breakdown of the Presidential Appointments Process.* Washington, DC: Brookings Institution, 2001.

Maltese, John. *Spin Control: The White House Office of Communications and the Management of Presidential News.* Chapel Hill: University of North Carolina Press, 1992.

Mansfield, Harvey C., Jr. *Taming the Prince: The Ambivalence of Presidential Power.* New York: Free Press, 1989.

Martin, Janet M. *The Presidency and Women: Promise, Performance, and Illusion.* College Station: Texas A&M University Press, 2003.

Mayer, Jane. *The Dark Side: The Inside Story of How the War on Terror Turned into a War on American Ideals.* New York: Doubleday, 2008.

Mayer, Kenneth R. *With the Stroke of a Pen: Executive Orders and Presidential Power.* Princeton, NJ: Princeton University Press, 2001.

Mayer, William G. and Jonathan Bernstein, eds. *The Making of the Presidential Candidates, 2012.* Lanham, MD: Rowman & Littlefield, 2012.

Mayhew, David. *Divided We Govern.* New Haven, CT: Yale University Press, 1991.

McClellan, Scott. *What Happened: Inside the Bush White House and Washington's Culture of Deception.* New York: Public Affairs, 2008.

McCullough, David. *Truman.* New York: Simon & Schuster, 1993.

McPherson, James M. *Tried By War: Abraham Lincoln as Commander In Chief.* New York: Penguin, 2008.

Meacham, Jon. *American Lion: Andrew Jackson in the White House.* New York: Random House, 2008.

Mearsheimer, John J. *Why Leaders Lie.* New York: Oxford University Press, 2011.

Merry, Robert W. *Where They Stand: The American Presidents in the Eyes of Voters and Historians.* New York: Simon & Schuster, 2012.

Milkis, Sidney M. *The President and the Parties.* New York: Oxford University Press, 1993.

Miroff, Bruce. *Pragmatic Illusions: The Presidential Politics of John F. Kennedy.* New York: David McKay, 1976.

———. *Icons of Democracy.* New York: Basic Books, 1993.

Morgan, Iwan W. *The Age of Deficits: Presidents and Unbalanced Budgets from Jimmy Carter to George W. Bush.* New York: Palgrave, 2009.

Morris, Irwin L. *The American Presidency: An Analytical Approach.* New York: Cambridge University Press, 2010.

Murray, Robert K., and Tim H. Blessing. *Greatness in the White House: Rating the Presidents, Washington through Reagan.* University Park: Pennsylvania State University Press, 1994.

Mycoff, Jason D., and Joseph A. Pika. *Confrontation and Compromise: Presidential and Congressional Leadership*. Lanham, MD: Rowman & Littlefield, 2008.

Nathan, Richard. *The Administrative Presidency*. New York: John Wiley and Sons, 1983.

Nelson, Dana D. *Bad for Democracy: How the Presidency Undermines the Power of the People*. Minneapolis: University of Minnesota Press, 2008.

Nelson, Michael, ed. *The Evolving Presidency: Landmark Documents*. 3rd ed. Washington, DC: CQ Press, 2008.

———. *The Presidency and The Political System*. 9th ed. Washington, DC: CQ Press, 2010.

Nemacheck, Christine L. *Strategic Selection: Presidential Nomination of Supreme Court Justices from Herbert Hoover through George W. Bush*. Charlottesville: University of Virginia Press, 2007.

Neustadt, Richard E. *Presidential Power and the Modern Presidents*. New York: Free Press, 1990.

———. *Presidential Power*. New York: Wiley, 1960.

Nye, Joseph S., Jr. *The Powers to Lead*. New York: Oxford University Press, 2008.

Obama, Barack. *The Audacity of Hope: Thoughts on Reclaiming the American Dream*. New York: Crown Publishers, 2006.

Patterson, Bradley H., Jr. *The White House Staff: Inside the West Wing and Beyond*. Washington, DC: Brookings Institution, 2000.

———. *To Serve the President: Continuity and Innovation in the White House Staff*. Washington, DC: Brookings Institution, 2008.

Patterson, Thomas E. *The Vanishing Voter: Public Involvement in an Age of Uncertainty*. New York: Alfred A. Knopf, 2002.

Peterson, Mark A. *Legislating Together*. Cambridge, MA: Harvard University Press, 1990.

Pfiffner, James P., ed. *The Strategic Presidency: Hitting the Ground Running*. 2nd ed. Lawrence: University Press of Kansas, 1996.

———. *The Managerial Presidency*. 2nd ed. College Station: Texas A&M University Press, 1999.

———. *Character and the Modern Presidency*. Washington, DC: Brookings Institution, 2001.

———. *Power Play: The Bush Presidency and the Constitution*. Washington, DC: Brookings Institution, 2008.

Phelps, Glenn A. *George Washington and the American Constitutionalism*. Lawrence: University Press of Kansas, 1994.

Pious, Richard M. *Why Presidents Fail: White House Decision Making from Eisenhower to Bush II*. Lanham, MD: Rowman & Littlefield, 2008.

Plouffe, David. *The Audacity to Win*. New York: Penguin, 2009.

Posner, Eric A., and Adrian Vermeule. *The Executive Unbound: After the Madisonian Republic*. New York: Oxford University Press, 2010.

Posner, Richard A. *An Affair of State: The Investigation, Impeachment, and Trial of President Clinton*. Cambridge, MA: Harvard University Press, 1999.

———. *Not a Suicide Pact: The Constitution in a Time of National Emergency*. New York: Oxford University Press, 2006.

Prior, Markus. *Post-Broadcast Democracy*. New York: Cambridge University Press, 2007.

Ragsdale, Lyn. *Presidential Politics*. Boston: Houghton Mifflin, 1993.

Rapoport, Ronald B., and Walter J. Stone. *Three's a Crowd: The Dynamics of Third Parties, Ross Perot, and Republican Resurgence*. Ann Arbor: University of Michigan Press, 2008.

Reich, Robert. *Locked in the Cabinet*. New York: Knopf, 1997.

Reagan, Ronald. *An American Life: The Autobiography*. New York: Simon & Schuster, 1990.

Risen, James. *State of War: The Secret History of the CIA and the Bush Administration.* New York: Free Press, 2006.

Robinson, Donald L. *"To the Best of My Ability": The Presidency and the Constitution.* New York: Norton, 1987.

Rockman, Bert. *The Leadership Question: The Presidency and the American System.* New York: Praeger, 1984.

———, and Richard W. Waterman., eds. *Presidential Leadership: The Vortex of Power.* New York: Oxford University Press, 2007.

Rossiter, Clinton. *Constitutional Dictatorship: Crisis Government in the Modern Democracy.* Princeton, NJ: Princeton University Press, 1948.

———. *The American Presidency.* New York: Harcourt, Brace and World, 1956.

Rozell, Mark J. *Executive Privilege: Presidential Power, Secrecy, and Accountability.* 2nd ed., rev. Lawrence: University Press of Kansas, 2002.

Rudalevige, Andrew. *Managing the President's Program: Presidential Leadership and Legislative Policy Formulation.* Princeton, NJ: Princeton University Press, 2002.

———. *The New Imperial Presidency.* Ann Arbor: University of Michigan Press, 2005.

Savage, Charlie. *Takeover: The Return of the Imperial Presidency and the Subversion of American Democracy.* Boston: Little, Brown, 2007.

Schier, Steven E., ed. *Transforming America: Barack Obama in the White House.* Lanham, MD: Rowman & Littlefield, 2012.

Schlesinger, Arthur M., Jr. *The Imperial Presidency.* Boston: Houghton Mifflin, 1973.

———. *The Cycles of American History.* Boston: Houghton Mifflin, 1986.

———. *War and the American Presidency.* New York: Norton, 2005.

Schumaker, Paul D., and Burdett A. Loomis, eds. *Choosing a President: The Electoral College and Beyond.* New York: Chatham House, 2002.

Shane, Peter M. *Madison's Nightmare: How Executive Power Threatens America's Democracy.* Chicago: The University of Chicago Press, 2009.

Shull, Steven A., ed. *The Two Presidencies: A Quarter Century Assessment.* Chicago: Nelson-Hall, 1991.

Shultz, George P. *Turmoil and Triumph: My Years as Secretary of State.* New York: Scribner, 1993.

Simonton, Dean Keith. *Why Presidents Succeed.* New Haven, CT: Yale University Press, 1987.

Skowronek, Stephen. *The Politics Presidents Make: Leadership from John Adams to George Bush.* Cambridge, MA: Belknap, 1993.

———. *Presidential Leadership in Political Time: Reprise and Reappraisal.* Lawrence: University Press of Kansas, 2007.

Sloan, John W. *FDR and Reagan: Transformative Presidents with Clashing Visions.* Lawrence: University Press of Kansas, 2008.

Smith, Hedrick. *The Power Game: How Washington Works.* New York: Random House, 1988.

Soderstrom, Jamin. *Qualified: Candidate Resumes and The Threshold For Presidential Success.* Bloomington, IN: iUniverse, Inc., 2011.

Sollenberger, Mitchel A. *Executive Branch Czars and the Erosion of Democratic Accountability.* Lawrence: University Press of Kansas, 2012.

———. *The President Shall Nominate: How Congress Trumps Executive Power.* Lawrence: University Press of Kansas, 2008.

———. *Judicial Appointments and Democratic Controls.* Durham: Carolina Academic Press, 2011.

Sorensen, Theodore C. *Watchman in the Night*. Cambridge, MA: MIT Press, 1975.

——. *Counselor: A Life at the Edge of History*. New York: Harper, 2008.

Spitzer, Robert J. *The Presidential Veto: Touchstone of the American Presidency*. Albany: State University of New York Press, 1988.

——. *President and Congress: Executive Hegemony at the Crossroads of American Government*. New York: McGraw-Hill, 1993.

Stuckey, Mary E. *The President as Interpreter-in-Chief*. Chatham, NJ: Chatham House, 1991.

Sundquist, James L. *Constitutional Reform and Effective Government*. Washington, DC: Brookings Institution, 1986.

——. *Dynamics of the Party System*, rev. ed. Washington, DC: Brookings, 1993.

Suskind, Ron. *Confidence Men: Wall Street, Washington and the Education of Presidents*. New York: Harper, 2011.

Thomas, Helen. *Watchdogs of Democracy? The Waning Washington Press Corps and How It Has Failed the Public*. New York: Scribner, 2007.

Thurber, James A., ed. *Rivals for Power: Presidential–Congressional Relations*. 3rd ed. Lanham, MD: Rowman & Littlefield, 2005.

——. *Obama in Office*. Boulder, CO: Paradigm Publishers, 2011.

Tulis, Jeffrey K. *The Rhetorical Presidency*. Princeton, NJ: Princeton University Press, 1987.

Troy, Gil. *See How They Ran: The Changing Role of the Presidential Candidate*. New York: Free Press, 1991.

Walsh, Kenneth T. *Feeding the Beast, the White House vs. Press*. New York: Random House, 1996.

Warshaw, Shirley Anne. *Powersharing: White House–Cabinet Relations in the Modern Presidency*. Albany: State University of New York Press, 1996.

——. *The Co-Presidency of Bush and Cheney*. Stanford: Stanford Politics and Policy, 2009.

Wayne, Stephen J. *Is This Any Way to Run a Democratic Election?* 3rd ed. Washington, DC: CQ Press, 2007.

——. *Personality and Politics: Obama For and Against Himself*. Washington, DC: CQ Press, 2012.

——. *The Road to the White House, 2008*. Boston: Thomson, 2008.

Weisberg, Jacob. *The Bush Tragedy*. New York: Random House, 2008.

Weko, Thomas J. *The Politicizing Presidency: The White House Personnel Office, 1948–1994*. Lawrence: University Press of Kansas, 1995.

Westen, Drew. *The Political Brain: The Role of Emotion in Deciding the Fate of the Nation*. New York: Public Affairs, 2007.

Wills, Garry. *Certain Trumpets: The Call of Leaders*. New York: Simon & Schuster, 1994.

Witcover, Jules. *Crapshoot: Rolling the Dice on the Vice Presidency: From Adams and Jefferson to Truman and Quayle*. New York: Crown, 1992.

——. *Very Strange Bedfellows: The Short and Unhappy Marriage of Richard Nixon and Spiro Agnew*. New York: Public Affairs, 2007.

Wittes, Benjamin. *Law and the Long War: The Future of Justice in the Age of Terror*. New York: Penguin, 2008.

Yoo, John. *Crisis and Command*. New York: Kaplan, 2009.

——. *The Power of War and Peace*. Chicago: University of Chicago Press, 2005.

——. *War by Other Means*. New York: Atlantic Monthly Press, 2006.

NOTES

1. Barbara Tuchman, *The Distant Mirror* (New York: Knopf, 1978), p. xvii.
2. David Brooks, "The Bush Paradox," *The New York Times* (June 24, 2008): A23.
3. Howard Fineman, *The Thirteen Arguments* (New York: Random House, 2008), p. 245.
4. Alexis de Tocqueville, *Democracy in America*, Vol. II (Wordsworth Classics, 1998), chap. 5, p. 359.
5. See Harvey C. Mansfield, Jr., "The Ambivalence of Executive Power," in Joseph Bessette and Jeffrey Tulis, eds., *The Presidency in the Constitutional Order* (Baton Rouge: Louisiana State University Press, 1981), pp. 314–33; see also Gene Healy, *The Cult of the Presidency* (Washington, DC: Cato Institute, 2008).
6. See, for example, various modern yet differing conceptions of the presidency in Michael A. Genovese, ed., *Contending Approaches to the American Presidency* (Washington, DC: CQ Press, 2011).
7. See John J. Mearsheimer, *Why Leaders Lie* (New York: Oxford University Press, 2011), and Eric Alterman, *When Presidents Lie* (New York: Viking, 2004).
8. Andrew Rudalevige, *The New American Presidency* (Ann Arbor: University of Michigan Press, 2006), p. 259.
9. Benjamin A. Kleinerman, *The Discretionary President: The Promise and Peril of Executive Power* (Lawrence: University Press of Kansas, 2009), p. xi.
10. Woodrow Wilson, *Mere Literature and Other Essays* (New York: Grosset and Dunlap, 1896), p. 207.
11. We have expanded on these ideas in Thomas E. Cronin and Michael A. Genovese, *Leadership Matters: Unleashing the Power of Paradox* (Boulder: Paradigm Publishers, 2012), chap. 8.
12. Richard M. Nixon, *Leaders* (New York: Warner Books, 1983), p. 341.
13. Michael Walzer, *Thinking Politically* (New Haven, CT: Yale University Press, 2007), p. 279.
14. For a few books that treat both the moral and constitutional issues of the George W. Bush presidency, see Howard Ball, *Bush, the Detainees, and the Constitution: The Battle over Presidential Power in the War on Terror* (Lawrence: University Press of Kansas, 2007); Jack Goldsmith, *The Terror Presidency*

(New York: Norton, 2007); and Philippe Sands, *Torture Team* (New York: Palgrave MacMillan, 2008).

15. Saul Alinsky, *Rules for Radicals* (New York: Random House, 1971).

16. Alan Ehrenholt, "The Paradox of Corrupt Yet Effective Leadership," *The New York Times* (September 30, 2002).

17. Robert J. Morgan, A *Whig Embattled: The Presidency under John Tyler* (Lincoln: University of Nebraska Press, 1954).

18. See, in general, Gary Jacobson, *A Divider Not a Uniter* (New York: Pearson, 2007).

19. Quoted in *U.S. News and World Report* (January 28, 1985): 40.

20. James MacGregor Burns, *Leadership* (New York: Harper & Row, 1978).

21. For critical appraisals of JFK's pragmatism, see Bruce Miroff, *Pragmatic Illusions: The Presidential Politics of John F. Kennedy* (New York: David McKay, 1976); Nick Bryant, *The Bystander* (New York: Basic Books, 2006); and Henry Fairlie, *The Kennedy Promise* (Garden City, NY: Doubleday, 1973). For generally positive evaluations of Kennedy's leadership, see Ted Sorensen, *Counselor* (New York: HarperCollins, 2008); Robert Dalleck, *An Unfinished Life* (Boston: Little, Brown, 2003); and Chris Matthews, *Jack Kennedy: Elusive Hero* (New York: Simon and Schuster, 2011).

22. Jonathan Darman, "True or False? Candidates Should Never Flip-Flop," *Newsweek* (July 7/July 14, 2008): 30. See also, in general, Amy Gutman and Dennis Thompson, *The Spirit of Compromise: When Governing Demands It and Campaigning Undermines It* (Princeton: Princeton University Press, 2012).

23. William Davison Johnston, *TR, Champion of the Strenuous Life* (Oyster Bay, NY: Theodore Roosevelt Association, 1958), p. 95.

24. Christopher Matthews, *Jack Kennedy: Elusive Hero* (New York: Simon and Schuster, 2011), p. 375.

25. Roger Martin, *The Opposable Mind* (Boston: Harvard Business School Press, 2007), p. 144.

26. See Michael Scherer, "Obama's Boldness Rap," *Time* (December 12, 2011): 54.

27. See Garry Wills, "What Makes a Good Leader?," *The Atlantic Monthly* (April 1994), pp. 63–80.

28. Laski, *The American Presidency*, p. 93.

29. See the useful analysis by George C. Edwards, *Overreach: Leadership in the Obama Presidency* (Princeton: Princeton University Press, 2012).

30. Quoted in Robert A. Caro, *Lyndon Johnson and The Passage of Power* (New York: Knopf, 2012) p. xv.

31. John Keegan, *The Mask of Command* (New York: Penguin Books, 1987).

32. Scott McClellan, *What Happened* (New York: Public Affairs, 2008), p. 268. See also Stephen J. Farnsworth, *Spinner-in-Chief: How Presidents Sell Their Polices and Themselves* (Boulder, CO: Paradigm Publisher, 2009).

33. McClellan, *What Happened*, p. 208. See also Roger Draper, *Dead Certain* (New York: Free Press, 2007), and Jacob Weisberg, *The Bush Tragedy* (New York: Random House, 2008).

34. Robert S. McNamara, *In Retrospect* (New York: Random House, 1995), p. 333; see also the award-winning documentary that interviews McNamara called *Fog of War* (2003).

35. David Brooks, "The Bush Paradox," *The New York Times* (June 24, 2008): A23.

36. Duberstein, quoted in Kenneth T. Walsh, "When It's Gut-Check Time in the Oval Office," *U.S. News and World Report* (November 3, 2008): 32.

37. *Boston Globe* (January 7, 1976).

38. Bob Woodward, *The Agenda: Inside the Clinton White House* (New York: Simon & Schuster, 1994), p. 164.

39. This is how one of our students aptly put it in a class discussion a few years ago.

40. Obama initially objected to this "Change We Can Believe In" slogan, complaining "Do you really think it says enough? Nothing about issues at all." But his message team prevailed. See David Plouffe, *The Audacity To Win* (New York: Penguin, 2009), p.103.

41. George C. Edwards, *On Deaf Ears: The Limits of the Bully Pulpit* (New Haven, CT: Yale University Press, 2003), p. 247. See also, Brendan Doherty, *The Rise of the President's Permanent Campaign* (Lawrence: University Press of Kansas, 2012).

42. George Edwards summarizes reflections of political scientist Hugh Heclo in *On Deaf Ears*, p. 247.

43. Stephen Skowronek, *The Politics President Make: Leadership from John Adams to George Bush* (Cambridge, MA: Belknap, 1993), and his *Presidential Leadership in Political Time: Reprise and Reappraisal* (Lawrence: University Press of Kansas, 2008).

44. See J. David Greenstone, *The Lincoln Persuasion: Remaking American Liberalism* (Princeton, NJ: Princeton University Press, 1993).

45. Stephen Skowronek, *Presidential Leadership in Political Time* (Lawrence: University Press of Kansas, 2008), p. 95.

46. Reagan, in 1989, quoted in Skowronek, *Presidential Leadership*, p. 95.

47. Skowronek, *Presidential Leadership*, p. 78.

48. Andrew Gelman et al., *Red State, Blue State, Rich State, Poor State: Why Americans Vote the Way They Do* (Princeton, NJ: Princeton University Press, 2010), Introduction.

49. Gelman, p. 165.

50. See Robert D. Putnam and David E. Campbell, *American Grace: How Religion Divides Us and Unites Us* (New York: Simon and Schuster, 2010).

51. Putnam and Campbell, p. 369.

52. Nelson Mandela, *Long Walk to Freedom* (Boston: Back Bay Books, 1993), p. 625.

53. Michael Kinsley, "The Trouble with Optimism," in his *Please Don't Be Calm* (New York: W. W. Norton, 2008), pp. 260, 261.

54. Howard Gardner, *5 Minds for the Future* (Boston: Harvard Business Press, 2008), p. xiii.

55. See James M. McPherson, *Tried by War: Abraham Lincoln as Commander in Chief* (New York: Penguin Press, 2008), and Doris Kearns Goodwin, *Team of Rivals: The Political Genius of Abraham Lincoln* (New York: Simon & Schuster, 2005).

56. See, for example, Edward S. Corwin, *The President: Office and Powers* (New York: New York University Press, 1957); Arthur M. Schlesinger, Jr., *The Imperial Presidency* (Boston: Houghton Mifflin Company, 1973); Andrew Rudalevige, *The New Imperial Presidency* (Ann Arbor: University of Michigan Press, 2006); and James P. Pfiffner, *Power Play* (Washington, DC: The Brookings Institution, 2008).

57. Walter Berns, "The American Presidency: Statesmanship and Constitutionalism in Balance," *Imprimis* (January 1983): 3.

58. Jon Meacham, *American Lion: Andrew Jackson in the White House* (New York: Random House, 2008), p. 211.

59. Ibid., p. 303.

60. See David H. Donald, *Lincoln* (New York: Simon & Schuster, 1995), pp. 128–29. See also James M. McPherson, *Tried by War: Abraham Lincoln as Commander-in-Chief* (New York: Penguin, 2008).

61. For a useful history of the Whigs, see Michael F. Holt, *The Rise and Fall of the American Whig Party* (New York: Oxford, 1999).

62. See Woodrow Wilson, *Constitutional Government in the United States* (New York: Columbia University Press, 1908). See also Jeffry Tulis, *The Rhetorical Presidency* (Princeton, NJ: Princeton University Press, 1987).

63. For analysis of public opinion mood cycles, see James A. Stimson, *Public Opinion in America: Moods, Cycles, and Swings* (Boulder, CO: Westview, 1999).

64. James L. Sundquist, *The Decline and Resurgence of Congress* (Washington, DC: The Brookings Institution, 1981), p. 33. See also William Howell, *Power Without Persuasion* (Princeton, NJ: Princeton University Press, 2003).

65. This is not to say that all of the nineteenth-century presidents were passive. Several did rally public opinion and went public in winning support for their initiatives. See Mel Laracy, *Presidents and the People* (College Station: Texas A&M, 2002).

66. For a fascinating reappraisal of Reagan and the Reagan era, see Sean Wilentz, *The Age of Reagan* (New York: Harper, 2008).

67. See Stephen Skowronek, *The Politics Presidents Make: Leadership from John Adams to Bill Clinton* (Cambridge: Harvard University Press, 1997); also Erwin C. Hargrove and Michael Nelson, *Presidents, Politics, and Policy* (New York: Knopf, 1984); and Stephen Skowronek, *Presidential Leadership in Political Time* (Lawrence: University Press of Kansas, 2008).

68. Mike Kimel and Michael E. Kanell, *Presimetrics* (New York: Black Dog and Leventhal Publishers, 2010), p. 233.

69. See the instructive review by Louis Fisher, "Teaching the Presidency: Idealizing a Constitutional Office," *PS: Political Science & Politics* (January 2012): 17–31.

70. Data and analysis from www.gallup.com/poll, 149636, "Americans Want Leaders to Follow Public's Views More Closely," September, 23, 2011.

71. Lyn Ragsdale, *Presidential Politics* (Boston: Houghton Mifflin, 1993), p. 143.

72. Gary King and Lyn Ragsdale, *The Elusive Executive* (Washington, DC: Congressional Quarterly Press, 1988), p. 290.

73. Paul Gronke and Brian Newman, "FDR to Clinton, Mueller to?: A Field Essay on Presidential Approval," *Political Research Quarterly* (December 2003): 508.

74. See Gary C. Jacobson, *A Divider Not a Uniter* (New York: Pearson, 2007), and George C. Edwards and Desmond S. King, eds., *The Polarized Presidency of George W. Bush* (New York: Oxford, 2007).

75. See, among other sources, Scott McClellan, *What Happened: Inside the Bush White House and Washington's Culture of Deception* (New York: Public Affairs, 2008), and Charlie Savage, *Takeover: The Return of the Imperial Presidency and the Subversion of American Democracy* (Boston: Little, Brown, 2007).

76. Gary C. Jacobsen, "Obama and the Polarized Public" in James A. Thurber, ed., *Obama in Office* (Boulder: Paradigm, 2011) pp. 32–33.

77. Paul Brace and Barbara Hinckley, *Follow the Leader* (New York: Basic Books, 1992), p. 1.

78. George Edwards, *The Public Presidency* (New York: St. Martin's Press, 1983), p. 233.

79. For instructive analysis of presidential fiascoes, see Richard M. Pious, *Why Presidents Fail* (Lanham, MD: Rowman and Littlefield, 2008).

80. Stephen Farnsworth, *Spinner in Chief* (Boulder, CO: Paradigm, 2009), and Scott McClellan, *What Happened.*

81. Jeffrey E. Cohen, *Presidential Responsibilities and Public Policy* (Ann Arbor: University of Michigan Press, 1997), p. 247.

82. See Brandice Canes-Wrone, *Who Leads Whom? Presidents, Policy and the Public* (Chicago: University of Chicago Press, 2006).

83. Jeffery E. Cohen, *The Presidency in the Era of 24-Hour News* (Princeton, NJ: Princeton University Press, 2008).

84. Paul Gronke and Brian Newman, "Public Evaluations of Presidents," in George Edwards and William Howell, eds., *The Oxford Handbook of The American Presidency* (New York: Oxford University Press, 2009), p. 246.

85. George C. Edwards, III, *On Deaf Ears: The Limits of the Bully Pulpit* (New Haven, CT: Yale University Press, 2003). See also Edwards, *The Strategic Presidency* (Princeton, NJ: Princeton University Press, 2009).

86. Edwards, *On Deaf Ears*, p. 254.

87. Quoted in George C. Edwards and Stephen Wayne, *Presidential Leadership,* 3rd ed. (New York: St. Martin's Press, 1994), p. 90.

88. Arthur M. Schlesinger, Jr., "The Ultimate Approval Rating," *The New York Times Magazine* (December 15, 1996): 51.

89. James W. Ceaser, "The Reagan Presidency and American Public Opinion," in Charles O. Jones, ed., *The Reagan Legacy: Promise and Performance* (Chatham, NJ: Chatham House, 1988), p. 220.

90. Drew Westen, *The Political Brain* (New York: Public Affairs, 2007), p. 310.

91. See, for example, Alvin S. Felzenberg, *The Leaders We Deserved: Rethinking the Presidential Rating Game* (New York: Basic Books, 2008); and the helpful essays in Meena Bose and Mark Landis, eds., *The Uses and Abuses of Presidential Rankings* (Hauppauge, NY: Nova, 2003). See also Robert W. Merry, *Where they Stand: The American Presidents in the Eyes of Voters and Historians* (New York: Simon & Schuster, 2012).

92. James Lindgren, *Rating the Presidents of the United States, 1789–2000: A Survey of Scholars in History, Political Science, and Law* (Washington, DC: The Federalist Society, 2000), mimeographed report. See also James Lindgren and Steven Calabresi, "Ranking the Presidents," *The Wall Street Journal* (November 16, 2000): A26, and *The Wall Street Journal* (September 12, 2005): A17. See also Bose and Landis, *Uses and Abuses.*

93. John Balz, "Ready to Lead on Day One: Predicting Presidential Greatness from Political Experience," *PS: Political Science and Politics* (July 2010): 487.

94. Jamin Soderstrom, *Qualified: Candidate Resumes and The Threshold for Presidential Success* (Bloomington, Indiana: iUniverse, 2011), p. 214.

95. See Fred Greenstein, *Inventing the Job of President* (Princeton, NJ: Princeton University Press, 2009), p. 3. See also *The Presidential Difference* (New York: Free Press, 2000). See also Dean Keith Simonton, *Why Presidents Succeed* (New Haven, CT: Yale University Press, 1987) and Michael A. Genovese, *Presidential Prerogative: Imperial Power in an age of Terrorism* (Stanford, CA: Stanford University Press, 2011).

96. This list, paraphrased, comes from Alvin S. Felzenburg, *The Leaders We Deserved (and a Few We Didn't): Rethinking the Presidential Rating Game* (New York: Basic Books, 2008), pp. 372–377.

97. Jay Hobbs, "Bad Boys" Research paper for Colorado College 'Leadership and Governance' seminar, April 20, 2011, p. 2. We are indebted to Hobbs for this general idea.

98. Ivan Elaud, *Recarving Rushmore: Ranking the Presidents on Peace, Prosperity and Liberty* (Oakland, CA: The Independent Institute, 2009), p. 428.

99. Ibid., p. 429.

100. Bruce Miroff, *Icons of Democracy: Heroes, Aristocrats, Dissenters, and Democrats* (New York: Basic Books, 1993).

101. See Thomas E. Cronin and Michael A. Genovese, *Leadership Matters* (Boulder, CO: Paradigm, 2012), and George Edwards, *The Strategic Presidency* (Princeton, NJ: Princeton University Press, 2009), and Robert W. Merry, *Where They Stand*, op cit.

102. George F. Will, "The Presidency in the American Political System," *Presidential Studies Quarterly* (Summer 1984): 328–29. See also Garry Wills, "What Is Political Leadership?" *Atlantic Monthly* (April 1994): 63–80. See also Thomas A. Bailey, *Presidential Greatness* (New York: Appleton-Century, 1966), p. 259.

103. See David Plouffe, *The Audacity to Win: The Inside Story and Lessons of Barrack Obama's Historic Victory* (New York: Viking, 2009), and John Heilemann and Mark Halperin, *Game Change* (New York: Harper Collins, 2010).

104. See Lara M. Brown, *Jockeying for the American Presidency: The Political Opportunism of Presidents*, (Amherst, NY: Cambria Press, 2010).

105. See the excellent voting studies scholarship in Michael S. Lewis Beck et al., *The American Voter Revisited* (Ann Arbor: University of Michigan Press, 2008); Richard R. Lau and David Redlawsk, *How Voters Decided* (New York: Cambridge University Press, 2006); and Bryan Caplan, *The Myth of the Rational Voter* (Princeton, NJ: Princeton University Press, 2008).

106. Drew Westen, *The Political Brain* (New York: Public Affairs, 2007) pp. xv, 35, 119, 120.

107. Ibid., pp. 125, 138, 305.

108. See George Lakoff, *The Political Mind* (New York: Viking, 2008).

109. See Jonah Lehrer, *How We Decide* (Boston: Mariner Books, 2009).

110. James David Barber, *The Presidential Character*, rev. ed. (New York: Prentice-Hall, 1992).

111. James P. Pfiffner, *The Character Factor* (College Station: Texas A&M University Press, 2004).

112. Martin Walker, book review of Robert Wilson's *Character Above All*, in *The Washington Monthly* (April 1996): 54; Robert A. Wilson, ed., *Character Above All* (New York: Simon and Schuster, 1995).

113. Emmett H. Buell, Jr., "The Invisible Primary," in William G. Mayer, ed., *In Pursuit of the Presidency* (Chatman, NJ: Chatman House, 1995).

114. See Stephen J. Farnsworth and S. Robert Lichter, *The Nightly News Nightmare: Media Coverage of U.S. Presidential Elections 1988–2008* (Lanham, MD: Rowman & Littlefield, 2010).

115. Quoted in *New York Times* (October 19, 1974): E18.

116. Nelson W. Polsby and Aaron Wildavsky, *Presidential Elections: Strategies and Structures of American Politics*, 9th ed. (Chatham, NJ: Chatham House, 1995), p. 69.

117. Anthony Gierzynski, *Money Rules* (Boulder, CO: Westview, 2000).

118. 558, U.S. 09–205 (2010).

119. 494 U.S. 652 (1990).

120. 540 U.S. 93 (2003).

121. See Jane Mayer, "Attack Dog," *The New Yorker* (February 13 & 20, 2012): 40–49.

122. Quoted in Jasper B. Shannon, *Money and Politics* (New York: Random House, 1959), p. 35.

123. Jane Mayer, "Inside the Money Machine," *The New Yorker* (February 3, 1997): 32–37; and Anthony Corrado, "Financing the 1996 Elections," in Gerald Pomper, ed., *The Election of 1996* (Chatham, NJ: Chatham House, 1997).

124. Virginia Hefferman, "Clicking and Choosing: The Election According to YouTube," *The New York Times Magazine* (November 16, 2008): 22–24.

125. Richard L. Fox and Jennifer M. Ramos, *iPolitics: Citizens, Elections, and Governing in the New Media Era* (New York: Cambridge University Press, 2012).

126. See Markus Prior, *Post. Broadcast Democracy* (New York: Cambridge University Press, 2007).

127. Adam Nagourney, "The '08 Campaign: Sea Change for Politics as We Know It," *The New York Times* (November 3, 2008): 1.

128. Nagourney, p. 1.

129. Arthur T. Hadley, *The Invisible Primary* (Englewood Cliffs, NJ: Prentice-Hall, 1976), pp. 14–15.

130. See, for example, "Primary Reforms," an editorial in the *New York Times* (June 8, 2008): 11; and Sean Wilentz and Julian Zelizer, "A Rotten Way to Pick a President," *The Washington Post Weekly Edition* (February 25–March 2, 2008): 26.

131. Ryan Lizza, "Romney's Dilemma," *The New Yorker* (June 6, 2011): 38–43.

132. One of the most useful and most balanced studies of the presidential primaries is found in William R. Keech and Donald R. Matthews, *The Party's Choice* (Washington, DC: Brookings Institution, 1976). See also William J. Crotty, *Political Reform and the American Experiment* (New York: Crowell, 1977), chap. 7. Also, see the provocative analysis in Robert D. Loevy, *The Flawed Path to the Presidency 1992: Unfairness and Inequality in the Presidential Selection Process* (Albany: State University of New York Press, 1995).

133. Wayne P. Steger, "Who Wins Nominations and Why?," *Political Research Quarterly*, Vol. 60, No. 1 (March 2007): 91–99.

134. See Christopher Hall, *Grassroots Rules: How the Iowa Caucus Helps Elect American Presidents* (Palo Alto, CA: Stanford Law and Politics, 2007).

135. See Stephen J. Wayne, *The Road to the White House, 2008*, 8th ed. (Boston: Thompson, 2008).

136. H. L. Mencken, *The Mencken Society* (Baltimore, MD: www.mencken.org).

137. Richard Pious, "The Presidency and the Nominating Process," in Michael Nelson, ed., *The Presidency and the Political System* (Washington, DC: CQ Press, 2005).

138. Edward R. Tufte, *Political Control of the Economy* (Princeton, NJ: Princeton University Press, 1978), pp. 2–3.

139. Laura R. Olson and John C. Green, *Beyond Red State, Blue State: Electoral Gaps in the Twenty-First Century American Electorate* (Upper Saddle River, NJ: Pearson, 2008); see also the splendid essays in Jody C. Baumgartner and Peter Francia, *Conventional Wisdom and American Elections* (Lanham, MD: Rowman & Littlefield, 2008).

140. Robert A. Dahl, "Myth of the Presidential Mandate," *Political Science Quarterly,* 105 (Fall 1990): 335–72; Patricia H. Conley, *Presidential Mandates: How Elections Shape the Natural Agenda* (Chicago: University of Chicago Press, 2001).

141. Jimmy Carter comments at a meeting in Atlanta, March 26, 2001, quoted in Jack N. Rakove, "The E-College in the E-Age," in Jack N. Rakove, *The Unfinished Election of 2000* (New York: Basic Books, 2001), p. 201.

142. Jack N. Rakove, ibid.; Shlomo Slonim, "Designing the Electoral College," in Thomas E. Cronin, ed., *Inventing the American Presidency* (Lawrence: University Press of Kansas, 1989); Thomas E. Cronin, "Foreword: The Electoral College Controversy," in Judith A. Best, ed., *The Choice of the People? Debating the Electoral College* (Lanham, MD: Rowman & Littlefield, 1996), pp. vii–xxv.

143. Norman Ornstein, "No Need to Repeal the Electoral College," *State Legislators Magazine* (February, 2001).

144. George Will, "Forward," in Tara Ross, *Enlightened Democracy: The Case for the Electoral College* (Dallas, TX: Colonial Press, 2004), p. xi.

145. Tara Ross, Ibid., pp. 34–59, 172.

146. Arthur Schlesinger, Jr., "The Electoral College Conundrum," *Wall Street Journal* (April 4, 1977). See also his "It's a Mess, But We've Been Through It Before," *Time Magazine* (November 20, 2000): 64.

147. Editorial, "Drop Out of the Electoral College," *The New York Times* (March 14, 2006): A30.

148. See *Electing the President: A Report of the Commission on Electoral College Reform* (Chicago: American Bar Association, 1967).

149. Editorial, "Flunking the Electoral College," *New York Times* (November 20, 2008): A32.

150. George C. Edwards III, *Why the Electoral College is Bad for America* (New Haven, CT: Yale University Press, 2004).

151. Ibid., p. 39.

152. Polsby and Wildavsky, note 116, p. 3.

153. Stephen J. Wayne, "Let the People Vote Directly for President," in Stephen J. Wayne and Clyde Wilcox, eds., *The Quest for the White House* (New York: St. Martin's Press, 1992), pp. 313–14.

154. A strong case is made for the direct vote system in Lawrence D. Longley and Neal R. Pierce, *The Electoral College Primer 2000* (New Haven, CT: Yale University Press, 1999). See also the helpful analyses in Paul D. Shumaker and Burdett A. Loomis, eds., *Choosing a President: The Electoral College and Beyond* (New York: Chatham House, 2002).

155. See, for example, Douglas Amy, *Real Choices/New Voices: The Case for Proportional Representation in the United States* (New York: Columbia University Press, 1993); and Stephen J. Brown, *The Presidential Election Game* (New Haven, CT: Yale University Press, 1978).

156. See William Keech, *Winner Take All: Report of the Twentieth Century Fund Task Force on Reform of the Presidential Election Process* (New York: Holmes and Meier, 1978). See also Thomas E. Cronin, "Choosing a President," *The Center Magazine* (September–October, 1978): 5–15; and Thomas E. Cronin, "The Direct Vote and the Electoral College: The Case for Meshing Things Up!," *Presidential Studies Quarterly* (Spring 1979): 144–63.

157. Such a system was supported by a group called the Center for Voting and Democracy, as well as by the Ralph Nader inspired Public Interest Research Group. See www.votersdecide.com. Australia uses a similar system for its parliamentary elections, and Ireland uses it to elect their president, the ceremonial head of state.

158. William Poundstone, *Gaming the Vote: Why Elections Aren't Fair and What We Can Do About It* (New York: Hill and Wang, 2008).

159. Bruce Miroff, *Icons of Democracy: American Leaders as Heroes, Aristocrats, Dissenters, and Democrats* (New York: Basic Books, 1993).

160. Samuel P. Huntington, *American Politics: The Promise of Disharmony* (Cambridge, MA: Harvard University Press, 1981), pp. 4, 33.

161. Clinton Rossiter, *Conservatism in America* (New York: Vintage, 1962), p.72.

162. Max Lerner, *America as a Civilization* (New York: Knopf, 1957), p. 718.

163. Alexis de Tocqueville, *Democracy in America* (New York: Knopf, 1999), p. 430.

164. George W. Bush, Address to Airline Employees, O'Hare International Airport, Chicago, Illinois. September 27, 2001; Available at The American Presidency Project, http://www.presidency.ucsb.edu/ws/?pid=65084.

165. George W. Bush, *Decision Points* (New York: Crown Publishing, 2010), p.444.

166. Robert Bellah, Richard Masden, William Sullivan, Ann Swindel, and Steven Tipton, *Habits of the Heart* (New York: Harper & Row, 1985); Arthur M. Schlesinger, Jr., *The Disuniting of America* (New York: Norton, 1991).

167. Stephen Skowronek, *The Politics Presidents Make* (Cambridge, MA: Belknap Press, 1993).

168. Stephen Skowronek, "Presidential Leadership in Political Time," in Michael J. Nelson, ed., *The President and the Political System*, 3rd ed. (Washington, DC: CQ Press, 1990), pp. 117–162.

169. Valerie Bunce, *Do New Leaders Make a Difference?* (Princeton, NJ: Princeton University Press, 1981).

170. Paul C. Light, *The President's Agenda* (Baltimore, MD: Johns Hopkins University Press, 1982).

171. Arthur M. Schlesinger, Jr., *The Cycles of American History* (Boston: Houghton Mifflin, 1986), pp. 22–27.

172. Ibid., p. 34.

173. See Stephen Skowronek, *The Politics Presidents Make: Leadership from John Adams to George Bush* (Cambridge, MA: The Belknap Press of Harvard University Press, 1993).

174. Edward S. Corwin, *The President: Office and Powers*, rev. ed. (New York: New York University Press, 1957).

175. de Tocqueville, note 163, p. 126.

176. Lyndon Johnston to Richard Nixon, quoted in Bobby Baker with Larry Nixon, *Wheeling and Dealing* (New York: Norton, 1978), p. 265.

177. This work has gone through several revisions: Richard Neustadt, *Presidential Power. The Politics of Leadership with Reflections on Johnston and Nixon* (New York: Wiley & Sons, 1976). The latest edition (New York: Free Press, 1990) includes commentary up to and including the Reagan presidency. All quotes are drawn from the 1976 edition. See also Charles O. Jones, ed., *Preparing to be President: The Memos of Richard E. Neustadt* (Washington, DC: AEI Press, 2000);

Robert Y. Shapiro et.al, eds., *Presidential Power: Forging the Presidency for the Twenty-First Century* (New York: Columbia University Press, 2000).

178. Niccolo Machiavelli, *The Prince* (New Haven, CT: Yale University Press, 1997), chapter XVII.

179. Ibid., p. 229.

180. Ibid., p. 230.

181. L. Gordon Corvitz and Jeremy A. Rabkin, eds., *The Fettered Presidency: Legal Constraints on the Executive Branch* (Washington, DC: America Enterprise Institute, 1989). See also the helpful revisionist commentary on Neustadt's analysis by Fred Greenstein, *The Presidential Difference* (New York: Free Press, 2000), pp. 251–53; and Gene Healy, *The Cult of the Presidency* (Washington, DC: Cato, 2008). See also Ryan J. Barilleaux, "Conservatives and the Presidency," in Michael A. Genovese, ed., *Contending Approaches to the American Presidency* (Washington, DC: CQ Press, 2012), pp. 30–49.

182. See Benjamin A. Kleinerman, *The Discretionary President: The Promise and Peril of Executive Power* (Lawrence: University Press of Kansas, 2009); Phillip J. Cooper, *By Order of the President: The Use and Abuse of Executive Direct Action* (Lawrence: University Press of Kansas, 2002); and John M. Carey and Matthew Soberg Shugart, *Executive Decree Authority* (Cambridge, England: Cambridge University Press, 1998).

183. William G. Howell, *Power Without Persuasion: The Politics of Direct Presidential Action* (Princeton, NJ: Princeton University Press, 2003).

184. Michael A. Genovese, *Memo to a New President: The Art and Science of Presidential Leadership* (New York: Oxford University Press, 2008).

185. See George C. Edwards, *The Strategic President: Persuasion and Opportunity in Presidential Leadership* (Princeton, NJ: Princeton University Press, 2009).

186. Paul J. Quirk, "Presidential Competence," in Michael Nelson, ed., *The Presidency and the Political System* (Washington, DC: CQ Press, 2006). pp. 136–69.

187. Robert Shogan, *The Riddle of Power: Presidential Leadership from Truman to Bush* (New York: Dutton, 1991), p. 5.

188. James P. Pfiffner, *The Strategic Presidency: Hitting the Ground Running*, 2nd ed. (Lawrence: University Press of Kansas, 1996).

189. James MacGregor Burns, *Roosevelt: The Lion and the Fox* (San Diego: Harcourt Brace Jovanovich, 1956), p. 197; Ronald Heifetz, *Leadership Without Easy Answers* (Cambridge, MA: Belknap Press, 1994).

190. Corwin, note 174.

191. See John W. Sloan, *FDR and Reagan: Transformative Presidents With Clashing Visions* (Lawrence: University Press of Kansas, 2008).

192. Some studies cast doubt on the ability of presidents to move public opinion; See George C. Edwards III, *On Deaf Ears: The Limits of the Bully Pulpit* (New Haven, CT: Yale University Press, 2003).

193. See Fred I. Greenstein, *The Presidential Difference: Leadership Style from FDR to Clinton* (New York: Martin Kessler Books, 2000).

194. Thomas E. Cronin and Michael A. Genovese, *Leadership Matters: Unleashing the Power of Paradox* (Boulder, CO: Paradigm, 2012).

195. Quoted in Sidney Blumenthal, "The Education of a President," *The New Yorker* (January 24, 1994): 33.

196. Erwin C. Hargrove, "Presidential Personality and Leadership Style," in George C. Edwards, John H. Kessel, and Bert A. Rockman, eds., *Researching the Presidency:*

Vital Questions, New Approaches (Pittsburgh: University of Pittsburgh Press, 1993), p. 70; Erwin C. Hargrove, *The President as a Leader* (Lawrence: University Press of Kansas, 1998).

197. Hargrove, "Presidential Personality and Leadership Style," p. 82.

198. Richard M. Pious, *Why Presidents Fail* (Lanham, MD: Rowman & Littlefield, 2008).

199. Pfiffner, note 188, p. 4.

200. Gene Healy, *The Cult of the Presidency: America's Dangerous Devotion to Executive Power* (Washington, DC: Cato Institute, 2008); Dana D. Nelson, *Bad for Democracy: How the Presidency Undermines the Power of the People* (Minneapolis: University of Minnesota Press, 2008).

201. *The Cult of the Presidency*, pp. 3 and 7.

202. *The Cult of the Presidency*, p. 3.

203. Nelson, op. cit., pp. 10–11.

204. Louis Fisher, "Teaching the Presidency: Idealizing a Constitutional Office," in *PS: Political Science* (January, 2012): 17–31.

205. Willard Sterne Randall, *Thomas Jefferson: A Life* (New York: Henry Holt, 1993); Merrill D. Peterson, ed., *The Portable Thomas Jefferson* (New York: Viking Press, 1975).

206. Hamilton, Madison, and Jay, *The Federalist Papers*, No. 51 (New York: New American Library, 1961), p. 322.

207. Madison, *Federalist Papers*, No. 45; Hamilton, *Federalist Papers*, No. 70, respectively.

208. Edward S. Corwin, *The President: Office and Powers, 1978–1984*, 5th ed. (New York: New York University Press, 1984); Joseph M. Bessette and Jeffrey Tulis, *The Presidency in the Constitutional Order: An Historical Examination* (Baton Rouge: Louisiana State University Press, 1981); Louis Fisher, *The Constitution Between Friends* (New York: St. Martin's Press, 1978).

209. James P. Pfiffner, *The Modern Presidency* (New York: St. Martin's Press, 1993), p. 13.

210. Glenn A. Phelps, *George Washington and American Constitutionalism* (Lawrence: University Press of Kansas, 1993).

211. Leonard White, *The Federalists: A Study in Administrative History* (New York: Macmillan, 1967), p. 99.

212. Stephen Skowronek, *The Politics Presidents Make: Leadership from John Adams to George Bush* (Cambridge, MA: The Belknap Press of Harvard University Press, 1993).

213. Willard Sterne Randall, *Thomas Jefferson: A Life* (New York: Henry Holt, 1993).

214. Robert V. Remini, *Andrew Jackson* (New York: Harper & Row, 1966).

215. Herman Belz, *Lincoln and the Constitution: The Dictatorship Question Reconsidered* (Fort Wayne, IN: Louis A. Warren Lincoln Library and Museum, 1984); James G. Randall, *Constitutional Problems Under Lincoln*, rev. ed. (Urbana: University of Illinois Press, 1951); David Donald, *Lincoln* (New York: Simon & Schuster, 1995).

216. Jeffrey K. Tulis, *The Rhetorical Presidency* (Princeton, NJ: Princeton University Press, 1987).

217. Theodore Roosevelt, *The Autobiography of Theodore Roosevelt* (New York: Charles Scribner's Sons, 1941), p. 197–98.

218. Arthur S. Link, *Wilson and the New Freedom* (Princeton, NJ: Princeton University Press, 1956); Kendrick A. Clements, *The Presidency of Woodrow Wilson* (Lawrence: University Press of Kansas, 1992).

219. William E. Leuchtenburg, *In the Shadow of FDR: From Harry Truman to Ronald Reagan* (Ithaca, NY: Cornell University Press, 1983); see also Philip Abbott, *The Exemplary Presidency* (Amherst: University of Massachusetts Press, 1990).

220. Fred I. Greenstein, *The Hidden-Hand Presidency: Eisenhower as Leader* (New York: Basic Books, 1982).

221. Arthur M. Schlesinger, Jr., and Alfred De Grazia, *Congress and the Presidency: Their Role in Modern Times* (Washington, DC: American Enterprise Institute, 1967).

222. Larry Berman, *Lyndon Johnson's War* (New York: Norton, 1989).

223. Sir Michael Howard, "Smoke on the Horizon," *Financial Times* (London: September 6, 2002): 16.

224. Spencer Ackerman and John B. Judis, "The First Casualty: The Selling of the Iraq War," *The New Republic* 228 (June 2003): 14–25.

225. Ibid.

226. John F. Kennedy, quoted in Richard Nixon, *RN: Memoirs of Richard Nixon* (Grosset & Dunlap, 1978), p. 235.

227. Richard Nixon, quoted in Theodore White, *The Making of the President 1968* (Atheneum, 1969), p. 147.

228. Leonard Garment, quoted in Theodore H. White, *The Making of the President 1972* (Atheneum, 1973), p. 52.

229. Aaron Wildavsky, "The Two Presidencies," in *Trans-Action* (December, 1966): 7. See also Barbara Kellerman and Ryan J. Barilleaux, *The President as World Leader* (New York: St Martin's Press, 1991); and Cecil V. Crabb and Kevin V. Mulcahy, *American National Security: A Presidential Perspective* (Pacific Grove, CA: Brooks-Cole, 1991).

230. Edward S. Corwin, *The President: Office and Powers, 1787–1984,* 5th rev. ed., Randall W. Bland, Theodore T. Hindson, and Jack W. Peltason, eds. (New York: New York University Press, 1984) p. 201.

231. Meena Bose, "The Presidency and Foreign Policy," in Lori Cox Han, ed., *New Directions in the American Presidency* (New York: Routledge, 2011), pp. 180–197.

232. Louis Fisher, *Presidential War Power* (Lawrence: University Press of Kansas, 1995).

233. Jon R. Bond and Richard Fleisher, *The President in the Legislative Arena* (Chicago: University of Chicago Press, 1990), p. 171.

234. Marcia Lynn Whicker, James P. Pfiffner, and Raymond A. Moore, eds., *The Presidency and the Persian Gulf War* (Westport, CT: Praeger, 1993).

235. James M. McCormick, "The Obama Presidency: A Foreign Policy of Change?," in Steven E. Schier, ed., *Transforming America: Barack Obama in the White House* (Lanham, MD: Rowman & Littlefield, 2012); James Mann, *The Obamians: The Struggle Inside the White House to Redefine American Power* (New York: Viking, 2012); and David Sanger, *Confront and Conceal: Obama's Secret Wars and Surprising Use of American Power* (New York: Crown, 2012).

236. Meena Bose, "The Presidency and Foreign Policy," in Lori Cox Han, ed., *New Directions in the American Presidency* (New York: Routledge, 2011), pp. 180–197.

237. Richard M. Pious, "Prerogative Power in the Obama Administration: Continuity and Change in the War on Terrorism," *Presidential Studies Quarterly* (June 2011): 263–290.

238. George W. Bush, *Decision Points* (New York: Crown Publishing, 2010) p. 440.

239. This bill passed the House with no Republican votes, and received only three Republican votes in the Senate.

240. Iwan W. Morgan, *The Age of Deficits: Presidents and Unbalanced Budgets from Jimmy Carter to George W. Bush* (Lawrence: University Press of Kansas, 2009). See also the critique in Noam Scheiber, *The Escape Artist: How Obama's Team Fumbled the Recovery* (New York: Simon and Schuster, 2012).

241. Raymond Tatalovich, "The Obama Administration and the Great Recession: Relief, Recovery, and Reform Revisited," in Steven E. Schier, ed., *Transforming America: Barack Obama in the White House* (Lanham, MD: Rowman & Littlefield, 2012).

242. George W. Bush, *Decision Points* (New York: Crown Publishers, 2010), p. 330.

243. Paul C. Light, "Domestic Policy Making," *Presidential Studies Quarterly* 30 (1, 2000): 109–132.

244. Mitchell Sollenberger, *Executive Branch Czars and the Erosion of Democratic Accountability* (Lawrence: University Press of Kansas, 2012).

245. David Shafie, "The Presidency and Domestic Policy," in Lori Cox Han, ed., *New Directions in the American Presidency* (New York: Routledge, 2011), pp. 166–179.

246. Jonathan Alter, *The Promise: President Obama's First Year* (New York: Simon and Schuster, 2010).

247. Gary C. Jacobson, "Legislature Success and Political Failure: The Public's Reaction to Barack Obama's Early Presidency," *Presidential Studies Quarterly* (June 2011): 220–243.

248. Richard Brookhiser, *Founding Father: Rediscovering Washington* (New York: Free Press, 1996).

249. Quoted in Arthur M. Schlesinger, Jr., *A Thousand Days* (Boston: Houghton Mifflin, 1965), p. 127.

250. See Irving I. Janis, *Victims of Groupthink* (Boston: Houghton Mifflin, 1972).

251. G. Calvin Mackenzie, "The Politics of the Appointment Process," mimeo, 1977, pp. 66–67. See also F. V. Malek, *Washington's Hidden Tragedy* (New York: Free Press, 1978), chap. 4.

252. Benjamin Ginsberg and Martin Shefter, *Politics by Other Means* (New York: Basic Books, 1990), pp.164–65.

253. Marver H. Bernstein, "The Presidency and Management Improvement," *Law and Contemporary Problems* (Summer 1970), p. 516. See also Otis I. Graham, Jr., *Toward a Planned Society: From Roosevelt to Nixon* (Oxford University Press, 1976).

254. Hugh Heclo, *A Government of Strangers: Executive Politics in Washington* (Washington, DC: Brookings, 1977).

255. James S. Young, *The Washington Community, 1800–1828* (New York: Columbia University Press, 1966), pp. 75–76.

256. Emmet John Hughes, *The Living Presidency: The Resources and Dilemmas of the American Presidential Office* (New York: Coward, McCann & Geoghegan, 1973), p. 208.

257. For example, see Gary Andres and Patrick J. Griffin, "Successful Influence: Managing Legislative Affairs in the Twenty-First Century," in James A. Thurber, trans., *Rivals for Power: Presidential-Congressional Relations* (New York: Rowman & Littlefield, 2002); and Brad Lockerbie, Stephen Borelli, and Scott Hedger, "An

Integrative Approach to Modeling Presidential Success in Congress," *Political Research Quarterly* 51 (1998): 155–172.

258. Robert J. Spitzer, *President and Congress: Executive Hegemony at the Crossroads of American Government* (New York: McGraw-Hill, 1993) p. xx.

259. Clinton Rossiter, *The American Presidency* (New York: Harcourt, Brace & World, 1980), p. 26.

260. George C. Edwards III, *At the Margins: Presidential Leadership of Congress* (New Haven, CT: Yale University Press, 1989).

261. *Youngstown Sheet and Tube Co. v. Sawyer*, 343 US 579, 635 (1952).

262. As *Federalist Papers,* No. 47, reminds us, "The executive magistrate forms an integral part of the legislative authority."

263. See Keith Krehbiel, *Pivotal Politics: A Theory of U.S. Lawmaking* (Chicago: University of Chicago Press, 1998).

264. Paul J. Quirk, "The Legislative Branch: Assessing the Partisan Congress," in *A Republic Divided*, Annenberg Democracy Project (Oxford, England: Oxford University Press, 2007), pp. 121–156.

265. David R. Mayhew, *Divided We Govern: Party Control, Lawmaking, and Investigations, 1946–1990* (New Haven, CT: Yale University Press, 1991).

266. Paul J. Quirk and Bruce Nesmith, "Divided Government and Policymaking: Negotiating the Laws," in Michael Nelson, ed., *The Presidency and the Political System*, 8th ed. (Washington, DC: CQ Press, 2000), pp. 508–31.

267. Shawn Zeller, "Historic Success, At No Small Cost," *CQ Weekly* (January 11, 2010): 112.

268. Diana Dwyre, "Old Games, New Tricks: Money in the 2010 Elections," *Extensions* (Summer 2011): 18–24.

269. Lester G. Seligman and Cary R. Covington, *The Coalitional Presidency* (Chicago: The Dorsey Press, 1989).

270. Roger H. Davidson and Walter J. Oleszek, *Congress and Its Members* (Washington, DC: Congressional Quarterly Press, 1981), p. 282. See also Mark A. Peterson, *Legislating Together: The White House and Capitol Hill from Eisenhower to Reagan* (Cambridge, MA: Harvard University Press, 1990), and David Mayhew, *Divided We Govern: Party Control, Lawmaking, and Investigations, 1946–1990* (New Haven, CT: Yale University Press, 1991).

271. Samuel Kernell, *Going Public: New Strategies in Presidential Leadership* (Washington, DC: CQ Press, 1986).

272. George C. Edwards III, *On Deaf Ears: The Limits of the Bully Pulpit* (New Haven, CT: Yale University Press, 2003).

273. Brandice Canes-Wrone, "The President's Legislative Influence from Public Appeals," *American Journal of Political Science* 45(2) (2001): 313–29. See also Matthew Eshbaugh-Soha and Jeffrey S. Peake, "Presidential Influence over the Systemic Agenda," *Congress and the Presidency*, Vol. 31 (2004): 181–201; Andrew W. Barrett, "Gone Public: The Impact of Going Public on Presidential Legislative Success," *American Politics Research*, Vol. 32, No. 3 (May 2004): 303.

274. George Edwards III, *At the Margins: Presidential Leadership in Congress* (New Haven, CT: Yale University Press, 1989); Jon Bond and Richard Fleisher, *The President in the Legislative Arena* (Chicago: University of Chicago Press, 1990).

275. Paul Brace and Barbara Hinckley, *Follow the Leader* (New York: Basic Books, 1992); Brandice Canes-Wrone, *Who Leads Whom? Presidents, Policy, and the*

Public (Chicago: University of Chicago Press, 2006), p. 192; George C. Edwards III, *On Deaf Ears: The Limits of the Bully Pulpit* (New Haven, CT: Yale University Press, 2003), pp. 241–46, 253–54; Diane J. Heith, *Polling to Govern: Public Opinion and Presidential Leadership* (Palo Alto, CA: Stanford University Press, 2003); Lawrence R. Jacobs and Robert Y. Shapiro, *Politicians Don't Pander: Political Manipulation and the Loss of Democratic Responsiveness* (Chicago: University of Chicago Press, 2000); Douglas Rivers and Nancy Rose, "Passing the President's Program: Public Opinion and Presidential Influence in Congress," *American Journal of Political Science* 29 (May 1985): 183–96.

276. Jon R. Bond and Richard Fleisher, *The President in the Legislative Arena* (Chicago: University of Chicago Press, 1990), p. 218; George Edwards, *At the Margins*; and Aage R. Clausen, *How Congressmen Decide: A Policy Focus* (New York: St. Martin's, 1973).

277. Terry Sullivan, "Headcounts, Expectations, and Presidential Coalitions in Congress," *American Journal of Political Science* 32:3 (August 1988): 567–89.

278. George Edwards, *At the Margins*, p. 216.

279. Gary C. Jacobson, "Partisan Polarization in Presidential Support," *Congress and the Presidency* 30 (Spring 2003): 1–7; Matthew J. Dickinson, "The President and Congress," in Michael Nelson, ed., *The Presidency and the Political System*, 8th ed. (Washington, DC: CQ Press, 2000), pp. 455–80.

280. James P. Pfeiffer, "The President and Congress at the Turn of the Century," in James A. Thurber, ed., *Rivals for Power: Presidential-Congressional Relations*, 2nd ed. (Lanham, MD: Rowman & Littlefield 2002), pp. 34–45; see also: Robert Draper, *Do Not Ask What Good We Do: Inside the U.S. House of Representatives* (New York: Free Press, 2012); and Thomas E. Maren and Norman J. Ornstein, *It's Even Worse than It Looks: How the American Constitutional System Collided with the New Politics of Extremism* (New York: Basic Books, 2012).

281. Matthew N. Beckmann, "The President's Playbook: White House Strategies for Lobbying Congress," *Journal of Politics* 70 (April 2008): 407–19.

282. Andrew Rudalevige, *Managing the President's Program: Presidential Leadership and Legislative Policy Formulation* (Princeton, NJ: Princeton University Press, 2002).

283. See Matthew N. Beckmann, *Pushing the Agenda: Presidential Leadership in U.S. Lawmaking: 1953-2004* (New York: Cambridge University Press, 2010); and Jasmine Farrier, *Passing the Buck: Congress, the Budget, and Deficits* (Lexington: University Press of Kentucky, 2004).

284. James W. Davis, *The President as Party Leader* (New York: Praeger, 1993), pp. ix–x.

285. Robert V. Remini, "The Emergence of Political Parties and Their Effect on the Presidency," in Philip C. Dolce and George H. Skau, eds., *Power and the Presidency* (New York: Columbia University Press, 1959), 24–34. See also Jon Meacham, *American Lion* (New York: Random House, 2008).

286. Remini, "The Emergence of Political Parties," p. 33. See also Robert Remini, *Martin Van Buren and the Making of the Democratic Party* (New York: Columbia University Press, 1959).

287. Quoted in Arthur B. Tourtellot, *The Presidents on the Presidency* (Garden City, NY: Doubleday, 1964), p. 387.

288. Ibid., p. 5.

289. James MacGregor Burns, *Running Alone: Presidential Leadership–JFK to Bush II: Why It Has Failed and How We Can Fix It* (New York: Basic Books, 2006); and Robert Harmel, "President–Party Relations in the Modern Era: Past, Problems, and Prognosis," in R. Harmel, ed., *Presidents and Their Parties: Leadership or Neglect* (New York: Praeger, 1984), p. 250. See also Burns, *Running Alone*, footnote 3.

290. On the veto power, see Robert Spitzer, *The Presidential Veto* (Albany: State University of New York Press, 1988).

291. See Charles M. Cameron, *Veto Bargaining: Presidents and the Politics of Negative Power* (New York: Cambridge University Press, 2000).

292. Leonard W. Levy, *Original Intent and the Framers' Constitution* (New York: Macmillan, 1988), p. 30.

293. Stephen A. Ambrose, "The Presidency and Foreign Affairs," *Foreign Affairs* (Winter 1991–92), p. 137.

294. Ibid., p. 136; see also Richard M. Pious, *Why Presidents Fail* (Lanham, MD: Rowman & Littlefield, 2008).

295. *The National Security Strategy of the United States of America* (Washington, DC: The White House, 2002), p. 29.

296. Arthur M. Schlesinger, Jr., *The Imperial Presidency* (Boston, MA: Houghton Mifflin, 1973).

297. On the importance of executive orders and similar direct presidential actions, see Phillip J. Cooper, *By The Order of the President* (Lawrence: University Press of Kansas, 2002); and Kenneth R. Mayer, *With the Stroke of a Pen* (Princeton, NJ: Princeton University Press, 2001).

298. James Sundquist, *The Decline and Resurgence of Congress* (Washington, DC: Brookings Institution, 1981).

299. John Hart Ely, *War and Responsibility* (Princeton, NJ: Princeton University Press, 1993); Louis Fisher, *Presidential War Power* (Lawrence: University Press of Kansas, 1995).

300. See Louis Fisher and David Gray Adler, "The War Powers Resolution: Time to Say Goodbye," *Political Science Quarterly,* Vol. 113, No. 1 (Spring 1998): 1–20.

301. President Barack Obama, Report to Congress, "United States Activities in Libya," June 15, 2011.

302. Mitchel Sollenberger, "Congress Needs to Reassert Its War Powers," *Roll Call* (March 17, 2009).

303. Michael Ross, "House Defeats GOP Effort to Kill War Powers Act," *Los Angeles Times* (June 8, 1995): A4.

304. William G. Howell and Jon C. Pevehouse, *While Dangers Gather: Congressional Checks on Presidential War Powers* (Princeton, NJ: Princeton University Press, 2007); see also Andrew Rudalevige, *The New Imperial Presidency: Renewing Presidential Power after Watergate* (Ann Arbor: The University of Michigan Press, 2005); and James P. Pfiffner, *Power Play: The Bush Presidency and the Constitution* (Washington, DC: Brookings Institution, 2008).

305. See Michael J. Gerhardt, *The Federal Appointments Process: A Constitutional and Historical Analysis* (Durham, NC: Duke University Press, 2003); and G. Calvin Mackenzie, ed., *Innocent Until Nominated: The Breakdown of the Presidential Appointment Process* (Washington, DC: Brookings Institution, 2001).

306. Christopher J. Deering, "Damned If You Do and Damned If You Don't: The Senate's Role in the Appointments Process," G. Calvin Mackenzie, ed., *The In-and-Outers: Presidential Appointees and Transient Government in Washington* (Baltimore, MD: Johns Hopkins Press, 1987), chap. 5.

307. See Christine L. Nemacheck, *Strategic Selection: Presidential Nomination of Supreme Court Justices from Herbert Hoover Through George W. Bush* (Charlottesville: University of Virginia Press, 2007).

308. Stephen L. Carter, *The Confirmation Mess* (New York: Basic Books, 1994).

309. John Massaro, *Supremely Political: The Role of Ideology and Presidential Management in Unsuccessful Supreme Court Nominations* (Albany: State University of New York Press, 1990); Charles Willis Pickering, *Supreme Chaos: The Politics of Judicial Confirmation and the Culture War* (Macon, GA: Stroud and Hall Publishers, 2006); Nemacheck, *Strategic Selection*.

310. Massaro, *Supremely Political*.

311. Stephen L. Elkin, "Contempt of Congress: The Iran-Contra Affair, and the American Constitution," *Congress and the Presidency* 18, No. 1 (Spring 1991): 3.

312. Lloyd Cutler, "Party Government under the Constitution," in Donald L. Robinson, ed., *Reforming American Government: The Bicentennial Papers of the Committee on the Constitutional System* (Boulder, CO: Westview Press, 1985); Donald L. Robinson, *To the Best of My Ability: The Presidency and the Constitution* (New York: Norton, 1987).

313. James L. Sundquist, *Constitutional Reform and Effective Government* (Washington, DC: The Brookings Institution, 1986), p. 15.

314. Sundquist, *Constitutional Reform and Effective Government*, pp. 203–204.

315. Sundquist, *Constitutional Reform and Effective Government*, p. 205.

316. James M. Burns, *The Power to Lead: The Crisis of the American Presidency* (New York: Simon and Schuster, 1984), p. 117; James M. Burns and Georgia J. Sorenson, *Dead Center: Clinton-Gore Leadership and the Perils of Moderation* (New York: Scribner's, 1999).

317. Peri E. Arnold, *Making the Managerial Presidency* (Princeton, NJ: Princeton University Press, 1986), p. 361.

318. See Richard M. Pious, *Why Presidents Fail* (Lanham, MD: Rowman & Littlefield, 2008); Irving L. Janis, *Groupthink: A Psychological Study of Foreign Policy Decisions and Fiascoes* (Boston: Houghton-Mifflin, 1982); and Lawrence E. Walsh, *Firewall: The Iran-Contra Conspiracy and Cover-Up* (New York: Norton, 1997).

319. See MaryAnne Borrelli, *The President's Cabinet: Gender, Power, and Representation* (Boulder, CO: Lynne Rienner, 2002); Shirley Anne Warshaw, *Powersharing: White House–Cabinet Relations in the Modern Presidency* (Albany: State University of New York, 1996); and Anthony J. Bennett, *The American President's Cabinet: From Kennedy to Bush* (New York: St. Martin's, 1996). Finally, see Robert B. Reich's curious memoir from the Clinton years, *Locked in the Cabinet* (New York: Knopf, 1997).

320. Jimmy Carter, *Keeping Faith: Memoirs of a President* (New York: Bantam, 1982), p. 60.

321. Henry Learned, *The President's Cabinet: Studies in the Origin, Formation and Structure of an American Institution* (New Haven: Yale University Press, 1912, reissued in 1972), p. 119. See also Mary L. Hinsdale, *A History of the President's*

Cabinet (Ann Arbor: University of Michigan Press, 1911). The best study of the cabinet in mid-twentieth century was Richard Fenno, *The President's Cabinet: An Analysis in the Period from Wilson to Eisenhower* (New York: Vintage, 1959).

322. Lyndon B. Johnson, quoted in Charles Maguire, oral history, August 19, 1969, Lyndon B. Johnson Presidential Library, Austin, Texas, p. 28.

323. See Calvin G. Mackenzie, ed., *Innocent Until Nominated: The Breakdown of the Presidential Appointments Process* (Washington, DC: The Brookings Institution, 2001). See also Paul C. Light, "Nominate and Wait," *The New York Times* (March 24, 2009): A25.

324. See Stephen Hess, *What Do We Do Now?* (Washington, DC: The Brookings Institution, 2008), p. 81.

325. Robert B. Reich, *Locked in the Cabinet* (New York: Knopf, 1997), pp. 51–2.

326. Shirley Anne Warshaw, *Powersharing: White House–Cabinet Relations in the Modern Presidency* (Albany: State University of New York Press, 1996).

327. Reich, *Locked,* note 325, pp. 43–4.

328. McGeorge Bundy, *The Strength of Government* (Cambridge, MA: Harvard University Press, 1968), p. 39.

329. Bradley H. Patterson, Jr., *The President's Cabinet: Issues and Questions* (Washington, DC: American Society for Public Administration, 1976), pp. 17–18. See also his *The White House Staff: Inside the West Wing and Beyond* (Washington, DC: The Brookings Institution, 2000).

330. Charles Dawes, quoted in Kermit Gordon, "Reflections on Spending," in J. D. Montgomery and Arthur Smithies, eds., *Public Policy* (Cambridge, MA: Harvard University Press, 1966), p. 15.

331. Walter J. Hickel, *The New York Times* (May 7, 1970): C18.

332. Quoted in *U.S. News and World Report* (March 29, 1982): 28. For a Reagan cabinet member's perspective, see the instructive memoir by Secretary of Education "Ted" Bell, who served from 1981 to 1985, when he was unceremoniously let go; Terrel H. Bell, *The Thirteenth Man: A Reagan Cabinet Member* (New York: Free Press, 1988).

333. See Anne E. Kornblut, "White House Moving to Repair Troubled Relationship with Cabinet" *The Washington Post* (March 9, 2011) [online version]. See also the essays in James A. Thurber, ed., *Obama in Office* (Boulder, CO: Paradigm, 2011).

334. Interview at the White House, with Thomas E. Cronin.

335. Carter, *Keeping Faith*, p. 59.

336. Griffin B. Bell with Ronald J. Ostrow, *Taking Care of the Law* (New York: Morrow, 1982), p. 47.

337. See Ron Suskind, *Price of Loyalty: George W. Bush, the White House, and the Education of Paul O'Neill* (New York: Simon and Schuster, 2004), and Scott McClellan, *What Happened: Inside the Bush White House and Washington's Culture of Deception* (New York: Public Affairs, 2008).

338. Quoted in Richard H. Rovere, "Eisenhower: A Trial Balance," *The Reporter* (April 21, 1955): 19–20.

339. For Rubin's own overview of his White House and cabinet years, see Robert E. Rubin, *In an Uncertain World: Tough Choices from Wall Street to Washington* (New York: Random House, 2003). For James Baker's memoir, see James A. Baker III, *The Politics of Diplomacy: Revolution, War, and Peace, 1989–1992* (New York: Putnam, 1995).

340. See James P. Pfiffner, "Organizing the Obama White House," in James A. Thurber, ed., *Obama in Office*; and Jodi Kantor, *The Obamas* (New York: Little, Brown, and Company, 2012); and Ron Suskind, *Confidence Men: Wall Street, Washington, and the Education of a President* (New York: Harper Collins, 2011).

341. See Stephen J. Wayne, *Personality and Politics* (Washington, DC: CQ Press, 2012), and Ryan Lizza, "The Obama Memos: The Verdict on Malpractice," *The New Yorker* (January 30, 2012): 36–49.

342. Pfiffner, "Organizing The Obama White House," in Thurber, ed., *Obama in Office*, p. 81.

343. See, for example, several essays in George C. Edwards III and William G. Howell's, *The Oxford Handbook of the American Presidency* (New York: Oxford University Press, 2009); and Kenneth Mayer, *With the Stroke of a Pen: Executive Orders and Presidential Power* (Princeton, NJ: Princeton University Press, 2001); and Phillip Cooper, *By Order of the President: The Use and Abuse of Executive Direct Action* (Lawrence: University Press of Kansas, 2002).

344. See, for example, James E. Pfiffner, *Power Play: The Bush Presidency and the Constitution* (Washington, DC: The Brookings Institution, 2008), and William G. Howell, *Power without Persuasion: The Politics of Direct Presidential Action* (Princeton, NJ: Princeton University Press, 2003).

345. Mayer, *With the Stroke of a Pen*.

346. See the heated debate on this between legal scholars Peter M. Shane and Nelson Lund in Richard J. Ellis and Michael Nelson, eds., *Debating The Presidency*, 2nd ed. (Washington, DC: CQ Press, 2010), pp. 137–153.

347. Myra Gutin, *The President's Partner* (New York: Greenwood Press, 1989); Edith Mayo, "The Influence and Power of First Ladies," *The Chronicle of Higher Education* (September 15, 1993); Lewis L. Gould, "Modern First Ladies and the Presidency," *Presidential Studies Quarterly* 20 (1990): 677–83; and Karen O'Connor, Bernadette Nye, and Laura van Assendelft, "Wives in the White House: The Political Influence of the First Ladies," *Presidential Studies Quarterly* 26 (1996): 835–53.

348. See Robert P. Watson, *The Presidents' Wives* (Boulder, CO: L. Rienner, 2000), and Robert P. Watson and Anthony J. Eksterowicz, *The Presidential Companion: Readings on the First Ladies*, 2nd ed. (Columbia: University of South Carolina Press, 2006).

349. See Mary Van Rensselaer Thayer, *Jacqueline Kennedy, The White House Years* (Boston: Little, Brown and Co., 1967).

350. Donald Young, American Roulette: The History and Dilemma of the Vice Presidency (New York: Viking, 1974), p. 134.

351. Lois Scharf, *Eleanor Roosevelt: First Lady of American Liberalism* (Boston: Twayne Publishers, 1987), p. 110.

352. *The New York Times* (July 16, 1985): 1.

353. On Hillary Clinton's role in public policy matters in Bill Clinton's first years in the White House, see Jacob Hacker, *The Road to Nowhere: The Genesis of President Clinton's Plan for Health Security* (Princeton, NJ: Princeton University Press, 1998).

354. Indeed, one biographer suggests she caused exasperation among several of the President's top West Wing advisers. Many of these White House aides left midway into the first term. It is not clear if they left because of her disappointment

or whether her husband shared her disappointment or whether they were just burned out. Probably a mix of factors was involved. Tensions in the Obama White House staff are discussed in Jodi Kantor, *The Obamas.*

355. See Richard M. Pious, *Why Presidents Fail* (Lanham, MD: Rowman & Littlefield, 2008).

356. Barack Obama, quoted in *The New York Times* (December 2, 2008): A20.

357. See Ron Suskind, *Confidence Men.*

358. James P. Pfiffner, "The President's Chief of Staff: Lessons Learned," *Working Paper 92,* Institute of Public Policy, George Mason University (October 1992), p. 19.

359. Summarizing interviews with White House aides, Charles E. Walcott, Shirley Anne Warshaw, and Stephen Wayne, "The Office of Chief of Staff," in Martha Joynt Kumar and Terry Sullivan, eds., *The White House World* (College Station: Texas A&M University, 2003), p. 136.

360. See Mark Leibovich, "White House Message Maven Finds Finger Pointing at Him," *The New York Times* (March 6, 2010): 1, 19; and Noam Scheiber, "What' Really Eating David Axelrod? The Disillusionment of Obama's Political Guru," *The New Republic* (October 14, 2010): 10–15.

361. Helen Thomas, *Watchdogs of Democracy* (New York: Scribner, 2006), p. 36.

362. Mark Leibovich, "What Kind of Relationship Will the Obama White House Have with the Media?," *The New York Times Magazine* (December 21, 2008): 34.

363. Stephen J. Farnsworth, *Spinner-in-Chief: How Presidents Sell Their Policies and Themselves* (Boulder, CO: Paradigm Publishers, 2009), p. 95. See also Scott McClellan, *What Happened.*

364. Fred I. Greenstein, *The Presidential Difference* (New York: Free Press, 2000), p. 195.

365. See Alexander L. George and Eric K. Stern, "Harnessing Conflict in Foreign Policy Making: From Devil's to Multiple Advocacy," *Presidential Studies Quarterly* (September 2002): 484–508. See David Gergen, *Eyewitness to Power: The Essence of Leadership: Nixon to Clinton* (New York: Simon & Schuster, 2000). See also Richard M. Pious, *Why Presidents Fail* (Lanham, MD: Rowman & Littlefield, 2008), chaps. 10 and 11.

366. John M. Broder, "Energy Secretary's Challenge" *The New York Times* (March 23, 2009): A13.

367. John W. Gardner, testimony before the Senate Government Operations Committee, *Congressional Record,* 92nd Congress, 1st session, June 3, 1971.

368. Paul C. Light, *Vice Presidential Power: Advice and Influence in the White House* (Baltimore, MD: Johns Hopkins University Press, 1984), p. 1. See also Jody C. Baumgartner, *The American Vice Presidency Reconsidered* (Westport, CT: Praeger, 2006); Barton Gellman, *Angler: The Cheney Vice Presidency* (New York: Penguin Press, 2008); and Joel K. Goldstein, "The Rising Power of the Modern Vice Presidency," *Presidential Studies Quarterly* (Sept. 2008), 374–389.

369. See, for example, Jules Witcover, *Very Strange Bedfellows: The Short and Unhappy Marriage of Richard Nixon and Spiro Agnew* (New York: PublicAffairs, 2007).

370. Allan P. Sindler, *Unchosen Presidents: The Vice-President and Other Frustrations of Presidential Succession* (Berkeley: University of California Press, 1976), p. 41. See also Jules Witcover, *Crapshoot: Rolling the Dice on the Vice Presidency* (New York: Crown, 1992); and Vance R. Kincade, Jr., *Heirs Apparent: Solving the Vice Presidential Dilemma* (Westport, CT: Praeger, 2000).

371. Henry Kissinger, *White House Years* (Boston: Little, Brown, 1979), p. 713.

372. Doris Kearns Goodwin, *Lyndon Johnson and the American Dream* (New York: Harper & Row 1976), p. 164.

373. Jack K. Goldstein, "The Rising Power of the Modern Vice Presidency," *Presidential Studies Quarterly* (September 2008): 374–389; and Harold C. Relyea, "*The Law:* The Executive Office of the Vice President: Constitutional and Legal Considerations," *Presidential Studies Quarterly* (June 2010): 327–341.

374. See Jody C. Baumgartner, *The American Vice Presidency Reconsidered.* For two biographies of Dick Cheney, see Barton Gellman, *Angler: The Cheney Vice Presidency* (New York: Penguin, 2008), and Stephen Hayes, *Cheney: A Revealing Portrait of America's Most Powerful and Controversial Vice President* (New York: HarperCollins, 2007).

375. The most comprehensive account of the Twenty-Fifth Amendment is by John D. Feerick, *The Twenty-fifth Amendment: Its Complete History and Earliest Applications* (New York: Fordham University Press, 1976).

376. *Time* (January 20, 1975): 23.

377. Donald Young, *American Roulette: The History and Dilemma of the Vice Presidency* (New York: Holt, Rinehart & Winston, 1972), pp. 353–54.

378. James F. Byrnes, *All in One Lifetime* (New York: McMillan, 1974), pp. 263–64.

379. Joseph E. Kallenbach, *The American Chief Executive: The Presidency and the Governorship* (New York: Harper & Row, 1966), pp. 234–35.

380. Michael Novak, *Choosing Our King: Powerful Symbols in Presidential Politics* (New York: Macmillan, 1974), pp. 263–64.

381. For a semi-revisionist view of Aaron Burr, see Nancy Isenberg's *Fallen Founder: The Life of Aaron Burr* (New York: Viking, 2007).

382. James MacGregor Burns, *Roosevelt: The Lion and the Fox* (New York: Harcourt, Brace, 1956), p. 414.

383. Agnew was forced to resign as a result of tax evasion and political bribery. See Jules Witcover, *Very Strange Bedfellows.* For Agnew's own more complicated assessment of his final year in office, see Spiro T. Agnew, *Go Quietly... or Else* (New York: William Morrow and Co., 1980).

384. Arthur M. Schlesinger, Jr., "Is the Vice Presidency Necessary?," *Atlantic* (May 1974): 37.

385. Hubert H. Humphrey, "A Conversation with Vice President Hubert H. Humphrey," National Educational Television, April 1965. See also Hubert H. Humphrey, *The Education of a Public Man: My Life in Politics* (Minneapolis: University of Minnesota Press, 1991).

386. Gerald R. Ford, *A Time to Heal: The Autobiography of Gerald R. Ford* (New York: Harper & Row/Reader's Digest, 1979), p. 327.

387. Ibid., p. 328. For the Rockefeller side of this story, see Joseph E. Persico, *The Imperial Rockefeller: A Biography of Nelson A. Rockefeller* (New York: Simon & Schuster, 1982); and Michael Turner, *The Vice President as Policy Maker: Rockefeller in the Ford White House* (Westport, CT: Greenwood Press, 1982).

388. Walter F. Mondale, quoted in *National Journal* (December 1, 1979): 2016.

389. Walter F. Mondale, lecture on "The American Vice Presidency" at the University of Minnesota, Minneapolis, February 18, 1981, mimeo, p. 3. See, too, the useful reflections by a top Mondale aide: Richard Moe, "The Making of the Modern Vice

Presidency: A Personal Reflection," *Presidential Studies Quarterly* (September 2008): 390–400.

390. Adapted and condensed from Mondale lecture, cited in footnote 22, p. 7.

391. *The Houston Post* (May 1, 1983): 1.

392. E. J. Dionne, Jr., "Bush's Presidential Bid Is Shaky..., Poll Finds," *The New York Times* (July 26, 1987): 1, 14.

393. See, for instance, Joe Klein, *The Natural: The Misunderstood Presidency of Bill Clinton* (New York: Doubleday, 2000), pp. 200–201.

394. Charlie Savage, *Takeover* (New York: Little, Brown, 2007), pp. 8–9. See also David Bromwich, "The Co-President at Work," *The New York Review of Books* (November 20, 2008): 29–33. For a more sympathetic biography of Cheney, see Stephen F. Hayes, *Cheney: The Untold Story of America's Most Powerful and Controversial Vice President* (New York: HarperCollins, 2007).

395. See his memoir, Dick Cheney, *In My Time* (New York: Threshold, 2011).

396. For overviews of the Bush–Cheney views on anti-terrorism, torture, detainees, and constitutionalism, see Jane Mayer, *The Dark Side: The Inside Story of How the War on Terror Turned into a War on American Ideals* (New York: Doubleday, 2008); and James P. Pfiffner, *Power Play: The Bush Presidency and the Constitution* (Washington, DC: The Brookings Institution, 2008). See too, Dick Cheney, *In My Time*. See also Shirley Ann Warshaw, *The Co-Presidency of Bush and Cheney* (Stanford: Stanford Politics and Policy, 2009).

397. David Bromwich, "The Co-President at Work," *The New York Review of Books* (November 20, 2008): 33. See also Bruce P. Montgomery, *Richard B. Cheney and the Rise of the Imperial Vice Presidency* (New York: Praeger, 2008).

398. Cheney, quoted in Gellman, *Angler*, p. 110.

399. Rachael L. Swarns, "Cheney, Needling Biden, Defends Bush's Record on Executive Power," *New York Times* (December 22, 2008): A14.

400. Cheney, quoted in Gellman, *Angler*, p. 160.

401. Staunch conservatives praised the Cheney vice presidency while others considered him a dangerous influence. Al Neuharth, founder of *USA Today*, called him the worst vice president since Spiro Agnew. *USA Today* (September 20, 2011): 13A. See, too, James P. Pfiffner, *Torture as Public Policy* (Boulder, CO: Paradigm, 2010). See also Shirley Ann Warshaw's assessments in *The Co-Presidency of Bush and Cheney*.

402. Bush, quoted in Gellman, *Angler*, p. 384.

403. Ibid. See also, in general, George W. Bush, *Decision Points* (New York: Crown, 2010).

404. James P. Pfiffner, *Torture as Public Policy* (Boulder, CO: Paradigm, 2010), p. 143.

405. See Jack Goldsmith, "Wrong Mission Accomplished," *New York Times* (Sept. 18, 2011): 15.

406. David Plouffe, *The Audacity to Win: The Inside Story and Lessons of Barack Obama's Historic Victory* (New York: Viking, 2009), p. 289.

407. Bush, quoted by one of his speech writers, Matt Latimer, *Speech-less: Tales of a White House Survivor* (New York: Crown, 2009), p. 268.

408. See, for example, Jodi Kantor, *The Obamas* (New York: Little, Brown, 2012), and Ron Suskind, *Confidence Men: Wall Street, Washington, and the Education of a President* (New York: Harper Collins, 2011).

409. See James Traub, "Foreign Policy Sage, Sounding Board…Joe Biden Could Be the Second-Most-Powerful Vice President in History AFTER CHENEY," *The New York Times Magazine* (November 29, 2009): 34–41, 48–49.

410. Thomas M. Durban, *Nomination and Election of the President and the Vice President of the United States* (Washington, DC: U.S. Government Printing Office, 1998). See also Bruce Ackerman, "Abolish the Vice Presidency," *Los Angeles Times* (October 2, 2008): A23.

411. Jules Witcover, *Crapshoot.*

412. See *Official Report of the Vice Presidential Selection Commission of the Democratic Party*, December 19, 1974, mimeo. See also "Hearings of the Vice Presidential Selection Commission of the Democratic National Committee," *Congressional Record* (October 16, 1973), S19245 ff; and Allan P. Sindler, *Unchosen President.*

413. Arthur M. Schlesinger, Jr., *The Imperial Presidency* (New York: Popular Library, 1974), p. 481. For an earlier version of this notion, see Lucius Wilmerding, Jr., "The Vice Presidency," *Political Science Quarterly* (March 1953): 17–41. Theodore Roosevelt was also among those who suggested abolishing the vice presidency. Yale Law School professor Bruce Ackerman endorsed this reform in 2008, writing "Mexico and France see no need for a vice president. We should designate the secretary of state to be in charge until a special election can be held to replace a president." Ackerman, "Abolish the Vice Presidency," *Los Angeles Times* (October 2, 2008): A23. See also political scientist Douglas L. Kriner, "Resolved, the Vice Presidency Should Be Abolished" in Richard J. Ellis and Michael Nelson, eds., *Debating the Presidency: Conflicting Perspectives on the American Executive* (Washington, DC: CQ Press, 2010), pp. 172–179.

414. Schlesinger, Jr., *The Imperial Presidency*, p. 493. See also on this point the provocative advocacy book by law professor Sanford Levinson, *Our Undemocratic Constitution* (New York: Oxford, 2006).

415. Joel Goldstein, *The Modern Vice Presidency: The Transformation of a Political Institution* (Princeton, NJ: Princeton University Press, 1982), p. 89. See also Jody C. Baumgartner, "The Veepstakes: Forecasting Vice Presidential Selection in 2008," *PS: Political Science & Politics* (October, 2008): 765–72.

416. Jay Winik, *April 1865: The Month that Saved America* (New York: Perennial, 2002), p. 262.

417. Ibid., p. 267.

418. See, for example, Ashby Jones, "Who Reigns in Succession Crisis: Confusion, Perhaps," *The Wall Street Journal* (November 13, 2008): A14.

419. John D. Feerick, "The Proposed Twenty-fifth Amendment to the Constitution," *Fordham Law Review* (December 1965): 197. See also Feerick's *The Twenty-fifth Amendment: Its Complete History and Earliest Applications* (Bronx, NY: Fordham University Press, 1976); and Herbert L. Abrams, "Shielding the President from the Constitution: Disability and the 25th Amendment," *Presidential Studies Quarterly* (Summer 1993): 533–53.

420. For a negative assessment of the Twenty-Fifth Amendment and some alternative remedies, see Herbert L. Abrams, *The President Has Been Shot: Confusion, Disability, and the 25th Amendment in the Aftermath of the Attempted Assassination of Ronald Reagan* (New York: W. W. Norton, 1992). See also "Preserving our

institutions: Presidential Succession" (Continuity of Government Commission, June 2009) www.continuityofgovernment.org/SecondReport.

421. See John M. Murphy and Mary E. Stuckey, "Never Cared to Say Goodbye: Presidential Legacies and Vice Presidential Campaigns," *Presidential Studies Quarterly* (March 2002): 46–66.

422. David Gray Adler and Michael A. Genovese, eds., *The Presidency and the Law: The Clinton Legacy* (Lawrence: University Press of Kansas, 2002).

423. See James Macgregor Burns, *Packing the Court: The Rise of Judicial Power and the Coming Crisis of the Supreme Court* (New York: Penguin), 2009.

424. See Sarah Binder and Forrest Maltzman, *Advice & Dissent: The Struggle to Shape the Federal Judiciary* (Washington, DC: Brookings Institution, 2009); Christine L. Nemacheck, *Strategic Selection: Presidential Nomination of Supreme Court Justices from Herbert Hoover Through George W. Bush* (Charlottesville: University of Virginia Press, 2007); Mitchel A. Sollenberger, *The President Shall Nominate: How Congress Trumps Executive Power* (Lawrence: University Press of Kansas, 2008); and Mitchel A. Sollenberger, *Judicial Appointments and Democratic Controls* (Durham: Carolina Academic Press, 2011).

425. See, for example, Albert R. Hunt, "Symmetry in Judicial Nominations," *Wall Street Journal* (February 20, 2003): A13; Christine L. Nemacheck, *Strategic Selection: Presidential Nominations of Supreme Court Justices from Herbert Hoover to George W. Bush* (Charlottesville: University of Virginia Press, 2007).

426. Terry Eastland, *Energy in the Executive: The Case for the Strong Presidency* (New York: Free Press, 1992), p. 235.

427. Jan Crawford Greenburg, *Supreme Conflict: The Inside Story of the Struggle for Control of the United States Supreme Court* (New York: Penguin, 2007).

428. Selections from the *Correspondence of Theodore Roosevelt and Henry Cabot Lodge, 1884–1918* (New York: Charles Scribner's Sons, 1925), Vol. II, p. 519. For a good study of President Harding's appointment of a Supreme Court Justice, see David J. Danelski, *A Supreme Court Justice Is Appointed* (New York: Random House, 1964).

429. Henry J. Abraham, *Justices and Presidents: A Political History of Appointments to the Supreme Court*, 2nd ed. (New York: Oxford University Press, 1985), p. 65. See also Robert J. Steamer, *Chief Justice: Leadership and the Supreme Court* (Columbia: University of South Carolina Press, 1986). For a useful study of Lyndon B. Johnson's criteria and political decision making in the appointment of judges, see Neil D. McFeeley, *Appointment of Judges: The Johnson Presidency* (Austin: University of Texas, 1987), esp. chaps. 5 and 6.

430. Stephen L. Carter, *The Confirmation Mess: Cleaning Up The Federal Appointments Process* (New York: Basic Books, 1994).

431. Janet Malcolm, "The Art of Testifying: The Confirmation Hearings as Theatre," *The New Yorker* (March 13, 2006): 72–79.

432. Jane Mayer and Jill Abramson, *Strange Justice: The Selling of Clarence Thomas* (New York: Houghton Mifflin, 1994); John C. Danforth, *Resurrection: The Confirmation of Clarence Thomas* (New York: Viking, 1994). For a reaction to both the Bork and Thomas nominations, see Stephen L. Carter, *The Confirmation Mess*.

433. Quoted in David G. Savage, "Bush's Judicial Nominations Go 28 for 80 in the Senate," *The Los Angeles Times* (December 31, 2002): A12.

434. James Gerstenzang, "Bush Urges Judicial Process Changes," *The Los Angeles Times* (October 31, 2002): A10.

435. See David Yalof, *Pursuit of Justices: Presidential Politics and the Selection of Supreme Court Nominees* (Chicago: The University of Chicago Press, 1999); Lee Epstein and Jeffrey A. Segal, *Advice and Consent: The Politics of Judicial Appointments* (New York: Oxford University Press, 2005); Richard David, *Electing Justice: Fixing the Supreme Court Nomination Process* (New York: Oxford University Press, 2005); Christine L. Nemacheck, *Strategic Selection: Presidential Nomination of Supreme Court Justices from Herbert Hoover through George W. Bush* (Charlottesville: University of Virginia Press, 2008); Mitchel A. Sollenberger, "The President 'Shall Nominate': Exclusive or Shared Constitutional Power?" *Presidential Studies Quarterly* (December 2006).

436. Robert Scigliano, *The Supreme Court and the Presidency* (New York: The Free Press, 1971), pp. 146–47. Another study concludes that most presidents by and large do rather well in appointing individuals who will be supportive of the administration that supports them, at least during their first few years on the Court. "After that initial period, there is an apparent falling off." See Roger Handberg and Harold F. Hill, Jr., "Predicting the Judicial Performance of Presidential Appointments to the United States Supreme Court," *Presidential Studies Quarterly* (Fall 1984): 538–47.

437. *Marbury v. Madison*, 5 U.S. (1 Crouch) 137 (1803); *Ex-parte Milligan*, 4 Wall. 2 (1966); *Youngstown Sheet and Tube Co. v. Sawyer*, 343 U.S. 579 (1952); and *U.S. v. Nixon*, 418 U.S. 683 (1974).

438. Scigliano, *The Supreme Court and the Presidency*, p. 159. This view is also echoed in David M. O'Brien, *Storm Center: The Supreme Court in American Politics* (New York: Norton, 1986) chap. 2.

439. Quoted, *Time* (May 23, 1969): 24.

440. Stanley K. Kutler, *The Wars of Watergate: The Last Crisis of Richard Nixon* (New York: Knopf, 1994); Fred Emery, *Watergate: The Corruption of American Politics and the Fall of Richard Nixon* (New York: Touchstone, 1994).

441. Theodore Draper, *A Very Thin Line: The Iran-Contra Affairs* (New York: Touchstone Books, 1991); Jane Mayer and Doyle McManus, *Landslide: The Unmaking of the President, 1984–1988* (Boston: Houghton Mifflin, 1988).

442. See Nancy V. Baker, *Conflicting Loyalties: Law and Politics in the Attorney General's Office, 1789–1990* (Lawrence: University Press of Kansas, 1992); Katy J. Harriger, *Independent Justice: The Federal Special Prosecutor in American Politics* (Lawrence: University Press of Kansas, 1992); Rebecca Mae Salokar, *The Solicitor General: The Politics of Law* (Philadelphia: Temple University Press, 1992); Jack L. Goldsmith, *The Terror Presidency: Law and Judgment Inside the Bush Administration* (New York: W. W. Norton, 2007); and Jane Mayer, *The Dark Side: The Inside Story of How the War on Terror Turned into a War on American Ideals* (New York: Doubleday, 2008).

443. See Harold Hongju Koh, *The National Security Constitution: Sharing Power after the Iran-Contra Affair* (New Haven, CT: Yale University Press, 1990).

444. Frederick Schauer, "Should Presidents Obey the Law?" in Terry L. Price and J. Thomas Wren, eds., *The Values of Presidential Leadership* (New York: Palgrave MacMillan, 2007).

445. See Hamilton, Madison, and Jay, *The Federalist Papers*, No. 48.

446. Geoffrey P. Miller, "The President's Power of Interpretation: Implications of a Unified Theory of Constitutional Law," *Law and Contemporary Problems* 56, No. 4 (Autumn 1993); David A. Strauss, "Presidential Interpretation of the Constitution," *Cardozo Law Review* 15 (1993).

447. Daniel P. Franklin, *Extraordinary Measures: The Exercise of Prerogative Powers in the United States* (Pittsburgh: University of Pittsburgh Press, 1991).

448. See Richard A. Posner, *Not a Suicide Pact: The Constitution in a Time of National Emergency* (New York: Oxford University Press, 2006).

449. Abe Fortas, "The Constitution and the Presidency," *Washington Law Review* 49 (August 1974): 100.

450. Edward S. Corwin, *Total War and the Constitution* (New York: Knopf, 1947) p. 80.

451. See Harold Hongju Koh, "Why the President Almost Always Wins in Foreign Affairs," in David Gray Adler and Larry George, eds., *The Constitution and the Conduct of American Foreign Policy* (Lawrence: University Press of Kansas, 1996).

452. Richard Longaker, "'Introduction' to Clinton Rossiter," *The Supreme Court and the Commander in Chief*, expanded ed. (Ithaca, NY: Cornell University Press, 1976), p. xii.

453. Ryan C. Hendrickson, *The Clinton Wars: The Constitution, Congress, and War Powers* (Nashville, TN: Vanderbilt University Press, 2002); Louis Fisher, "The Law: Legal Disputes in the Clinton Years," *Presidential Studies Quarterly* (September 1999) pp. 697–707; Adler and Genovese, note 1.

454. See Nancy V. Baker, "The Law: The Impact of Antiterrorism Policies on Separation of Powers: Assessing John Ashcroft's Role," *Presidential Studies Quarterly* (December 2000): 765–78.

455. See, for example, David G. Adler, "Foreign Policy and the Separation of Powers Under the Constitution: The Influence of the Judiciary," paper delivered at the 1987 Annual Meeting of the Western Political Science Association, Anaheim, CA, March 26–28, 1987; and his more specialized book, *The Constitution and the Termination of Treaties* (New York: Garland, 1986). See also Francis D. Wormuth and Edwin B. Firmage, *To Chain the Dog of War: The War Power of Congress in History and Law* (Dallas: Southern Methodist University Press, 1986). For a more modified verdict, see Louis Fisher, *The Politics of Shared Power*, 2nd ed. (Washington, DC: CQ Press, 1987).

456. R. Shep Melnick, "The Courts, Jurisprudence, and the Executive Branch," in Joel D. Aberbach and Mark A. Peterson, eds., *The Executive Branch* (New York: Oxford University Press, 2005), pp. 452–85.

457. *The Prize Cases*, 67 U.S. (2 Black) 635 (1863).

458. *In re Neagle*, 135 U.S. 1 (1890).

459. *United States v. Curtiss-Wright Export Corporation*, 299 U.S. 304 (1936).

460. *United States v. Belmont* 301 U.S. 324 (1937).

461. Eugene V. Rostow, book review, *The Washington Post National Weekly Edition* (January 2, 1984): 34. See also Peter Irons, *Justice At War: The Story of the Japanese American Internment Cases* (New York: Oxford University Press, 1983).

462. William H. Rehnquist, *All the Laws but One: Civil Liberties in Wartime* (New York: Knopf, 2001).

463. Michael Genovese, *The Supreme Court, The Constitution, and Presidential Power* (Lanham, MD: University Press of America, 1980), p. 121.

464. *Marbury v. Madison*, 1 Cranch, 137, 2 L. Ed. 60 (1803).

465. *Little v. Bareme*, 2 Cranch 170 (1804).

466. *Humphrey's Executor v. United States*, 295 U.S. 602, 628 (1935).

467. Louis Fisher, "Congress and the Removal Power," *Congress and the Presidency* (Spring, 1983): 64–65.

468. Robert J. Donovan, *Tumultuous Years* (New York: Norton, 1982), p. 387.

469. Ibid., p. 391.

470. *New York Times Co. v. United States* 403 U.S. 713 (1971).

471. Ibid.

472. *United States v. U.S. District Court*, 407 U.S. 297 (1972).

473. *Clinton v. Jones*, 520 U.S. 681 (1977).

474. Jack Goldsmith, *The Terror Presidency: Law and Judgment Inside the Bush Administration* (New York: Norton, 2007); Jane Mayer, *The Dark Side: The Inside Story of How the War on Terror Turned into a War on American Ideals* (New York: Doubleday, 2008).

475. *Rasul v. Bush*, 542 U.S. 466, 2004.

476. *Hamdi v. Rumsfeld*, 542 U.S. 507, 2004.

477. *Hamdan v. Rumsfeld*, 548 U.S. 557, 2006.

478. *Boumediene v. Bush*, 553 U.S. 723, 2008.

479. Jonathan Mahler, *The Challenge: Hamden v. Rumsfeld and the Fight over Presidential Power* (New York: Farrar, Straus, and Giroux, 2008); Benjamin Wittes, *Law and the Long War: The Future of Justice in the Age of Terror* (New York: The Penguin Press, 2008).

480. Michael Lind, "The Out-of-Control Presidency," *The New Republic* (August 14, 1998): 21; see also Jane Mayer, *The Dark Side: The Inside Story of How the War on Terror Turned into a War on American Ideals* (New York: Doubleday, 2008), and Charlie Savage, *Takeover: The Return of the Imperial Presidency and the Subversion of American Democracy* (Boston: Little, Brown, 2007).

481. Theodore C. Sorensen, *Watchmen in the Night* (Cambridge, MA: MIT Press, 1975).

482. James Madison, *Federalist Papers*, No. 51 (1788).

483. Benjamin R. Barber, "Neither Leaders nor Followers: Citizenship Under Strong Democracy," in Michael Beschloss and Thomas E. Cronin, eds., *Essays in Honor of James MacGregor Burns* (Englewood Cliffs, NJ: Prentice Hall, 1989), p. 117.

484. Quoted in Larry Berman, *The New American Presidency* (Boston: Little, Brown, 1987), p. 344.

485. Larry L. Sabato, *A More Perfect Constitution: 23 Proposals to Revitalize our Constitution and Make America a Fairer Country* (New York: Walker & Company, 2007), chap. 2, "Perfecting the Presidency." See also Sanford Levinson, *Our Undemocratic Constitution: When the Constitution Goes Wrong (And How We the People Correct It)* (New York: Oxford University Press, 2006). For an older and more radical rewriting of the Constitution, see Rexford Tugwell, *The Emerging Constitution* (New York: Harper's Magazine Press, 1974).

486. See *George Washington Law Review*, which contained a symposium on the no-confidence proposal (January 1975): 328–500.

487. Diamond, quoted in Thomas L. Friedman, "Third Party Rising," *New York Times* (October 3, 2010): 8, Sunday Opinion Section.

488. Friedman, "Third Party Rising," p.8.

489. Ross K. Baker "Third Party in 2012? Forget About It," *USA Today* December 7, 2011. www.usatoday.com/news/opinion/forum/story/2011-12-07/tird-party-independent-president.

490. George Will, "The Empty Promise of 'No labels' ", *The Denver Post*, December 10, 2010, 5D.

491. Michael J. Korzi, *Presidential Term Limits in American History: Power, Principles, and Politics* (College Station: Texas A & M University Press, 2011).

492. Clinton Rossiter, *The American Presidency*, 2nd ed. (New York: Harcourt, Brace, 1960), p. 232.

493. James R. Hedtke, *Lame Duck Presidents: Myth or Reality?* (Lewiston, NY: E. Mellen Press, 2002).

494. Ibid., p. 236.

495. We borrow here from ideas in Thomas E. Cronin and Jeffrey J. Weill, "An Item Veto for the President?," *Congress and the Presidency* (Autumn, 1985): 127–51.

496. Bruce Bartlett, http://bartlett.blogs.nytimes.com (accessed March 15, 2006).

497. Fisher, quoted in Gregory Korte, "Lawmakers Modify Idea of Line-Item Veto," *USA Today* (December 9, 2011): 6A.

498. See James Madison's notes on June 19, 1787, from "The Debates in the Federal Convention of 1787."

499. Louis Fisher, *Presidential War Power*, 2nd ed. (Lawrence: University Press of Kansas, 2004); David Gray Adler, "The Constitution and Presidential Warmaking," in David Gray Adler and Larry N. George, *The Constitution and the Conduct of American Foreign Policy* (Lawrence: University Press of Kansas, 1996), pp. 183–226.

500. Quotation from Gaillard Hunt, ed., *The Writings of James Madison*, Vol. 6 (New York: G. P. Putnam's Sons, 1900–1910), pp. 312–14.

501. See Richard A. Posner, *An Affair of State: The Investigation, Impeachment and Trial of President Clinton* (Cambridge, MA: Harvard University Press, 1999). See also Peter Baker, *The Breach: Inside the Impeachment and Trial of William Jefferson Clinton* (New York: Scribner, 2000); and Jeffrey Toobin, *A Vast Conspiracy: The Real Story of the Sex Scandal That Nearly Brought Down a President* (New York: Touchstone, 1999).

502. See, for thoughts on this debate, Lawrence Lessig, *Republic, Lost: How Money Corrupts Congress—and a Plan to Stop It* (New York: Twelve, 2011); Thomas E. Mann and Norman J. Ornstein, *It's Even Worse Than It Looks: How the American Constitutional System Collided with the New Politics of Extremism* (New York: Basic Books, 2012); and Ezra Klein, "Our corrupt politics: It's not all money" *The New York Review of Books* March 22, 2012, 43–45.

503. Gene Healy, *The Cult of the Presidency: America's Dangerous Devotion to Executive Power* (Washington, DC: Cato Institute, 2008).

504. Dana Nelson, *Bad for Democracy: How the Presidency Undermines the Power of the People* (Minneapolis: University of Minnesota Press, 2008).

505. It is believed that the first use of the term "elective kingship" dates to Henry James Ford's *The Rise and Growth of American Politics: A Sketch of Constitutional Development* (New York: Macmillan, 1898), p. 293: "In the presidential

office…American democracy has revived the oldest political institution of the race, the elective kingship. It is all there: the precognition of the notables and the tumultuous choice of the freemen, only conformed to modern conditions."

506. Arthur M. Schlesinger, Jr., *The Imperial Presidency* (New York: Houghton Mifflin Company, 1973), p. x; Arthur M. Schlesinger, Jr., *The War and the Presidency* (New York: W. W. Norton, 2005); and the astute conservative position from Richard A. Posner, *Not a Suicide Pact: The Constitution in a Time of National Emergency* (New York: Oxford University Press, 2006).

507. Such a solution is championed in an appealing if unconvincing way by Sanford Levinson, *Our Undemocratic Constitution: Where the Constitution Goes Wrong (and How We the People Can Correct It)* (New York: Oxford University Press, 2006). See also previously cited works by Sabato and Tugwell.

508. Stephen J. Farnsworth, *Spinner in Chief: How Presidents Sell Their Policies and Themselves* (Boulder, CO: Paradigm Publishers, 2009); and Charlie Savage, *Takeover: The Return of the Imperial Presidency and the Subversion of American Democracy* (Boston: Little, Brown, 2008).

Presidential Election Results, 1789–2012				
Year	Presidents/Vice-Presidents/Other Candidates	Party	Popular Vote	Electoral Vote
1789	George Washington			69
	John Adams			
	John Adams			34
	Others			35
1793	George Washington			132
	John Adams			
	John Adams			77
	George Clinton			50
	Others			5
1796	John Adams	Federalist		71
	Thomas Jefferson			
	Thomas Jefferson	Democratic-Republican		68
	Thomas Pinckney	Federalist		59
	Aaron Burr	Democratic-Republican		30
	Others			48
1800	Thomas Jefferson	Democratic-Republican		73
	Aaron Burr			
	Aaron Burr	Democratic-Republican		73
	John Adams	Federalist		65
	Charles C. Pinckney	Federalist		64
1804	Thomas Jefferson	Democratic-Republican		162
	George Clinton			
	Charles C. Pinckney	Federalist		14
1808	James Madison	Democratic-Republican		122
	George Clinton			
	Charles C. Pinckney	Federalist		47
	George Clinton	Independent-Republican		6
1812	James Madison	Democratic-Republican		128
	Elbridge Gerry			
	DeWitt Clinton	Federalist		89

Presidential Election Results, 1789–2012

Year	Presidents/Vice-Presidents/Other Candidates	Party	Popular Vote	Electoral Vote
1816	James Monroe	Democratic-Republican		183
	Daniel D. Tompkins			
	Rufus King	Federalist		34
1820	James Monroe	Democratic-Republican		231
	Daniel D. Tompkins			
	John Quincy Adams	Independent-Republican		1
1824	John Quincy Adams	Democratic-Republican	108,740(30.5%)	84
	John C. Calhoun			
	Andrew Jackson	Democratic-Republican	153,544(43.1%)	99
	Henry Clay	Democratic-Republican	47,136(13.2%)	37
	William H. Crawford	Democratic-Republican	46,618(13.1%)	41
1828	Andrew Jackson	Democratic	647,231(56.0%)	178
	John C. Calhoun			
	John Quincy Adams	National Republican	509,097(44.0%)	83
1832	Andrew Jackson	Democratic	687,502(55.0%)	219
	Martin Van Buren			
	Henry Clay	National Republican	530,189(42.4%)	49
	William Wirt	Anti-Masonic		7
	John Floyd	National Republican	33,108(2.6%)	11
1836	Martin Van Buren	Democratic	761,549(50.9%)	170
	Richard M. Johnson			
	William H. Harrison	Whig	549,567(36.7%)	73
	Hugh L. White	Whig	145,396(9.7%)	26
	Daniel Webster	Whig	41,287(2.7%)	14
1840	William H. Harrison	Whig	1,275,017(53.1%)	234
	John Tyler			
	Martin Van Buren	Democratic	1,128,702(46.9%)	60
1844	James K. Polk	Democratic	1,337,243(49.6%)	170
	George M. Dallas			
	Henry Clay	Whig	1,299,068(48.1%)	105
	James G. Birney	Liberty	63,300(2.3%)	
1848	Zachary Taylor	Whig	1,360,101(47.4%)	163
	Millard Fillmore			
	Lewis Cass	Democratic	1,220,544(42.5%)	127
	Martin Van Buren	Free Soil	291,163(10.1%)	
1852	Franklin Pierce	Democratic	1,601,474(50.9%)	254
	William R. King			
	Winfield Scott	Whig	1,386,578(44.1%)	42
1856	James Buchanan	Democratic	1,838,169(45.4%)	174
	John C. Breckinridge			
	John C. Fremont	Republican	1,335,264(33.0%)	114
	Millard Fillmore	American	874,534(21.6%)	8
1860	Abraham Lincoln	Republican	1,865,593(39.8%)	180
	Hannibal Hamlin			
	Stephen A. Douglas	Democratic	1,381,713(29.5%)	12
	John C. Breckinridge	Democratic	848,356(18.1%)	72
	John Bell	Constitutional Union	592,906(12.6%)	79
1864	Abraham Lincoln	Republican	2,206,938(55.0%)	212

Presidential Election Results, 1789–2012

Year	Presidents/Vice-Presidents/Other Candidates	Party	Popular Vote	Electoral Vote
	Andrew Johnson			
	George B. McClellan	Democratic	1,803,787(45.0%)	21
1868	Ulysses S. Grant	Republican	3,013,421(52.7%)	214
	Schuyler Colfax			
	Horatio Seymour	Democratic	2,706,829(47.3%)	80
1872	Ulysses S. Grant	Republican	3,596,745(55.6%)	286
	Henry Wilson			
	Horace Greeley	Democratic	2,843,446(43.9%)	66
1876	Rutherford B. Hayes	Republican	4,036,571(48.0%)	185
	William A. Wheeler			
	Samuel J. Tilden	Democratic	4,284,020(51.0%)	184
1880	James A. Garfield	Republican	4,449,053(48.3%)	214
	Chester A. Arthur			
	Winfield S. Hancock	Democratic	4,442,035(48.2%)	155
	James B. Weaver	Greenback-Labor	308,578(3.4%)	
1884	Grover Cleveland	Democratic	4,874,986(48.5%)	219
	T. A. Hendricks			
	James G. Blaine	Republican	4,851,931(48.2%)	182
	Benjamin F. Butler	Greenback-Labor	175,370(1.8%)	
1888	Benjamin Harrison	Republican	5,444,337(47.8%)	233
	Levi P. Morton			
	Grover Cleveland	Democratic	5,540,050(48.6%)	168
1892	Grover Cleveland	Democratic	5,554,414(46.0%)	277
	Adlai E. Stevenson			
	Benjamin Harrison	Republican	5,190,802(43.0%)	145
	James B. Weaver	Peoples	1,027,329(8.5%)	22
1896	Wiliam McKinley	Republican	7,035,638(50.8%)	271
	Garret A. Hobart			
	William J. Bryan	Democratic; Populist	6,467,946(46.7%)	176
1900	William McKinley	Republican	7,219,530(51.7%)	292
	Theodore Roosevelt			
	William J. Bryan	Democratic; Populist	6,356,734(45.5%)	155
1904	Theodore Roosevelt	Republican	7,628,834(56.4%)	336
	Charles Fairbanks			
	Alton B. Parker	Democratic	5,084,401(37.6%)	140
	Eugene V. Debs	Socialist	402,460(3.0%)	0
1908	William H. Taft	Republican	7,679,006(51.6%)	321
	James S. Sherman			
	William J. Bryan	Democratic	6,409,106(43.1%)	162
	Eugene V. Debs	Socialist	420,820(2.8%)	0
1912	Woodrow Wilson	Democratic	6,286,820(41.8%)	435
	Thomas R. Marshall			
	Theodore Roosevelt	Progressive	4,126,020(27.4%)	88
	William H. Taft	Republican	3,483,922(23.2%)	8
1916	Woodrow Wilson	Democratic	9,129,606(49.3%)	277
	Thomas R. Marshall			
	Charles E. Hughes	Republican	8,538,211(46.1%)	254
1920	Warren G. Harding	Republican	16,152,200(61.0%)	404

Presidential Election Results, 1789–2012

Year	Presidents/Vice-Presidents/Other Candidates	Party	Popular Vote	Electoral Vote
	Calvin Coolidge			
	James M. Cox	Democratic	9,147,353(34.6%)	127
	Eugene V. Debs	Socialist	919,799(3.5%)	0
1924	Calvin Coolidge	Republican	15,725,016(54.1%)	382
	Charles G. Dawes			
	John W. Davis	Democratic	8,385,586(28.8%)	136
	Robert M. La Follette	Progressive	4,822,856(16.6%)	13
1928	Herbert C. Hoover	Republican	21,392,190(58.2%)	444
	Charles Curtis			
	Alfred E. Smith	Democratic	15,016,443(40.8%)	87
1932	Franklin D. Roosevelt	Democratic	22,809,638(57.3%)	472
	John Nance Garner			
	Herbert C. Hoover	Republican	15,758,901(39.6%)	59
	Norman Thomas	Socialist	881,951(2.2%)	0
1936	Franklin D. Roosevelt	Democratic	27,751,612(60.7%)	523
	John Nance Garner			
	Alfred M. Landon	Republican	16,681,913(36.4%)	8
	William Lemke	Union	891,858(1.9%)	0
1940	Franklin D. Roosevelt	Democratic	27,243,466(54.7%)	449
	Henry A. Wallace			
	Wendell L. Wilkie	Republican	22,304,755(44.8%)	82
1944	Franklin D. Roosevelt	Democratic	25,602,505(52.8%)	432
	Harry S. Truman			
	Thomas E. Dewey	Republican	22,006,278(44.5%)	99
1948	Harry S. Truman	Democratic	24,105,812(49.5%)	303
	Alben W. Barkley			
	Thomas E. Dewey	Republican	21,970,065(45.1%)	189
	J. Strom Thurmond	States' Rights	1,169,063(2.4%)	39
	Henry A. Wallace	Progressive	1,157,172(2.4%)	0
1952	Dwight D. Eisenhower	Republican	33,936,234(55.2%)	442
	Richard M. Nixon			
	Adlai E. Stevenson	Democratic	27,314,992(44.5%)	89
1956	Dwight D. Eisenhower	Republican	35,590,472(57.4%)	457
	Richard M. Nixon			
	Adlai E. Stevenson	Democratic	26,022,752(42.0%)	73
1960	John F. Kennedy	Democratic	34,227,096(49.9%)	303
	Lyndon B. Johnson			
	Richard M. Nixon	Republican	34,108,546(49.6%)	219
1964	Lyndon B. Johnson	Democratic	43,126,233(61.1%)	486
	Hubert H. Humphrey			
	Barry Goldwater	Republican	27,174,989(38.5%)	52
1968	Richard M. Nixon	Republican	31,783,783(43.4%)	301
	Spiro T. Agnew			
	Hubert H. Humphrey	Democratic	31,271,839(42.7%)	191
	George C. Wallace	American Independent	9,899,557(13.5%)	46
1972	Richard M. Nixon	Republican	46,632,189(61.3%)	520
	Spiro T. Agnew			
	George McGovern	Democratic	28,422,015(37.3%)	17

Presidential Election Results, 1789–2012

Year	Presidents/Vice-Presidents/Other Candidates	Party	Popular Vote	Electoral Vote
1976	Jimmy Carter Walter F. Mondale	Democratic	40,828,587(50.1%)	297
	Gerald R. Ford	Republican	39,147,613(48.0%)	240
1980	Ronald Reagan George H. W. Bush	Republican	42,941,145(51.0%)	489
	Jimmy Carter	Democratic	34,663,037(41.0%)	49
	John B. Anderson	Independent	5,551,551(6.6%)	0
1984	Ronald Reagan George H. W. Bush	Republican	53,428,357(59%)	525
	Walter F. Mondale	Democratic	36,930,923(41%)	13
1988	George Bush James D. Quayle III	Republican	48,881,011(53%)	426
	Michael Dukakis	Democratic	41,828,350(46%)	111
1992	Bill Clinton Albert Gore	Democratic	38,394,210(43%)	370
	George Bush	Republican	33,974,386(38%)	168
	H. Ross Perot	Independent	16,573,465(19%)	0
1996	Bill Clinton Albert Gore	Democratic	45,628,667(49%)	379
	Bob Dole	Republican	37,869,435(41%)	159
	H. Ross Perot	Reform	7,874,283(8%)	0
2000	George W. Bush Richard Cheney	Republican	50,456,169(48%)	271
	Al Gore	Democrat	50,996,116(48%)	266
2004	George W. Bush Richard Cheney	Republican	60,040,610 (50.73%)	271
	John Kerry	Democrat	59,028,439 (48.27%)	251
2008	Barack Obama Joseph Biden	Democrat	69,499,428 (52.8%)	365
	John McCain	Republican	59,950,323 (45.6%)	173
2012	Barack Obama Joseph Biden	Democrat	62,610,003 (50.6%)	332
	Mitt Romney	Republican	59,133,398 (47.8%)	206

INDEX